Women's Literary Feminism in Twentieth-Century China

WOMEN'S LITERARY FEMINISM IN TWENTIETH-CENTURY CHINA

Amy D. Dooling

palgrave
macmillan

First published in 2005 by
PALGRAVE MACMILLAN™
175 Fifth Avenue, New York, N.Y. 10010 and
Houndmills, Basingstoke, Hampshire, England RG21 6XS
Companies and representatives throughout the world.

PALGRAVE MACMILLAN is the global academic imprint of the Palgrave Macmillan division of St. Martin's Press, LLC and of Palgrave Macmillan Ltd. Macmillan® is a registered trademark in the United States, United Kingdom and other countries. Palgrave is a registered trademark in the European Union and other countries

ISBN 1–4039–6733–4

Library of Congress Cataloging-in-Publication Data

Dooling, Amy D.
    Women's literary feminism in twentieth-century China / by Amy D. Dooling.
        p. cm.
    Includes bibliographical references and index.
    ISBN 1–4039–6733–4
        1. Chinese literature—Women authors—History and criticism. 2. Chinese literature—20th century History and criticism. 3. Feminism in literature. I. Title: Women's literary feminism in 20th-century China. II. Title.

PL2278.D66 2004
895.1'099287'0904—dc22   2004049000

A catalogue record for this book is available from the British Library.

Design by Newgen Imaging Systems (P) Ltd., Chennai, India.

First edition: January 2005

10 9 8 7 6 5 4 3 2 1

Printed in the United States of America.

For Peter and Molly

Contents

ACKNOWLEDGMENTS

This book, which grew out of my doctoral dissertation, has been a long time in the making and would not have come to fruition without all the help and encouragement I received along the way.

I would like to thank the original readers of my dissertation, Marilyn Young, Marsha Wagner, Shang Wei, and Tomi Suzuki, and above all my primary advisor David Der-wei Wang, who has continued to provide invaluable mentoring since my days at Columbia University. Special thanks also to Peter Hitchcock, C.T. Hsia, Hu Mingliang, Mab Segrest, Kristina Torgeson, Deborah Sang Tze-lan, and Ellen Widmer, for their support of this project as it evolved and for their invaluable help on specific aspects of individual chapters. Comradely critiques and feedback from Susan Mann, Rebecca Karl, Kathryn Bernhardt and other participants at the New Directions in Chinese Women's History Conference organized by Dorothy Ko at Columbia University in 2001, and from members of the China Gender Studies Workshop at the Harvard Fairbank Center, where I presented portions of my work, were especially useful at a critical juncture in the project. A special thanks to Ellen Widmer and Christina Gilmartin for their encouragement and advice on pursuing publication. Spirited discussions about the Chinese women's literary tradition with Liu Jianmei, Megan Ferry, Joan Judge, Zhang Jingyuan, and Wang Lingzhen at various conferences over the years have also been inspirational. And my colleagues in Gender and Women's Studies at Connecticut College have been a continual source of guidance and wisdom in thinking through questions of feminist cultural practices.

The research and ideas presented in this book owe a great deal to the work of many other scholars who have pioneered the study of women's cultural history and feminism in China. I would like to acknowledge, in particular, Christina Gilmartin, Rey Chow, Wendy Larson, Tani Barlow, Yi-tsi Feuerwerker, Elisabeth Croll, Meng Yue, and Dai Jinhua, whose work informs my inquiry in profound ways. Although I engage critically with some of their arguments, my aim has been to build on the invaluable interventions their scholarship has made in this field.

Sincere thanks are due to the reference librarians at the C.V. Starr East Asian Library at Columbia University, Beijing University Library, Beijing Library, KMT Party History Archives, National Central Library in Taibei, the Institute of Modern History at Academia Sinica, and at Connecticut College for their assistance in helping me track down obscure Chinese journals and texts. And finally, my gratitude to Toby Wahl, my excellent editor at Palgrave Macmillan, and the anonymous readers who endorsed the project.

Financial support for the initial research I conducted in Taiwan and Mainland China in 1994–1995 came from the Fulbright Commission and the American Council of Learned Societies. A Mellon Dissertation Fellowship allowed me to devote myself fully to writing in 1995–1996. A postdoctoral award from the Chiang Ching-kuo Foundation enabled me to work on revisions to the manuscript in 2001–2002.

My deepest appreciation goes to my family: my late Grandfather Evarts Loomis, whose tales of life in Yunnan Province in the 1940s sparked my initial interest in China; my remarkable mother Margaret and stepfather Bob; my sisters Daniella, Charlotte, Jennifer, Eleanor, and Maggie, and above all to Peter, who provided extraordinary intellectual and emotional sustenance throughout every single step of this book's development. With infinite affection I dedicate this book to him and to our beloved Molly, who has arrived in our lives just in time to see this book go to press.

Introduction: Women and Feminism in the Literary History of Early Twentieth-Century China

This study undertakes a critical inquiry into the powerful connections between emergent feminist ideologies in China and the production of "modern" women's writing in the period spanning the demise of the last imperial dynasty and the founding of the People's Republic in 1949. Proceeding through a series of primarily formal and historical analyses of literary examples drawn from a variety of narrative genres, I accentuate both well-known and under-represented literary voices who intervened in the heated gender debates of their generation and historically contextualize the formal strategies used in imagining alternative stories of female experience and potential. My analysis investigates two overarching questions: first of all, how the advent of enlightened views of gender relations and sexuality influenced the literary practices of the small elite of modern-educated "new women" who made their debuts in the cultural public sphere at the time, in terms not only of narrative content but also the narrative forms and strategies they deployed, the readership they sought to address, and the publication venues of which they availed themselves. Second, it analyses how, in turn, these representations themselves attest to the various ways in which early twentieth-century female literary intellectuals engaged and expanded contemporary social and political concerns by self-consciously writing women into stories of national salvation, social transformation, and revolution. Throughout, I reexamine the critical paradigm of feminism's subordination to the modernizing discourses of Nation and Revolution and instead build on contemporary research while presenting new evidence that the early paradigm fails to account adequately for the creative strategies China's new female literary intellectuals employed as they questioned dominant gender ideologies *within* a moment of revolutionary social transformation. But in order to understand why the literary history of women and feminism in early-twentieth-century China should be recast we will need to come to terms with the crucial theoretical and conceptual coordinates that inform this important branch of literary study. The aim is not simply a revisionist literary history, but the development of an analysis that will cement a broader, richer knowledge of the period by augmenting recent theoretical readings with a significantly expanded set of primary materials. If a new paradigm is to take hold it might fruitfully employ a whole range of formal and historical sources.

*   *   *

Some notable scholarship on the subject of "women and gender" in modern China paints a discouraging picture of the feminist project of challenging the power and logic of patriarchal ideology. To the extent that the conditions of women's material lives have undergone any significant improvement in China since the beginning of the twentieth century, this is apparently in spite of, not because of, the work of feminism (*feiminieshimu; nüquan zhuyi; nüxing zhuyi, nannü pingdeng zhuyi, nüquan yundong; funü yundong*).[1] Historians have documented at least two troubling patterns. First, while from the late nineteenth century onward the goal of female liberation[2] was quickly (and often conspicuously) absorbed into progressive political discourse on a theoretical level, in practice specific feminist agendas tended to be subordinated to or, to borrow Margery Wolf's apt phrase, perpetually "postponed" by the ostensibly more pressing political struggle at hand (be it national salvation, anti-imperialist resistance, or socialist state-building [Beahan, 1976; Croll, 1979; Andors, 1983; Stacey, 1983; Wolf, 1985; Gilmartin, 1995[3]]). Second, the gestures made by late Qing reformers, May Fourth intellectuals, or Communist Party officials were underpinned by a persistent paternalism that casts serious doubt on just how "feminist" was the modern Chinese discourse of female emancipation. With respect to the latter, the point, in my opinion, is not that men can't occupy a legitimate place in the feminist project or lend genuine support to women's struggles; however, insofar as male radicals have dominated both intellectual debates and the political management of modern gender reform in China, women have arguably remained as disenfranchised and marginal as ever, the passive beneficiaries of male authority. Few would deny that the legal rights and expanded opportunities in the economic sphere which this "imposed" liberation brought, marks a vast improvement over traditionally sanctioned modes of female subjection; feminist transformation, however, it is not.

In the arena of cultural politics (a primary focus in this book), feminism has fallen under similarly valid scrutiny. The recent surge of critical interest in the representation of gender in twentieth-century Chinese fiction and film on the part of contemporary scholars has focused long overdue attention on the ways in which the apparently "enlightened" narrative treatments of women (ranging from critical realist exposés of female suffering under the traditional Confucian order to socialist celebrations of empowered working-class heroines) were often complicit in consolidating repressive modern ideologies of gender. That is to say, in spite of radical innovations in both the content and form of narrative representations of women in the modern period, there are startling continuities with inherited gender assumptions. It has been persuasively argued, for instance, that gender liberation served as an immensely fertile *rhetorical* terrain through which self-styled modern male intellectuals were able to work through and articulate their disavowal of traditional forms of authority. In other words, their (almost) obsessive preoccupation with the female condition (and hence persistent urge to write about or otherwise represent women) arose not so much from deep allegiance to a feminist political or social agenda (with concrete ideas and ideals about women's equality or self-determination) *per se*, as from a desire to come to terms with modernity in general. In recent rereadings of canonical works that seem to indict traditional Chinese patriarchy, for instance, critics have revealed that in many cases the figure of the afflicted female victim functions as a pretext to showcase the enlightened emotional and political stance of a male narrator/protagonist, supplying an object through which to register the modern male subject's moral outrage at social injustice in general and *his* desire for social change (Chan, 1988; Wang, 1989; Chow, 1991; Yue, 1993; Lieberman, 1998; Zhang, 1999; Louie, 2002).[4] Similarly, narratives of female liberation (the many stories inspired by Ibsen's Nora in the 1920s, for instance, or the popular legend of the white-haired girl (*Baimao nü*) that circulated widely during the Sino-Japanese war), inscribed "woman" as the object of heroic male rescue, whether that hero be in the guise of the sympathetic May Fourth intellectual or the benevolent Communist Party cadre.[5] Hence, even if what one critic calls the "salvation impulse" driving such narratives may be said to reflect an important emergent consciousness of women's *problematic* social position, the gender hierarchy these fictions implicitly reinforced—male as active savior/female as helpless victim—seems to leave the conventional symbolic structures of masculine power/authority more or less intact.

Yet another troubling rhetorical pattern contemporary scholars have duly discerned in the modern Chinese literary and film canon is the enlistment of the image of the oppressed female body as an allegorical space on which to inscribe (his)stories of the nation: would-be "feminist" concerns about women's physical mutilation (foot binding, in particular), rape, prostitution, female suicide, and so forth have found vivid expression in twentieth-century cultural narratives but routinely operate on a symbolic or metaphorical level to articulate the violation of China's *national* body, rather than specific instances of *women's* experience of physical and sexual violence (Ma, 1989; Liu, 1994; Liu Kang, 1993; Zhang, 1999).[6] Even if such texts can be said to contain a latent critique of patriarchy, in pointing to or standing in for other levels of meaning—for example, the brutality of traditional culture, the nation's plight vis-à-vis imperialist aggression, class exploitation—that critique is again either perpetually "postponed" as a matter of lesser urgency or dissolved into an imaginary resolution of China's political liberation.

The influential view of the failure of Chinese feminism—both as a social movement and as a cultural politics—is informed by at least two historical contexts. First, it owes much to the rise of feminist theory in the field of Chinese studies beginning in the late 1980s and to the increasing sophistication of critical methodologies being brought to bear on issues of women and gender. In literary studies, this has sparked a reevaluation of canonical texts and engendered greater sensitivity to the complexities of the sexual–textual politics underlying modern Chinese representations of women and men and the ideological contexts in which these were/are embedded (Chow, 1991; Barlow, 1994; Zhang, 1996; Larson, 1993, 1998; Lieberman, 1998; Zhong, 2000; Louie, 2002). Accordingly, not unlike the development of feminist literary studies of the Anglo-European tradition, there has been a marked shift from predominantly empirical, content-based interpretations to a critical engagement with the historically contingent meanings of form, genre, and language in relation to modern constructions of gender difference.[7] The prevalence of seemingly "positive" representations of women (whether via a sympathetic rendering of their victimization or affirmative depictions of female empowerment) in mainstream twentieth-century Chinese literature, we have now come to better appreciate, does not necessarily reflect a nascent feminist consciousness; on the contrary, it may be one of the very factors that most inhibited such a political consciousness from truly taking root.

Second, the critique of feminism's failure in the Chinese context is informed by the post-Mao challenges to the official rhetoric of the Chinese Communist Party (CCP) that claims credit for having successfully realized the modern project of "liberating" women (*jiefang funü*). According to the assumptions that inform the latter, the key to achieving gender equality resides in women's entry into the productive workforce. For, as was proclaimed at the First All-China Women's Congress in 1949, "only through active participation in production can women raise and consolidate their position; improve a step further their own living standard . . . and free themselves from the feudal yoke."[8] Thus, insofar as Chinese women were widely integrated into social production after the founding of the People's Republic, the logic goes, their status no longer remains a problem. Adding to this rosy picture has been official government endorsement of women's equal rights and abilities. The basic policy on women, voiced by official state organs such as the Women's Federation, or *Fulian*, has worked as a powerful obstacle in fully confronting the realities of gender inequities and identities in the PRC.[9] For this reason, efforts to expose the state's mythology on women's liberation and to rearticulate gender as a relevant political category clearly remain of central importance to Chinese feminists and feminist Sinological research.[10] Critique strategically focused on the gaps and contra-dictions between the official party line on women and the historical record, and on the incommensurability of the modern rhetoric and realities of gender, undertakes the vital task of repoliticizing gender as an arena of unresolved conflict and struggle.

In delineating the limits and contradictions of the ostensible endeavors to transform gender relations in China over the course of the twentieth century, however, we need to be mindful of the pitfalls of another potentially dangerous, and equally monologic, countermyth; namely, the myth of a masculine modernity. It is one thing to critique the ways in which women and women's liberation have been strategically appropriated by contending modernizing discourses, it is quite another to conclude that such processes effectively precluded women from asserting their own visions, voices, and desires as historical subjects.

Without diminishing the value of feminism to the recent study of Chinese literature and culture, I would suggest that it has sometimes played into precisely such a myth.[11] Neglectful of what literary scholar Patricia Yaeger refers to as "moments of emancipation and empowerment" in women's cultural productions,[12] some scholarly accounts unwittingly give the impression of an omnipotent patriarchy that condemned modern Chinese women to silence. Nothing much has changed for, let alone been changed *by*, women over the past century since, it is contended, women ceased being objects within the masculine Confucian symbolic order only to be reobjectified by its Communist correlative. Thus, in the words of one contemporary critic, "Women's emancipation in China failed not only because a new patriarchal order attempted to replace an old one by using women's representational power, but also because Chinese women, for lack of gender awareness, could not sufficiently resist their reductive roles as representations of masculinist ideology."[13] Appearing in the preface to a collection focused on twentieth-century Chinese literature, the implication would seem to be that the Chinese women writers (journalists, novelists, playwrights, poets, translators, cultural commentators, and critics) who actively protested discriminatory gender attitudes and practices in the twentieth century not only failed as agents of social change but in fact served as unwitting conspirators in the modern reinscription of patriarchy.

But assuming that the women referred to in the above quotation are not Chinese women in general, but the elite cosmopolitan female intellectuals, artists, and writers who in actuality enjoyed expanding opportunities to assert their own "representational power" as a result of historic changes in women's education, in public literary culture, and in politics in the early decades of the twentieth century, how much is currently known about the various ways in which they resisted (or failed to resist) the structures of silence that threatened to render them the mute metaphors of China's self-styled "new" men? On what grounds can it be claimed that such women were insufficiently self-conscious of the new politics of gender being negotiated during this complex historical juncture, or that they ultimately failed to transcend their inherited status as the mere objects of masculinist discourse? And why should we take for granted that the intense focus concentrated on women and feminine experience in the pre-1949 era arose chiefly as a product of male endeavors to reshape their own history?

A great deal of recent feminist literary scholarship, while offering theoretically astute rereadings of the modern canon and analyses of post-Mao women's writing, has evinced comparative disinterest in the cultural interventions Chinese women themselves have undertaken at earlier points in the past century.[14] Even as current archival work by contemporary Mainland Chinese scholars radically reshapes the contours of twentieth-century literary history—bringing back into print the work of long-forgotten female authors, and enabling the recent publication of the first comprehensive modern women's literary histories—Western-based critics tend to focus on a relatively small handful of writers (Ding Ling, Bing Xin, Xiao Hong, and, most recently, Zhang Ailing), to the detriment of a broader understanding of the modern period.[15] This raises other important questions: for instance, is the apparent lack of women's representational power in China simply a result of powerful local patriarchies? That is to say, to the extent that women's roles in the formation of modern literary culture appear restricted to that of figures of representation, could this not also have something to do with prevailing literary historiographic practices that, for example, either severely limit the number of women writers who are considered, or persist in taking male-authored texts as the privileged site of analysis? While the cultural productions of early-twentieth-century urban female intellectuals "on" women were undoubtedly influenced, sometimes overwhelmingly so, by the masculinist logic permeating the cultural discourses of modernity in China, the construction of the recent past as an inevitable story of male domination is excessively pessimistic.[16]

My point is not to advocate a conventional model of writing-as-resistance to interpret the practices of the new breed of literary women that the modern historical era produced, but that we need to acknowledge and account for the counterexamples that disrupt the historical narrative of the past hundred years as an unchanging continuum of male domination.[17] Surely, to construe women as the inevitable victims of modern Chinese men is to construct a *critical discourse* that replicates the very logic of silence feminism deplores? Rather than presume that feminist cultural interventions were doomed to failure, we might instead ask: How did the young female intellectuals who turned to creative literature to critically articulate issues and themes of gender discrimination in novels, autobiographies, and dramas in the late nineteenth and early twentieth centuries register awareness of the fraught ideological context that relentlessly impinged upon their portraits of female suffering and exploitation? What effect did mainstream literary appropriations of the repertoire of imagery and rhetoric conventionally claimed by feminists elsewhere have on the emergence of an effective oppositional discourse of gender in twentieth-century China? How, if indeed at all, did radical women intellectuals and writers meaningfully articulate and critically oppose practices of gender discrimination at a moment when the very images and narratives of female suffering and victimization were being co-opted for other cultural–political agendas, imbued with symbolic meanings and connotations often at odds with the values and interests of feminism itself? Did they realize how their textual representations might have played into rather than against the masculinism they were consciously seeking to overturn? Is it possible, finally, to understand Chinese women not only as discursive constructs or textual configurations but also as active producers of stories and histories of their own making?

Historian Wang Zheng's recent *Women in the Chinese Enlightenment* (1999) provides invaluable insights into the lives of radical women prior to 1949 that, among much else, force us to rethink many of our assumptions about female historical agency at that time. Intended as a revision of "gender-blind" accounts of the May Fourth movement, including Vera Schwartz's seminal *The Chinese Enlightenment* (1986), the study reassesses the advent and impact of emancipatory gender discourses in the pre-1949 period by tracing the historical construction of the so-called New Women's (*xin nüxing*) subjectivity. Rather than treat New Women as merely a male-formulated textual trope, Wang investigates how alternative terminologies, concepts, and images of womanhood circulating in the urban media beginning in the teens and twenties were absorbed and, in turn, transformed by the (newly) educated young women who comprised the female readership that many New Culturalists targeted. To answer these questions, Wang relies primarily on extensive interviews conducted in the early 1990s with veteran activists whose lived experiences of attending modern secondary schools and colleges, involvement in political and social movements, and career pursuits make them representative of their generation of middle- and upper-class urban Chinese women. The resulting oral histories, in which women emerge as historical protagonists, offer an immensely provocative narrative of the May Fourth era. More specifically, they begin to illuminate a crucial chapter in the history of modern Chinese feminism, by demonstrating the centrality of the liberal-humanist feminist discourses to women's self-definitions, the meanings they attributed to their professional achievements, and to their personal memories and recollections of this formative era. In other words, contrary to standard accounts that credit the Party for having "liberated women" (*jiefang funü*), Wang argues that New Culture feminism altered the lives and indelibly imprinted the consciousness of the generation of new women who came of age at the time.

Like *Women in the Chinese Enlightenment*, the present study is motivated by an interest in the formation of women's feminist subjectivities in the early twentieth century and a desire to help break from the literary historical narrative that has long obscured the record of the "new" women's cultural work and activism. Whereas Wang Zheng usefully examines agency in terms of a reconceptualized notion of women as readers, I argue that we must also take into account the ways in which such women participated in literary culture *as authors* to confront orthodox gender assumptions and to construct more empowering definitions of female identity.[18] Specifically, then, this study addresses women's emerging discursive power to imagine and inscribe new possibilities of gender through a critique of feminist resistance in literature by modern Chinese women writers from the period spanning the collapse of the last imperial dynasty and the consolidation of the modern socialist state (1900s–early 1950s). It considers the complex historical matrix under which "woman" was appropriated as a central trope in both the modern literary and political imaginary, and the specific implications of this imaginative centrality for female authors committed to improving women's domestic and public roles and status. While I take seriously the charge leveled by critics that at times this centrality, paradoxically, entailed a certain erasure of women as subjects, this study proposes that our critique must nevertheless account for the concrete ways some women writers themselves began to engage with the politics of gender during the first half of the twentieth century. The socio-historical impediments progressive writers encountered as they struggled to claim a public voice in feminism were often considerable, as I outline below; these obstacles did not, however, preclude effective literary opposition to male domination. By showing, via close readings of selective texts, how specific writers drew upon, challenged, and transformed the emergent narrative plots and rhetorical patterns shaping modern definitions of "woman," the four central chapters propose a more nuanced and complex account of women's relationship to the literary and political debates around gender in the period.

This study explores the historical challenges women writers in early twentieth-century China faced, but also the narrative solutions they fashioned, in claiming woman as a subject of feminist representation. Despite the misogynist legacy of the Confucian orthodoxy and the masculinist logic lurking beneath the emergent discourses of modernity, there are important examples of literary women writing from self-consciously anti-patriarchal perspectives, which reveal a keener, more inventive and imaginative feminist cultural praxis than has previously been analyzed. Availing themselves of the vast resources of the burgeoning modern literary culture, Wang Miaoru (1877–1903), Qiu Jin (1875–1907), Bai Wei (1894–1987), Lu Yin (1898–1934), Shi Pingmei (1902–1928), Chen Xuezhao (1906–1991), Xie Bingying (1906–2000), Yang Jiang (1911–), Su Qing (1917–1982), and others critically appropriated existing narrative forms, from utopian fantasy to autobiography, in order to address the problems facing contemporary women and to articulate a desire for historical change. In so doing, they also negotiated with the powerful patterns and conventions underpinning the narrativization of "woman" in modern fiction, expanding and embellishing alternative plots, while critically contesting others. Their writing, while often directly engaged with the central concerns of dominant culture (nation-building, personal subjectivity, political revolution, and so forth), also departs in subtle and often significant ways from much of that writing in that it resists the tropes of gender that had come to inform its narrative practices. More importantly, it afforded new perspectives on these very concerns—producing bold new narratives and meanings of concepts of nation, the individual, and revolution.

The relationship between feminist literary discourse and narrative practice invariably evolved as the political–cultural matrix shifted over the course of the early twentieth century. Who constituted the intended target audience of the feminist writer and what her/his creative motivations were, underwent subtle and profound permutations as both material and ideological circumstances changed for writers and readers alike. On a primary level, then, my investigation is historical, in that I strive to recontextualize particular textual practices within the immediate political and literary landscapes they inhabited, as well as the conditions affecting women as producers and consumers of literary texts. The point is not merely to supply pertinent background material against which to read discrete textual examples. Literary texts, as they are understood in this study, are embedded within ideological and social formations, in the sense of being both shaped by and helping to shape such historical dynamics. Moreover, as a literature that by definition engages a politics of personal and social transformation, feminist writing is not content to passively reflect its historical setting but instead actively wrestles with present conditions, even as it may be constrained by them. In order to appreciate the significance of both the narrative forms different writers appropriated and the array of rhetorical strategies they practiced, therefore, it is imperative to locate them within the historical fabric of which they were a part.

By foregrounding both well-known and some relatively unknown women writers active in the decades spanning the end of Qing dynasty to the founding of the People's Republic of China (PRC), this study also seeks to contribute to current efforts in the field of Chinese studies to broaden the scope of our knowledge about women's roles in and contributions to the formation of modern literary culture. Let me emphasize, however, that my intent is not to make claims for a "female tradition" in general, nor even to systematically trace a feminist sub-tradition within modern women's writing.[19] Rather, what I attempt to provide is a critical understanding of specific problems in the evolving relationship between feminism and women's narrative practices during an era of enormous historical turmoil and transformation in China. Given the dominant discursive patterns that continually threatened to co-opt woman, what strategies did female writers use to circumvent or subvert them? What were the contexts that enabled or empowered them to do so? To what extent were they successful in preserving an oppositional edge in their feminist writing? To answer these questions, I will provide in-depth analyses of works by nearly a dozen women writers and the narrative genres they deployed: fantasy, realism, autobiography, and comedy. At the same time, these analyses give occasion to reflect on subsequent mechanisms that have worked to obscure the literary struggles, achievements, and perspectives of feminist women.

Here I will address the ways in which the category of feminist narrative is currently being theorized within feminist literary criticism as well as articulate the basic assumptions that underlie my own treatment of the category "feminist narrative." I will then provide a conceptual overview of the salient issues surrounding feminism and literary representation in modern China prior to 1949 in order to establish a framework for the readings to follow.

THEORIZING FEMINIST FICTION

In spite of its keen interest in the politics of women's literary production, feminist criticism has paid relatively scant attention to the category of feminist fiction as such. According to Maria Lauret, who attempts to redress this gap in her book *Liberating Literature* (1994), there are at least two reasons for this critical lacuna.[20] First, feminist scholars have tended to

conceptualize women's writing *in general* as politically subversive, and
therefore have not felt compelled to differentiate between literary practices
arising from the marginalized position from which women have historically
written in patriarchal traditions and those that derive from more or less
self-consciously held ideological views vis-à-vis the constructed nature of
gender. It is not difficult to discern this tendency in many of the most
influential feminist studies of women's writing from the past few decades: in
a work that has shaped the field, Gilbert and Gubar's pioneering *Mad
Woman in the Attic* (1979), for instance, the authors trace what they describe
as a tradition of palimpsestic writing, whereby nineteenth-century female
authors employed covert narrative strategies to articulate ideas and desires at
variance with those proscribed by the dominant culture.[21] A sequel of sorts
to this book, Rachel DuPlessis's equally influential study *Writing Beyond the
Ending* (1985) argues that twentieth-century Anglo-European women's
writing carries on this subversive project but is marked by a more overtly
transgressive impulse to rewrite the master-narratives (in particular, the
heterosexual romance plot), which have traditionally scripted patriarchal
gender roles.[22] This influential paradigm of women's writing as a subversive
literature[23] is also manifest in some feminist analysis of the Chinese female
literary tradition. In *Fuchu lishi dibiao* (Emerging on the horizon of history)
(1989), for example, a major critical study of modern Chinese women's
writing, Meng Yue and Dai Jinhua endorse the definition of *nüxing wenxue*
as a rupture from dominant culture.[24] This break is explained as a
coming-to-consciousness by women intellectuals in the modern era to both
their historically marginalized gender status and to their feminine
"difference," which in turn is inscribed in their texts.

Second, Lauret points out, as feminist critical methodology and theory
grow more sophisticated, the sometimes didactic and propagandistic bent of
feminist fiction render it an unappealing object of literary study. This is
understandable, to a certain degree. Still, she suggests, as contemporary
scholars become increasingly attuned to theoretical problems of textuality,
subjectivity, and ideology many now view the preference for realist forms
among self-styled feminist writers—autobiographical fiction, the confessional
novel, the female *bildungsroman*—as something of an embarrassment. Such
literary practices have been subject to frequent attack by theorists for being
naively "embedded in traditional conceptions of identity and referential
modes of representation; [they] merely reproduced conventional constructions of reality instead of challenging them."[25] Lauret is right that much of
this approach has followed the rise of postmodernist aesthetics and the high
value subsequently accorded to linguistic and formal modes of experimentation. It should be pointed out, however, that even less theoretically inclined
literary critics like Elaine Showalter seem to find explicitly feminist writing
objectionable: in the evolutionary schema she sees at work in the British
tradition of women's writing (or, alternatively, within the personal evolution
of the individual female author), the feminist phase is defined by an
instrumental use of literature as a didactic vehicle for social and political

protest.[26] In Showalter's opinion, such writing is fueled by the rage the politicized woman writer harbors toward society and the narrow roles to which she has been assigned, and therefore lacks the aesthetic merits of other modes of women's literature.

For other critics, however, the literary practices generated by the historical advent of feminism deserve more rigorous consideration than they have typically received. An important dimension of women's literary history, feminist writing is not synonymous with women's writing; and while always political, it is never simply the transparent medium for feminist ideology. In addition to Rosalind Coward's significant early essay "Are Women's Novels Feminist Novels?" (1980), key studies exploring the intersection between feminism and literature include Rita Felski's *Beyond Feminist Aesthetics: Feminist Literature and Social Change* (1989); Anne Cranny Francis' *Feminist Fiction: Feminist Uses of Generic Fiction* (1990); Ann Ardis's *New Women: New Novels* (1990); Gayle Greene's *Changing the Story: Feminist Fiction and the Tradition* (1991); Maria Lauret's *Liberating Literature: Feminist Fiction in America* (1994); Eve Taylor's *The Domestic Revolution: Enlightenment Feminisms and the Novel* (2000); Anna Wilson's *Persuasive Fictions: Feminist Narrative and Critical Myth* (2001).[27]

While different in important respects, these studies share certain key premises. Most obvious, perhaps, is the need to resist eliding the cultural productions by women in general and those by feminists. Gayle Greene enunciates this view in no uncertain terms: "[f]eminist fiction is not the same as 'women's fiction' or fiction by women; not all women writers are 'women's writers', and not all women writers are feminist writers, since to write about 'women's issues' is not necessarily to address them from a feminist perspective. Nor are feminist writers necessarily so all of the time . . ."[28] Such demarcations may sound self-evident when they are articulated in as blunt terms as these, but in fact the distinctions have potentially far-reaching implications for feminist literary critique: above all, they shift the focus of inquiry away from a totalizing and vaguely defined conception of "gender"—how the woman writer's gendered social position or feminine subjectivity supposedly informs her oppositional writing practices–to the more specific role of political ideology in shaping feminist writing. The former approach (which links the otherwise dissimilar literary theories of gynocriticism and *écriture féminine*)[29] attempts to posit "a necessary or privileged relationship between female gender and a particular kind of literary structure, style, or form," which is in turn valorized for its opposition to masculinist culture.[30] By contrast, the latter view holds that feminist narrative effects are not the natural, automatic product of a "female aesthetic" emanating from the woman author's biological gender or gendered experience, but are brought about as a result of political motivation and/or the ideological (consciously or unconsciously), which determine how a writer narrates a given story, the manner in which she organizes its constituent elements, the mode of address she adopts vis-à-vis her implied reader, and the formal strategies she decides to use. This nonessentialized approach to the notion of feminist writing helps us account for why not all women writers are feminists; why a given author's *oeuvre* may contain both feminist and nonfeminist work; why feminist effects can emerge in a literary text at an unintended or unconscious level; and why some male authors produce feminist literature.

One possibility Greene overlooks is whether feminist writers must by definition be *women* writers. The issue of male authors engaging sympathetically with feminist ideas may be justifiably bracketed in the Western context on grounds that, with few exceptions, feminism has developed as a form of dissident politics by and on behalf of women themselves. Such is clearly not the case in China (nor indeed in many other modernizing Asian nations), where male radicals emerged as vocal advocates of women's interests from the initial stages of feminism's history in the 1890s.[31] Many of the most influential works of modern fiction depicting the struggles of women under the cruel tyranny of Confucian patriarchy ("Zhufu" [New year's sacrifice, 1926]) and the psychological and sexual quandaries of the "New Women" (*Hong* [Rainbow, 1930]), not to mention countless polemical tracts and essays on women's liberation, were in fact authored by reform-minded men. This phenomenon (to which I will return below) is further evidence that feminism is after all a matter of ideology not female biology; yet, it poses a certain paradox: how can the cycle of male domination be broken by men? That is to say, can men authorize the end of patriarchy without assuming authority over women? The well-known May Fourth women writer Lu Yin once commented on the extraordinary zeal with which China's "new men" had taken up feminist issues in a way that highlights this quandary. Referring to a photo taken at Beijing Women's Normal College of the Alliance for Women's Rights, she wonders sardonically "nearly two-thirds [of those in the photo] are men while a mere third are women. How truly astounding: could it be that Chinese men are exceptionally open-minded? Instead of being the enemies of women they express their utter sympathy for us; and such being the case, women don't even need their own movement."[32] Lu Yin, like many of her contemporaries, lamented the apparent political apathy of modern Chinese women; what her remarks here reveal is that this may, in part, be one of the stifling effects of the male co-optation of feminism. Her view was not unique. Educated women throughout this period, from the pioneers of the feminist press in the late Qing to Su Qing in the 1940s, articulated a similar distrust of the conspicuously male voice of Chinese feminism. In my view, this reminds us of the strategic value of incorporating some notion of women's cultural agency within our definition of feminist literature. It is not that men cannot produce effective feminist texts, but that it is clearly more significant, politically and culturally, when women write as feminists to challenge male "authority" over women's images.

But what does it mean to define feminist literature as a political cultural praxis? Is the author's oppositional stance articulated only on the level of content, that is, in the thematic representation of male–female relations and women's experience, or is it inscribed on the formal dimensions of her text as well? And, to the extent that meaning is generated in the encounter between the text and its reader, what conditions make feminist texts possible? Obviously these are complex questions. They relate to ongoing debates on the relationship between aesthetics and politics, the meaning of literary form, and the role of literature as an agent of social change. Their difficulty is further compounded by the fact that feminism itself has historically encompassed an immense range of ideological positions, practices, and tactical strategies—all of which arise and change in conjunction with specific social and cultural constellations, thus making definitive answers all the more elusive.

Indeed, precisely because of feminism's historically contingent nature, critics like Rita Felski propose that an understanding of its literature(s) cannot be sought in a fixed notion of "feminist aesthetics." That is to say, there can be no *a priori* feminist styles, contents, or formal practices, only those deriving from and in response to the ideologies and practices of particular cultural formations. If, on its most elementary level, feminist literature expresses resistance to the subordination of women, the ways in which that resistance is given expression are determined not by some intrinsically feminist sensibility or consciousness, then, but by the political (and other) imperatives of particular moments. Accordingly, how and what the specific dynamics were in early-twentieth-century China that engendered the feminist literary practices of women writers will be carefully examined in the course of this study. The "dominant" culture, however, is hardly an unambiguous concept in the context of Chinese feminism. Western critics, for instance, have often taken for granted that feminist cultural practices exist in what is described as a "politically and aesthetically hostile environment" that, in turn, provides the point of reference against which "oppositional" strategies (including textual ones) are developed.[33] The early rise of feminism in China, by contrast, coincided with a wholesale reassessment of traditional values, practices, and textual conventions by intellectuals and political reformers. Arguments in support of gender equality, far from being contentious ideas that pitted female activists against a disapproving or hostile male establishment, were from the outset vigorously embraced in the name of national salvation, modernization, and eventually revolution. Consider, for example, the manifesto put forth by the "Woman Question Research Association" (*Funü wenti yanjiuhui*), an organization comprised of May Fourth male intellectuals:

That the world has a Woman Question is the ignominy of humanity; that China has only in recent years discovered the Woman Question is China's ignominy. The woman problem is the historical result of men's unjust oppression of woman; the discovery of the woman problem is the awakening of humanity to the harms of this oppression. Until the individuality (renge) of the female half of the population is properly recognized, and they fully achieve freedom and are able to participate in culture, no matter how much progress society makes it stills lack humanity; and no matter how developed a culture, it still will be a prejudiced one. Therefore the women problem is the world's greatest problem, not just the problem of one segment of humanity.[34]

If this statement betrays a certain connection between feminism and male anxieties about Chinese modernity (note here, for instance, how the woman problem is invoked as evidence that China has "caught up with" with the rest of the world), it also reveals the centrality accorded to women's issues in that historical project. This is not to say that feminism's war was won before it was even fought; on the contrary, it made (and continues to make) the lines of conflict more difficult to trace and should be seen as one of the complex conditions with which women feminists in China had to contend.

Foucault's notion of reverse discourse may be instructive here, insofar as it offers a compelling hypothesis of how dominant cultures may actually work to open up discursive space for voices of dissent and opposition. Citing the example of nineteenth-century homosexuality in western European society, he argues in *The History of Sexuality* (1980) that the various mechanisms of power and prohibition (including modern discourses and practices of science and medicine) that sought to discipline sexual practice had the simultaneous effect of generating a new social category whose subjects, in turn, "began to speak on [their] own behalf, to demand that [their] legitimacy or 'naturality'" be acknowledged."[35] In terms of Chinese feminism, then, the fact that the ideal of the emancipated woman was from the outset "mainstreamed" may well mean that the conditions conducive to the emergence of a subversive female subject never fully materialized. It may help explain, for instance, the thwarted formation of autonomous cultural institutions—presses, magazines, bookstores, and so forth—through which women themselves could promote and represent issues of importance to them. Such institutions arose out of necessity in other national cultures where feminism met resistance, but they also proved (and have continued to prove) crucial in providing alternative and autonomous discursive spaces for women to develop the forms of gender self-awareness and political experience that are, after all, central to the feminist project. In China of course there were successive endeavors by early activist women to carve out just this kind of space—the pioneering founders of the feminist magazines (*nübao*) in the late Qing, for instance, defended the need for separate women's publications on the grounds that, in their view, the reform press had not adequately addressed their needs. (On the other hand, one finds nothing equivalent in scope to, say, *Seito* [Bluestocking, 1911–1916], the influential woman-run feminist literary journal founded in Japan by Hiratsuka Raicho).[36] Another important, though less well-known example is the Women's Bookstore (*Nüzi shudian*), a publishing collective comprised mostly of women intellectuals who ran a bookstore and a small press in Shanghai from 1933–1936.[37] In addition to actively promoting women's writing, the Women's Bookstore also provided social service-type assistance to young women in need. Such examples, while vital testimony of the neglected story of women's contributions to Chinese literary feminism, were nevertheless exceptions at a

time when women writers, including political writers, were courted by
the mainstream press that was all too eager to cash in on their modern
"difference."

In certain respects, Elaine Showalter's vision of the propagandist who
commandeers the literary text to protest on behalf of wronged womanhood
is not an entirely inaccurate description of the feminist writer. An instrumental view of the role of literature in gendered social transformation has to
a greater or lesser degree stimulated feminist textual practice—like the early
suffragette fiction Showalter examines, the "new novels" promoting the
advancement of female education and equal rights that appeared in the late
Qing, for example, were blatantly intent on delivering new ideas and
information to the female readers to whom they were addressed.[38]
Ultimately, to view the feminist text as merely the transcription or articulation of a political ideology that preexists independently of and outside the
realm of fiction, however, is to fail to address literature's own role as a
specific form of meaning production.

For, beyond overt political proselytizing, feminist writing also engages in
complex, nuanced, and often highly self-conscious ways with the *narrative
tradition* of which it is a part, as several of the above-mentioned critics
demonstrate. The New Women novelists of Victorian England, for instance,
contested the conventional romance plot in which female characters had
long been contained by inventing fictional heroines who aspire to erotic,
political, or professional goals beyond the yoke of marriage (Ardis, 1990).
The feminist practitioners of popular fiction studied by Cranny-Francis
appropriate familiar popular narrative genres in order to play upon reader
expectation and thereby "make visible within the text the practices by which
conservative discourse such as sexism are seamlessly and invisibly stitched
into the textual fabric, both into its structures and into its story, the weave
and the print."[39] Similarly, the contemporary writers of feminist metafiction
examined in Gayle Greene's study incorporate self-reflexive commentary on
narrative structure and technique to draw attention to the manner in which
imaginative literature encodes gender roles and hence to its complicity in
maintaining the patriarchal symbolic order. The "political" intervention a
given feminist text makes, in other words, should not simply be seen solely
in terms of its ideological opposition to the external sociopolitical order but
also in terms of its engagement with language and narrative as important
battlegrounds in resisting male authority. Maria Lauret thus broadly defines
feminist fiction as having a twofold function: it is writing that not only con-
tests "dominant meanings of gender" but, in interrogating the boundaries of
genre and narrative convention, also challenges "established standards of
'literariness.' "[40]

The emphasis on the textual politics of feminist fiction is not simply a
formalist ruse designed to deflect attention from the "real" contradictions of
the material world. Rather, it is predicated on the theory that narrative
participates in the cultural construction (and maintenance) of sexual difference. According to this view, narrative constitutes one of the fundamental

semiotic practices shaping human perception, knowledge, and desire—through the selective highlighting of events and information, their organization into patterns of coherence, and the assignment of value and significance. The prevalence of particular narrative conventions and paradigms naturalize certain versions of reality over others and, simultaneously, render deviations or disruptions from dominant stories abnormal, implausible, or even simply unimaginable.

Adapting and elaborating on these insights in its analysis of patriarchal gender ideology, feminist criticism posits a number of fundamental polemics: first, traditional (or dominant) narrative representations of women have tended to support and sustain sexist configurations of society by producing feminine subject positions in accordance with those configurations. Again, the claim here is that narrative never *simply* reflects the hierarchical relations of power between men and women in society, but that it actively enables and authorizes those relations by providing the emotional, ethical, cognitive, and imaginary structures that induce individuals to accept and identify with their "proper" gender assignments. Indeed, elucidating the ideological function of narrative enables feminist critics to explain (at least in part) why patriarchy has been so successful historically in reproducing itself and, in particular, why women (and women writers) themselves so often become subjectively invested in the norms of a system based on assumptions and structures of male superiority.[41]

But narrative, however effective a mechanism in perpetuating normative values and assumptions, is neither the exclusive domain of masculine culture nor impervious to resistance and contestation. This is the second major point that needs to be emphasized. Rather than reject narrative as an inherently patriarchal mode (as was the case of feminist avant-garde artists in the United States and Europe the 1970s and, more recently, some French theorists who call for an "anti-narrative" aesthetic) there is a continuing need to confront and unravel the alliance between patriarchy and narrative discourse. This can occur either through feminist literary critique, which works to uncover the patriarchal effects of formal strategies in artistic expression and in turn helps to construct new "resisting" readers,[42] or through alternative representational practices that deliberately undermine the "coherence" of dominant narrative conventions. As Teresa de Lauretis comments, "Because of their capacity to inscribe desire and to direct, sustain, or undercut identification (in all senses of the term), [narrative and narrativity] are mechanisms to be employed strategically and tactically in the effort to construct other forms of coherence, to shift the terms of representation, to produce the conditions of representability of another—and gendered—social subject."[43] With regard to the latter, however, it is emphasized that the aim goes beyond formal experimentation and stylistic innovation, which do not in and of themselves "bear any necessary relationship to the political and social goals of feminism."[44] Rather, one objective of the feminist writer is to inscribe new ways of narrating reality so as to heighten political consciousness, to expand imaginative possibilities, and to produce new forms of subjectivity.

Analysis of the intersections between literary practice and feminist politics thus requires an approach that can attend to the historical, and cultural, specificity of the conditions under which a given text is produced and circulated. For, like any oppositional political aesthetic, feminist writing can never be known in advance on the basis of a fixed style, content, or formal practice, but only by the styles, contents, or forms that emerge in conjunction with particular historical exigencies and material conditions. To understand how the feminist text generates meaning, moreover, requires attention not just to the manifest level of thematic content, but investigation into the formal workings of the text in relation to dominant literary discourse. That is to say, how meaning is produced and reproduced in a particular patriarchal context is crucial to an understanding of how a given feminist writer devises strategies of intervention in her own representation of "reality." This includes, of course, the ways in which she addresses her reader, a topic that remains implicit in the following chapters.

CONCEPTUALIZING FEMINISM AND LITERATURE IN PRE-49 CHINA

Having elaborated in general terms my approach to the category of feminist literature, let me turn now to the specific cultural and historical contexts to be examined in this book.

The appearance of feminist literary texts in China at the end of the nineteenth century coincided with political endeavors among treaty port elites, including a small but growing number of educated women, to elevate the status of women in Chinese society in conjunction with national modernization efforts. As late Qing reformers began to take concrete action to reform female education and abolish foot binding (the two earliest causes to garner wide public support), many also turned to the nascent periodical press to promote women's causes among a broader urban audience. Glimmers of a proto-feminist consciousness have been traced in Chinese fiction and drama prior to this period, the most notable example being the 1828 fantasy novel *Jinghuayuan* (Flowers in the Mirror) by Qing literati-writer Li Ruzhen.[45] For the most part, however, the critiques these texts offered tended not to be anchored in a vision calling for a major overhaul of gender–power relations in Confucian culture but focused on discrete social practices (foot binding and concubinage, for instance). Nor were they coterminous with an organized women's movement that provided new opportunities and avenues for women's public political activism. For these two reasons, then, such literature in my view is to be differentiated from the politicized fiction calling for a "new women's world" (*xin nüjie*) that burst on the literary scene around the turn of the century.

Unlike the rise of feminism in the West, where enlightenment philosophy precipitated in the eighteenth–nineteenth centuries a social movement for women's individual political and civic rights, in China feminism arose in the context of national modernization projects that swept the country in the wake of European and Japanese imperialism in the late 1800s and early 1900s. Before the founding of the PRC in 1949 and the consolidation of all women-related agendas under the aegis of the Communist Party's *Quanguo fulian* (All-China women's federation), what came to be known as the women's movement loosely encompassed numerous organizations, groups, and individuals representing a fairly wide spectrum of anti-patriarchal platforms and practices. Some, such as the anti–feet binding societies of the 1890s and the suffrage associations founded in the Republican era, were organized around quite specific sociopolitical issues. Others were aligned with major political parties such the *Gongchandang* (CCP) and the *Guomindang* (KMT), which sought reform on a national scale. Despite significant heterogeneity, what ties these various strands of feminism together in the pre-49 era was the shared belief in the relevance of women's liberation to national modernization.[46]

This fundamental linkage had discernible but always complex consequences in the urban cultural sphere. In ways that were unprecedented in the Chinese tradition, the oppression of women became a serious, but simultaneously fashionable, topic of debate among self-styled "modern" intellectuals, launching an avalanche of writings in the early decades of the century of such magnitude that the subject soon acquired its own label—the *funü wenti* (or *nüzi wenti*). Under the rubric of the *funü wenti* (Woman Question) fell discussions of immense variety and breadth: as early as the late 1890s, articles regarding women's educational and vocational opportunities, political rights, freedom in marriage and divorce, physical health, foot binding, dress reform, superstition, self-esteem, sexual morality, political organization, labor issues, and more appeared in the progressive urban periodical press.[47] The earliest women's magazines, or *nübao*, such as *Nüzi shijie* (Women's world), *Zhongguo xin nüjie* (New Chinese women), *Zhongguo nübao* (The Chinese women's journal), which were explicitly aimed at bringing these debates to female readers, also began cropping up at this time. By the early 1920s, the "Woman Question" had materialized as a leitmotif of the May Fourth assault on the traditional Confucian family and in the cultural enlightenment project launched by New Culture intellectuals. *Xin qingnian* (New youth), the vanguard journal of May Fourth thought, set the tone by declaring its allegiance to women's liberation in its manifesto in 1919: "we believe that to respect women's personality and rights is a practical need for the social progress at present" wrote the editors, "and we hope that they themselves will become completely aware of their duty to society."[48] Hu Shi, one of *Xin qingnian*'s chief contributors and the period's leading advocate of linguistic/literary reform, included the "position of women" as one of the rich subject areas modern writers were to mine as part of the "reformed" literary practice he advocated.[49] Periodicals and newspapers quickly followed suit by adding special issues and columns (*zhuanlan*) featuring fiction, articles, and translations of foreign works on women's issues.[50] Dozens of smaller radical magazines and journals dedicated entirely to combating women's oppression also flooded the market. Some, such as

Xiandai funü (Modern women), which was cosponsored by the *Funü wenti yanjiuhui* (Woman question research society) and the *Zhonghua jieyu yanjiushe* (Chinese birth control research society), were published by small feminist organizations.[51] Others, like *Funü pinglun* (Women's review) which started out as a weekly supplement to *Shanghai minguo ribao* (Republican daily), were attached to major urban newspapers, a fact which gives further indication of the widening circulation such writings now commanded.[52] Major publishing houses such as the influential Shanghai Commercial Press also launched several women's books series (*Funü congshu* and the *Xiandai funü congshu*) featuring such titles as *The Women Question, Women and the Family, The Women's Movement; On Women's Professions and Motherhood; Women and Socialism; Women's Past and Future*; and *The Birth Control Movement*. In a rather irreverent reflection on this unprecedented publishing trend, the novelist Mao Dun wrote at the time: "I often joke that in China it's so easy to discuss the Woman Question because there isn't anything that can't be attacked. You name it, marriage, the family system, the question of female personality (*renge wenti*), concubinage . . . countless topics of every kind, all one has to do is give it a good cursing and turn it into an essay, and when real young men and women see it they'll be ecstatic and applaud 'hooray, hooray, oh joy, oh joy!' "[53]

Indeed, by the mid-1920s, it was clear that feminism sold and the publishing industry (along with savvy modern advertisers and film-makers) quickly capitalized on the phenomenon. Even the mainstream *Funü zazhi* (Ladies' journal), the successful magazine sponsored by the Shanghai Commercial Press, had abandoned its moderate home economics approach to appeal to the new political orientation of its urban readership by the early 1920s, devoting special issues to feminist themes: the January issue in 1923 (*Funü yundong hao*), for instance, focused on the women's movement and featured detailed articles introducing readers to the ins and outs of feminism in China and abroad.[54]

New research shows that the rising influence of the cultural left in the literary/intellectual arena in the late 1920s and early 1930s did not stifle feminist publishing activities; indeed there is evidence of renewed interest in promoting what some referred to as women's culture (*funü wenhua*). It was at this very moment, for instance, that the Women's Bookstore (*Nüzi shudian*) first opened its doors in the French concession district of Shanghai to launch an avowedly nonpartisan magazine, the *Nüzi yuekan* (Women's monthly) and a press devoted to advancing feminist goals and women's writing. In addition to an impressive series of scholarly monographs on gender-related subjects and the international feminist movement,[55] the press also issued literature by contemporary Chinese women, among them Feng Yuanjun, Lu Yin, Zhao Qingge, and Wu Shutian. Two other prominent feminist magazines, both edited by women, were also launched in Shanghai in the early 1930s and served as important forums for the heterogeneous ideas and viewpoints of female activists, artists, and writers at the time: *Nüsheng* (Women's voice) edited by Wang Yiwei (1905–1993), ran from 1932–1935 (resuming publication briefly after the defeat of Japan), and *Funü shenghuo* (Women's life), launched by Shen Zijiu (1898–1989) in 1935 and relocated to Chongqing after the outbreak of war. Having noted these developments, it is important not to overestimate the social impact of feminist debates in the Chinese press in the early decades of the twentieth century, which were largely confined to urban intellectual elites, even if they do mark a major rethinking of gender relations.

Given the coterminous advent of a new view of fiction as a particularly effective instrument of sociopolitical reform, it is perhaps not surprising that the so-called *xin xiaoshuo* (new novel) was quickly harnessed as one of the favored media for exploring these issues. Critics dubbed the genre the *funü wenti xiaoshuo*. Fiction (short stories and novels) and drama that took as their central theme the problematic aspects of women's experience, *funü wenti xiaoshuo* were featured in journals and magazines specifically addressed to female readers: a number of the earliest ephemeral periodicals that comprised the so-called *nübao* at the turn of the century began featuring sections for fiction,[56] a pattern that was continued in several of the more commercially successful women's magazines of the May Fourth period such as *Funü zazhi*. But the Woman Question fiction also (and in fact more systematically) appeared in leading cutting-edge publications of the day sponsored by cosmopolitan male intellectuals: the new presses associated with the New Fiction movement in the 1890s such as *Xiaoshuolin* (Fiction grove), *Mingming xueshe* (Enlightened academy), and *Zuoxin she* (Renewal society) for instance, published works of this nature, as did many of the most influential May Fourth journals.

Because the particular ways in which progressive gender discourse evolved in the first half of the twentieth century are fundamental to an understanding of the fiction that emerged in conjunction with it, let me briefly outline what I consider to be four major (and overlapping) contexts relevant to the project of women's feminist representation and its analysis.

I would begin by pointing to the unusually dominant male tenor of early Chinese feminism. In sharp contrast to the American and Anglo-European contexts, where the birth of feminism and the New Woman figure initially associated with it were generally regarded by the intellectual and political establishment as alarming signs of political turmoil and moral decadence (and accordingly resisted, ridiculed, and condemned in the mainstream periodical press and literature), in China (as in numerous other non-Western modernizing nations) feminism was from its inception vigorously embraced by the male intellectual vanguard as a progressive force that would contribute to the much-desired salvation, transformation, and revitalization of the beleaguered Chinese nation.[57] Whether one examines the incipient rise of the nationalist movement at the end of the Qing dynasty, the antitraditional Cultural Enlightenment project of the May Fourth era, or the patriotic resistance culture that developed in response to the Sino-Japanese War, male intellectuals claimed a central role in—seemingly to the point of monopolizing—progressive gender discourses. In the late 1800s, for example, it was reform-minded male literati such as Kang Youwei (1858–1927) and Liang Qichao (1873–1929) who were the primary instigators behind the anti–foot binding movement (by founding so-called natural feet societies in which they enrolled their daughters or to which they swore allegiance by refusing to marry, or have their sons marry, women with bound feet), as well as the most vocal advocates of formal education for women. During the May Fourth movement, young male iconoclasts, Chen Duxiu (1879–1992), Mao Dun (1896–1981), and Ye Shengtao (1899–1988) among them, again assumed a leading public role in bringing the problem of gender discrimination to the fore of social debate by writing extensively about issues such as the misogyny of the traditional Confucian family system and the need to expand women's political and economic rights. Not only were such subjects fervently discussed in articles and fiction in key New Culture magazines like *Xin qingnian* and *Xiaoshuo yuebao* (Short story monthly), but also in journals and newspaper columns founded for the express purpose of addressing the so-called *funü wenti*. In this context, it is not surprising that both of the major organized political parties—the KMT and CCP—that came into existence in the early decades of the twentieth century actively courted female members and almost immediately established women's divisions within their party structures with the stated purpose of "representing" female interests.

The tremendous interest many early-twentieth-century Chinese male intellectuals expressed in feminist ideals and, in particular, the reasons why female liberation emerged as a recurrent theme in their endeavors to fashion a new national culture is a complex and fascinating issue. Historians and literary scholars of China have offered a variety of explanations for this phenomenon, ranging from the economic pressures to mobilize women into the modern workforce to the growing currency of Western political philosophy that posited links between gender and national progress. Social Darwinist Herbert Spencer's tract "Women's Rights," which was first translated into Chinese in 1902, for instance, related social progress to the status of women, while Friedrich Engels' "On the Origins of Private Property" (parts of which were also first translated in the late Qing) also helped popularize the notion that the condition of women offered a barometer by which to measure society's advancement toward liberty and civilization in general. In the context of growing Western hegemony, the freedoms European and American women ostensibly enjoyed—widely reported on at the time in the Chinese reform press—lent further credence to the view that female emancipation was integral to social development and thus a phenomenon that would necessarily and naturally occur within China's own modernizing process. Thus in the preface to a British book originally entitled *The Women's Movement*, for example, one of many translations to introduce Chinese readers to the subject of Western feminism, the editor notes that he initially intended to entitle the work *The Emancipation of Western European Women*, to reflect the specifically European content of the book. In light of the fact that women's rights constitute a universal aspect of *modernity*, the editor explains, he ultimately decided against the geographically specific term in favor of the more inclusive noun "world" (*shijie*).[58] Championing the cause of women, in other words, can be seen in part as a form of cultural capital, one that imparted to the male intellectual the aura of a whole array of new values, including modernity, progressivity, enlightenment, and Westernization.

A slightly different explanation for the phenomena of male feminist advocacy suggests that, at least during the early May Fourth era, iconoclastic youths experienced a special sense of allegiance, even emotional identification, with women on the basis of their own intensifying feelings of injury and vulnerability vis-à-vis the traditional Confucian family. As Vera Schwartz maintains, "by delving into what it felt like for women to be so thoroughly at the mercy of family arrangements, these young men deepened and sharpened their own awareness of the problem of self-emancipation."[59] Along similar lines, Christina Gilmartin has documented the fact that many of the early Marxists personally suffered as a result of arranged marriages and attributes their ardent embrace of a feminist vision (evident in their prolific articles and essays on female oppression in such journals as *Xin qingnian, Juewu* [Awakening], and *Funü pinglun*) to first-hand conflicts with the repressive old-style family system.

Other examples could be cited to illustrate how an "enlightened" preoccupation with women's status permeated the masculine cultural imaginary throughout this historical era.[60] What most concerns me here, however, is not so much why the cultural establishment took such interest in women's status as what the implications were for women in feminism. Did the male arrogation of feminist discourse in the early twentieth century ultimately reduce that discourse to a paternalistic discussion among men about women? Are we to assume that the male appropriation of the voice of feminism effectively preempted the development of female agency in general and fostered, to the contrary, a damaging passivity and dependency among modern Chinese women with regard to gender transformation?

Examples that attest to the fact that many of China's "new men" (as one outspoken May Fourth female intellectual facetiously referred to them) desired gender reform (but often on their own terms) have been amply cited by critics. But it is one thing to make the claim that there were inherent contradictions in the paternalistic modes of feminist consciousness of some male intellectuals, and quite another to conclude that it completely thwarted women's attempts to articulate their own feminist perspectives and opinions. In fact, when we shift our focus of attention away from the former and look at what female writers and intellectuals themselves were actually thinking and writing about, it becomes clear that, at the very least, many were keenly aware of the potential problems or disadvantages of *being liberated by men*.[61] During the first wave of the women's movement in China during the late Qing, for example, the radical female anarchist He Zhen made an acute insight into the importance of the historical agency of women in feminist politics. She writes:

> Chinese society in recent years has seen a little liberation of women. But has this women's liberation truly come from women's being active agents

(*zhudongzhe*)—or from their being passive agents (*beidongzhe*)? What is "being an active agent"? Is it women struggling for liberation with their own might. What is "being a passive agent"? It is men's granting liberation to women. When we look at the liberation of Chinese women today, most of it has come about from being passive and less of it from being active agents. What active forces there have been have come from men and as a result the benefits to women have not equaled those garnered by men.

He Zhen was not alone in voicing concern over who would best "represent" Chinese women in their struggle for liberation. Several decades later, veteran feminist activist Liu-Wang Liming reiterated the view that feminist change had to come from women themselves. In her book on the urban Chinese women's movement she reflected on the subject:

> Over the past thirty or forty years, revolutionary thought has engulfed the nation, and has been accompanied by the development of democratic thought and a clamor for women's emancipation . . . .from the beginning, there have been many men who sympathized with oppressed women, such as Li Ruzhen, Liang Qichao, Chen Duxiu and others, who have advocated female resistance and equal rights in their books. However, if women want to achieve real emancipation and to benefit women themselves as well as humanity, they must depend on their own organization and effort.[62]

During the height of May Fourth period, the concept of female "self-emancipation" itself, it should be pointed out, was commonly invoked by male radicals who, like Mao Dun, now insisted that meaningful liberation depended significantly on women themselves.[63] But whether or not one sees this as men attempting to dictate the terms of feminist change (i.e., we men demand that you women emancipate yourselves), the fact remains that feminism in China was accompanied by an important new consciousness of the importance of women's historical agency. As the following chapters will show, not only do we find repeated statements expressing the considerable apprehension women activists and intellectuals felt about a bestowed liberation (as opposed to one demanded and sought of women's own accord) and about the perennial lip-service they felt their male contemporaries paid to the feminist cause, but also, in their fiction writers often depicted self-professed "new men" as part of the perilous social terrain the modern heroine must cautiously navigate and overcome in her bid for emancipation.

Obstacles to women's cultural agency in Chinese feminism of course were never just a matter of literary representation but of material practice. Of equal, if not greater, consequence than the fact that male writers included feminist issues as part of their literary–political agenda, I would argue, is that they did so from a privileged position of cultural authority. While the early twentieth century was marked by the rapid expansion of public literary opportunities for women, men had at their disposal considerably more cultural capital and continued throughout this era to occupy key roles in the literary arena as publishers and editors, critics, and cultural commentators. Thus, even if certain male intellectuals now asserted their influence and position to encourage and support women writers, their highly vocal and visible stance within the unfolding public discourse on gender put women at a distinct disadvantage in terms of setting the feminist agenda. And in the long run, it had the effect of overshadowing and marginalizing women's own literary feminism in the history of this era.

A second major context in which the problem of feminist representation needs to be situated pertains to the tremendous symbolic power that "woman" accrued—particularly the dichotomous tropes of the oppressed female victim and the liberated modern woman—in China's modern cultural discourse. Alice Jardine, in a book theorizing a phenomenon she calls "gynesis," or the putting of "woman" into discourse, suggests that the symbolic associations of the feminine with what is marginal or repressed by hegemonic culture renders it a particularly potent signifier in times of "epistemological crisis," embodying whatever new or transgressive values have arisen to displace the old order. Referring to the case of twentieth-century French culture, she comments "such rethinking has involved, above all, a reincorporation and reconceptualization of that which has been the master narratives' own 'nonknowledge,' what has eluded them, what has engulfed them. This other-than-themselves is almost always a 'space' of some kind (over which the narrative has lost control), and this space has been coded as feminine, as woman."[64] To be sure, the multifarious crises of Chinese modernity have been far from only philosophical, but Jardine's notion of the powerful affinity between femininity and a cultural logic of transgression may be useful in explaining the recurring preoccupation with the figure of woman that we find in early-twentieth-century Chinese culture. As contemporary China scholars have often observed, the overriding concerns of writers and artists of this period—tradition, nation, class, and social revolution—were often articulated *by means of* the figure of woman. The enduring fascination with Ibsen's Nora, for instance, attests to the centrality of the image of "liberated woman" in the modern Chinese political imagination, but also how malleable that image proved to be: Nora was as easily enlisted by liberal thinkers like Hu Shi to personify the notion of wholesome individualism as by leftists like Lu Xun to emphasize the necessity of socioeconomic transformation.[65] Leftist cinema in the 1930s appropriated the sexualized female body—often embodied by the figure of the prostitute—as a key battleground for contending (male) ideologies at the time. And resistance drama during the Sino-Japanese War is marked by a proliferation of female resistance symbols whose purpose was to mobilize the masses to stand up against Japanese agression. Among the most prevalent tropes in plays from this period are those of the patriotic courtesan and the woman warrior, both familiar traditional character types whose impressive integrity, courage, and uncompromising patriotism serve to highlight (and chasten) their less determined male counterparts. In some ways, these rebellious female heroines (such as Ge Neniang in A Ying's [1939] *Mingmo yihen* [Sorrow for the fall of the Ming], for instance] seem consistent with the May Fourth attack on Confucian gender ideology, but ultimately the feminist implications of the story are subsumed by the nationalist content such that, for example, women's equality is construed as the equality to defend the nation.[66]

The deployment of "woman" as a trope in social–political critique is not a uniquely *modern* Chinese literary convention.[67] There is a long-standing tradition of male literati appropriations of the female voice or the female predicament to vent frustration and protest against the system, including most famously the *Li Sao* (Encountering sorrow) and *Hongloumeng* (Dream of the red chamber). But if the symbolizing potential of femininity can be shown to have traditional antecedents, the cultural implications such symbolism took on in the twentieth century prove very different. For one thing, femininity was not merely a rhetorical symbol in literature but simultaneously the site of conscious ideological concern and contestation for those—including many women writers—who genuinely believed that gender reform was integral to China's modernization. At issue, then, is what effect the feminization of oppression—whereby woman is constructed as the quintessential symbol of the "oppressed" or "marginalized"—may have had on Chinese literary feminist discourse.

The marketing and critical reception of Xiao Hong's novel *Shengsi chang* (The field of life and death) in the mid-1930s, as Lydia Liu has cogently analyzed, offers a particularly telling example in this regard. First published in 1935, the novel explores in haunting detail the physical traumas of rape, pregnancy, childbirth, illness, and death as experienced by women in rural Manchuria. Xiao Hong sets her grim vignettes against the historical backdrop of the Japanese invasion of northern China but, as Liu astutely points out, the author defies the conventional nationalist narrative that exploits women's struggles purely for their symbolic value subverting, in particular, "the nationalist appropriation of the female body."[68] Instead of projecting the violated woman as a metaphorical extension of China's besieged landscape, Xiao Hong's realist description captures the literal, brutalized existence poor women endured not just during but prior to the outbreak of war. Yet in spite of this, Liu goes on to argue, it was not Xiao Hong's unsentimental indictment of rural patriarchy, but precisely the theme of nationalist awakening as it emerges toward the end of her novel that contemporary male critics privileged in their readings. For instance, Lu Xun, who invoked fresh memories of the Japanese bombing of Shanghai in 1932 in his preface to the first edition of the novel, promised readers that the novel would imbue them with "the strength to persevere and resist," while Hu Feng (who penned the epilogue) lauded the work in nationalist terms for its depiction of "a persecuted people in a pillaged land." According to Liu, this framing, in combination with the heightened patriotic climate of the mid-1930s, promoted a specific (mis)reading of the novel as an allegory of the suffering of the Chinese population and their struggle against Japanese imperialism.

I find Liu's analysis instructive for a number of reasons. For one thing, it underscores the power of the gendered nationalist imaginary at the time which, in this case, shaped not only the contemporary reception of Xiao Hong's novel but, as it turns out, secured the author's subsequent reputation as a "patriotic" writer. It is precisely this imaginary that enabled and validated the kind of rhetorical slippage between gender-based forms of oppression and other modes of subjugation manifest in the comments of the male critics who promoted the novel. And, having reduced women's gendered oppression to a symbolic construct of China's national plight, such readings seemed to work to contain or circumscribe the feminist valence of Xiao Hong's narrative. At the same time, however, I would note that Liu's own rereading points to the ways a feminist perspective readily opens onto the alternative narrative of woman and the nation that Xiao Hong knowingly inscribed in her text. Implicit in Liu's argument, in other words, is the potential of seeing women's literary work as a discursive arena where women writers flexed their own linguistic powers to redeploy language in new ways and to invent strategies to defy and disrupt the ways dominant culture wrote women out of history. In this sense, we can go even further in understanding the contemporary reception of the novel and read Lu Xun and Hu Feng's rhetorical maneuvers not just as imposing closure upon or limiting the meaning of Xiao Hong's novel, but as evidence of Xiao Hong's victory in drawing male (nationalist) critics into a public dialogue that exposes that theirs was but "one among many possible modes of speech."[69] If it is only recently that we have strong critical voices (like Liu's) to elaborate the feminist intervention Xiao Hong makes to literary historical accounts of this period, one of the aims of this study is to build on such insights and argue that the project of making women legible in new ways powerfully originates in women's feminist writing itself.

The issue of the (masculine) rhetorical appropriation of feminism needs to be distinguished from the deliberate ways in which early Chinese feminists sought to examine sexual oppression in relation to other forms of social domination. A third context to bear in mind in the course of this inquiry, then, is that the politics of feminism in early-twentieth-century China were seldom exclusively about sexual oppression. As was the case of many modernizing Asian nations facing the external threat of foreign imperialism and internal domestic unrest in the late nineteenth and early twentieth century, feminism in China did not arise (or proceed to develop) as a discrete politics of gender, stemming from a singular critical awareness of gender discrimination and difference, but because the advancement of women's roles was widely perceived to be coimplicated in the project of social transformation in general.[70] If their responses varied according to changing perceptions of China's historical malaise, Chinese feminists typically envisaged the eradication of female oppression as encompassing a struggle against traditional practices of male domination but also resistance to the other relations of domination suppressing Chinese women as well. Thus, in the words of veteran liberal activist Liu-Wang Liming, who published a highly informative insider account of the women's movement in 1934, the goal of Chinese feminism was to achieve human rights for women *and*, simultaneously, to empower women to create a more just society: "we don't only want to emancipate two hundred million women, we also want to join hands with awakened men and strive towards a happier world."[71] At the turn of the century, for instance, the impending threat of China's demise in the clutches of western imperialism compelled pioneer feminists like Qiu Jin and Chen Xiefen to ally themselves with the anti-Manchu nationalist movement. By the 1920s, as the labor movement began to organize women workers, some focused on the connections between gender and social–economic relations, and many were inspired to join the CCP. Xiang Jingyu, an early leader of the Communist-led women's movement, was typical in arguing that without fully confronting the class-based inequities experienced by female peasants and the working poor, feminism would effect little impact on the lives of the vast majority of Chinese women. Throughout this historical era, moreover, activist women were not alone in emphasizing the interconnections between their desires for gender justice and the goals of other contemporary progressive social–political causes; as mentioned earlier, the predominantly male leadership of both the nationalist and communist movements actively courted female support with promises of commitment to the feminist agenda(s).

In practice, as Elizabeth Croll, Judith Stacey, Chris Gilmartin, and other historians concur, the shifting alliances between the politics of feminism and the two major political movements of this century—nationalism and socialism, were fraught with tension. There is a sense that the overtures both parties made to women were probably as much pragmatic bids to harness an increasingly indispensable political force as they were a product of genuine resolve vis-à-vis the feminist cause. Gilmartin has suggested, alternatively, that the obstacles the CCP faced in promoting gender reform were born not so much of an ideological conflict between Marxist and feminist objectives, but from "the incorporation of traditional hierarchical gender patterns into the Chinese Communist polity" (203) itself—in particular, the male domination of feminist ideology and the implicit assumption of a masculine prerogative to speak on behalf of women.

Whether such tensions were of an ideological or institutional nature, a number of salient questions need to be asked of the feminist literature produced at the time. For instance, insofar as women's liberation was not envisaged as an end in itself, but as an integral part of the larger political project to build a new China, to what extent were those feminist issues that did not directly (or obviously) pertain to the overthrow of the existing social order get articulated and acknowledged? Did feminist writers voice concerns about the conflicts they encountered in struggling simultaneously against gendered and other forms of violence and oppression? And what became of feminist writers who voiced dissent from the dominant political ideologies of their day?

A critical engagement with feminist literary texts in pre-49 China, then, must be attentive to the manner in which women's issues were being formulated and confronted within the context of other on-going social and political struggles at the time. Just as activists took up a variety of efforts and causes, in many cases writers who addressed female subordination in fictional and autobiographical narratives assumed that gender issues constituted but one layer of women's overall predicament. Some writers, for example, sought to elaborate the connections between issues of gender and nation, or gender and class, explicitly on the level of thematic content; others alluded to the broader sociopolitical context and social movements that characterized the contemporary era in more indirect and subtle ways. Still others depicted the sexism and discrimination women activists experienced in the political arena in an attempt to bring greater attention to potential sites of tension and to underscore the relevance of sexual politics within the revolutionary process. While the degree to which these authors were successful in conveying their vision can only be judged through a critical evaluation of actual texts, the main point I wish to emphasize here is that a narrow definition of feminism as about sexuality and rights (basically, the liberal position) will not be sufficient given the historical framework in which the politics of gender were lived and written about in China at the time.

To elucidate feminist literary/cultural praxis in China involves, finally, a reexamination of the masculinist assumptions and paradigms that undergird some cultural–historical approaches to modern China. For the difficulty of identifying moments of cultural resistance by women would appear to stem not just from the specific contexts in which Chinese feminism historically unfolded, but also from certain literary historiographic practices, which may be implicated in under-emphasizing women's/feminist cultural agency. One may see this in some work that brackets women and feminist issues as separate from major topics such as modern narrative (Chen, 1990) and realism (Anderson, 1990; Wang, 1992), but it is also in evidence in examples of feminist scholarship. I focus the following comments on the latter.

Certainly, as even a cursory survey of bibliographies of contemporary research would attest, there has been no dearth of scholarly attention to Chinese women or gender-related matters. Yet, for all the exciting archival discoveries and keen critical insights that such research has begun to yield, there remains a need to understand the basic protocols of mainstream Chinese literary history that can marginalize women's literary feminism.[72] Without questioning this critical framework—including inherited perspectives on historical periodization, genre, authorship, and thematic "obsessions"—our attempts to comprehend the roles women played in producing modern culture will be thwarted. To cite one example, by uncritically adopting a periodization that locates the origins of cultural modernity in the May Fourth era, feminist research can overlook the pioneer generation of female radicals in the pre-Republican period who helped pave the way for May Fourth feminism.[73] Another tendency in current discussions of gender and feminism in modern Chinese culture is the over-privileging of male-authored texts at the expense of women's perspectives. Obviously, the conspicuous championing of feminist ideologies on the part of modern male literary intellectuals continues to warrant serious critical attention, especially since their work was often not what it seemed (Chan, 1988; Yue Mingbao, 1993; Lieberman, 1998). Yet, by focusing exclusively on what men had to say about such issues, women's participation in these historical debates can be critically undervalued. Meng Yue and Dai Jinhua observe in their study of women's writing,

> For a number of reasons many of the key images of women in modern Chinese literary history initially came from the hands of male authors. This is not to suggest that there is something particularly amazing about male inscriptions of women but that many of the new concepts of women are owed to male masters. For example, the conception of the traditional Chinese woman is inseparable from Xianglin Sao (Lu Xun's "Zhufu"), the conception of the May Fourth woman is inseparable from Zijun, and the image of the new woman of the Communist Party in the 1920s comes from Mao Dun's *Shi*, and that of the liberated woman from [Tian Han's] *The White Haired Girl*. (4)

One of the key reasons (though not one these authors cite) is that literary historians have selectively privileged these texts: more is known about the male constructions of "woman" because, quite simply, women's writing has not been adequately represented in official accounts of modern Chinese literature and culture. Although Meng and Dai's study represents an important (and promising) countertrend, the persistent masculinist focus of literary history has too often been mistaken for confirmation of women's historical absence from gender debates. Thus, in his forceful critique of the discourse on the "New Woman" (*xin nüxing*) in May Fourth fiction, Stephen Chan brackets "female writers like Ding Ling" in order to devote his attention to Lu Xun, Mao Dun, and Yu Dafu, only then make a series of sweeping claims about the impossibilities of the new women's self-representation. His critical objective, to his credit, is to unveil the masculinism operative in the works of established May Fourth male authors, but to what extent may it be said that his own critical practice unwittingly repeats the marginalization and silence he critiques? What about Ding Ling and her unnamed contemporaries?

* * *

The chapters that follow proceed in roughly chronological order. In chapter 1, I begin with the emergent moment of Chinese feminism and the women's movement in the late Qing (1895–1911), a moment marked by an unprecedented flowering of journalistic and literary activities among a small number of politically oriented women writers. Liberally educated daughters and wives from elite families, some of whom had studied abroad in Japan, such writers seized upon on the reform press and fiction to extend the current nationalist discussions on women and political reform to a much broader range of feminist concerns. The major themes they tackled—nearly all of which would be echoed in the ensuing decades—included: women's political rights and responsibilities, family and marriage, the repressive double standards of Confucian sexual morality, female education, professional occupations, and physical liberation from conventional practices like foot binding. My analysis focuses, in particular, on two utopian literary fantasies of female liberation, *Nüyuhua* (Flowers in the female prison, 1904) and *Jingweishi* (Stones of the Jingwei bird, 1907) by women writers Wang Miaoru (1877–1903) and Qiu Jin (1875–1907). While their appropriation of this popular fiction genre was undoubtedly encouraged by the New Fiction (*xin xiaoshuo*) debate initiated by reform-minded late Qing literati, I argue that the imaginary projection of egalitarian futures may also be seen as a specific means by which these writers endeavored to defamiliarize traditional gender boundaries and to construct for their readers a fresh vantage point from which to perceive women's roles in society. Reminiscent to a certain degree of the didactic Confucian literature for women of earlier periods, the implied reader is the object of intense pedagogical effort: both authors use their texts to dispense specific information and models of feminine conduct for the reader to emulate. What is decidedly different, however, is an acute awareness that the transgressive content of their texts competes with inherited knowledges and modes of consciousness that have long underpinned women's subordination. In this sense, their fiction posits and engages the notion that feminist transformation is not just a matter of enacting external measures of legislative or social reform, but requires internal, psychological change on the part of women.

Not surprisingly, given the alarming expansion of Western imperialism in China at the time, coupled with the perceived shortcomings of the ruling Manchu regime, the issue of national salvation figures prominently in this fiction, as Charlotte Beahan and others have documented with regard to the early women's press (*nübao*) in general. But the ways in which creative writers dramatized key feminist concerns of the day in their fiction also challenge the common assumption that this pioneer generation "subordinated" such concerns to the agenda of nation-building as envisioned by male reformers. The personal empowerment of the activist heroine(s) at the center of their novels, for instance, is never merely a matter of fulfilling patriotic duties, but is represented as hinging on her awakening to her subordinate position in the family and marriage.

The formation of an educated, cosmopolitan female elite that, by the 1920s, was familiar with a wide variety of imported feminist theories and the earnest homegrown polemics focused on the *funü wenti* is key to understanding the New Women writers (*xin nüxing pai zuojia*) explored in chapter 2. Described as the female literary vanguard by critics and publishers who championed their "bold" and "candid" depictions of romance, desire, and female sexuality, Lu Yin (1898–1934), Feng Yuanjun (1900–1974), Chen Xuezhao (1906–1991), and other New Women authors addressed their audience as an enlightened peer group with shared concerns and aspirations, rather than as complacent subjects in need of ideological conversion. Not that their fiction relinquished designs upon the reader: at a moment when the New Culturalists vied to stake claims over the meaning(s) of China's modern womanhood, these writers developed literary devices (including a quasi-confessional narrative voice that sought to elicit the reader's sense of identification and sympathy) to promote and validate their own version of the "new realities" of female life. The feminist issues they thematized in their narratives overlapped with, but also often interrogated, the May Fourth gender discourse: in fiction centering on the highly topical subject of modern marriage, for instance, they challenge the increasingly common view that marriage based on free love embodied the solution to the inequities associated with the old Confucian family system. In story after story, marriage is represented in terms of loss and isolation for the modern woman, a site of reconfigured patriarchal relations and therefore an obstacle rather than the answer in her search for independence and a self-actualized, meaningful life. My analysis attempts to recontextualize the New Women writers' experimentation with subjective realist forms—most notably the diary short story and epistolary fiction—alongside the literary/aesthetic debates about notions of realism and representation current at the time and suggests that these self-consciously textual forms reflected, while at the same time reinforced, an emergent valuation of women's authority vis-à-vis the domain of female experience. However, while the production of short stories and novels by and about the New Woman continued well into the 1930s (a clear indication of an enduring market for such fiction), it is male authors such as Mao Dun, Ba Jin, and Lu Xun who have been credited in official literary histories for creating the figure of the liberated modern heroine (even as contemporary critics begin to enunciate a more critical perspective on the reasons why these authors professed such interest in this new literary figure in the first place). Throughout the chapter I thus also reflect on the process of canon formation in relation to feminism's ongoing interest in promoting women's self-representation.

In chapter 3, I turn to the fraught intersection between feminist sexual politics and leftist literary culture of the 1930s in order to reassess the assumption that gender issues were largely abandoned as progressive intellectual women increasingly sought to put their fiction at the service of revolution. To be sure, such writers found themselves in a literary/ideological environment that had changed considerably from the previous decade. Once encouraged to add their voices to the chorus of debate on the "Woman Question," writers now risked being discounted by leftist critics for continuing to dwell on domestic subjects, as Wendy Larson has assiduously documented.[74] And, though gender equality remained on the revolutionary agenda, literary radicalism no longer offered any clear direction on how to address women's concerns as part of the broader social struggle. Under these circumstances, it is hardly surprising that some writers (Ding Ling is often cited in this regard) began to bracket gender issues in their work. Yet this is only part of the story, for other radical women writers chose to confront this erasure, often foregrounding in their work the travails of female activists immersed in a movement seemingly insensitive—if not altogether indifferent—to their dilemmas. Stories tracing the trauma of pregnancy and its impact on

political commitments, for instance, resist the new boundaries being erected
between private and public experience and problematize the revolutionary
narrative in which female desire is mobilized on behalf of national salvation.[75] For these writers, meaningful transformation of the social order was
not to be achieved by transcending the problem of gendered subjectivity but
instead required the transformation of gender subjectivity itself. In particular, I focus on two of the most prominent "activist" writers of the period, Bai
Wei (1894–1987) and Xie Bingying (1906–2000), both of whom published
autobiographies at this very moment—a gesture that clearly defies the
simplistic opposition that was being set up between personal struggle
and political change. Through careful consideration of Bai Wei's mammoth
Beiju shengya (Tragic life, 1936) and Xie Bingying's *Nübing zizhuan*
(Autobiography of a woman soldier, 1936), I address the use of autobiographical narrative to redefine the female self as a social construct and to
reassert the interconnections between individual and social, personal and
political, transformation against a revolutionary aesthetic that increasingly
trivialized gendered experience.

Finally, chapter 4 explores the appearance of comic narrative strategies in
works by Yang Jiang (1911–), Su Qing (1917–1982), and Zhang Ailing
(1920–1995), three women who became active in literary culture under the
Japanese occupation of Shanghai in the early 1940s. The central themes of
their writing were by then familiar ones: criticism of the patriarchal family,
the dilemmas of marriage and divorce, the experience of motherhood, and the
question of women's vocations and economic autonomy. What was markedly
different from earlier treatments of such themes, however, was the subversive
humor that underlies their narrative stance. Neither sentimental in its
engagement with the new woman's struggles, as seen in May Fourth
women's writing, nor doggedly polemical in the manner of a Qiu Jin or Bai
Wei, what we find now is a more detached, even cynical, comic vision and a
more playful approach to literary expression, which foregrounds not the
unrelenting power of patriarchy but its abject absurdity. In this regard, this
literature is clearly consistent with the "antiromantic" trend Edward Gunn
has traced in Shanghai literary culture during the war.[76] Gunn attributes this
development to the convergence of a number of historical factors—the
growing political skepticism of a "disillusioned" and "war-fatigued" public,
the commercialization of urban culture, and the constraints of political
censorship. All are similarly relevant in elucidating the forms feminist literary
expression assumed at the time, though to this list I would add: a heightened
self-consciousness about gender ideology that evoked new responses to
patriarchy. By the 1940s, one could argue that the "rhetoric" of liberation
had become an overly predictable feature of both political and cultural
discourse; to write about the plight of women without acknowledging this
would not only have seemed naive but risked eliding the engagement of a
potentially large and generally receptive public audience.

The sexual stereotypes that are mocked in these writers' works, for
instance—Yang Jiang's silly romantic suitors (*Nongzhen chengjia* [Forging

the truth], 1944) and Zhang Ailing's practical *femme fatales* (*Qingcheng zhi lian* [Love in a fallen city], 1943)—reflect a similar self-reflexivity, calling attention less to the social "realities" of gender relations than to the ways in which patriarchal culture has imagined itself in fiction. But if the comic elements of this writing are symptomatic of a particular historical juncture, they are also literary strategies that produce particular effects. They include, for example, an increasing use of irony to deflate patriarchy's authority. Thus, although the fictional world depicted is still very much a man's world, the men who populate it have been demoted from their tyrannical stature as villains who control women's lives to self-deluding buffoons whose author-ity is more illusory than real. Joining the gallery of twentieth-century femi-nist character-types, one also finds a new laughing heroine: neither suffering victim nor radical revolutionary, she disrupts the rules of patriarchal culture by playing its games to her own advantage, mimicking feminine stereotypes to outwit her would-be oppressors.

In general, this writing shows more attention to language and form and offers a new maturity in feminist literary articulations. It can also be viewed, however, as a contradictory retreat from politics at the very moment when self-consciousness would seem to urge the opposite. But one should go further by analyzing the formal attributes of such fiction and drama. Here, for instance, the comic techniques employed include a destabilizing of the dichotomy of male power/female powerlessness. Thus, what might seem a withdrawal from the politics of the public sphere may represent a renegotia-tion of its terms within an expanded and innovative literary method. It is precisely to these contradictions and possibilities of political and literary expression that the central chapters are dedicated.

While the new challenges faced by women as writers and as feminists in the Maoist era (1949–1976) fall beyond the scope of the present study, in the conclusion I lay out a series of questions that serve as potential avenues for future research. These include: what became of the writers and veteran activists involved in gender politics in the post-49 era? How and to what extent did the advent of state feminism, in particular the All-China Women's Federation, support and promote cultural work as part of its agenda? For example, can the massive distribution of storybooks to promote knowledge among rural women of the newly enacted Marriage Law in the early 1950s be seen as a new mode of feminist cultural practice? How do the types of per-sonal narratives and memoirs featured in the *Fulian*-sponsored magazines such as *Xin Zhongguo funü* (New Chinese women) compare with women's self-writings of the previous decades? These questions do not constitute a blueprint, but they are meant to offer a sense of the continuities and breaks that exist between the period I analyze (1900–1949) and the Maoist era that follows. Thus, I see this study not just as an intervention in its own period focus but as a provocation for cultural critique beyond it.

CHAPTER 1

NATIONAL IMAGINARIES: FEMINIST FANTASIES AT THE TURN OF THE CENTURY

> The Darkness. Darkness is when there is no truth, no knowledge, nor any proper human thought or action. In the chilling context of the darkness, there are a million unthinkable dangers. But the truest danger of all is oblivion to danger; oblivion to danger *is* the great darkness.
>
> Qiu Jin, 1907

> When you're a woman before there is a language of feminism, trying to understand what it's like to be a woman, you have no concepts, no vocabulary for even understanding your own situation.
>
> Marge Piercy, 1986

In the premiere issue of *Zhongguo nübao* (Chinese women's journal), one of several dozen feminist magazines that flourished briefly in late imperial China, Qiu Jin (1875–1907) conjures up a stark image of the condition of women in China as a "darkness" (*hei'an*) steeped in ignorance and injustice. The plight of her female contemporaries, she contends, arises not only from the narrow prescriptions of Confucian femininity or the social practices attending orthodox gender roles, but also from the state of self-delusion engulfing women themselves. Having internalized inherited gender ideologies, Chinese women had come to embrace the conditions of subjugation as a preordained social order. Indeed, according to the self-appointed feminist vanguard of late Qing China, the vast majority of Chinese women, or *nüjie*, were blissfully oblivious to their demeaned status as the playthings (*wanwu*), slaves (*nuli*), or chattel of men, to use the pointed terminology of the day. Feminist transformation, in other words, would lie not just in the arena of concrete sociopolitical reform but, crucially, required change at the deepest psychological levels: in order for women to begin to overcome their oppressed existence, they would have to first learn to imagine themselves, their experience, and their future potential in a radically different light.

For the great majority of late Qing feminist writers, including Qiu Jin, the "darkness" carried a dual significance: it referred both to the specific gendered experiences of women, and to their immediate plight as members of what was increasingly perceived to be a nation encumbered by decaying culture, official corruption and, above all, mounting foreign colonial aggression. As they often lamented, in their present state Chinese women were, in fact, doubly victimized—as the "slaves of slaves"—ensnared by both domestic bondage and the fetters of foreign domination.

By the time the nascent elite feminist movement had begun to stir at the turn of the century, China had suffered a series of humiliating military and territorial losses to the imperialist powers of Western Europe, Russia, and Japan, and the so-called scramble for concessions seemed to continue unabated. Foreign nationals were now free to take up residence in newly designated treaty port cities, exempt from Chinese law under the imposed provisions of extra-territoriality; Western economic incursions penetrated ever further inland bringing, among other things, the "legalized" traffic of opium; domestic industry faltered under fierce international competition. Accordingly, late Qing advocates of women's emancipation almost invariably articulated their mission not just in terms of gender reform exclusively but as an integral part of the urgent task to redress the sources of national subjugation and to transform China into a "modern" nation.[1] Thus the editors of *Zhongguo xinnüjie* (China's new women), one of the more successful feminist periodicals at the turn of the century, explicitly linked these two agendas in the inaugural issue in 1907:

> For thousands of years, the Chinese women's world has been subjected to conservative ancient teachings, and it is difficult to overcome the accumulated weight [of such traditions]. Even though we belong to an era of international communication and fierce competition, the custom of gender inequality has chronically blocked knowledge and evil practices of injuring the body are still entrenched in society. [These things] are deeply rooted and won't be easily eradicated. Those with superficial views say that such things have no bearing on the progress of the nation. Don't they know that although China's population is large, the majority—two hundred million—are women? Such is the case, yet while China has the most female citizens, it lacks the spirit of female citizens. So although there are citizens [min] is it tantamount to having no citizens.[2]

Another early women's publication, the *Liuri nüxuehui zazhi* (Magazine for the overseas female students' association in Japan), drew a somewhat different connection between feminism and nationalism by linking China's current political crisis to the traditional status of women.[3] In their mission statement (*fakanci*), the editors point out that since women are likely to suffer equally under the conditions of colonialism, the burden to resist this "peril" also falls on their shoulders; more polemically, they posit a causal link between the current inequities women were thought to endure and their historically poor record of civic participation:

> . . . men are not the only ones subjected to the peril of China being cut up like a melon. And therefore men are not the only ones with a duty to eliminate this menace. It is apparent that for thousands of years women have been completely muddleheaded: they have lived in dependency, taken obedience as their duty; they know nothing about the affairs of the nation, and have no idea what the relationship between women and the nation is. Therefore they have relinquished all national rights and their autonomy in relation to men.[4]

Perhaps not surprisingly, statements like these, which clearly privilege the nation (that it is on behalf of the national good that women ought to be liberated and that women would somehow overcome their social subjugation simply by dedicating themselves to this cause) have made scholars of early Chinese feminism justifiably wary of the motives of the late Qing women's emancipation movement.[5] The prevailing view that has emerged maintains that the pioneer generation of women activists who became vocal in political reform around the turn of the century ultimately failed to transcend the (masculinist) political struggle for national transformation because their specifically gendered concerns were invariably subsumed by their preoccupation with the plight of China-as-nation. Even if their unconventional activities sometimes went beyond the enlightened domesticity envisioned by their fellow male reformers, and even if they successfully broadened the parameters of the contemporary debate on female citizenship, it is maintained, they basically remained the dutiful handmaidens of the nationalist movement.

Historian Charlotte Beahan, for instance, whose groundbreaking essay on the early feminist press in China remains one of the most comprehensive accounts of the subject in English, concludes that the journals that appeared between the years 1898 and 1911 ultimately situated feminism within a framework of national politics in such a way that, "Women's rights were henceforth a cause which was indissolubly linked with, yet *subordinate to and defined by*, the interests of the nation" [my emphases].[6] In a more recent article, Tani Barlow, who cites Beahan's pioneering work, avoids the term feminist altogether in designating the "late Confucian women" who called for women's liberation in the radical press. While she concedes that such women positioned themselves differently from men (a positioning which, according to Barlow, is indicative of an important discursive shift in the gendered category of *funü* that occurs during this era), she reiterates Beahan's thesis that their primary focus of concern was China's nationalist liberation from foreign, including Manchu, imperialism, rather than the dismantling of patriarchal gender relations *per se*. As she ultimately contends, the new patriotic inscription of woman (which presumably includes that inscription in the work of the female journalists she mentions) in effect left dominant gender hierarchies intact.[7]

Feminism's alleged "subordination" to nationalist politics in the late Qing era has gained such wide currency that contemporary scholarship on issues of women, gender, and feminism in modern China tends to bypass this complex historical juncture altogether (or, at most, nod cursorily to the narrow nationalist-gender reforms espoused by male intellectuals like Kang Youwei and Liang Qichao); instead, what gets foregrounded are the subsequent May Fourth and post-May Fourth periods (Feuerwerker, 1975; Meng and Dai, 1989; Barlow, 1993).[8] Although this pattern of omission has clearly been compounded by other factors (not the least of which is the entrenched notion of May Fourth as the "origin" of modern Chinese culture), it has been partly rooted in the assumption that the women activists who made their debut in public politics beginning in the 1890s somehow failed (in a way their May Fourth successors allegedly did not) to locate an "authentic" position from which to express themselves as women or as feminists. To cite another example, Meng Yue and Dai Jinhua maintain in their groundbreaking study of modern women's writing, *Fuchu lishi dibiao*, that remarkable women like the cross-dressing Qiu Jin may have "emerged on the horizon of history" at the turn of the century by joining the realm of national political debate, but they did so by posing and speaking as men: it was not until May Fourth, it is contended, that women made history as women.[9]

The questions that these and other examples of scholarly research have raised about the relationship between feminism and nationalism in late Qing China and, by extension, about the politics of early feminist writing are important: Was feminism fundamentally a subordinate—or utilitarian—arm of the nationalist movement that sought to bring women into its fold in order to bolster its own "manpower"? Did the pioneer generation of women activists ultimately (if perhaps unwittingly) play out modern male political fantasies in their involvement in reform and revolutionary circles and in their literary imaginings on women? For instance, was their formulation of the female citizen (*nüguomin*), women who would assert their "rights" and fulfill their "duties" to serve the nation, in fact little more than an updated version of the age-old Mulan paradigm—that is, the (ultimately conservative) idealization of the self-sacrificing daughter who effaces her identity as a woman in order to save her (father's) nation?

While I fully concur with prevailing interpretations that the nation-problem profoundly shaped and even, in certain cases, detrimentally dominated late Qing feminist discourse, an examination of feminist literary writing of this key historical juncture does not entirely support the theory that efforts to liberate women were necessarily subsumed or constrained by the project to bolster China's national interests. Specifically, I would argue that while feminist writers undeniably helped produce a new national conception of women— by defining the *nüjie* as a political force that was to be mobilized in new ways to modernize or strengthen China, for example—in their myriad investigations of the effects of the dominant gender ideology and its social practices and in their utopian visions of alternative feminine futures, they also promoted a critical reconceptualization of women as a specifically oppressed group, whose transformation was predicated on but not synonymous with national liberation.

This can be registered on a number of different levels in the late Qing women's press, which I will briefly note here: first, along with a new lexicon articulating women's incipient identity as national subjects (*guomin zhi mu; nü guomin; guomin yiwu*; and so forth), one finds in the small corpus of feminist literature of this period an emerging terminology to specifically define women as a subordinate sexual category in relation to men: the darkness of the women's world (*nüjie zhi hei'an*); the slaves of slaves (*nuli zhi nuli*); gender discrimination (*nanzun nübei*); separate spheres (*nanwai nünei*); the toys of men (*nanzi de wanwu*); male tyranny (*nanren zhuanzhi*); women's rights (*nüquan*); gender equality (*nannü pingdeng*). These neologisms, a good deal of them introduced via Japanese translations of Anglo-European literature, marked the initial formation of a "language of feminism" that, as Marge Piercy's quotation at the beginning of this chapter suggests, is essential in fashioning new ways of naming and, hence, perceiving gendered experience within a patriarchal context.

Second, proliferating narratives of national women in the women's press reveal innovative plots of female experience, not solely of patriotic feminine self-sacrifice for the sake of the nation (though, to be sure, tales of Chinese-style Joans of Arc or modern Mulans were in abundance).[10] They feature the afflictions of wives and mothers, daughterly rebellions against the patriarchal domestic sphere, and struggles for self-fulfillment beyond the conventionally appointed feminine roles. Indeed, in a sharp departure from the familiar myth of Hua Mulan who temporarily masquerades to take her father's place in battle, only to subsequently resume her traditional feminine role (and garb), the newly imagined female citizen represented in many late Qing feminist narratives seems to embody a radical metamorphosis of feminine consciousness. Her desire to save the nation is mobilized less by a sense of virtuous duty to preserve and protect the dominant sociopolitical order (and thus her "proper" domestic place within it) on behalf of men, than by an enlightened desire to *transform* the nation by fundamentally altering the relations of power between women and men.

And third, many early feminist texts are marked by a self-conscious effort to inscribe a new kind of reading position for the women to whom they were explicitly addressed. Even when utilizing the new national nomenclature such as *nütongbao* or *nüguomin*, such texts interpellated women readers as *feminists* in a twofold manner. First, they invite the identification of the reader as a subject of systemic abuse affecting all Chinese women. And second, they encourage a recognition of this oppression as a historical (rather than a permanent or inherent) condition that had to be overcome, both for the sake of women in particular *and* for the national good.

Late Qing feminist writers deployed a stunning array of textual forms and rhetorical modes, both old and new, in their endeavor to "rewrite" women—everything from polemical essays to revolutionary poetry to international and domestic news reports—and I touch upon these briefly in an overview of the fin-de-siècle women's press below. My main focus in the present chapter, however, is the production of feminist literary fantasies, which I discuss via two primary textual examples:Wang Miaoru's *Nüyuhua* (Flowers in the female prison, 1904) and Qiu Jin's *Jingweishi* (Stones of the Jingwei bird, 1905), with occasional comparative reference to a third novel, *Nüziquan* (Women's rights, 1907), by the little-known male author Siqi Zhai.[11] Symptomatic of the curious confluence of popular culture and reform discourse in the final decades of the Qing dynasty, the feminist appropriation of fantasy—in the form of utopian tales of enlightened immortals who rescue women from the shackles of Chinese patriarchy, adventure stories of intrepid super-heroines who champion women's rights, and futuristic fictions of egalitarian societies in which feminine subordination exists only as a nightmare of the past—can be seen on one level as a strategic adaptation of a pleasurable narrative form in order to convey didactic political content. Like other contemporary writers, the authors I examine in this chapter were no doubt drawn to the genre in part due to its resemblance to the indigenous *chuanqi* tradition but also because of the refreshing novelties introduced to the genre through newly imported translations of works by European authors like Edward Bellamy, Jules Verne, and H.G. Wells. What interests me in particular, however, is how fantasy as a narrative mode can be read as a response to a specific historical need of the emergent feminist movement: namely, the need identified by Qiu Jin and echoed widely throughout the late Qing women's press to disrupt and challenge inherited and ingrained notions of "normal" gender arrangements—or, as Qiu Jin puts it, the "darkness."

The literature of fantasy, as Rosemary Jackson theorizes, accentuates "the basis upon which cultural order rests, for it opens up, for a brief moment, on to disorder, on to illegality, on to that which lies outside the law, that which is outside dominant value systems."[12] Extending this view to feminist literary practice, fantasy may be understood as a means by which the logic of a patriarchal cultural order is laid bare, by temporarily pulling back the ideological fabric that cloaks the subordination of women and, in turn, by subversively suggesting alternative feminine potentials. In radically reenvisioning women's experience within the late imperial social order as an experience of oppression and euphorically imagining more ideal modes of feminine existence beyond the confines of the Confucian domestic sphere, Wang Miaoru and Qiu Jin enlisted fantasy to call into question the gender status quo, to interrogate its seeming naturalness, and to generate new social and political desires for its demise. If I emphasize the subversive potential of feminist fantasy, I should also note that literary fantasy may also be put to extremely conservative ends. As theorists of the genre are quick to point out, political fantasy walks a fine line between engagement and escapism, inasmuch as the reader's political desires may be as easily diverted or dissipated as activated through their fictional wish-fulfillment. Moreover, as David Wang argued in his study of late Qing literature, *Fin-de-siècle Splendor* (1997), for all their high-minded rhetoric about the instructional value of the so-called new fiction, many late-nineteenth- and early-twentieth-century novelists, fantasy novelists included, actually reveal a marked ambivalence with regard to the reader's moral and political edification. Thus, in a novel such as Haitian Duxiaozi's *Nü Wa shi* (Stone of the goddess Nüwa, 1905), ostensibly a work on women's liberation, the plot gets repeatedly sidetracked by entertaining descriptions of super high-tech gadgets and, arguably, the social message is ultimately lost amid the outlandish escapades of the heroine.[13] In evaluating the potential ideological effects of feminist fantasy, then, this tendency is certainly something that must be kept in mind. On the other hand, the generic pitfalls of fantasy seem to have been anticipated by the authors I examine, for in each case strategies are developed to prevent readers from, as Qui Jin's narrator puts it, treating the narrative in question as mere "fiction."

In the examples treated below, a utopian vision of feminist liberation is represented as a movement toward a more perfect nation of the future, either directly as part of the narrative action or through interpolated commentary by an explicitly patriotic narrator or character who time and again interprets the significance of gender transformation in national terms. *Nüyuhua* is a short episodic novel that depicts a two-stage gender revolution in China, beginning with a militant insurrection against male tyranny and culminating in the peaceful liberation of women through educational reform. Informing the author's vision is a particular theory of revolution prevalent among late Qing thinkers, as proceeding from a violent stage of struggle to harmonious social evolution; the tale, however, is also a cautionary one, calling for a reformed national order organized along egalitarian principles by way of a dystopian view of the potential menace of radical feminist separatism. *Jingweishi* (1905–1907), Qiu Jin's unfinished *tanci* dramatizing the amazing metamorphosis of five sheltered "talented beauties" into a rebellious sisterhood, suggests that women's liberation from the patriarchal domestic sphere constitutes the very foundation of national revolution. Inspired by the enlightened Huang Jurui, the young ladies steal the money and jewelry set aside for their dowries, travel abroad to Japan where they align themselves with exiled radicals, and eventually return home to China to take part in a successful feminist-national revolution.[14]

Differences notwithstanding, these works of fiction undertake a far more complex negotiation of the problems of national and gender transformation than the prevailing hypothesis of feminism's subordination to nationalist politics in the late Qing period might lead us to expect. Thus in each case, the symbolic relocation of the heroine(s) from domestic spaces into the public realm is precipitated not by the national emergency but, crucially, by a crisis in the patriarchal family itself. The heroine's transgression of conventional feminine roles is represented, accordingly, not as a temporary foray into forbidden male territory nor as an expanded enactment of feminine virtue, but as a result of dissatisfaction with the limits and liabilities of such roles (e.g., domestic confinement, arranged marriage, lifelong dependency on men) on the one hand, and desires for a wider range of opportunities for self-fulfillment (access to higher education, economic autonomy, unfettered public mobility, and romantic choice, for instance) on the other. In *Jingweishi*, for example, the five dutiful daughters are mobilized in response to the physical suffering and intellectual frustration they endure in the "fragrant boudoir." The imposed frailty of the female body, the gender bias inherent in Confucian moral and sexual codes, stifled intellectual potential, and other issues fuel the heroines' disenchantment with their assigned roles, although the concrete impetus for mutiny comes when Huang Jurui's parents arrange for her to marry the debauched son of a rich merchant. The decision to run away from home is thus propelled first and foremost by a longing to break out of the enclosed, debilitating domestic existence to which their lives would otherwise be confined.

Similarly, *Nüyuhua* begins as a tale of domestic rebellion in which the heroine awakens to the inherent role limitations within the family and marriage and then abandons home in search of more independent modes of feminine identity within the social world. As in *Jingweishi*, the heroine's quest is not cast primarily as a search for individual liberation, as would become typical in May Fourth fiction, but is represented as a collective enterprise for Chinese women in general. In both, the importance of collective change—no doubt partly inspired by discussions of *qun*, or association, among late Qing reformers—finds expression in the formation of public alliances of all sorts.[15] Whereas the domestic space is now associated with debilitating isolation, the heroine's journey into the social landscape brings her in contact with a supportive female community, in political coalitions, newspaper and magazine editorial boards, anti–foot binding organizations, revolutionary cells, women's schools, labor unions, even the international women's movement. Rather than private ties of kinship, these networks are based on intellectual and ideological affiliations, and not only provide a new way of imagining women outside of their conventional male-determined identities as wives, mothers, or daughters but valorize a new sense of gender identification among women based on empowering political bonds and solidarity against their common experience as subordinated subjects.[16]

By arguing that feminist fantasies operated as an ideological space through which, on the one hand, the patriarchal "real" was subjected to radical scrutiny and, on the other, visions of a new female subject (as self-determining historical agent) were given shape, a major aim of the present chapter is to revisit the issue of feminism's relationship to the nation in the late Qing. And here the insights of contemporary cultural theories of nationalism come in useful. For it is proposed that despite the way in which "the nation" is commonly invoked—as objective geo-political entities that emerge with the advent of "modernity" or as the construct of nationalist ideologies— nations are the products of far more ambivalent, variegated, and fluid processes of naming, narrating, imaging, and remembering. They are, in Benedict Anderson's phrase, "imagined communities," which are given form and imbued with meaning by, among other things, the myriad fictions members of a given culture produce about its collective self—past, present, and future. And while these multiple fictions are almost invariably muted by the privileged narrative that eventually becomes official History, the *diverse* stories produced at any given point in time bear witness to the heterogeneous, and always contentious, voices of "the people" and their struggles over what (and who) the ideal political community might be and how that might best be achieved.

What theorists of nationalism can no longer ignore, thanks in no small measure to the work of feminist critics, is that national imaginaries are also inherently gendered discourses.[17] On the one hand, gendered metaphors of sexual difference, desire, and family have tended to figure prominently (albeit in culturally specific ways) in representations of nationhood, helping to render in putatively natural terms particular political interests and configurations of power. On the other hand, never fixed or unmalleable in the first place, gender categories themselves are particularly open to ideological contest during moments of social transition, not the least by the women intellectuals and activists who have been historically mobilized in national movements of modernizing states. To neglect the historic role of women and gender in creating the national imaginary is to perpetuate masculinist discourse for "if nationalism is not transformed by an analysis of gender power," writes one leading critic, "the nation-state will remain a repository of male hopes, male aspirations, and male privilege."[18]

It is from this more nuanced approach to the "nation" that I propose that the emergent moment of feminism in China might be better understood by asking a slightly different question than the one that has shaped the inquiry up to now. It is not simply whether or not early feminists were centrally engaged with the question of "China-as-nation" (which they undeniably were). The crucial point is how, in their various struggles to effect positive change in the sphere of gender relations, they helped produce or invent their own "myths of the nation?"[19] In other words, rather than continue to assume that feminism simply served the nationalist agenda of the radical male intelligentsia by replicating its visions of enlightened wives and patriotic mothers, we investigate how feminist writers actively constructed their own narratives of patriotic feminist emancipation and, in the process, significantly altered the plot of the "story" of Chinese national transformation. How did their calls for domestic revolution (*jiating geming*) shift the site or scene of national crisis? By placing their specific agenda of emancipating the *nüjie* at the center of their narratives of national development, what version of "China" did feminist writers project? How do the national heroines who star in their stories act out narratives of social change which encode gender in accordance with a more emancipatory discourse on women? And, how did feminist visions of women's role in transforming the nation challenge the dominant nationalist notions of enlightened wives and modern mothers?

Before moving on to analyze the ways in which Wang Miaoru and Qiu Jin utilized the genre of fantasy to project visions of an ideal Chinese nation in order to reveal the limited, imperfect nature of women's present realities at the turn of the century, I want to briefly examine the ways in which "woman" and "nation" were being articulated in the late Qing press, particularly in the "women's press" (*nübao*). As I suggest, if this period witnessed new links being forged between woman and nation, it also saw a new relationship emerge between women and writing.

* * *

WOMEN, NATION, AND THE FEMINIST PRESS

The surge of political and cultural anxiety at the *fin-de-siècle* about the plight of the Chinese nation was, as is by now well known, accompanied by historically unprecedented alarm over the conditions of Chinese women and vigorous calls for specific gendered social reforms (Rankin, 1975; Ono, 1978; Zarrow, 1988; Liu, 1989, Lü, 1990). To some degree, this is hardly surprising: in an era of tremendous political turmoil, when China's geographical borders were being constantly redrawn as territory fell to the imperialist powers of Europe and Japan, age-old institutions replaced by new forms of social and political allegiance, and fundamental cultural assumptions and beliefs challenged by the heady influx of western ideas (often filtered via Japan) ranging from anarchism to social evolution, why should the dominant attitudes toward femininity have remained intact? Shaped to a large degree by the imported ideas of liberal political philosophers Herbert Spencer and John Stuart Mill who postulated that women's oppression hindered social progress, from the outset the gender debate was inextricably linked to the project of nation-building.[20] Thus as the writings of nationalist-reform intellectuals like Kang Youwei, Liang Qichao, and Zhang Zhidong amply testify, reevaluations of "woman" were informed by perceptions of political decline, moral degeneration, and racial weakness: everything from women's economic dependence on men, to widespread female illiteracy, to the prevalent practice of foot binding was now condemned as a source of China's malaise and, in particular, China's increasingly obvious vulnerability vis-à-vis the imperialist West. Accordingly, their utilitarian visions of enlightened wives and modern mothers—reformed females with healthy (re)productive bodies, disciplined minds, and patriotic loyalties—were projected with an eye to China's national transformation.

Two specific causes captured the nationalists' attention: the abolition of foot binding and the improvement of female education. Relying on the urban print media and local activist organizations, nationalists pressed eagerly for reforms in these two areas on grounds that they were vital to the mission of "strengthening the nation and preserving the race" (*qiangguo baozhong*). Thus, in the typical hyperbole of late Qing political discourse, one commentator called for the eradication of foot binding by connecting the survival of the Chinese race to the fate of the female foot: "In order to save the nation, we must save our race; in order to save the race, we must get rid of that which hurts the race, and is there anything more harmful to the race than foot binding?"[21]

Aside from the common complaint that foot binding was a national embarrassment (physical proof to the world of China's "uncivilized" ways), foot binding was regarded, along with female illiteracy, as an obstacle to the production and reproduction of a modern male citizenry. These two practices, it was widely held, not only bred an unhealthy form of female parasitism which unduly burdened men, but produced mothers and wives unfit to nurture the new kind of men China desperately required to turn itself into a modern nation-state. As most historians would agree, early nationalists were ultimately less interested in empowering women *per se* than in empowering women to better serve men; from their point of view, what China needed were women who could, in the words of Liang Qichao, "support their husbands and instruct their sons" and in those capacities "help the family and improve the race."[22]

By the turn of the century, however, male nationalists were not alone in reassessing dominant paradigms of femininity or in proclaiming connections between women and China's political destiny. Marking an important turning point in the history of Chinese literature, the late 1890s witnessed the emergence of a unique corpus of explicitly feminist writing (much though not all of which by women) for a newly constructed national audience of female readers, the so-called *nüjie*.[23] Starting in 1898 with the founding of *Nüxuebao* (Journal of women's education) in Beijing by a group of women closely associated with leading male reformers,[24] women activists turned to the modern media as a way of participating in the process of sociopolitical transformation. For the most part, such women appear to have been highly privileged, well-educated daughters and wives from the elite classes who had been exposed to politically progressive ideas circulating at this time among the enlightened literati. Between 1898 and 1911, over thirty periodicals dedicated to bringing women—as writers and readers—and women's issues into the arena of public debate were launched in treaty port cities of China and in Tokyo, which had become an important hub for progressive Chinese students and intellectuals as early as the 1870s. While this number is admittedly modest in comparison to the hundreds of political journals launched by male intellectuals during this same period,[25] it is important to keep in mind that the value of female literacy (not to mention the vocal participation of women in public forums) was far from being universally accepted, even among the scholarly elite. Independent political publications by and for women also mark a historical first: educated gentry women and high-level courtesans had begun participating in public literary culture with increasing visibility since the late Ming and, as Kang-i Sun Chang has recently shown, late imperial women on occasion even took on editorial roles in the compilation of poetry anthologies. Nonetheless, the fact that even a small handful of women self-consciously took it upon themselves or, in other cases, worked in collaboration with male intellectuals, to raise funds, establish editorial boards, compose and edit contributions, and oversee the printing and distribution of their own magazines marked a new level of literary and political autonomy among Chinese women.[26]

It was far from easy. In addition to political censorship (*Nübao*, for example, was forced to suspend publication due to its affiliation with the anti-Manchu paper *Subao* in Shanghai in 1903, while *Zhongguo xinnüjie* was banned in Tokyo, allegedly for having featured an article on female assassins[27]), financial constraints also brought a premature end to many early publications. Before her execution for involvement in a conspiracy to overthrow the Qing dynasty, Qiu Jin's *Zhongguo nübao*, for instance, was on the verge of financial collapse even after she pawned a valuable family heirloom to fund the second issue.[28] In general, it seems that no publication lasted for more than a few years, while many folded after just a few months. Just a decade later, China would witness the first commercially successful women's magazines, but in the late Qing women's magazines were financed largely by the founding editors and their generous friends (whose donations are often gratefully acknowledged in the magazines), rather than by revenues generated from advertising or subscriptions.[29]

Circulation figures for late Qing feminist periodicals have been difficult to estimate. *Nüxuebao* (1898) allegedly sold around 1,000 copies per issue, and *Zhongguo xinnüjie* (1907), the only other publication for which any estimates are currently available, is believed to have commanded the widest circulation of 5,000, all of which indicates that the feminist press reached a minuscule readership.[30] Yet, if the subscription locations such magazines listed are any indication, it would appear that however small the actual numbers of subscribers their geographical reach was not insignificant: these include major Chinese cities (Shanghai, Beijing, Nanjing, Tianjin, Guangzhou, Changsha, and Wuchang), Tokyo and, in the case of the slightly later *Shenzhou nübao* (Shenzhou women's paper) (1912–1913), London, Paris, and Champagne/ Urbana.[31] In terms of readership, it is probably fair to assume that a good portion were men; however, from a number of factors—including editorial statements of purpose and the prevalent use of explicitly gendered modes of address to readers as the *nüjie* or *nütongbao* in the actual contents of the magazines—one can infer that the primary target audience was female. Furthermore, the deliberate incorporation of texts written in *baihua* as well as simple songs and poetry (on such novel themes as "natural" feet and "civilized" marriage) would also suggest that such publications at least aspired to reaching as wide a female audience as possible. Some, like *Beijing nübao* (Beijing women's journal) openly advertised themselves as vernacular publications geared specifically for women with only a rudimentary level of education. Seldom adopted in a systematic fashion, even within a single magazine, the use of vernacular mandarin (the northern spoken dialect) in the feminist press, however, may reflect more than a practical response to the (perceived) educational limits of its female readership. For it would also appear to be part of the incipient effort—to be carried out more vigorously in the May Fourth—to foster the development of a national language, a common language which would, among other things, serve as a unifying force among the *nüjie*.[32]

Feminists availed themselves of the modern press under the inspiration of the cultural–political discourse of the enlightened late Qing elite. Faced with the dismal prospects of political reform (which came to a head with the

spectacular failure of the 1898 reform movement), high hopes were pinned
on the circulation of news and information, in addition to the celebrated
"new novel" (*xin xiaoshuo*), as the primary vehicles for affecting serious
social change. Expanding literacy among the urban masses of China's treaty
ports had already created a substantial market for the popular periodical press
(newspapers, tabloids, and fiction magazines) and many leading reformers
now came to believe that the very key to national renewal lay in tapping into
and transforming this audience. As Liang Qichao declared, with his characteristic confidence, in 1896: "the more the people read the press, the more
intelligent they become: the greater the press, the stronger the nation."[33]
The founders of the feminist press appropriated this logic (and the utopian
rhetoric) and proclaimed their mission to be nothing less than the transformation of all Chinese women. In the editorial statement to the magazine she
launched in Shanghai in 1906, Qiu Jin suggested:

> Who is responsible for controlling the force of public opinion and taking
> charge of guiding the citizens of the nation if not the press? Today, this maga-
> zine will unite our two hundred million women by circulating our news and
> serving as our general headquarters. It will enliven the *nüjie* and arouse their
> spirits.[34]

Like Qiu Jin's *Zhongguo nübao*, most women's magazines defined their
goals in national terms but, at the same time, underscored the need for a specific forum for women's issues. Indeed, according to Luo Yanbin, editor of
the successful Tokyo-based *Zhongguo xinnüjie*, the women's feminist press
was imperative precisely because male nationalists had failed to grasp the central importance of women's emancipation to China's national survival:

> The two best known political party publications boast of their own theories and
> bicker constantly; yet they do not discuss women . . . how, then, can they help
> China progress? . . . Do they not know that with China split into the categories
> of "male" and "female" the idea that China can prosper without raising the sta-
> tus of women is like a man who alls in half of his body but who still finds that
> he is unable to get out of bed? But they never see this.[35]

The theme that China's national progress hinged on ameliorating women's
social status was, accordingly, a hallmark of the feminist press. Yet crucially,
the vision of such change or indeed how it was to occur was by no means
unified. The wide array of political approaches to the problem of women and
the nation—from essays foregrounding women's innate rights to those
focusing on their civic responsibilities, from discussions on the need for
women's economic autonomy to demands that women exercise their power
through consumer boycotts of foreign goods, and from articles advocating
improved moral, physical, and scholarly training of women to those expound-
ing the unique qualifications of female assassins in times of revolutionary
struggle—reflects the extent to which such journals provided a valuable

discursive space for women to engage in public debates with one another about the very meanings of "feminist" and "national" change.

The nationalist inflection of the late Qing women's press has, as previously noted, been singled out by scholars as both its defining characteristic and evidence of the limits and constraints on feminist discourse of this period (Beahan, 1975; Zarrow, 1988; Barlow, 1991). An alternative interpretation of the dynamic and multivalenced debate that "national crisis" generated in these magazines might suggest, to the contrary, that nationalist discourse (with its attendant concepts of national salvation [*jiuguo*], citizenship [*guomin*], human rights [*renquan*], association [*qun*], social evolution [*jinhua*], and so forth) constituted an enabling force, which facilitated the construction of a new emancipatory discourse on women. First, somewhat analogous to the pioneer feminists of eighteenth-century Europe who appropriated the terms of liberal democratic philosophy to argue for the rights of women, late Qing feminists extended the logic of the nationalist debate in order to problematize the social subordination of women and to justify alternative social, economic, and political roles for women. Second, by framing their critique of the feminine condition in terms of the national interest they were able to legitimize an otherwise potentially threatening heterodox gender discourse that challenged many of the most cherished values of Confucian culture. Third, and what is of particular relevance to the question of women's *writing*, by calling upon women to assume a more public voice, nationalist ideology in an important sense "authorized" women to express themselves in much more public forums and across a far greater spectrum of literary genres than previously available to them.

The last point emphasizes that one salient characteristic of late Qing women writers was the sheer diversity of perspectives and approaches brought to bear on the mission of transforming women. If their agenda was, in the last instance, always political, they did not necessarily carry this out through overtly political writing. In addition to the steady fare of rhetorically charged exhortations to women readers to reform the *nüjie* and China and somber musings on the interconnections of gender and national crisis, such journals also provided an eclectic range of practical information (e.g., how to unbind bound feet or matriculate into a girls' school, solve common math problems or control household pests); news updates on women at home and abroad (e.g., the opening of new female schools in Shandong or the latest developments in the suffrage movement in England); biographies of eminent women of China and abroad[36] and profiles of prominent contemporary figures; translations; propaganda poetry and songs; and a variety of fictional forms, including drama and short stories. Reflective of the broad ambitions of early feminists, this formal diversity thus points to the extent to which the feminist press afforded an important creative space for the women writers associated with it. Not only did it give them literary license to experiment with multiple textual modes—philosophical essays, polemical tracts, pedagogical instruction, journalistic reports, historical biography, imaginative literature—but, as Beahan notes, it provided an unprecedented opportunity to showcase their literary versatility.

Recent efforts to trace the roots of Chinese literary modernity in the cultural transformations that occurred in the late Qing period have already drawn important attention to the shuffle within traditional literary hierarchies, the politicization of fictional content, innovations in narrative point of view and the voracious consumption of "translated" fictions from abroad.[37] What I have attempted to suggest here is that the late Qing was also marked by an important reconfiguration of the relationship between gender and writing. For this moment witnessed not only an explosion of new narratives about women but, in addition, the historically unprecedented debut of women writers who actively engaged in literary production as a form of political and public resistance to inherited ideologies of gender. Needless to say, how this "sexual/textual" revolution illuminates the explosion of interest in questions of women and women's writing in the subsequent May Fourth era is an area that clearly also deserves further examination.

Such writers were undoubtedly exceptional women. In the articles they contributed to radical newspapers and journals, the magazines they published, and the fiction they wrote, however, they confidently declared their mission to be nothing less than the transformation of *all* Chinese women. And, although this ultimate mission may have been as naive as it was ambitious—since after all, the vast majority of the *nüjie* at the time were illiterate women with neither the financial means nor the educational background to consume this new corpus of revolutionary writing—the textual productions of the first generation of feminist writers were nevertheless significant for a number of reasons: (1) they broadened the narrow nationalist discussion on women to many of the gender issues that would inform feminist debates for decades to come; (2) they developed new modes of narrative and nonnarrative writing, among them women's news, biographies of rebellious public women, and what we might call feminist fiction; (3) and, what I now turn to in an analysis of specific examples of this fiction, they helped construct a new female readership by calling into question conventional modes and standards of femininity and, at the same time, by presenting alternative visions as possible historical realities.

* * *

FEMINIST FANTASIES OF WOMEN'S LIBERATION

There are many over-determined reasons why fiction, a literary genre that had gained steadily in popularity over the course of the Ming and Qing dynasties, became the textual mode of choice among the late Qing reform literati, not the least of which is that it helped sell the reform magazines such as the ones I have just discussed. Another argument that surfaces in articles promoting the *xin xiaoshuo* at the time emphasized its status as a popular cultural form. Specifically, with its accessible colloquial syntax and wide popular appeal, vernacular fiction was deemed to be among the most effective media for reaching and teaching the semiliterate and literate reading public. Indeed, for fervent nationalists like Liang Qichao, dismayed by the prospects of political reform, fiction took on enormous importance in the project of national transformation. Thus he declared in his famous manifesto:

> To renovate the people of a nation, the fictional literature of that nation must be first renovated. Thus to renovate morality, we must renovate fiction; to renovate religion, we must first renovate fiction; to renovate manners, we must first renovate fiction; to renovate learning and the arts, we must first renovate fiction, and even to renew the people's hearts and remold their character, we must first renovate fiction. Why? It is because fiction exercises a power of incalculable magnitude over humankind.[38]

For writers specifically interested in the pedagogical potential of texts for female audiences, the question of accessibility was all the more pertinent: recent scholarship has revealed that elite women had benefitted from more lenient attitudes toward female literacy from the late Ming dynasty onward, and that new avenues for intellectual and creative pursuits gave rise to an identifiable female literary community. Building on these trends, the late Qing campaign for modern education reform brought even wider social acceptance of female literacy. Nevertheless, it is fair to say that at the end of the nineteenth century, higher learning was still largely an elite male prerogative. Even those gentry women fortunate enough to have received some schooling, either from a private tutor at home or at one of the newly established Western-style academies for girls, were often unlikely to have studied much beyond an elementary level. For this reason, the presumed advantages of fiction were deemed especially significant by feminist writers. Wang Miaoru, for instance, composed *Nüyuhua* in a deliberately unembellished style of vernacular Chinese, almost certainly with this kind of female reader in mind. Praising fiction as a democratic form, her heroine claims toward the end of the novel:

> To change the world, there is nothing greater than fiction; for while there are people who don't read the classics, there are none who don't read fiction. People with limited learning can't read the difficult classics, and even if they try it is extremely taxing. Only fiction, with its colloquial language, can be understood by all. (65)

Yet, even this is a gross overstatement. For the obvious fact remains that for the vast majority of Chinese women at the time, written texts, no matter how elementary or colloquial their syntax, were no more accessible than before. At a moment when their intended audience lacked basic literacy skills, how, then, could practitioners of the new feminist fiction carry out their emancipatory mission?

It is no coicidence that Qiu Jin, who established her reputation as a leading feminist agitator on the strength of her public lectures as well as the polemical essays she wrote about women for the radical press, adopted the popular oral poetic-narrative form of the *tanci* for what she intended to be her most extensive appeal to women.[39] Qiu Jin herself appears to have never directly elaborated on the link between the performative potential of the *tanci* form as such and female illiteracy; however, in an article contributed to *Baihua bao* (The vernacular news) around the time she first started composing *Jingweishi*, she put forth a strong argument on the value of oratory in promoting social change.[40] In addition to extolling the power of the spoken word to reach audiences beyond the literate elite, she asserts that, compared to the periodical press (so celebrated by Liang Qichao, among others), the oral message affords greater accessability because it is cost free and can be communicated regardless of time and place. What Qiu Jin is specifically defending in this particular essay is the practice of public speaking, one of the new political practices women activists in China (and Europe) were trying out.[41] Implicit in her argument, however, is an acute awareness of the inherent limits of the "literary revolution" envisaged by late Qing reformers (i.e., using written fiction to transform the largely illiterate masses) along with a highly pragmatic acknowledgment of the pedagogical potential of popular oral forms.

Commonly considered mere entertainment that catered primarily to women,[42] by the late Qing *tanci* fiction was among the many traditional cultural forms that had come to be seen as an detrimental influence in urgent need of reform. In the preface to *Ershi shiji nüjie wenmingdeng* (The torch of civilization of the twentieth-century women's world), a feminist tanci published in 1910, for instance, the author Zhong Xinqing asserts, in classic late Qing hyperbole:

> In today's society, people of all classes compete in the art of the *tanci*; in Shanghai alone, there are over 100 locations [where they can be heard]. But it is women who are particularly influenced by the *tanci*. Frequently they gather in crowds, laughing and talking as they listen; they sing at the beginning but during the silences there is none who is loud. And when it is over, they dwell upon it with great relish, describing it over and over with words and gestures; some even dream about it. That is how deeply the *tanci* moves people. However, the *tanci* literature is comprised of no more than the stories of illicit romance like *Sanxiao Yinyuan* and *Luo Jinshan* which are euphemistically described as "*caizi jiaren*" stories. These tales dazzle and dizzy the audience, who in turn pass them on approvingly by word of mouth. These tales are then imitated in real life, and that is why society is so degenerate.[43]

Insofar as the *tanci* tradition encompassed a wider thematic range than just *caizi jiaren* (scholar-beauty) romances, and in fact had proven more amenable to exploring adventurous topics than many other high-brow poetic genres, Zhong presents a somewhat misleading characterization of the form. His statement, nevertheless, reflects the emerging anxieties about the specific gendered effects of culture that seem in part to have propelled the search of late Qing feminists for new, or at least revised, aesthetic practices for women.

Concern for the perceived influence that the *tanci* form, in particular the romantic *caizi jiaren* genre, exerted over female audiences, then provides yet another reason why writers like Qiu Jin may have been drawn to the form: that is, they sought to counter its potentially harmful effects by reappropriating it as a feminist ideological practice.

The contradictions underlying the textual practices of late Qing feminism can be registered in other ways as well, among them the somewhat ambivalent representation of textual agency in emancipating Chinese women. On the one hand, the narratives under question are punctuated with optimistic references to the new urban print media—newspapers, magazines, manifestoes, and novels—which time and again are shown to play a pivotal role in the political awakening of the female protagonists and in their ensuing crusades to save fellow downtrodden women. Heroic credentials, furthermore, inevitably entail literary ability—though no longer in the style of exquisite feminine poetic talent of *cainü* of days past. *Nüyuhua*'s Sha Xuemei authors a scathing exposé of male domination entitled *The Book of Revenge*, while in Siqi Zhai's *Nüziquan* the heroine even earns herself the title "China's Spencer" (Zhongguo Sibinsai) for her forceful manifesto on the social consequences of women's subordination. The narrative emphasis, however, tends to fall less on the act of writing *per se* (as we will find in May Fourth fiction) than on the impact a text has on its female readers. Repeated scenes highlight the liberating effects of reading. Huang Jurui (*Jingweishi*) derives critical insight into the possibility of alternative social roles for women through the foreign books her tutor Master Yu, a proponent of new learning (*xinxue*), regularly supplies. And thanks to the enlightened ideas in *On the Rights of Women* (a copy of which she rather implausibly chances upon in her husband's library), Sha Xuemei is jolted into awareness of her subordinated position as a wife.[44] Clearly, these are examples of "fantasy" providing an imaginary resolution to a real problem.

On the other hand, underlying this highly idealistic view of textual agency is a rather less sanguine recognition that the (elite) literate female public was not a docile, malleable mass who could be easily or automatically manipulated. Both *Jingweishi* and *Nüyuhua* begin by projecting a naive female reader who (due to her allegiance to orthodox values) threatens to misinterpret or simply fail to comprehend the significance of the stories represented and, by extension, the urgency of feminist reform in the real world looming beyond the fiction text. *Jingweishi* thus opens with a passionate lament by the narrator who bemoans the fact that the women of China—the *nüjie*— remain utterly unaware of their subordination to men, complacent in their insipid domesticity. She writes:

> I am often pained that my sister compatriots remain in the World of Darkness, as though drunk or dreaming, oblivious to the changes around them. Even though there are now schools for women, few enroll in them. Let me ask you, of our twenty million women, how many still grovel at the feet of tyrannical men? Alas, today they continue to powder and paint themselves, chatter about

their hairdos and bind their feet, adorn their heads with gold and pearls, and drape their bodies in brocade. Toadying for favor, they ingratiate themselves to men—obeying their commands like chattel. They are no more than the servile and shameless playthings of men. But though they are subjected to immeasurable oppression, they are unaware of their pain; they suffer abuse and humiliation, yet they have no shame. They are completely blind and ignorant, saying with foolish serenity: this is our fate. They feel no shame begging like slaves and groveling on their knees. (121)

Even though the narrator goes on to point out that there are new books which could potentially instruct Chinese women otherwise (Qiu Jin perhaps had in mind here such groundbreaking tracts as Jin Yi's *Nüjiezhong* (Women's bell) (1903), the first book-length analysis of the subjection of Chinese women, or Ma Junyu's translation of Herbert Spencer's *The Rights of Women* (1902), both of which had recently been published), women's ignorance and their "narrow realm of experience" render the possibility for new forms of female self-knowledge exceedingly difficult.[45] There still exists, in other words, a significant gap between women's own perception of their lives and the views of enlightened authors. Similarly, *Nüyuhua* is prefaced with a grim assessment of women's failure to learn from the revolutionary literature now available to them; rather than take seriously these new works, they have simply "paid them no heed, refusing to give them any thought or make any effort to reclaim their own rights to autonomy." Thus she soberly concludes, "women have grown so accustomed to being slaves they're unconscious of their own suffering" (1).

The problem articulated by Qiu Jin and Wang Miaoru (and widely decried throughout the feminist press of the time),[46] namely, women's internalized identification with their subjugated roles, provides an important key to understanding the use of fantastic narrative techniques among the pioneer generation of Chinese feminist writers. Whereas for the subsequent May Fourth generation the so-called *funü wenti* would become a more or less fixed (albeit not uncontested) facet of intellectual discourse, late Qing feminists evince a keen awareness of the daunting task of having to bring into being a whole new way of apprehending women, of finding, to use the words of American feminist Adrienne Rich, "the language and images for a consciousness [they were] just coming into."[47] That is to say, they recognized the difficult but urgent challenge of deconstructing the patriarchal myths that had hitherto molded women's subjectivity and replacing them with new "fictions" by which to imagine their relation to the world.[48]

Nowhere is this challenge captured more forcefully than in a dream episode from Wang Miaoru's novel *Nüyuhua*. In this vividly described scene, the protagonist Sha Xuemei dreams that she has been ushered into a grand hall where she is ordered to kneel on the floor with a throng of women and livestock. Beside them lie torture devices of all sorts. Certain that she has committed no offence and doesn't deserve such punishment, she stands up to protest, whereupon the assembly of men sitting at the front of the hall order her to resume her deferential pose because, so they declare, such is her female "nature." Unlike the complacent women around her, who appear to have surrendered to this mandate, Xuemei again resists, appalled by the blatant inequity. She is on the verge of going to their rescue when she awakes. Despite the seeming transparency of its symbolism, in attempting to decipher the nightmare the following day, Xuemei and her disciples fail to establish any connection between her macabre vision and their own gendered "reality." Only later in the story, after Xuemei is forced to give up her vocation as a martial arts instructor by a husband who expects her to take up more conventional feminine pursuits, does the relevance of the dream to her own predicament become clear to her. Significantly, it is at the very point at which she identifies with the oppressed figures of the dream that marks the beginning of her feminist adventures.

As a rudimentary reflection of how hegemony operates, this scene captures the problem of the feminine subject under patriarchy: on the most obvious level, the dream itself illustrates how women themselves become, as a result of culturally enforced fictions of natural feminine subservience, the complicit subjects of masculine domination. What is even more salient, however, is Xuemei's initial (mis)interpretation of the dream. Read allegorically, Xuemei's failure to decode the spectacle of feminine subservience elucidates the bind presented by the naive reader initially posited by both Qiu Jin and Wang Miaoru's texts. That is, how can alternative images of women and women's lives make sense to (let alone inspire) an audience conditioned by patriarchal "realities," for whom being "women" was not yet considered problematic? By what means can the writer divest such readers of dominant ideologies? And how can these readers be made to recognize themselves in representations of oppression or, to borrow an Althusserian concept, how can they be interpellated as feminist subjects?

Obviously these are major questions that lie at the core of ongoing debates on feminist aesthetics, and I do not presume to offer simple answers here. In the space remaining, however, let me turn to some of the formal devices these particular authors developed to dismantle the dominant gendered subjectivities in which Chinese women were presumed to have become so invested. In my reading, these strategies mark an attempt to construct a new feminist reading position that invites (often in patently didactic fashion) the reader to reassess the norms governing gender relations so as to grasp the necessity/possibility of action leading to social change.

The initial strategy the authors of *Nüyuhua* and *Jingweishi* adopt, a convention they share in common with many New Fiction writers, is the projection of a defamiliarized vision of contemporary Chinese society, in each case one that draws into sharp focus the marginalization of women. *Jingweishi* begins with a thinly disguised allegory of Chinese history depicting an amazingly decadent nation branded by the international community as Slumberland (*Shuiguo*). Ruled by an emperor who can barely stay awake and bureaucrats who mysteriously develop symptoms of dementia and myopia as soon as they take office, the throne has been usurped by foreigners, a troubling development that, astonishingly, no one seems to have noticed. The narrator's main concern, however, focuses on Slumberland's long-standing tradition of sexual inequality. As she explains, despite the fact that women and men were originally endowed with equal intellectual and physical potential, over the inglorious course of Slumberland's history, powerful men "fabricated" spurious doctrines of female subordination by proclaiming, for instance, that "Heaven had mandated the superiority of men and the inferiority of women" (126). Duped by this and an array of other myths, in time women themselves acquired what is described as a "slave nature" (*nulixing*) and began to voluntarily consent to male authority, even enduring the "mutilation of flesh and bones" (127) in order to cater to the perverse male desire for tiny bound feet. Yet, even though these "slave women" now readily fulfill their demeaning duties, they are still subjected to innumerable abuses. Such is the suffering of the women of this land that rising clouds of grievances finally alert the Taoist immortal Queen Mother of the West to their plight.[49] Outraged by the "reckless tyranny of men," she dispatches a troupe of illustrious immortals on a divine mission to liberate the women of Slumberland (and rescue the nation from foreigners at the same time). Thus concludes the allegory.

Making little attempt to disguise the fact that she is representing China, Qiu Jin's dystopian vision examines prevailing gender practices of her own day: not only does the narrator expose the truisms and familiar tenets of womanly virtue and obedience as blatant masculinist ideologies, but she reenvisions women's compliance to normative feminine standards as a form of learned servility. One way this is carried out, a standard rhetorical maneuver of feminist writing of the period, is through a careful strategy of renaming. Thus the time-honored Confucian classics that contained and perpetuated the codes of proper feminine conduct are here designated contemptuously as "barbaric books" (*yeman shuji*), which rationalized the suppression of women (*shufu nüzi*), while popular precepts like the "three obediences and four virtues" (*sancong side*) are denounced as deliberate lies designed to keep women in their place and render them passive and ignorant. Far from mere linguistic play, what is demonstrated here is that insofar as language has been instrumental in the maintenance of the gender asymmetry, it is also crucial to gender reform: only by disassociating key terms from their habitual semantic usage, the author seems to imply, can women overcome their self-alienation. Qiu Jin uses this scene, moreover, to defamiliarize the reading process itself: having prepared the reader for a *deus ex machina* whereby the immortals are to descend to Slumberland to abolish gender discrimination, the narrator then proceeds to disrupt this comforting resolution by inserting a caustic reminder that divine intervention is a *fictional* device and that human agency alone can change the course of history. Like the fictional heroines in the tale that follows, the woman reader must shed superstitious fancies that "fate" is dictated by deities and supernatural forces and instead resolve to assume responsibility for her own future.

Nüyuhua also begins by projecting a highly dystopian view of women's status in Chinese society in order to highlight the injustice of the dominant gender order. This occurs in the symbolic dream sequence described earlier in which the protagonist is confronted with an alarming spectacle of female servility. Although quite different in formal structure and style from Qiu Jin's pseudo-historical allegory, this scene relies on many of the same tropes of captivity to reimagine women as patriarchal subjects. As in Qiu Jin's narrative, for instance, women are explicitly likened to slaves, draft animals, and prisoners in order to convey the utterly disempowered and undignified state to which they have been reduced. The author makes clear that such roles have been imposed (the horrifying instruments of torture scattered throughout the hall, for instance, are a blunt allusion to the consequences of disobedience or deviation from normative roles); but emphasis is again placed on how women themselves have been so thoroughly inculcated by the values of hegemonic culture that they are completely unaware of their exploitation. Just as Qiu Jin's narrator decries the fact that women have "surrendered every bit of talent and ceded the superior position to men" (126), Wang Miaoru draws particular attention to the issue of female complicity: complacent in their degradation, the female figures depicted in the dream display no overt signs of resistance to the inhuman manner in which they are treated and completely ignore Xuemei when she makes an attempt to save them.

Needless to say, neither Qiu Jin nor Wang Miaoru's visions of the utter benightment of women are meant to be taken at face value: for to the extent that they suggest an all-pervasive system of domination that has incapacitated women (mentally, physically, and verbally), would that not (paradoxically) preclude the possibility of any, including their own, counter stance? The stark imagery and rhetoric they deploy, I would argue, are intended to grab the reader's attention and to first, make her question whether she too has unwittingly accepted or internalized the servile mode of feminine subjectivity problematized by the narrative; and second, radically reorient her perception of unexamined aspects of her own life (e.g., physical beauty, marriage, and so forth).[50]

Both *Jingweishi* and *Nüyuhua* open with a critical exposé of sexist social relations and the psychological (and other) damage this inflicts on women. At the center of their main narratives, however, stand utopian heroines who not only dramatically alter the course of their own lives but, through advancing the cause of women's liberation on a national scale, the course of Chinese history itself. Traditional Chinese fiction admittedly abounds with powerful women who transgress Confucian ideals of feminine obedience and cloistered domesticity to venture into forbidden masculine terrains of military battle and public officialdom. From the legendary woman warrior Hua Mulan, who replaces her father in battle and saves the state, to the ambitious Meng Lijun,[51] who poses as a scholar and successfully ascends to the top echelons of the imperial bureaucracy, gender-bending heroines had long provided entertaining (albeit safe) scenarios of exceptional women who excelled across the sexual borderline. Safe, because while such unruly women, armed with impressive physical prowess, intellectual acumen, and adventurous spirits triumph beyond a prescribed feminine domain, more often than not they do so by masquerading as honorary men—hence, the recurring literary trope of female transvestism—and because the narrative resolution to their escapades typically celebrated a conspicuous *redomestication* of the heroine who, in the end, returns to her orthodox role of daughter/wife/mother.[52] In the late Qing, however, as radical writers self-consciously appropriated fantasy as a vehicle for social and political critique, an important shift seems to occur. In the hands of certain authors at least, the fantasy heroine came to be a figure through which traditional gendered divisions of power and identity were *self-consciously* explored, questioned, and contested. Accordingly, the actions of the heroines are no longer plotted as temporary transgressions or daring deviations from their customary gender assignments, but rather as a serious challenge to the ideological and social structures that tradition-ally regulated women's confinement and subordination within the family and home.

This is not to say the classical female knight-errant (*nüxia*) did not continue to offer an important source of inspiration for late Qing authors. Huang Jurui, who is herself described as looking "chivalric like clear spring moun-tains and as dignified as cold autumn water," openly admires the bravery of Mulan, Hong Yu, and Sun Guan, while Sha Xuemei's training in the martial arts not only affords her a vocation (as an instructor to the local children) but accounts for her remarkable physical prowess. At the same time, how-ever, much in the same way Ibsen's Nora was to capture the imagination of May Fourth writers in the 1920s, foreign figures unmistakably contributed to the new image embodied by the late Qing fantasy heroine.[53] The most notable, as other scholars have pointed out, being the Russian anarchist Sophia Perofskaya and French revolutionary Madame Roland, both of whom were frequently held up as exemplary models in the late Qing press, not to mention featured as the subjects of several works of fiction. Revolutionary spirit was not the only trait admired in foreign women, however: among others, Harriet Beecher Stowe (1811–1896) (who makes an appearance as an immortal in one *tanci*), was highly regarded for her political writing; Mary Lyon (1797–1849) and Florence Nightengale (1820–1910) (whose photographs adorn the study of Wen Dongren, one of Xuemei's associates) were also emulated for their respective pioneering work in women's higher education and the nursing profession.

As utopian figures who herald the triumph of an alternative social order, the late Qing fantasy heroine differs in important respects from her May Fourth successors—tortured *xin nüxing* whose feminist desires are more often than not thwarted by the intractable feudal mentality of the society around them or by their own psychological turmoil. Here no matter how challenging the obstacle (authoritarian Confucian fathers, abusive husbands, persecution by the law, incarceration) or far reaching their missions, their efforts invariably end in triumph. The valiant Huang Jurui (*Jingweishi*), who appropriately assumes the new sobriquet Huang Hero-of-the-Han, for instance, mobilizes her well-bred companions into a rebellious sisterhood, then helps found an egalitarian Chinese Republic; the gallery of extraordinary heroines in *Nüyuhua* awaken the *nüjie* and universalize education and healthcare for women.

The super-heroine is not constructed along realist lines as a historically plausible character endowed with psychological or emotional depth, but is instead a fantastic device for delivering the author's oppositional message. Unencumbered by the constraints which allegedly enslave the rest of the *nüjie*, the heroine's privileged position of knowledge and agency enables her to both apprehend and oppose the perceived injustice of the present gender order. On the level of plot, the utopian heroine acts as the mentor or guide for the unenlightened women on whose behalf she struggles; time and again, we find her delivering impassioned speeches about the origins of women's degradation, arguing the pros and cons of possible modes of redress with interlocutors, firing off political documents, and dispensing advice to anyone who will listen. As a heuristic device, such interludes constitute a key formal strategy, which allows the author to incorporate lengthy philosophical and political discussions of the current gender debates into the narrative while at the same time anticipating possible questions the text may spark in the minds of readers. Staging philosophical and political exchanges between characters over the nature of women's oppression and the meaning of feminist emancipation contributes to the feminist reading position in another important way as well: by interrupting the flow of dramatic action, these pedagogical digressions prevent the reader from becoming overly engrossed in the fictional world presented, or treating it, as Qiu Jin's narrator remarks, as mere fiction.

Nothing illustrates this better than the climactic scene in *Jingweishi* in which the main characters assemble together for the first time in the private chambers of Little Jade. The scene is structured in such a way as to first arouse the reader's sympathy through the emotional outpourings of the young ladies as they tearfully lament their stifled existence and, in particular, the bleak future of arranged marriage that awaits them. Stirred by Little Jade's confession that she had been severely beaten by her older step-brother the day before, one after another, the heroines vent their frustration over the systematic mistreatment of women. The issues they individually explore—which include the tyranny of the traditional system of arranged marriage; the enforced economic dependency of women through the deprivation of education, employment and property rights; the physical and mental enervation brought on by the meaningless feminine "arts" of needlework and sewing; the double sexual standard that condones prostitution, polygamy, concubinage, and wife-abuse while strictly enforcing female chastity—together comprise a stark inventory of the contradictions and constraints of traditional femininity the likes of which was rare in Chinese fiction up to that point. Yet, for all their indignation, a crucial element is missing from their conversation: namely, the ability to conceive alternative possibilities. Thus, when Huang Jurui belatedly arrives, for instance, the best advice her friend Little Jade can muster regarding the former's impending (and patently unsuitable) marriage is that she might as well concede to her parent's wishes: "I must urge you to stop taking things so hard," Jade says, "This is all your parents' doing and it's impossible to break off an engagement" (155).

Huang's reaction to this comment and the passionate argument she then proceeds to deliver to the assembled young ladies (and obviously the reader) on women's liberation, however, serve to introduce precisely such a perspective. Whereas her friends appear more or less passively resigned to their feminine fate, Huang Jurui is described early on by the narrator as possessing an innate aversion to the injustices of women's lives; perhaps even more crucially, she also has the distinct advantage of having studied under an open-minded tutor, Master Yu, who regularly supplies her (unbeknownst to her conservative Confucian father) with radical literature on women's rights in the West. Thus with her arrival, the discussion shifts abruptly from an anguished lament over women's woes to an affirmative lesson in the possibilities of alternative female roles within a new social order. Much to the amazement of her friends, Jurui discloses her defiant scheme to break off her engagement and go abroad to study, along with a detailed justification of her decision. (And, just in case the reader fails to take it all in the first time, Qiu Jin records the speech in full for a second time in the following chapter, when an eavesdropping maid reports it back to one girl's mother.)

Interestingly, Huang's oration draws heavily on examples of the allegedly advanced state of women's education and employment in Europe and America. Western women, as she informs them, enjoy schooling equal in quality and content to that of men, and compete on level playing fields in all academic disciplines, whether it be philosophy, chemistry, physics, or the arts. This training prepares them for professional occupations, most notably careers in business and teaching, which in turn earns them respect from their husbands (oftentimes former classmates with whom they have become acquainted prior to marriage). So great in fact is the respect that women command in Western society at large, not only for their accomplishments, but also because of their vital role as "mothers of the nation" that men stand whenever a woman enters a room and even go so far as to give up their seats to them in public venues! Needless to say, one could easily find fault with Qiu Jin's (mis) representation of Western women at the turn of the century. A more important observation is that, as a fanciful projection, it arms her heroine with a valuable mythology that verifies the possibility of gender relations other than the ones currently available (and currently imaginable) to the fictional heroines and again the implied reader.[54] (While I won't take up this issue here, it might also be observed that, complicating the notion of "Western influence" in China at the time, a fascinating new question arises: how did the "West" become the productive site of China's own fantasies of modernity?)

While the girls are duly impressed by Huang's amazing revelations (they declare in unison "It is as though we have just awoken from a dream!" 157), they are not entirely convinced. This lends some verisimilitude to the episode but it also serves as a rhetorical ploy by the author to persuade readers to readjust their views on current gender practices. When Zhenhua, for instance, balks at Huang's proposal that they all unbind their feet for fear that it might look unattractive, Huang promptly reels off a list of harmful effects caused by this longstanding custom as well as the multiple advantages of so-called natural feet. (Her explanations might strike readers today as all too obvious insofar as foot binding has come to epitomize women's oppression in traditional China; however, the considerable attention the text devotes to the issue underscores the extent to which women's investment in traditional standards of beauty and sexual attractiveness still hindered efforts to abolish the practice on the basis of its deleterious physical effects.)

Wang Miaoru also relies extensively on the use of reported dialogue and debate among her characters to explore current social and political problems facing women and to impress upon the reader the urgency of their resolution. Consider, for example, an episode that occurs after the woman warrior Sha Xuemei finds herself incarcerated in a women's prison for accidentally killing her husband during a domestic dispute. A highly symbolic setting, most of the chapter dwells on the heroine's attempt to rouse her fellow inmates (virtually all of whom have been wrongfully accused by jealous or malicious husbands) by delivering a fiery diatribe against the institution of arranged marriage and its various reprehensible consequences (among them, abusive mother-in-laws, prostitution, polygamy, and the cult of female chastity). Like Qiu Jin's narrator, rhetoric itself becomes for Xuemei a powerful instrument of attack, as we see in way she dissects the social category "wife" to reveal its resemblance to the less respectable images of slaves and criminals:

> Outside the home they treat us like slaves, while inside the home they treat us like criminals; think about it, who else but women make their beds, fold their quilts, serve their tea and cook their dinners? We are never suspicious about what they do outside the home, yet if we utter a few trivial words to a man, they suspect us of adultery, so they guard over us vigilantly. Men don't treat us like their wives but as though we were scheming servants. These multiple inequalities make me bristle with anger. (22)

Whereas Qiu Jin's text ultimately endorses a single perspective as the "truth" (after being enlightened by Huang's rousing lecture, the girls become sworn sisters, vowing to pursue their common goal to the end), *Nüyuhua* seems to acknowledge the possibility of competing political viewpoints. Debates in the latter novel do not necessarily result in consensus among the characters, and thus the reading position it inscribes is one that invites the reader's intellectual engagement with the issues rather than the simple identification solicited in *Jingweishi*.

One key scene in *Nüyuhua*, for instance, involves the chance encounter between the two lead heroines, the radical anti-male revolutionary Sha Xuemei and Xu Pingquan (literally, "Allow-Equal-Rights"), a liberal champion of the cause of women's education. Prior to this, the two have never met in person, although Xuemei has been eager to meet Pingquan ever since reading her feminist poetry at a roadside tavern. Yet despite the fact that the two heroines share a deep concern for the welfare of Chinese women, as their heated debate demonstrates, their interpretation of the very meaning of "revolution" (*geming*) and "liberty" (*ziyou*) couldn't be more different. Their main disagreement hinges on two fundamental questions: the present capability of Chinese women to emancipate themselves, and what liberty will entail. Xuemei vehemently insists that the ruthless sexism of contemporary society has reached such intolerable levels that a violent backlash by women is imminent. For her, the relation between the sexes is inherently one of domination and subordination, thus permanently locking men and women in an antagonistic competition for power: "Men are our eternal foes and enemies"; she maintains, "we can only kill them, not marry them" (21). The empowerment of women in other words, is contingent on the enslavement of men and vice-versa. In response, Pingquan points out that even were such a clean reversal of power relations desirable (which is not, in her estimation), at this stage of social evolution women have been socialized as the intellectual and physical inferiors of men and are thus incapable of prevailing over men. In her view, the apocalyptic change Xuemei predicts is therefore historically implausible. Besides, Pingquan argues, social liberty is not simply a matter of power but, rather, constitutes an entitlement accompanied by certain public responsibilities. As such, it is to be enjoyed by those suitably qualified. Women, who are currently "as ignorant as chattel," will only become qualified to share in the privileges of civil liberty along with men when they have received the proper moral, physical, and intellectual training. Paradoxically, given Pingquan's apparent espousal of a gradualist model of social evolution, she nevertheless sees some strategic value in Xuemei's radicalism: specifically (consonant with a certain vision of historical transformation current at the time), she views it as a necessary catalyst of change that will awaken women from their "foolish dreams."

The narrative plays out Pingquan's formulation of feminist change—sadly, Xuemei and a legion of her most loyal disciples commit suicide by immolation after the mass insurrection fails to materialize, though their spectacular self sacrifice proves an invaluable wake-up call to the female public. This, in turn, paves the way for Pingquan's reformist program, which she implements on a national scale upon her return from abroad. The earlier debate between these two women activists, however, which ends in an abrupt stalemate when Xuemei storms out of the room, highlights contending visions of the basis of women's subordination and its social remedy. Moreover, by presenting a range of views, the text invites the reader to recognize the issue as a significant debate with widely divergent points of view.

Siqi Zhai's *Nüziquan*, I would briefly note, contains similarly stark allusions to the potentially more violent strains of feminist politics. One of the heroine's first setbacks occurs when a band of militant women in Xinjiang storm a police station, killing several officers; when a copy of her newspaper is discovered at their headquarters, the authorities arrest her. For the most part, however, exchanges between female characters are used in this novel to present the reader with a concrete blueprint for social action. For instance, when Zhenniang addresses the Chinese Provincial Association in St. Petersburg (now home to a large overseas Chinese population), she details *how* women can achieve independence. In her speech, which as we would expect is recorded within the text (49–50), she attributes women's subordination to their socialization as dependent subjects who lack both the capacity for autonomy (*buneng zizhi*) and self-sufficiency (*buneng ziyang*). Her specific advice is to make use of the modern print media (specifically, vernacular newspapers) and the public lecture circuit to inculcate women with the principles of self-reliance and to promote vocational training. Like the heroines of the other two fantasies I have discussed here, Zhenniang is depicted as a pioneer leader of sexual reform; she is not, however, represented as the *sole* source of knowledge or social agency: on her global travels, she plays the dual role of disseminating information about the plight of Chinese women to the world and collecting useful ideas and financial support from the remarkable women she encounters. One young woman in attendance at her lecture in Russia, for instance, proposes that she circulate an international petition to pressure the Chinese parliament to enact constitution legislation, a measure that Zhenniang not only adopts but that turns out to be the linchpin in accomplishing her goals. Zhenniang's international journey, while perhaps less riveting than the extraterrestrial trips (*Yueqiu shimin di* [Moon colony, 1904]) or subaquatic expeditions (*Xin shitouji* [New story of the stone, 1908]) depicted in other contemporary fantasy novels, nevertheless yields an impressive arsenal of innovative political ideas, strategies, and resources: in Russia, at a conference convened by female labor unions, she realizes what a fully developed women's workforce entails (and how far China is from achieving that goal); in Berlin, she grasps the value of forging political alliances with progressive men; in New York, she gets her first taste of fund raising, and lands her first major donation from a wealthy widow. In short, going even further than the vision of collective action seen in either *Jingweishi* or *Nüyuhua*, *Nüziquan* imagines a broadly collaborative global "sisterhood," whereby women of multiple nationalities as well as the Chinese diaspora cooperate in pooling knowledge, experience, and material resources to effect change for the women of China.

    The final narrative strategy of the fantastic that I consider is the utopian resolution. Sharply contrasting the tragic outcomes that, as we shall see in the next chapter, typically befall the new women of May Fourth fiction, in these novels the heroines' quests invariably culminate with the acquisition of an ideal future in which the impediments to women's full participation in society as equal, autonomous subjects have been completely overcome.[55] Of course, to the extent that these visions of change were confined to the major concerns of late Qing feminism—educational reform, female employment, marriage, political rights, physical health, traditional morality—these endings represent what Angelika Bammer has termed a "partial" utopian vision.[56] Issues of female sexuality, for instance, are explored superficially, in terms of a reformed insitution of compassionate heterosexual marriage (i.e., one based on free choice, equal standards of sexual morality, and mutual respect) while the possibilities of sexual relations outside the institution of marriage, reproductive freedom, divorce, and other problems remain beyond their vision of change. Another glaring lacuna is the matter of class difference. Although we have seen that each of these authors envisions gainful employment as an indispensable measure for ensuring women's economic autonomy, none imagined economic transformation more radical in scope which would eliminate the exploitation of one class over another. In fact, while the heroines routinely discuss the importance of women's full access to work, we never actually encounter female laborers, only trained professionals such as doctors, journalists, and teachers. Or, as another example, consider the conspicuous exclusion of the intelligent and compassionate Xiurong, the indentured servant of Little Jade, from the "sisterhood" Huang Jurui mobilizes. Xiurong would appear to qualify as a sure candidate for the group, sharing both the high intelligence of the other girls as well as their deep empathy for suffering women, yet she is inexplicably left out of their plan of action. Needless to say, this smacks of a certain elitism in Qiu Jin's feminist vision.

Limits notwithstanding, the triumphant endings of these novels—in which conventional feminine roles in the Confucian family and arranged marriage have been supplanted by new modes of personal interaction and public participation, universal education and equal rights for women have been secured, and antagonistic gender relations replaced by progressive heterosexual cooperation—reveal much about the political desires of their authors. For as a narrative strategy, the projection of an ideal future world functions in (at least) a twofold manner: first and most obviously, it operates as a "critique of what is present," identified by Ernst Bloch as the "essential function" of utopia.[57] These futures draw into focus the inadequacies and contradictions of the gender status quo and, concomitantly, reveal that status quo to be a flawed historical condition rather than a preordained, permanent order of reality. In this way, these endings encourage the reader to question the "truth" of her present status and identity as a woman and to speculate about alternative possibilities. Just as the fictional heroines derive key insights into their predicaments as women in China through their glimpses into "other" worlds (whether via books or travels to distant lands), so too is the reader made to contemplate "reality" anew from the fictional presentation of what "might" or "could" be.

Second, as the narrative telos achieved through the active struggles of the female protagonists themselves, the utopian resolution emphasizes not only that social transformation is the product of historical struggle but, more crucially, that women's agency is central to the process of historical change. Thus unlike Kang Youwei's *Datongshu* (Treatise of grand unity, 1884–1885), for instance, a major utopian text of the late Qing period, which simply features liberated womanhood as a component of (his version of) the future ideal polity without offering any explanation of *how* women participated in realizing that state, these texts privilege the steps leading toward the more perfect society, a movement propelled by the raised consciousness of women and their dedicated work in the social and political arenas in bringing that society into existence.[58] It is important to note, in this regard, that although each of the narratives explored here also features pro-feminist men, they occupy conspicuously peripheral roles in the narrative action, as if to foreground the agency of the heroines themselves in undertaking their feminist-nationalist endeavors.[59]

Envisioning women as agents of historical change, rather than simply inert recipients of gains made on their behalf by progressive men underscores the fundamental agenda shared by all three writers: to galvanize women (readers) themselves to assume the responsibility as arbiters of their own destinies, specifically, to become aware of and in turn to overcome the structures of their oppression.

*   *   *

The utopian impulse of early Chinese feminism was extremely short-lived. With the founding of the Republic in 1911, political realities and new trends in literary fashion conspired to more or less extinguish the euphoric tenor expressed in the fiction explored above. Despite Sun Yatsen's promises otherwise, the National Assembly refused to recognize the principle of female equality or women's right to vote (even after, in an event deliberately evocative of the British suffragists, members of the newly formed Women's Suffrage Alliance stormed the parliamentary building in Nanjing). With Yuan Shikai's presidency such goals became all the more remote: in 1913, he officially banned women from joining political associations, attending political events, and contributing to radical publications. Such measures did not put a halt to feminist activism; they did, however, put a considerable damper on hopes that the "new" China would usher in better conditions for Chinese women. In literature, the new values accorded to realist modes of representation also led to an eschewal of the utopian sensibilities of the previous generation: the implications of this turn for politically committed women writers will be taken up in the next chapter.

CHAPTER 2

THE NEW WOMAN'S WOMEN

It is precisely due to the contributions of women writers that we are able know the New Woman who is in the process of being created.

Woman Writer Magazine, Shanghai, 1929

Today she was terribly upset because she had endowed an extremely level-headed and rational woman in her novel with unduly passionate emotions. Also, she had let a touch of melancholy slip in. This was definitely not the character she had intended to create, but it was the flaw in woman that she was able to understand best. She didn't know what would be better, to tear up the manuscript and start over, or to go on writing but *not* sympathize with the woman.

"Yecao," Ding Ling (1929)

As exemplary models and vehicles of instruction, the prototypical enlightened new women heroines of late Qing feminist fiction function less as a mimetic representation of reconfigured gender roles than as a feminist topos of antic-ipated change. By the early Republican era, however, the new woman existed not just as a literary construct but constituted an emerging social category. Despite the political setbacks encountered by the organized feminist move-ment in the early Republican era, particularly on the issue of women's suffrage, vigorous modernization efforts brought women greater access to education, including institutions of higher learning such as the Beijing Women's Normal College, which first opened its doors in 1918, professional opportunities (in such fields as teaching, medicine, and journalism), and expanded personal and political options. Such gains of course were to remain confined largely to the ranks of middle- and upper-class urban women, but the phenomenon of the *xin nüxing* (*xin funü; xinxing funü*), or New Women, as they came to be known, exerted a visible impact on the social, political, and cultural landscape of 1920s and 1930s China.

Literature, once again the focus of the reform agenda, also underwent significant change through the presence of the *xin nüxing*, not only because this new breed of women lent a compelling historical model for what were to become some of the most notable female protagonists of the May Fourth fiction canon, but because of their contributions as authors to contemporary feminist debates: they were journalists, translators, editors, essayists, cultural commentators, literary historians, and they were creative writers who turned in unprecedented numbers to the urban print media to experiment with a wide range of literary forms and genres to challenge and change cultural perceptions of gender difference and domination. It is somewhat ironic, given the May Fourth generation's own obsession with the linkages between textual representation and current social realities, that literary historical accounts of this period, while devoting considerable attention to the former aspect of the *xin nüxing*'s legacy has tended to overlook the latter. As a result, Lu Xun's Zijun, Mao Dun's Mei, and Ba Jin's Qin, not to mention Ibsen's Nora (probably the most popular feminist cultural icon in China at the time) are familiar figures; we know far less, however, about the actual literary women—writers such as Lu Yin (1898–1934), Feng Yuanjun (1900–1974), Shi Pingmei (1902–1928), Xie Bingying (1906–2000), Chen Xuezhao (1906–1991), and Bai Wei (1894–1987)—who self-consciously defied Confucian gender ideals both in their personal lives and in what they wrote at the time.

In this chapter, I begin by briefly examining the rise of realist literary aesthetics and how gender emancipation came to be embraced as one of its most salient new subject matters. As part of my discussion, I comment on the predominance of the new woman theme in male-authored fiction of the time and the recent feminist critique of the representational practices of May Fourth male "emancipators." I then shift my attention to consider the ways in which this era's conception of realism's proximity to truth and authenticity granted women writers unprecedented authority (at least temporarily) within the cultural project of redefining women's social and political identities. For it was in this context that the New Women writers (*xin nüxing pai nüzuo-jia*), the label critics bestowed upon the young female authors who broke from a Confucian ethical and familial framework to thematize women's sexual and economic emancipation in their fiction, strove to advance their own version of modern gender "realities." Their prevalent use of subjective narrative forms, notably fictionalized diaries and letters, is consistent with contemporary concerns regarding the self and individual psychology but, as I will argue, also worked to promote a specifically feminist understanding of these issues by illustrating how women's subjectivity continued to be significantly determined by gender inequities in everyday interactions in the family, marriage, and society.

The narrative practices of New Women writers also reflect (and simultaneously assert) a new sense of urgency around the specific act of female self-representation. At a moment when the classical textual tradition had come under full-scale indictment for having produced and maintained highly disempowering feminine identities, but also at a moment when male new culturalists wielded increasing power in the gender debate, New Women writers implicitly insisted on the importance of articulating their own analyses and solutions to contemporary gender inequities. As self-reflexive textual forms, fictionalized letters and diaries repeatedly enact the process of the modern woman's self-examination and self-interpretation, and in so doing posit a crucial link between authorship (authorial control over meaning) and the project of female (self)emancipation. Wendy Larson has recently argued that May Fourth women's literary production was underwritten, at least initially, by an anxiety stemming from traditional prohibitions against female creativity, and reads the mediated forms female authors adopted as emblematic of a struggle they had in envisioning themselves *as authors*.[1] While I find Larson's study illuminating on numerous levels, not least of which is her interrogation of the May Fourth's projected self-image as a radical rupture with preexisting cultural formations, my own analysis offers an alternative explanation.

* * *

As Marston Anderson and David Wang have noted, proponents of Western-style literary realism who came forward as part of the New Culture Movement in the early 1920s were far from united in their opinions as to how the realist mode operated or how, exactly, it was to contribute to the project of China's cultural modernization.[2] Even before the heated "Revolutionary Literature" debate erupted at the end of the decade and spawned more overtly political genres of proletarian realism (*puluo xianshi zhuyi*) or new realism (*xin xianshi zhuyi*), literary realism was hotly contested territory. For Mao Dun, arguably the period's foremost realist novelist and, incidentally, one of the harshest critics of contemporary women writers, realism was predicated centrally on what he called "objective observation" (*keguan guancha*). Linking the rise of realism in the West to the practices of modern science, he comments, "Because the scientific spirit emphasizes the pursuit of truth, literature also takes the pursuit of truth as its sole purpose. Just as the approach of the scientist emphasizes objective observation, that of the literary artist emphasizes objective description. In accordance with the pursuit of truth, in accordance with emphasizing objective description, it follows that whatever meets one's eyes will determine what one writes."[3] For others at the time, such as Mao Dun's close friend Ye Shaojun, what mattered most was the writer's proper subjective orientation or, as it was sometimes described, authorial sincerity: the effective communication of external reality, in this account, requires first and foremost a highly cultivated moral sensibility on the part of the individual author. The difference between these two positions, as Marston Anderson observes, may at first seem considerable: the former, openly derived from European literary theory, singles out the descriptive powers of realism as its most valuable feature; the latter, a view more consistent with neo-Confucian epistemology, foregrounds realism's expressive dimension. But whether they emphasized the descriptive or expressive qualities of realism or, as was common, various combinations of the two, what virtually all May Fourth realists shared was an overriding concern with present social conditions and with the social efficacy of their writing. "Realism," thus concludes Anderson, "seemed the most progressive of Western aesthetic modes, in part because of its scientism, in part because realist works took as their subjects a far wider range of social phenomena than earlier more aristocratic forms did. The Chinese assumed that, once successfully transplanted, realism would encourage its readers to actively involve themselves in the important social and political issues confronting the nation."[4]

Of the myriad social and political issues confronting intellectuals in the 1920s and 1930s, one of the most striking—and hence oft-thematized topics in the so-called problem fiction that gained popularity in the early May Fourth era—was the Woman Question (*funü wenti*). What had originated as a relatively specific—if fervently explored—set of concerns of the elite feminist vanguard of the late Qing national reform movement now exploded as a major polemic in the May Fourth press. Magazines devoted to the "Woman Question" proliferated rapidly; key academic journals and national newspapers carried special columns to ponder women's issues; major publishing houses such as the Commercial Press (*Shangwu yinshuguan*) launched specific book series to delve more deeply into particular facets of the supposed feminine condition. In the bookstores of Shanghai and Beijing, urban consumers could now purchase histories tracing the origins of the Woman Question in China, translations of works by European and Japanese feminists, and handsomely illustrated volumes on such "scientific" topics as women's physical fitness and female anatomy. And naturally short stories, novels, plays, and eventually even films took women as a staple thematic source, dramatizing everything from the abuse of young wives at the hands of old-fashioned parents-in-law to the alienation of liberated New Women in modern urban society. Virtually every leading intellectual figure of the period weighed in at some point or another on the *funü wenti*, an indication of just how embedded gender had become within the overall iconoclastic New Culture movement (*xin wenhua yundong*).

Much of what was now discussed under the rubric of the *funü wenti* had been prefigured in late Qing feminism: political enfranchisement, inheritance and property rights, equality in marriage (including women's legal rights to divorce and child custody), the improvement of education, professional opportunities and so on had already been identified as important goals by the pioneer generation of activists and writers at the turn of the century. May Fourth feminist discourse, however, does exhibit certain distinguishing characteristics, not the least of which was the extent to which it evolved into a mainstream public debate, both in terms of where and by whom its ideas were circulated. Overall, too, one detects a marked shift away from the utopian orientation toward future transformations to a more pragmatic outlook focused on the existing material conditions and contradictions of the present. For instance, if late Qing feminists grasped the intrinsic connection between women's paid labor and their social liberation, it was only in the Republican era as women actually began to gain wide entry into the urban work force that analyses of concrete concerns materialized: with the rapid increase of female workers in the industrial labor force (notably, in cotton mills, tobacco processing plants, silk-filatures, and match factories) in the 1920s and 1930s, for instance, it now became evident that the factory floor was hardly the liberating site late Qing feminists had once imagined it to be. As the popular woman writer Lu Yin (1898–1934) points out in one of several essays she wrote about issues facing the contemporary Chinese women's movement, in addition to the many grievances they shared with working-class men about appalling work conditions, problems of unequal compensation, inadequate maternity leave and child-care, and sexual harassment at the workplace were among the routine conditions many women workers faced on the job.[5]

Labor concerns and awareness of the socioeconomic divisions among Chinese women were to become more pronounced over the course of the May Fourth and post-May Fourth eras, particularly as feminists began to ally themselves with the Chinese Communist Party (f. 1921) and to incorporate class into their analysis of women's oppression. For the liberal, and at the time still more dominant wing of the urban women's movement of the 1920s and early 1930s, however, the central focus of attention tended not to be women of working-class or peasant origins but the plight of newly educated, middle- and upper-class young women like Lu Yin herself, China's "Noras," as they were sometimes dubbed in the May Fourth press, or simply that group that came to be known as *xin nüxing*. How were the New Women who had recently declared their independence from sheltered Confucian family life supposed to support themselves financially? Which professions most suited them? How could they balance the demands of the domestic realm (motherhood, for instance) and their newly defined public roles? What were the ethical and psychological consequences of sexual freedom? This last question was among those most persistently raised in the contemporary periodical press and in modern fiction: at a moment when droves of New Women (and new men) rejected traditional marital practices for "modern" romances and conjugal unions based on love or redirected their individual energies into careers and public causes, countless articles on marriage and divorce, sexual morality, birth control, motherhood, and the highly controversial singlehood (*dushen zhuyi*) bore witness to the new importance of sexuality in May Fourth conceptions of modern gender emancipation, but also to the conception of these issues as bearing public and political significance.

Partially fueling the contemporary production of discourse on the New Woman's sexuality was the burst of translations of Western and Japanese texts, both nonfiction and fiction, as New Culturalists increasingly turned away from the domestic textual tradition in their search for a fresh vantage point from which to carry out their social critique. From works by August Bebel, Emma Goldman, Friedrich Engels, Charlotte Perkins-Gilman, Ellen Key, Olive Schreiner, Yosano Akiko, Alexandra Kollontai, Yamakawa Kikue, Henrik Ibsen, George Sand, and Virginia Woolf among others,[6] Chinese intellectuals selectively appropriated the ideas and idioms they found most useful in dislodging the normative gender ideology in order to fashion one more in keeping with their diverse modernizing agenda(s). As part of the fierce attack on the Confucian family structure in the early May Fourth period, for instance, Zhou Zuoren translated Japanese feminist Yosano Akiko's (1878–1942) powerful essay "On Chastity" (*Xin qingnian*, 1918).[7] In this essay, Yosano identifies the traditional code of female chastity as the primary means through which Japanese women had historically been controlled and confined within the domestic sphere (*ie*) and, in effect, reduced from human beings to sexual objects. She encouraged women to embrace a more empowering sense of their sexuality but, even more importantly, to aspire to an integrity of the self. Such ideas proved immensely inspiring to Zhou Zuoren who, along with his brother Lu Xun and Hu Shi, quickly incorporated them into their own condemnation of the Confucian family as morally bankrupt and fostering unhealthy, servile modes of human behavior.

Zhang Xichen, at the forefront the movement calling for a new sexual morality (*xin xingdaode*) and free love (*ziyou lian'ai*), promoted the ideas of Swedish feminist Ellen Key (1849–1926) by publishing translations of her work in *Funü zazhi* (The ladies' journal), which Zhang edited from 1921–1925, and later in his own journal *Xin nüxing*.[8] Key's theorization of ethical marriage predicated on mutual love (as opposed to purely economic or procreative concerns) resonated deeply with the modern Chinese vision of a restructured family dynamic including, especially, a more egalitarian partnership between the sexes. What seems to have appealed most to liberal thinkers like Zhang, however, was Key's conception of sexual difference. Although Key's vision of marriage presupposed certain economic and political equalities for women (and contained, in addition, a powerful defense of their right to divorce), she also posited a notion of a unique female nature that valorized, in particular, women's maternal capacities. Only a reformed domestic sphere, according to Key, would enable women to truly develop their special feminine qualities that, in turn, would enrich society at large.[9]

And, as a final example, the writings of Russian Bolshevik Alexandra Kollontai (1872–1952) fired the imagination of those inclined toward a more radical interrogation of the economic underpinnings of contemporary sexual politics, especially as a Marxist analytical framework gained currency in the late twenties. Li Junyi, for instance, favorably compared the feminism of Kollontai to that of Key in an article published in *Funü zazhi*, asserting that Kollontai represented the true "realist" as a social critic: whereas Key idealized women's maternal nature as a universal fact, Kollontai recognized that under current capitalist economic conditions only women of certain classes (i.e., the bourgeoisie) have at their disposal the means to devote themselves exclusively to the home and family.[10] Furthermore, because of the prevailing sexist division of labor within the domestic sphere, women employed outside the home tend to experience as profoundly contradictory their dual roles as wives/mothers and as workers. With regard to this last point, one important insight Kollontai offered (and one that many Chinese New Women writers would echo) was the enormous difficulty of overcoming inherited emotional/sexual identities that chain women to domestic life in the first place. These ideas were elaborated in her *Women and the Family System*, which was translated into Chinese in 1932, and well as in her fiction, which also appeared in Chinese journals in the early 1930s. The character Olga Sergeevna in her story "Three Generations" (translated by the woman scholar Li Lan), for instance, proves incapable of balancing family demands with her professional life and winds up reluctantly sacrificing the former, while another of her fictional heroines, Vasilisa Malygina (whom Li Junyi deems even more representative of contemporary Chinese women than the ever-popular Nora) similarly wavers between commitment to political work on the one hand and her powerful desire for her husband and the close intimacy and security he represents, on the other.

Amid the flurry of public debate and proliferating imported imagery around the issue of modern Chinese womanhood, as well as the urgent calls for a modern literature that was to represent marginalized and disempowered segments of society, male practitioners of May Fourth realism seized upon the New Woman as key literary figure. Writers such as Lu Xun, Ye Shengtao, Mao Dun, and Ba Jin depicted awakened heroines who resist traditional feminine destinies by rebelling against parental authority and social convention and sympathetically explored the constraints or impediments their female protagonists confronted in their struggle for sexual and financial independence. In Lu Xun's influential short story "Shangshi" (Regret for the past, 1925), for instance, the New Woman heroine Zijun asserts her independence by moving in with her boyfriend, though in the end, pregnant and depressed by her lover's sudden indifference, she retreats home again. Mei, the ambitious heroine of Mao Dun's classic New Woman novel *Hong* (Rainbow, 1929) who (characteristically) journeys from the provincial interior to Shanghai in search of self-fulfilment and freedom, finds herself faced with a painful choice between satisfying her erotic/sensual self and political/intellectual self, for this author two apparently irreconcilable modes of being for the new woman. It is not just events in the plot, however, that seem to thwart the New Woman's bid for self-emancipation; as a number of literary scholars have recently pointed out, careful consideration of the narrative *discourse* of such stories reveals a far more problematic logic of containment at work.

In his oft-cited article examining the treatment of women's emancipation by established May Fourth male authors, Stephen Chan (1988) identifies a telling dissonance manifest between the radical content of their fiction and the "objectifying mode" of the narrative text itself.[11] What appear at first to be oppositional stories *about* the liberated woman and her painful plight are, upon closer analysis, no more than extended explorations of the *male* consciousness that encounters such matters. In his analysis of Lu Xun's "Shangshi," for instance, Chan observes that Zijun's entire story is refracted through the recollections of her lover such that the reader is "allowed to know her only as Juansheng remembers her" (25). And crucially what is recalled is not so much Zijun's despair but the despair she caused him. For Chan, the recurring depiction of modern female failure (and her accompanying despair, vulnerability, and suffering) is *necessary* precisely because it enables the male narrator to give expression to the depth of his own complex, tortured subjectivity on the brink of modernity. As he observes and contemplates the cruel injustice heaped upon the female other of *his* society, the intellectual reaffirms (albeit characteristically in a self-deprecating manner) his own superior status as the dominant subject of history and its central agent of change: "'You' are therefore but an innocent scapegoat, paying for the crimes that society has committed day after day, generation after generation. The root of *your* suffering is to be found in *my* own inability to right the wrongs that society has done to *me*."[12]

Rey Chow's close reading (1991) of Mao Dun's *Hong* similarly emphasizes an underlying contradiction in the narrative representation of the new woman heroine.[13] On the one hand, Mao Dun privileges Mei's "inner drama" (104) over the external events in the plot to produce a quintessentially modern psychological novel. In scene upon scene the author dwells on the subjective feelings and self-perceptions of his protagonist. On the other, Mei's eroticized female body (in particular, Chow notes, her breasts) surfaces as a conspicuous narrative fixation, the site of excessive or superfluous descriptive detail at odds with the "modern" aesthetic of social relevance. Taken as a whole, Chow thus concludes, the novel exhibits a "gap between 'woman' as reflexive 'mind' and 'woman' as sexual 'body'. In the midst of the most radical change in Chinese literary language—an analytic openness in fiction writing—we are confronted with the return of woman as the traditional, visually fetishized object which, in spite of woman's new 'cerebral' developments, still fascinates in a way that is beyond the intellect, beyond analysis!" (107).

Mao Dun's fiction is put under further scrutiny by Sally Lieberman (1998), who persuasively argues that Mao Dun's appropriation of the New Woman for his realist literary project depends on a specific, and ultimately problematic, strategy of "unmothering."[14] The strategy is said to operate on two levels, representational and critical. The first—and here Lieberman takes as her specific example Mao Dun's earliest novella *Huanmie* (Disillusion, 1927)—involves the way Mao Dun narrates his heroine's development as a progressive evolution that entails overcoming identification with the mother and the realm of sentimental maternal love/values she embodies. Only when this disillusionment is complete is the heroine available for the "modern" plot of heterosexual romance; it is also at this very point in the novella that the heroine's body finally becomes fully accessible for realist description. That is to say, at the very moment she assumes the status of a modern New Woman she is (re)inserted into the text as an object of (male) desire. If the argument so far overlaps somewhat with Chow's, Lieberman's second point about Mao Dun's "unmothering" adds a significant new twist to the gendered critique of his work. Just as Mao Dun refuses to ascribe to the mother any affirmative role in the (figurative) birth of the New Woman in his fictional narratives, Lieberman contends, so too in his critical writings on contemporary female authors does he elide their considerable role in bringing to life the New Woman as a literary subject. On the contrary, in the essays he published at the time about high-profile writers Lu Yin and Bing Xin[15]— both of whom had dealt with the new woman theme long before Mao Dun himself took up fiction writing, he can barely disguise his disdain for their alleged aesthetic defects and lack of social orientation, let alone concede any creative debt he may owe to their work. With regard to Lu Yin, for instance, a hugely popular writer at the time whose short story collections and novels often went into multiple printings, he accuses her of having "stagnated" (*tingzhi*), producing a great many works but harping on the same "tedious" message, and with the same sentimentally drawn female characters. Yet, as Lieberman astutely notes, "[e]ven while denying Lu Yin's work the legiti- macy of art, he recoups her heroines as a 'social phenomena' (*shehui xianxiang*)" (126). Such a ploy, moreover, is necessary precisely because of the aesthetic premise of Mao Dun's realism: implicitly advancing his view of realism as a practice grounded in "objective observation" he "phrases his critique in such a way that her 'tedious' heroines remain accessible to him as raw material for proper realist fiction" (126). In light of the fact that, as noted earlier, Mao Dun's New Woman fiction has enjoyed an enduring legacy (in contrast to the relative obscurity of most fiction by New Women writers from the same period), this is not an insignificant observation.

The point I would emphasize here, however, is that what contemporary literary critics alert us to is the masculinism that may lurk, in the form of "residues of traditional representation" behind even the seemingly most enlightened and sympathetic narratives of the modern woman.[16] More provocatively, they identify a potential collusion between the narrative discourse of May Fourth fiction and the consolidation of modern forms of patriarchy. By underestimating how language itself plays a central role in sustaining and reproducing women's subordination in patriarchal culture, it is suggested, May Fourth writers inadvertently curtailed (and perhaps even undermined) the oppositional potential of the feminist "content" of their texts.

To be sure, it is of critical importance to uncover the extent to which the logic of traditional gender ideologies continued to inform May Fourth fiction, in spite of the subversive intentions of its authors; at the same time, however, we should be wary of the tendency to over-state the scope of the problem.[17] As Rita Felski, among many other feminist theorists, warns us, to posit language as inherently phallocentric is to render feminist resistance and struggle pointless, since the very necessity of language would thus predeter- mine complicity with patriarchy: "Whether it is men or women who speak and whatever the context and content of their language, in speaking discur- sively they are doomed to speak the masculine. This view thereby serves to reinscribe women in a position of speechlessness outside language, theory and the symbolic order, denying any potential power and effectivity to female discourse."[18]

With this warning in mind, therefore, I think it is worth seriously ques- tioning the implication that Chinese women were "doomed" in advance to carry on the tradition of masculinist ideology as simply figures of representation in May Fourth culture. Were the discursive habits of Chinese patriarchy so firmly entrenched and all-powerful as to preclude alternative inscriptions of gender? Does the unequal distribution of narrative power that recent critics of modern Chinese literature ascribe to May Fourth fiction universally characterize all writing on and/or by women at the time? If, as Chan pessimistically claims, writers failed to "recognize the connection between women and language," can we locate exceptions in May Fourth literature that challenged "the perpetuation of the silencing of female voices"?[19] And, more precisely and to the point of this chapter, how successful were the New Women writers themselves in devising, and revising, rhetorical strategies to carry out a realist critique of contemporary patriarchal culture without reproducing the masculinist logic that usurps the image of women for its own interests?

I would note, finally, that the charges leveled against May Fourth realist representations of gender seem to reflect the anti-referential bias of contemporary western feminist theory in general. As feminist critical discourse shifted its attention from a content-oriented analysis of female images to issues of textuality in the 1980s, the realist aesthetic has come under particularly harsh scrutiny for allegedly being a "predominantly conservative form" that conceals the nature of "its own signifying practice."[20] It is increasingly common to find in contemporary scholarship, for instance, the view that realism suppresses the relationship between language/ideology and reality, and hence inadequately problematizes their roles in sustaining patriarchal culture. Deemed naively mimetic and insufficiently subversive of the symbolic order itself, realism has thus been widely rejected as an effective feminist cultural practice by contemporary critics who favor more formally self-reflexive and stylistically experimental modes of writing. The latter are presumed, especially by proponents of French post-structuralist theories of *l'écriture féminine*, to undermine the phallocentric logic of the patriarchal symbolic order by challenging the very structures and conventions of representation. In their apparent ambivalence toward May Fourth realist representations of women and their calls for greater attention to the issue of "women and representation" scholars of modern Chinese literature partake of this critical trend.

Given the historical function realism has played within many feminist literary traditions, however, some scholars have challenged this trend. And, in their defense of feminist applications of realism, critics like Felski and Maria Lauret raise several valid points that I think are highly applicable to the case of May Fourth literature.[21] Chief among these is the reminder that what constitutes literary radicalism (in a feminist or any other sense) at any given moment in time can only be defined contextually: even highly self-reflexive modes of modernist representation privileged by certain feminist literary theorists, Felski points out, can be rendered mainstream and commonplace "as [they] come[s] to embody the new aesthetic norm at the level of both production and reception."[22] By the same token, realist literary practices can and have played an important role in challenging the dominant aesthetic and ideological conventions within specific sociohistorical contexts. Certainly for Chinese New Women writers of the 1920s and 1930s, realism helped not only to significantly expand the scope of the literary subject matter they could legitimately address, but proved to be an important representational practice through which they laid claim to a public voice to radically interrogate the dominant cultural stereotypes of feminine experience.

Our current preoccupation with matters of textual signification, in other words, is to some extent itself historically specific, and thus we should not automatically assume that the political currency nonrealist literary experimentation carries in critical discourse today can (or should) be projected back to earlier cultural contexts. My point here is not to suggest that we ignore the stylistic or formal maneuvers of May Fourth realism or the potential ideological effects of certain rhetorical devices and structures adopted in such texts, for these are likely implicated on some level in the politics of gender they promulgate. It is, rather, to suggest that perhaps we shouldn't be overly hasty in dismissing May Fourth feminist writers for being politically "naive" or "failing" because they adopted realist narrative strategies. Finally, we should not forget that there are many *realisms* to discuss in the Chinese context.[23] To invoke realism as a monolithic or stable discourse is to preclude the various possibilities writers at the time in fact could avail themselves of. With this in mind, let us turn now to a consideration of feminist realist texts in the May Fourth era.

*　*　*

As noted, scholars have recently suggested that one reason the sexual/textual politics underlying May Fourth realism remained problematic is that the relationship between women and writing was not sufficiently examined by intellectuals at the time. Indeed, while it is safe to say that women ranked among the leading preoccupations in progressive literature of the period, women *and* literature provoked relatively few sustained critical inquiries, at least initially. The first comprehensive study on the subject, Xie Wuliang's pioneering *Zhongguo funü wenxue shi* (The history of Chinese women's literature, 1916) was not followed up by research comparable in nature until 1928, with the publication of Huiqun Nüshi's *Nüxing yu wenxue* (Women and literature). That same year the journal *Zhenmeishan* put out an enormously successful issue on women writers, which placed the Chinese female literary tradition within an international frame by discussing Chinese writers alongside Japanese and European authors, although the complex questions this comparative approach raised remained implicit rather than explicitly confronted by the contributors.[24] *Funü zazhi*, the longest running women's magazine of the early twentieth century, did not devote a special issue (*zhuanhao*) to the topic of women's writing until 1931, long after other— apparently more pressing—subjects had been covered (among them prostitution, the women's movement, choosing a spouse, and domestic revolution). Again much of the issue concerned itself with European and American writers (including George Sand, Mme.de Stael, the Bronte sisters, Harriet Beecher Stowe, Agnes Smedley, Singrid Undset, Marietta Shaginian, and Lydia Seigullina), rather than women authors from China. In fact, in the lead article "Jinshi funü jiefang yundong zai wenxueshang de fanying" (The reflection of the modern women's emancipation movement in literature) author Jin Zhonghua displays an impressive knowledge of late-nineteenth- and early-twentieth-century European literature but cites not a single contemporary Chinese woman author as an example.[25] By the early and mid-1930s a small spate of studies on modern Chinese women's writing were available in the literary marketplace, most of them more descriptive than theoretical in focus, and only a few of which construed the subject as a polemic with significant contemporary implications.

At a moment when both the categories of Chinese literature and Chinese women were undergoing major reconceptualization, the fact that the two were not brought together for consideration more systematically may come as something of a surprise. Does this apparent critical indifference in fact mask the presence of deep-seated cultural taboos against female literacy that Wendy Larson has argued lingered on into the modern age?[26] Or, could it be, belying the popular myth of the May Fourth era as the true origin of women's literary history, that women's writing was actually no longer deemed so novel (or unsettling) a phenomenon as to require special attention? Clearly more work needs to be done on cultural developments throughout the nineteenth century and, especially, on the emerging evidence of the great volume of women's writing that period produced before we can more fully ascertain what literary modernity might mean in terms of intellectual/literary women. Still, from the occasional commentaries we do have from this era and the dynamics of the May Fourth literary world in general, certain shifts in attitudes toward women's writing can be detected, chief among them the incipient assumption that women writers were integral to the production of the much touted "new" realism.

It was Zhou Zuoren, in a speech first delivered in 1920 at the Beijing Women's Normal College and later printed in *Funü pinglun* and *Funü zazhi*, who perhaps best articulated this central premise.[27] Arguing that literature is "a form through which life is realized," he posits the need for modern writers to supplant the misogyny and conventional feminine stereotypes of the Chinese philosophic and religious tradition with what he describes as more truthful representations. As the product of the masculine imagination, Zhou contends, the classical textual tradition misrepresented the true nature of womanhood and, in this sense, failed in its mission to accurately express and represent human life. The problem was not just that Chinese men had historically monopolized literary culture; female authors themselves, having internalized the negative beliefs and values of hegemonic culture (including distorted views of themselves as inferior beings), had not fared much better in conveying the "realities" of Chinese womanhood. Paraphrasing John Stuart Mill, he avers that "all the books women have written about women aim to flatter men but do not portray women *as they really are*" (my emphasis). Built on the principle of individual equality, modern literature, however, was now to be seized by women to cultivate a spirit of critical self-awareness that, in turn, would enrich life itself by revealing (hitherto hidden) realities of female experience. As Zhou thus advises with confidence, "from now on, women should take advantage of artistic freedom to express their true feelings and thoughts and to dispel the age-old misunderstandings and confusion about women."

However naive it may strike us today, the last point—that women themselves constitute the ultimate authority on feminine experience—was a sentiment commonly voiced at the time. And like Zhou Zuoren, in attempting to valorize the "new" writing by women, commentators often elaborated upon the (perceived) difference between women's literature from the past and fiction by contemporary female authors. Tan Zhengbi (1931), deploying even stronger rhetoric to criticize what he considered the artifice and imitative quality of traditional women's writing, refers to the privileged literate female elite of traditional times as "parrots" who merely sought to please men (*chanmei nanxing*, 29) or, in other cases, to vent private frustration at having failed in this role.[28] In particular, Tan deplores the excessive sentimentalism of classical female poets on grounds that it is superficial, since literary women seldom suffered material hardships of any real significance. In his view, the conventional themes found in traditional women's poetry—the loss of love, departure of friends, fading of flowers and fullness of moon—lack substance and reveal little about the real conditions of women's lives. By contrast, female authors galvanized by the New Culture movement such as Lu Yin, Bai Wei, and Chen Xuezhao are said to have been awakened by modern thought (*xiandai sichao*) and represent an important breakthrough in terms of the subject matter they tackled. Women's writing, Tan thus optimistically proclaims, "is now moving forward on a bright road, and will never again resemble what it was in the past" (34).

The woman critic Tao Qiuying (1933), to cite another typical example, emphasized that the traits hitherto associated with women's writing (its extreme emotionalism, narrow formal and thematic range, sentimentality, and so forth) are not essential or innately "feminine" characteristics but in fact reflect unhealthy symptoms of women's socioeconomic subjugation in the past.[29] Socialized according to patriarchal norms (norms, as her argument underlines, established and fortified by the classics of antiquity such as the *Shijing* (Book of odes) and *Liji* (Book of rites) as well as the moral literature directed specifically at female readers), women writers have invariably produced literary works that bear the emotional, intellectual, and political imprint of their circumscribed upbringing. Unlike some of her more iconoclastic contemporaries, Tao expresses appreciation for the literary accomplishments of past women writers, in spite of the restrictions they faced; nevertheless, she feels their full creative *potential* had to a large degree been stifled. At the end of her study, Tao alludes to the ongoing contemporary assault on the patriarchal social order (*zongfa shehui zuzhi*) and Confucian ethics (*lijiao*), and urges her fellow women to take advantange of the opportunity literature offers to "to vent our true emotions and to create our new and rich imaginations . . . we will do our best to free our genuine sentiments from any bondage and will not say anything untruthful nor fake any unwarranted sentimentality, and will build our country into a bright and dazzling land of literature."[30]

Even critics who acknowledged variation *within* contemporary female literary practice tended to evaluate and rank women authors according to their success in having broken from the ostensibly stale literary orthodoxy. In a schematic overview of the contemporary literary scene, the critic Yi Zhen, for instance, prefaces his analysis with a characteristic allusion to the traditional constraints placed on female literary/intellectual activities, a fact to be lamented since in his view women's psychological and social life constitutes *terra incognita* that female authors alone can chart.[31] He then proceeds to divide women writers into three categories along a continuum, with highest praise going to those who reject established convention. The first is the so-called *guixiu* school of women writers, exemplified in his view by Bing Xin and Su Xuelin, who continued to write within the ideological framework of Confucian ethics. Of particular note was their conventional treatment of love which was limited primarily to maternal and conjugal contexts. Slightly more progressive, yet still not entirely divested of Confucian values were the "New *guixiu*" writers, notably Ling Shuhua, who depict women in a modern social context yet who ultimately adhere to conventional morality.[32] The third group, and the one alleged to have most successfully transcended tradition were the New Women writers (*xin nüxing pai de zuojia*). According to Yi Zhen, what defines these writers are two primary traits: first, their ideological affinities with the New Culture movement and; second, their frank articulation of matters concerning modern romance and sexual desire.

Highbrow critics like Zhou, Tan, and Tao were not the only ones making claims about the authenticity of "new" women's writing. Publishers eager to cash in on the public's growing infatuation with the modern woman also marketed the notion that female authors could provide unparalleled (self)revelations and insight into female life.[33] In *Nüzuojia xiaocongshu* (Women writers mini-book series) (1930), a dainty, boxed set of miniature books unmistakably tailored for the female consumer, for instance, the editor locates the value of the collection not in the political/intellectual views contained therein nor in the artistry of the writing, but in the biological sex of the authors. For it is this fact, or so it is claimed, that guarantees the work's *truthfulness*: "speaking of women's psychology, their secrets can not be fathomed by even those artists with keen feeling! Only women themselves can reveal their own lives and describe their grief and indignation, their depression, comforts, happiness and various deeds in an undisguised fashion; only this can be considered [women's] sincere feeling and the spirit that can move people, only these possess artistic value."[34]

From a contemporary critical perspective, the overly generalized characterizations of both the pre-twentieth-century women's literary tradition and

May Fourth writers by early-twentieth-century critics, literary historians, and publishers leave much to be desired.[35] In attempting to protest the mechanisms through which traditional Chinese culture suppressed female creativity, commentators often homogenized the past, reducing literary women of the imperial period to a narrow stereotype of the repressed poetess who survived hostile cultural conditions either by confining herself to private lyrical forms or by acquiescing to orthodox Confucian values. Such accounts, among much else, clearly underestimate the scope and variety of female literary endeavors prior to the twentieth century and the considerable permutations concepts of the woman writer or women's writing have undergone over the long course of Chinese literary history. By the same token, early champions of contemporary women authors often greatly exaggerated the emancipatory potential of "modern" female literature. Simplistically construed as the liberated voice of the hitherto inhibited and marginalized female self, this view of modern women's writing seems to maintain that literature simply communicates, rather than creates, meaning. And emphasizing literature's function in documenting everyday life (preferably its darker dimensions), it elides such thorny issues as ideology and aesthetic convention. In this way, the May Fourth discourse on women's writing relied on, but in the process also *constructed*, a highly problematic opposition between tradition and modernity, past and present, silence and expression in ways that obscured the continuities between historical eras and the fact that literary and artistic endeavors of women in the past helped pave the way for contemporary practices. So pervasive has this narrative become that one continues even now to find the common view that the May Fourth movement marks the birth of women's writing *in the true sense*.

As the product of a specific convergence of social, literary, and political trends, the May Fourth discourse on women's writing nevertheless embodies the newly constructed standards of cultural value and authority that had come to inform the publication and reception of contemporary women's texts. No longer judged strictly for their aesthetic merits or adherence to inherited moral precepts, female-authored texts were now valorized as documents authentically recording the real conditions of women's lives and their inner knowledge. In this conception, new women's writing was first and foremost to play a key role in the realist agenda of exposing readers to all manner of human experience, in this case by transmitting "accurate" and "honest" representations of feminine experience.

* * *

Used in reference to Ding Ling, Feng Yuanjun, Lu Yin, Shi Pingmei, Bai Wei, and Xie Bingying, among others, New Women writers almost invariably featured unconventional heroines who reject arranged marriage and traditional obligations to the Confucian family. Yet, in taking up the innovative themes of new-style romance and male–female relationships in their fiction, New Women writers expressed deep ambivalence about the contemporary

realities of modern sexual relations. Whereas the literary imaginings of many
of their male peers—most notably Xu Zhimo, Yu Dafu, and Jiang Guangci—
often celebrate modern romantic possibilities, in their fiction the New
Women writers were patently cautious as to the potential dangers that the
doctrine of "free love" posed to the newly liberated new woman. In their
stories, female protagonists who embark on modern relationships in the
hope of securing emotional, sexual, and intellectual fulfillment typically end
up disappointed, if not utterly devastated, by what they find instead. One
common scenario, for instance, involved the seduction of a naive and sexually inexperienced female protagonist by a male partner who manipulates her
with the (empty) language of liberation and love. In Lu Yin's "Qilu" (Forked
road, 1933), the heroine Zhang Lanyin triumphs over an old-fashioned
Confucian family to become an activist in the women's movement, only to
fall prey to a smooth-talking comrade who abandons her shortly after convincing her to move in with him. Pride prevents her from seeking support
from her family and eventually mounting debts force her into a life of prostitution.[36] Echoes of this theme would later appear in Lu Yin's extremely
popular novel *Xiangya jiezhi* (Ivory rings, 1934), which unfolds the story of
Qin Zhu, a spirited young school teacher in Beijing who is left emotionally
scarred when she discovers that the man with whom she has fallen madly in
love is already married.[37]

Another narrative New Women writers favored interrogated the supposedly
"reformed" institution of marriage by foregrounding the emotional discon-
tent of women in the new-style family. Chen Xuezhao's ironically titled
novella *Xingfu* (Happiness, 1933),[38] for instance, dramatizes the heroine
Yufen's belated realization that her new husband's "modernity" is but skin
deep: having mustered the courage to elope with Ziheng, a handsome school
teacher, Yu Fen's conjugal bliss is cut short when her mother-in-law moves
in and monopolizes Ziheng's attentions. Adding insult to injury, her husband eventually deserts her for a younger woman—after all, he reasons, as a
"New Woman" (*xin nüzi*) she should be capable of fending for herself and
their two children. "We dreamt of a new, happy family," thus muses the now
embittered heroine, "but we came up empty-handed, since there are some
contemporary Chinese men who don the mask of the new era without having shed the flesh and blood of the old era. But we mistook them for the real
thing, for ideal companions, and as a result got nothing" (57). Another hypocritical modern husband can be found in Lu Yin's "Yimu" (A scene, 1928),
which depicts a modern college professor who publically champions women's
equality, but behaves in utterly conventional fashion toward his wife in the
privacy of their home.[39]

Hypocritical "new" husbands were not the only ones who earned the
scorn of New Women writers; often referred to as *taitai*, educated modern
women who allowed themselves to sink into domestic complacency upon
tying the knot were also targeted as part of their feminist interrogation of
new domestic ideologies. Shi Pingmei's "Ouran lailin de guifuren"
(Unexpected visit of a distinguished lady), for instance, examines the

adverse effects that bourgeois family life has had on a former student activist.[40] Once a leading figure in the women's movement (*nüjie weiren*), she has been transformed into a chic society lady who flaunts the status and wealth she has achieved through marriage. As for "presiding over meetings, writing petitions, putting out leaflets, and holding demonstrations," she now dismisses such activities as "laughable." In "Neige qieruo de nüren" (That weak woman, 1931), Lu Yin voices subtle criticism of an educated woman who lacks the will and courage to leave her physically abusive husband, even though, as the I-narrator observes, she has recourse to live independently.

Still other narratives revolve sympathetically around the transgressive figure of the single woman in order to imagine the consequences of eschewing married life altogether for the sake of other ambitions. Countering contemporary critics who decried the phenomenon of single women as a violation of female nature and an alarming social problem, these stories typically present the espousal of "*dushen zhuyi*" as a deliberate—though often difficult—personal choice by women who prefer to devote their lives to something more significant than one man.[41] Ding Ling's heroine Yecao, for instance, struggles to restrain her physical passions because she has learned from experience that romantic entanglement impedes her literary pursuits ("Yecao," 1929). In Lu Yin's "Hechu shi guicheng" (Which way back?, 1927), one of several works in which she explores singlehood, the character Lu Sha is a despondent housewife who worries about the wasted potential of her own life while envying the career of an aunt who has chosen celibacy in order to dedicate herself to the women's movement.[42] News that the aunt has been made the subject of malicious gossip and ridicule, however, ultimately forces Lu Sha to concede that her idealized vision of this woman's lifestyle may be in need of readjustment. The most extended examination of the struggles of the single woman of this period, however, can be found in Chen Xuezhao's novel *Nanfeng de meng* (Dream of southern winds, 1929).[43] The narrative portrays the New Woman heroine Keming, a writer determined to carve out an independent life for herself as a single woman: she is romantically involved with the affluent intellectual Mu Ou but, as a staunch proponent of *dushen zhuyi*, refuses on principle to marry him. Her quest for independence takes her abroad to France, which provides an exotic backdrop to much of the narrative, but the story centers largely on her attempts to extricate herself from the control of her boyfriend, who remains in China. Composed of flashbacks of the heroine's complex relationship with this man and scenes of the present trials and tribulations she endures as a foreign student, the structure of the narrative emphasizes the difficulties of carving out an autonomous space as a woman in a patriarchal culture. Despite having realized her dream of studying abroad, a venture financed by her own writing, the heroine remains hopelessly restricted by her ties (economic and emotional) to Mu Ou. Indeed, the juxtaposition of past and present reveals that, even with the considerable geographic distance separating them, Mu Ou continues to exert a powerful authority over her life.

Frequently the New Woman protagonist evinces strong political proclivities, and is often shown to turn to political involvement *as a result* of disenchantment with conventional marriages or modern love affairs. More often than not, however, the romance of revolution proves equally disheartening, not because the heroine's political desires subside but because they are thwarted by the all-too-familiar "realities" of revolutionary culture. In Bai Wei's novel *Zhadan yu zhengniao* (A bomb and an expeditionary bird, 1928), the heroine Yue leaves behind a bad marriage forced upon her by tradition-bound parents to go to Wuhan, the center of revolutionary activity and a vigorous women's movement in the mid-1920s.[44] Eager to find freedom and purpose in her life away from her oppressive marriage, she is appalled by the shallowness of the women's bureau and the partisan wrangling of the KMT and the CCP in Wuhan. She eventually aligns herself with the latter, but her hard-won sense of political agency is damaged when she is assigned to seduce a KMT official to gather information. Still worse, the mission fails and she becomes a victim of rape. In "Manli" (1928), Lu Yin offers a similar, if somewhat less stark, critique of the gender politics of revolution. In this story, the title character bids farewell to the heady romantic milieu of Shanghai for a more purposeful revolutionary calling. Like Yue, however, Manli's ardent political ambitions and desires are almost immediately dashed by the rampant corruption and decadence she witnesses among her "comrades"; in the end, she suffers a mental breakdown and has to be hospitalized.

The thematic concerns of New Women writers—which also encompassed experiences of unwanted pregnancy (Xie Bingying's *Paoqi* [Abandoned, 1932]; Chen Ying's "Nüxing" [Woman, 1934]); sexual harassment (Ding Ling's "Mengke" [1927]) and Chen Xuezhao's *Xingfu*); venereal disease (Bai Wei's *Beiju shengya* [Tragic life, 1936]); marital infidelity (Lu Yin's "Shidai de xishengzhe" [Sacrificed to the era, 1928]) and divorce (Lu Yin's *Nüren de xin* [A woman's heart, 1934]), and the innovative character-types they constructed are too numerous to exhaustively cover here. What these examples serve to illustrate is that generally speaking New Woman narratives marked a departure from the utopian trajectory characteristic of late Qing feminist novels discussed in chapter one.[45] If they share a common desire for a transformed social order, New Women fiction gives expression to feminist desire not through the imaginary projection of (possible) emancipated futures but through starkly highlighting the ongoing impediments to alternative realities.

In her pioneering essay on women writers from the 1920s and 1930s, Yi-Tsi Feuerwerker (1975) attributes the bleak vision that infuses their fiction to the profound disillusionment many young female authors personally experienced as they came of age amid this tumultuous historical era: "The crumbling of the old structures made it possible for a few gifted women, the articulate, self-conscious vanguard, to break out into the open. There they discovered that whereas women had been repressed and confined under the old system, they were now in a precarious and exposed situation, and no less vulnerable."[46] Ding Ling, one of the writers she profiles, for instance, led an impoverished existence in Beijing and Shanghai, undergoing a series of unsuccessful work experiences (including a particularly unsavory foray in the film industry) before settling on a career as a writer. More recent literary historical research further substantiates Feuerwerker's observation that many New Women writers indeed faced considerable difficulties in their adult lives: Lu Yin, for example, defiantly married her lover Guo Mengliang in 1923 and moved to his home town to reside with his mother and his legal first wife, an awkward and at times unbearable living arrangement she reportedly soon regretted. Several years later Lu Yin, having been widowed, again faced wide public disapproval (and ridicule) for her scandalous romance with a Qinghua University student nine years her junior.[47] Chen Xuezhao became embroiled in a bitter financial dispute with her older brothers, who withheld the earnings from her publications to force her to return from Europe to get married.[48] And Bai Wei, whose harrowing autobiography I discuss in the following chapter, escaped the abuse of a tyrannical mother-in-law only to become entangled with a selfish and emotionally cruel poet, Yang Sao.

At a moment when aesthetic value was intimately bound up with the (perceived) proximity of the literary text to the author's lived experiences, details like these are not insignificant. At the very least, it is evident that they were of immense interest to contemporary readers as well as to critics, who often invoked biographical information and references to personality traits in their interpretation and evaluation of a writer's work. According to Cao Ye, for instance, the power of Bai Wei's work sprang from the austere years the author spent as an impoverished student in Japan and her subsequent experiences in revolutionary circles;[49] similarly, the emotional intensity of Lu Yin's work was frequently ascribed to the fact that she had experienced much emotional turbulence in her life.[50] Critics of Xie Bingying's work singled out its journalistic qualities, praising the way the author simply "narrates what she sees, hears, and thinks without artifice and without technique. It is written not with pen and ink but with hot blood and sad tears . . ."[51] To cite biographical evidence as the only source of literary meaning, however, has obvious explanatory limits, not the least of which is the fact that it feeds into the "autobiographical fallacy" that has often prejudiced critical evaluations of women's writing.[52] Indeed, as Wendy Larson has perceptively shown, it was precisely the (flawed) presumption that women did little more than transcribe the experiences of the private self that would eventually come to underwrite the rash of leftist attacks against May Fourth-style women's writing that began to appear in the periodical press in the early 1930s.[53]

In my analysis the points that I would emphasize then are as follows: first, while women writers frequently wove personal details into their stories and, in a few cases, even wrote full-length novels based on their own lives or the lives of close friends (e.g., Ding Ling's *Wei Hu* and Lu Yin's *Xiangya jiezhi*), it is ultimately more productive to read these and other formal maneuvers as rhetorical strategies that consciously aimed at creating the effect of personal disclosure rather than as markers of personal disclosure *per se*. The prevalent use of the first-person narrative voice; reliance on unadorned colloquial language and loose narrative structures foregrounding the text's emotional performance over plot; naming techniques identifying fictional characters with the author or real-life individuals associated with the author[54] and so forth—prominent conventions, of course, that were readily apparent in the modern vernacular fiction of many male writers at the time also—were techniques applied by New Women writers to achieve a quality of clarity and directness in their fiction that contributed to a reading of their texts as spontaneous candid confession. (In this sense, they fit the definition of what Maria Lauret refers to in her analysis of American feminist literature as "self-conscious fictions of subjectivity.")[55] Second, New Women writers adopted such narrative strategies in response to the prevailing May Fourth discourse on realism, including its claims to mimetic reference but also, on an important level, can be said to have been empowered by them. At a moment when historical challenges to dominant sexual codes had opened up the possibility of alternative cultural scripts for women, realism's claims authorized them to represent women. The use of subjective narrative forms and female I-narrators in their fiction gave added credibility to their account of modern female experience, and in turn appealed to the reading public's interest in revelations of personal experience. Third and perhaps most crucially, at least in the hands of the most accomplished New Women writers at the time, the female self that is textually "revealed" in fact functions more to raise questions about the possible social identities of the modern woman rather than to assert absolute definitions. As we shall see, the narrative context that precipitates the (fictional) act of confession typically involves a crisis of some sort that challenges the I-narrator's self-identity; the conflicts, contradictions, and possibilities she comes to feel about what it means to be a woman are what fuel the production of her text. The project of self-writing (both as it is enacted by and represented in these stories) does not present itself as the solution to the underlying causes of her predicament; insofar as it contributes to the self-awareness of the I-narrator and the reader (again, both actual and the fictional readers figured in the text), including significantly, an awareness of the gaps between feminist ideals and lived experience, however, it is figured as a significant social/political practice. In short, if the boundaries between fact and fiction, between lived realities and imagined ones are difficult to demarcate in New Women's fiction, then, it is this fluidity that helped legitimize female authorship. That subsequent critical attempts to devalue women's writing zeroed in on its "autobiographical" content should thus come as no surprise; for it this very quality that had enabled New Women writers to *expand* the content of the "literary" and the "real" by addressing areas of female experience hitherto marginalized by the cultural tradition and to challenge dominant literary stereotypes of women.

All this is not to say that women writers who experimented with realist fiction to address feminist concerns were unaware of the potential "limits" of the form. From the outset, one senses a certain creative ambivalence toward this particular literary mode. Consider, for example, Feng Yuanjun's controversial short story "Gejue" (Separation, 1923) and the two sequels she wrote, "Gejue yihou" (After the separation, 1923) and "Cimu" (The benevolent mother, 1924).[56] Among the earliest of her generation to begin publishing vernacular fiction, Feng achieved considerable literary celebrity for her supposed "bold" depictions of male–female relations.[57] The stories in question also reveal the author's dilemma over how to best to accentuate the heroine's conflict and to heighten the effect of her social critique. Briefly, "Gejue" addresses the then highly topical issue of "free love" (*ziyou lian'ai*) through the dramatization of a bitter confrontation between a young, sexually emancipated woman and her uncompromising mother. When the I-narrator/protagonist refuses to consent to a traditional arrangement, protesting that love must be sought freely, her mother literally imprisons her at home. With the support of a sympathetic cousin who agrees to smuggle out a letter to a lover back at college (the text that comprises the story, in fact), the heroine plots an escape; whether or not she prevails remains uncertain, for the narrative ends inconclusively with the completion of her letter, leaving the reader to speculate as to the events that may have ensued.

Praised for her compelling portrait of the internal emotional turmoil the protagonist experiences, torn between conflicting desires to fulfill her filial duties on the one hand and to pursue romantic love on the other, Feng herself evidently felt dissatisfied with the text as it stood, especially its ambiguous ending, for she almost immediately published a grim sequel. This time the text is narrated retrospectively from the perspective of the cousin: at the appointed hour, Naihua's escape plan went tragically awry, the reader learns, and lest she be married off to a complete stranger, the heroine commits suicide by swallowing poison. The revision is highly suggestive, especially given what transpired in the real-life story of the woman after whom Feng modeled her heroine, her cousin Wu Tian.[58] As it turns out, the young woman who inspired the story quarreled with her mother (Feng's aunt) for reasons similar to those explored in the story, only to a rather different outcome. Backed by two older brothers, Feng Yuanjun's cousin persuaded her mother to release her from her "prison" whence she returned to college (and presumably her lover) in Beijing. The death and despair that haunt the final pages of Feng's fictionalized account—the heroine Naihua's tragic suicide, her mother's anguish, the lover's tearful vow to follow her—in other words, must be seen as a conscious aesthetic choice on the part of the author. In this case one could argue, for example, that it enabled Feng Yuanjun to draw out with particular poignancy the intensity of the young woman's desire for the freedom to choose her own partner and to focus the reader's attention on the cruel tyranny of the "traditional family."

Yet Feng apparently had second thoughts about the negative implications of such a bleak ending as well. Less than a year after the publication of "Gejue" and its sequel, she rewrote the story altogether. In "Cimu" (1924), again a first-person narrative in the form of a diary, the I-narrator/protagonist returns home, reluctant and full of dread, to confront her mother about her impending arranged marriage. Through the close-up view we are afforded of the heroine's inner thoughts, we learn that she fears the worst (i.e., that her mother will force her to go through with an old-fashioned betrothal to a virtual stranger) and is mentally prepared to commit suicide should it come to that. She has even taken the precaution of stashing some poison in her suitcase in the event of just such a scenario. To her (and perhaps Feng's readers') surprise, however, her mother welcomes her back home. The formidable maternal image the narrator had conjured up in her mind melts away the instant she sees how frail her aging mother has become. More importantly, upon realizing how adamantly her daughter opposes the arranged marriage, the mother agrees to cancel the wedding. In sharp contrast to the tragic denouement of "Gejue yihou," this story concludes on a high conciliatory note as the mother sees the I-narrator off at the train station for her journey back to school and her modern lover. My point here in describing Feng's various revisions is not to suggest that one is more or less compelling in a "realistic" sense than the other; rather it is to indicate that implicit in the process of rewriting is a tension between the urge to register the enormous obstacles the modern heroine faces in defying the institutions of traditional family and marriage and the more ideological impulse to represent the possibility of their reform.

Known perhaps more than any other May Fourth woman writer for her melancholic sensibility, it was Feng Yuanjun's classmate Lu Yin who best articulated the need to strike a balance between the affective power of the tragic content of realist fiction and its didactic designs.[59] In 1921, at the height of an important early debate on realism among members of the Association for Literary Studies (*Wenxue yanjiuhui*) with which Lu Yin was affiliated, she published a brief article on the subject.[60] "[N]atural catastrophes and human misfortunes," Lu Yin writes, "are never-ending in the world today. Society is enshrouded in a cloud of sorrow and a fog of misery." Yet people "do not know how to search for the cause of their bitterness and depression, or to seek out light amid darkness."[61] For this reason, Lu Yin goes on to argue, the writer bears a certain moral obligation to her readers when it comes to depicting the tragic realities of the contemporary world:

> Creative writers should depict the tragedy in this kind of society with an intense sympathy and somber tone—both to provide the tormented with the absolute solace of profound sympathy and to raise their self-consciousness so they may fight ardently to find light in the midst of darkness, thus enhancing their pleasure in life. This is to take on the responsibility of the creative writer . . . However, at a time when people are suffering extreme hardship and pain, while the sympathy of a tragic portrayal may console them, a work should not dwell on the path of absolute despair . . . Hence a new road to life must be built amid the sorrow and pain.[62]

For a writer who consistently focused on women's lives, it is surprising that Lu Yin does not frame her critical remarks more specifically in terms of gender representation; two important concepts, however, both relevant to the feminist narrative strategies I turn to below, emerge in this passage. First, there is the principle of sympathy, or *tongqing*, a concept that appeared with some frequency in the theoretical writings of several other May Fourth intellectuals of this period.[63] Here, Lu Yin evokes the term in much the same way Ye Shaojun does; namely, not as mere pity for society's victims but as a conscientious gesture of empathy toward human suffering aimed at providing consolation to the reader (who presumably may have experienced such suffering herself). But for Lu Yin, the "solace" (*weiji*) a given text might extend to the reader is not sufficient in and of itself; having sympathetically portrayed the existence of suffering in society, it is in turn the writer's responsibility to proffer a vision of change, of alternative possibility, or what Lu Yin here describes simply as "a new road to life."[64]

"Women have long lamented their condition," feminist philosopher Sandra Bartky has recently commented, "but a lament, pure and simple, need not be an expression of feminist consciousness, as long as their situation is apprehended as natural, inevitable, and inescapable, women's consciousness of themselves, no matter how alive to insult and inferiority, is not yet feminist consciousness."[65] In their fictional depictions of women's suffering, Lu Yin and several other May Fourth women writers, I would argue, were not satisfied with merely evoking the reader's compassion for the plight of women but did so as part of a self-conscious attempt to forge what Lu Yin refers to as a "new road" for Chinese women. And it is in these rhetorical gestures beyond the current "reality" of suffering that the feminist significance of their writing may be found. Often featuring an empathetic encounter between a female narrator and a woman victim, the textual examples I examine do not reiterate the problematic asymmetrical division of narrative power (between a conscious, intellectual male and an inert, oppressed female) one often finds in the fiction of established male writers; rather, they rewrite the encounter as one of identificatory exchange between female characters who recognize in each other their collective predicament as women in a culture entrenched in masculine values. Nor does narrative closure provide a cathartic moment of release for either the I-narrator (or for the reader), as it does in, say, Lu Xun's early short stories;[66] instead, by starkly emphasizing the continuing persistence of patriarchy, they articulate a moral imperative for the reader's ongoing (emotional) engagement. My argument is not, therefore, that these texts supercede or dislodge the masculinist narrative logic described earlier by virtue of the fact that they were written by women or that they simply displaced the figure of the observing, intellectual male with a female one; rather, my readings strive to demonstrate that on a discursive level New Women writers inscribed the victimization of women in ways that do not necessarily replicate the rhetorical violence ascribed to May Fourth cultural depictions of women. Contemporary scholars have duly noted that the patriarchal hegemony continued to flourish, even amid the "progressive" cultural reforms undertaken in the name of women during the May Fourth era, but was masculinism so rampant and pervasive as to preclude *all* alternative, counter modes of writing women?[67]

*   *   *

An epistolary short story, Lu Yin's "Shengli yihou" (After victory, 1925) gives expression to the frustrations, anxieties, and bitter disappointments that a tight-knit circle of college graduates (reportedly modeled after Lu Yin's own clique of Nü Shida friends Wang Shiying, Chen Dingxiu, and Cheng Junying) experience as their high hopes for post-collegiate life are dashed by the sobering realities of dull modern marriages.[68] Quintessential New Women, all but one of them have achieved the ostensible "victory" of a marital union based on free will and romantic love—the goal this generation of rebellious youth hailed as tantamount to freedom itself. Married life, however, proves a far cry from the blissful, fulfilling state they imagined. In fact, as each one now painfully confesses, marriage (and the domestic arrangements it entails) acts as a barrier to their aspirations as New Women. Qinzhi, a newlywed, resents the way she feels distracted from her literary and intellectual pursuits; Xiaoyu worries that her ambition to become an active, meaningful participant in society has been eroded by the daily tedium and isolation of housekeeping and child rearing. And Lengxiu (Lu Yin's fictional incarnation) regrets having compromised her ideals and settling to become a second wife, despite her belief that her husband's first (arranged) marriage had nothing to do with love. For all of them, the emotional, or spiritual, sustenance they had eagerly anticipated from their modern male partners proves bitterly disappointing, far less sustaining in fact than the intimate, egalitarian friendships forged with one another in college. Unlike Lu Xun's Zijun, who adapts all too easily to her role of modern housewife, for the characters here the novelty of married life has long since worn off, giving way to feelings of emotional isolation, intellectual boredom, and personal insignificance. Positively contrasted to the debilitating domesticity of the present are references to feelings of personal freedom and reciprocity associated with the past: ironically, then, victory has spelled nothing but defeat and despair. Thus confesses the character Qinzhi, though she had long cherished ambitions to travel abroad and to pursue a meaningful vocation, she now feels hopelessly trapped "in the web of daily affairs" and regrets that she let her emotions get the better of her:

> We really were all so foolish. How heroic it seemed when we battled against our families and willingly sacrificed all for love! All of us managed to achieve this victory, but now after victory our joys are few and our troubles great. And we now have little to aspire to. What happiness is left in life, when all the thoughts that were once so comforting have suddenly been wiped away? (155)

In constructing the new-style nuclear family as a site of contradiction for the modern female intellectual, Lu Yin's story thematizes several salient issues of 1920s feminism. Steady advances in female education since the turn of the century, including the establishment of women's colleges and coeducational universities, had produced the first generation well-trained, politically self-conscious women. Impassioned calls for women's sexual equality and social liberties in the urban media also had the effect of raising young women's (and men's) expectations about restructured gender relations and roles. Yet, as the story suggests, May Fourth ideals and social realities were quite different. On the one hand, as Lu Yin would later elaborate in her essay "Jinhou funü de chulu" (The future of women, 1936), the so-called New Women, while capable of autonomy in theory, were all too often willing to settle for the trite comforts and security of home.[69] Thus wonders one character in the story, "What's the point of higher education for women if they abandon their work in society the minute they get married?" (151). On the other hand, women faced enormous difficulties in carving out an independent space for themselves in the public domain as a result of the limited career opportunities available to them. As a result, as the primary narrator Qinzhi later emphasizes, at present a professional career hardly guarantees women the sense of self-worth they so intensely desire: "We feel discouraged now," she admits in her letter, "not just because we can't free ourselves from housework, but also because society doesn't offer us anything to do" (151). (In her essay "Huaping shidai" [The flower-vase generation, 1933], Lu Yin goes so far as to suggest that in many cases middle-class women were considered nothing more than pretty adornments for the workplace, rather than as colleagues valued for their professional abilities.)[70]

The thrust of "Shengli yihou," however, is less an extended political analysis of the contemporary predicament facing educated women, than a sentimental recording of their *feelings* of injury and anxiety.[71] The main body of the text consists of a somber letter from the newlywed Qinzhi to her friend Qiongfang, in which she confesses ambivalence toward her new role as wife and records, by means of embedded letters and reported dialogues, the similar sentiments of three mutual friends. The epistolary structure of the text deserves comment: one of the most prevalent new forms of narrative fiction among writers—male and female—at the time, the letter form seems to have gained initial popularity after Guo Moruo translated Goethe's *Die Leiden des Jungen Werther* in 1921. But vernacular letter-writing also appears to have been considered a particularly preeminent "modern" practice associated with China's New Women, emblematic of their repositioning as social subjects. (So indispensable was letter writing thought to be to women's new social interaction [*jiaoji*], in fact, that this period saw the advent of instructional books such as *Xiandai nüzi shuxin* [Contemporary women's letters] that were explicitly marketed for emancipated women to hone their public communication skills.)[72] In Lu Yin's story, the epistolary format is significant for several reasons: first, it enables the author to displace the direct plotting of women's victimization in marriage with melancholic musings and nostalgic reminiscences of the female-I who self-consciously reflects on her present quandary. As a textual strategy, this shift away from the immediate scene of patriarchy in action to a more mediated interpretation of experience by women is worth noting, especially as it characterizes so many I-narratives of this period. For one thing, this strategy seems to temper the (potentially) harsh impact of an impersonal third-person narrativization of the wrongs inflicted on women in patriarchal culture. Above all, however, such a structure symbolically represents the mutual sympathy and moral support the women characters have for each other within an otherwise alienating world. Isolated and depressed as individual middle-class wives, the characters connect via their epistolary exchanges, recreating the supportive and self-enclosed space of female solidarity that they had once shared as friends in college. Notably, the multilayered text provides no entry for a male protector or savior: indeed, it constructs the illusion of a self-contained female world secure from male intrusion, a private conversation or text for female ears and eyes only. As in numerous fictional narratives by May Fourth women writers, here sensitive female friendship, both in the form of memory and as it is reconstituted in the epistolary narrative, comes to represent a powerful alternative to the disillusioning realms of marriage and career.[73]

But while the text unmistakably aims at evoking the reader's compassion for the female characters, Lu Yin is careful to avoid portraying women as conventional victims: here, the New Woman's emotional outpourings are not meant to harken back to earlier ideals of feminine suffering and self-abnegation (as Katherine Carlitz and others have shown to be the case in classical texts), but are represented as a specific response to thwarted public ambitions and desires.[74] This is crucial from a feminist point of view because it shows suffering to be a social condition that can and indeed must be resisted. Two potential solutions, moreover, are alluded to with respect to the problem of the educated woman's conflict between private and public aspirations and desires. The first, as intimated by the primary narrator Qinzhi, involves rejecting the romantic ideology that shores up the institution of marriage by idealizing love as the culminating achievement of a woman's life. There are, she insists in her letter to Qiongfang, "numerous other matters [in a woman's life] besides the 'big event' of marriage" (146). Hence women must not idealize marriage, but treat it as merely "one social arrangement" (146). Importantly, as a woman who is openly ambivalent about her own recent marriage and, in accordance with social custom, her new duties managing household affairs, Qinzhi's authority stems less from a superior moral stance of having achieved the independence she recommends than from her identity as a sympathetic confidante who shares with her friends anxiety about the negative impact marriage may well have on her own aspirations.

A more radical, if rather more tentative, suggestion the text offers is that there are valid social options available to New Women besides marriage; namely, "singlehood" or *dushen zhuyi*. Although Lu Yin only names the idea specifically toward the end of the story, the notion that women could retain their independence and professional opportunities through sexual abstinence was appealing to many New Women writers at the time.[75] As noted, among the five friends only one has managed to stave off married life and remains single. Wenqi, the reader learns, had initially resolved to pursue a meditative life of spiritual self-cultivation, but eventually accepted a demanding post as the principle of a provincial girls' school. From her letters, it is clear that she is well aware of the pitfalls of married life and, naturally, shows little interest in romance when her friends and family offer to introduce her to a potential suitor. As a device, Lu Yin uses this character both to contest the inevitability of the marriage plot and to subtly imply the possibility that a professional career holds out greater promise in satisfying the new woman's desire for individual purpose and meaning.

Lu Yin continues to explore the theme of female solace as an antidote to disappointing modern sexual relations in her 1927 story "Lantian de chanhuilu" (Lantian's confession).[76] A framed narrative that again sets up an enclosed structure of intimate confession between women, the occasion for this story is the recent acquisition by the I-narrator of a diary composed by her unfortunate acquaintance Lantian. The journal (whose cover bears the title of the story) had been kept by Lantian for about month during a severe bout of illness and depression, and in it she discloses not only her current troubled state of mind but also events in her personal history leading up to her mental and physical collapse. The reader learns that Lantian has avoided the usual "feminine" destiny of arranged marriage (in her case, narrowly escaping the fate of becoming the fourth wife of a much older man by leaving home to enroll in a college in Beijing) only to fall victim to a manipulative "new" man she meets in the city. After boldly moving in with her lover, a schoolmate who had won her affections and trust through his professed sympathy for her struggles, she is devastated to discover that he is already engaged to another woman. Emotionally distraught and mortified by the moral stigma of having openly cohabitated with a man who is not (and never will be) her legal husband, Lantian falls gravely ill. The protagonist's physical condition, therefore, is "realistically" explained as having been brought on by the emotional blow she has been dealt; as a whole, however, the text also clearly invokes illness as a metaphor of the New Woman's plight under the debilitating cultural environment of contemporary society.[77] Imbued with subversive desires for a self-actualized life, the protagonist ultimately lacks the power to achieve this, and it is this contradiction that illness seems to symbolize.[78]

The melodramatic plotting of Lantian's story—the early loss of her beloved mother, her struggle to complete her education, her betrayal by a "modern" man—follows a common pattern in "New Woman" narratives of the May Fourth period. What is striking about Lu Yin's account is the prominent role she gives in the narrative to the counter theme of female solidarity. Throughout the story, the power of female friendship is shown to be critical in empowering the protagonist to overcome the adversities that beset her. In recalling her life back home, for instance, Lantian records how her classmate Xiu not only consoled her, but encouraged her to resist her step-mother's cruel attempt to marry her off against her will. Later, the presence of a compassionate female ally provides support through her lengthy illness.

The diary describes Zhi, the close friend who tries to nurse her back to health, as the "only person in the world who pities" her (298) now that she has been branded a fallen woman (yige meiyou pinxing de duoluo nüzi, 301). Like the emotional support she once got from Xiu, Zhi's sympathy and encouragement sustain Lantian and keep her from succumbing to complete despair. "Her [words] were like a shot of some stimulant; they made me feel, amid my desperation, as though the future were not completely hopeless" (303). Significantly, it is Zhi to whom Lantian entrusts her diary as her condition takes a turn for the worse. Perhaps the most interesting—if somewhat implausible—instance of female solidarity in the text, though, occurs at the very end of the story, when the "other woman" unexpectedly pays Lantian a visit at her apartment. In an extraordinary display of female bonding (a scene Lu Yin would recapitulate in a later story "Shidai de xishengzhe" [Sacrificed to the era], 1928), the new wife of Lantian's ex-lover claims to identify with her, on the grounds that they have both been "sacrificed" by the machinations of a good-for-nothing man.

For Lantian, this gesture sparks a major epiphany; her faith in the future restored as she experiences a profound sense of sisterly solidarity with another "beleagured" woman. Crucially, it also produces unmistakable signs of an incipient feminist subjectivity, as her cynical disdain of society gives way to a sympathetic identification with "wronged women":

> It is true that I have always cursed humanity, but because of her sincerity, I immediately forgave all women and wept on their behalf. The reason is that to this day there have yet to be women who have not been toyed with and insulted by men. If only I could conquer this illness, for I now once again have new hope. Regrettably this hope is too feeble, yet if I could join hands with all the women of the world and forge a new era for women, then I would confess to my past crimes and at the same time struggle for the future. (305–306)

Lest the reader be carried away by Lantian's newfound optimism and lose sight of the grim condition of contemporary womanhood, the story ends ambiguously. Cutting back to the present, the I-narrator (whose own compassion, it should be noted, frames Lantian's narrative as a whole) learns after having read the diary that her friend's health had in fact continued to decline in spite of her renewed hope, and her chances of recovery are slim. But the message was likely not lost on the (implied female) reader of the story: as potential victims of men under patriarchy all women need to find a language of coexperiencing.

In contrast to more familiar examples from the modern canon such as Yu Dafu's "Chunfeng chenzui de wanshang" (Intoxicating spring nights, 1923) and Lu Xun's "Shangshi" (1925) in which the suffering woman functions as a static and often silent object of male sympathy, the epistolary form of "Shengli yihou" and the diary format of "Lantian de chanhuilu" enable Lu Yin to invest her female victims with voices of their own. Neither mute images onto which a modern male intellectual projects desire or probes his subjectivity, nor simply static "problems" through which the hero redeems his masculinity or legitimizes his political agenda, the women characters here give powerful testimony on their own behalf to the conflicts and inequities they have endured under patriarchal hegemony. At the same time, such narrative forms also allow the author to construct female friendship and sympathy as an important alternative to the alienating and disillusioning realities of modern society, showing woman-to-woman relationships to be an empowering source of moral, emotional, and practical support.

In both stories, however, it should be pointed out that the feminist critique has only extended to women similar in class and educational status to New Women writers themselves. One question that inevitably arises therefore is, to what extent do such writers succeed in avoiding conventional social hierarchies and gender stereotypes when it comes to representing "other" women?

In "Lin Nan de riji" (Lin Nan's diary, 1928),[79] a compelling short story by Shi Pingmei, it is neither the new man nor the new woman who verbalizes the plight of the woman trapped in a traditional extended family but the woman herself.[80] Lin Nan, the fictional author of the eight diary entries that comprise the story, is a literate but nevertheless semi-old-fashioned woman who has dedicated her life to serving as a dutiful daughter-in-law, wife, and mother. When her husband Lin, however, finally comes back home after a three-year absence, armed with newfound convictions about "free love" (*ziyou lian'ai*) and indignant at the ways (he now claims) his family has mistreated him, she suddenly finds herself an inconvenient burden.[81] That her husband's lover awaits him in the wings, a "New Woman" student named Miss Qian, makes him all the more miserable to be back home and impatient for a divorce. The diary, which begins in eager anticipation of Lin's impending arrival and covers their strained reunion before ending abruptly, delineates in compelling detail the heroine's tumult of thoughts and inner feelings as she copes with this unexpected rejection.

Referring to herself as a woman "left behind by the times" (241), the entries in Lin Nan's journal construct a far more complex consciousness of victimization than the usual May Fourth narrative of women in the traditional family. To begin with, the reader learns that the heroine feels utterly bewildered by the fact that her husband blames her for his unhappiness and that he has little appreciation of what she has endured in fulfilling her obligations as wife and mother. Conscious of the options available to the "New Women" such as her sister-in-law Dai, she is painfully aware of the cost of having complied with more conventional feminine roles. "What have I ever done to offend you?," she asks her husband in a conversation she records in the diary, "Surely you know that my living here at home is entirely for your benefit—serving your parents, raising the children, I have never complained once about any of it" (244). At the same time, Lin Nan feels deeply distressed by the prospect of divorce, a scenario with far graver consequences than her husband, whose concern apparently lies solely with his own happiness, seems willing to admit. Significantly, she does not see herself as a helpless victim, insisting in her journal that she could "get by" on her own were Lin to divorce her; what most troubles her, instead, is what would become of her elderly parents-in-law and her young children without her.

In a sharp departure from the popular May Fourth narrative decrying the plight of the enlightened intellectual battling the tyranny of the Confucian family system, Shi Pingmei examines the other side of the story by shifting attention to unwitting casualties of that process. Having been sacrificed to the maintenance of the established order, Lin Nan is now sacrificed once again in the name of freedom and reform. And in so doing, the author subtly implicates the New Youths (modern men and women alike) in bearing some moral responsibility for the predicament such women found themselves in.[82] The husband's claim—one that heroes of May Fourth fiction often echoed[83]—of victimization by the old arranged marriage custom rings hollow when Lin Nan contemplates the imbalance of power that defines their roles: "Oh God! I haven't the strength to quell the anguish burning in my heart. It is in Lin's power to determine what becomes of the rest of us; he could leave me, abandon me, ruin my life. I am clearly the most wronged and pathetic woman; how can they really go on loving each other without any misgivings?" (243).

An unframed narrative, "Lin Nan de riji" does not stage an encounter between a sympathetic female reader/listener and the wronged woman's story in the overt manner "Lantian de chanhuilu" does; rather, it attempts to create what Rita Felski (in discussing subjective forms in American feminist fiction) describes as "an illusion of face-to-face intimacy between author and reader."[84] As readers, we seem to experience unmediated access into the private thoughts of the protagonist. And it is precisely the heroine's longing for a confidante with whom to share her innermost woes that motivates the diary, not unlike Sophie in Ding Ling's classic story. A means of escaping the verbal and emotional restrictions under which she must conduct herself as a female member of an extended Confucian household, the diary provides a significant outlet—and powerful testimony—for otherwise unspoken inner realities. Indeed, in contrast to the quiet demeanor Lin Nan publicly exhibits in compliance with traditional feminine decorum when interacting with her husband's family, in the privacy of her own diary the protagonist freely vents the pent-up anger, anguish, and trepidation occasioned by Lin's behavior. As she bitterly confesses, "I can't even cry any more because if I do they'll curse me for 'driving him away.' Lin himself keeps saying that he can't stand these family woes for a second longer. But who has ever put themselves in my shoes for once?" (249).

There is no indication within the story that Lin Nan finds someone with whom to share her woes or to read her journal. On the other hand, it could be argued that the text itself can be seen as an experiment on the part of the author to put herself in Lin Nan's shoes, as it were. As the reading public would later learn through Lu Yin's fictionalized account of Shi Pingmei's love life, Shi Pingmei was ardently courted by Gao Junyu (1895–1925), one of the founding members of the Communist Party, during her years at Beijing Women's Normal College. By the time they first met and fell in love in 1923,

Gao was already married through a traditional arrangement to a woman in his hometown in Shanxi Province, not an unusual circumstance at the time. In her case, Shi Pingmei's sensitivity for the "other" woman, however, prompted her to stop the relationship from developing beyond a platonic friendship. In this fictional story, such concern manifests itself as a sympathetic imagining of what a woman "left behind by the times" might experience.

The pronounced split between the "traditional" and "modern" woman that marks so many works of realist fiction from the 1920s and 1930s is, furthermore, problematized by this story. Rather than depict Lin Nan as a passive victim oblivious to (or at least incapable of effectively communicating) the injustice of her circumstances, the author endows her protagonist with intelligence, insight and, obviously, literary ability. For Lin Nan, much like the breed of semi-old-fashioned women suspended between historical eras that Ling Shuhua (1900–1990), and even more notably Zhang Ailing (1921–1995), would write about, has enjoyed the distinctly twentieth-century privilege of attending school before ultimately complying with orthodox society's gender scripts. But if education has not sufficiently empowered (nor for that matter emboldened) the heroine to actively reject her prescribed role within the patriarchal order, it has opened her eyes to the various choices newly available to some women. Thus, despite doubting that she could ever achieve greater personal independence herself, she clearly admires her sister-in-law Dai, a confident, self-supporting schoolteacher: "How fortunate she is! If I were more like her, I would never have let Lin dominate my entire existence. I have practically become his plaything; when he loves me, I am content; when he loathes me, I suffer; and when he casts me aside, all I can do is sit here and cry. I would never dare take my anger and storm out the door like Ibsen's Nora" (247).

In highlighting Lin Nan's consciousness of the "New Woman" and the alternative lifestyle she so appealingly represents but also her inability to fully identify with this figure, this story offers a poignant gendered examination of women living at the margins of the progressive social reform movement. Along realist lines, it captures the psychological complexity and anguish of a woman newly attuned to heterodox ideologies and other plausible modes of feminine existence yet, in this case, so enmeshed in the everyday fabric of family life that following in the bold footsteps of Nora is not a viable option.[85] The confused array of emotion she conveys in her diary, from anxiety about the future to indignation at her husband's callous indifference to the larger implications of his actions, moreover, invite the reader to contemplate the more subtle and complex aspects of the May Fourth "rebellion" against the traditional (patriarchal) family. In short, instead of merely reproducing the narrative of never-ending female victimization, this story represents with keen insight the historically specific crisis of women impacted by the promising new ideologies of gender and romance, even as they remained bound to conventional roles and the duties these entailed.

* * *

As the previous examples have illustrated, a feminist-realist representation of the grievances and thwarted desires of modern women need not reproduce on a discursive level the dominant masculinist ideology. Contrary to the assumption implicit in much of the current scholarship on May Fourth gender discourse, the women writers I have examined thus far were clearly not unaware of questions of representation and textuality. A variety of formal strategies were employed in these narratives to challenge contemporary social practices even as they were rendered visible in agonizing detail by realism. This is not to say, however, that the repeated narrativization of women's plight in May Fourth fiction was without its detractors. In this penultimate section I thus turn to an instructive example by another prominent New Woman writer, Xie Bingying, who adopted a distinctly less sentimental view of the prevalent motif of female suffering to suggest the detrimental side of this cultural script. Like Ding Ling, who, as Yi-tsi Feuerwerker has commented, adopted in her early fiction a particularly "critical attitude toward the image of the suffering female,"[86] Xie Bingying explores the potential dangers of the discourse of female suffering and, in so doing, implicitly cautions that such rhetoric itself may be part of feminism's problem (and not simply its diagnosis).

In "Gei S- de yifeng xin" (A letter to S-, 1929),[87] Xie Bingying complicates the compassionate construction of the New Woman's subjectivity by attributing greater agency to her I-narrator-heroine. Like Lu Yin's "Shengli yihou," the text consists of an emotionally charged letter written to a woman friend by an I-narrator, a female activist who, as we might now have come to expect, bears a striking resemblance to the author herself: besides various personal details disclosed by the narrator that happen to coincide with Xie Bingying's own (well-known) biography, the letter is signed Ming, the author's childhood appellation. This technique, as discussed earlier, allows the author to exploit the close identification between narrator and author to enhance the truth-claims and authenticity of the fictional scenario.[88] Here, it makes the epistolary narration seem all the more vivid and direct and, insofar as the reader aligns herself with the "you" (i.e., Dear S-) addressed in the letter, rhetorically effective.

Ostensibly written as a final farewell, the narrator opens the letter by bluntly declaring that she wants nothing more to do with the addressee, a former classmate with whom she had once shared an intense attachment. The narrator admonishes S- for having betrayed her both personally and politically by becoming the concubine of a rich (and, as it turns out, exceedingly chauvinistic and abusive) military officer. The letter thus begins with these stinging words: "To put it bluntly, you are no longer fit to be my friend. Of all my friends now, who is as timid and weak-willed as you, or as incompetent, or as degenerate? I want to curse you, curse you because you shouldn't have sunk so low, and shouldn't have sunk into this sea of misery lured by your own vanity" (553). The bulk of the letter traces in language that is by turns nostalgic and contemptuous, the origins of their homoerotic affection and how it was nurtured by the warm atmosphere of a modern

girls' school (undoubtedly among the most important new public institutions instrumental in reshaping female identities in the early twentieth
century), and finally, the subsequent deterioration of their special bond.[89] It
was during the climatic patriotic student movement of 1926 (a specific
historical detail Xie Bingying incorporates into the story to further heighten
the sense of narrative veracity) that their schoolgirl intimacy first began to
unravel. At the time, the I-narrator recalls, she had been drawn into revolutionary politics and the new literature that was all the rage, and it was not
long before she decided to participate in the political process by enlisting in
the military. Meanwhile, S- remained steeped in a schoolgirl world of
romance and sentimental poetry. From the outset, the I-narrator now
confides, she had hoped that S- would undergo a change of heart and was
therefore delighted when S- finally joined the revolutionary bandwagon as a
nurse. Unfortunately, S- found the work both strenuous and boring, and
promptly quit. With her own deepening revolutionary commitments, not to
mention the geographical distance separating them, the I-narrator finally
became completely alienated from her former friend.[90] Now, several years
later, their paths by chance cross again and S-, unhappily married and
pregnant, clearly longs to restore their former relationship; it is in response
to their chance reencounter that the narrator writes the epistolary text we are
reading.

In thematizing modern female friendship, Xie's story echoes works
discussed earlier in this chapter. Explored through the lens of wistful nostalgia,
we see that for all her pride and conviction in her present political work,
personal happiness for the I-narrator remains synonymous with the halcyon
schooldays with S-. And, despite the stated purpose of the letter, the intense
emotions expressed in the letter betray a discernible desire on the part of the
narrator to reawaken her misguided friend by evoking memories of the close-
ness and compassion they once shared as girlfriends. Xie Bingying rewrites
the motif of female friendship in several important ways, however. Above all
is the explanation the I-narrator provides for the breakdown of that idealized
connection: whereas in Lu Yin's fictional world, for instance, modern
women are constrained by forces beyond their control (and agonize over
thwarted ambitions), here Xie accentuates the modern woman's *knowing*
capitulation. Contesting the narrative pattern of the innocent female victim,
the I-narrator offers extensive evidence of the ways in which S-'s own weakness and lack of will—her individual agency, in other words—has shaped the
course of her life. At the same time, she scoffs at S-'s lame rationalization that
she was *driven* into the arms of her present husband out of economic desperation and her attempt to claim the status of victim deserving of pity. "Of
course, the evil economy robbed you of your fully pure, happy, and hopeful
life, and inflicted a mortal wound upon you," the narrator writes
sardonically, "but, dear S-, your own inability to endure hardship and be
patient, your weak will and vacillating beliefs . . . these too ought to bear a
significant share of the blame" (566). She pointedly reminds her friend, for
instance, that she was fully aware of how reactionary her husband-to-be was

long before becoming his concubine, as well as the fact that once S- herself had rebuked him for his despicable treatment of women. She also reminds her of the choices available that would have enabled her to lead a more meaningful, independent existence: she could have become a nurse or teacher, for instance. In short, S- hardly qualifies as a purely innocent or helpless victim with whom the narrator can empathize, let alone rescue; on the contrary she emerges as a woman who needs to own up to her culpability in creating her present misery and her own power to effect change over her life.

Xie Bingying ends the story with a passionate, yet nevertheless stern, enjoinder to S- and women finding themselves in similar straights, to take responsibility for themselves: "Money, power, status—I wonder how many ambitious women they have misled! The academic degrees they earned have become the fashionable new bridal trousseau, while the lessons they learned at school are merely guides for their love letters. Consequently, Dear S-, though I sometimes feel sorry for you and want to find some way to rescue you, what can I do for someone like you who has developed a slavish nature (*nulixing*) and who refuses to fight back? I can't force you to be strong, and I can't force you to come back to life . . . Oh S-!" (568–569).

* * *

It is perhaps only fitting to conclude this chapter with a brief discussion of Ding Ling (1904–1986), without doubt the most famous authoress of twentieth-century Chinese literature, and whose literary career was launched with her brilliant portrait of the new woman in "Shafei nüshi de riji" (Miss Sophie's diary). The story, first published in 1928 in the prominent journal *Xiaoshuo yuebao*, received rave reviews at the time and has since become the single most frequently analyzed and anthologized work of female-authored May Fourth fiction. Adhering to the popular diary format, and unfolding entirely from the point of view of the first-person narrator, the story nevertheless exemplifies Ding Ling's unsentimental approach to the question of the New Woman's identity. The tormented protagonist Sophie agonizes in a perpetual state of doubt and indecision, but she is not presented to elicit readerly sympathy: if the diary's (ostensibly) uncensored and often unflattering realistic details underscore Shafei's quest for self-knowledge they also expose some of the more negative psychological qualities—extreme emotionalism, self-loathing and passivity, among them—patriarchy instills in women. Ding Ling's approach, as commentators have often noted, sprang not from political indifference to the emotional crisis of the modern woman, but from the author's concern that women's "victim mentality" all too often exacerbated their inability to respond effectively to their oppressive surroundings. Indeed, despite the great success of "Shafei nüshi de riji," most of Ding Ling's subsequent "subjective" realism shifts between internal and external narrative points of view, thus affording the author a greater ironic distance from the heroine than we have seen in the first-person fiction produced by other New Women writers.

One such work is "Yecao" (1929),[91] a short story that is of particular pertinence to the present argument because it thematizes the issue of the New Woman's self-representation. A young writer living on her own in Shanghai, the title character Yecao is depicted as a fiercely independent and strong-willed woman whose former disenchantment in romance has left her cynical about love and heterosexual relations, but also firmly resolved not to repeat her former mistakes. Unlike Sophie, who seems imprisoned in her own confused and contradictory tangle of erotic desires and emotions, Yecao refuses to be swept away by fleeting physical urges or declarations of love and instead exercises a high degree of self-control over her feelings and fantasies. Nor do we find much of the moral ambivalence Sophie struggles with in regard to her sexuality in the restraint this new woman imposes on herself: rather, Yecao has discovered that the rewards of a literary vocation far outstrip the transient pleasures of romance. Hence in the story, while a date in the park with an ardent suitor stirs up intense feelings of passion, the heroine is able to redirect these feelings as a source of artistic inspiration.

Significantly, we are first introduced to Yecao amid a moment of creative crisis, as she reproachs herself for the way she has portrayed the fictional heroine in the novel she is writing:

Today she was terribly upset because she had endowed an extremely level-headed and rational woman in her novel with unduly passionate emotions. Also, she let a slight touch of melancholy slip in. This definitely was not the character she had intended to create, but it was the flaw in woman she was best able to understand. She didn't know what would be better, to tear up the manuscript and start over, or to go on writing, but not sympathize with the woman. (105)

Although the narrative quickly shifts focus to Yecao's rendevous later that day with an infatuated suitor, this brief opening scene introduces the major theme framing the story; namely, the links among women, suffering, and textuality. The woman writer is dismayed to find that she has inadvertently ascribed to her heroine emotional characteristics that, as she then goes on to assert, the "social environment" overexaggerates in women (105). This is suggestive for several reasons. First of all, Yecao's authorial consternation stems less from having failed to realistically capture her heroine's pychological condition, than from an implicit aversion to a certain mode of femininity that, she implies, is a socially imposed construct. That she herself has suffered as a result of this culturally acquired sensibility makes her especially knowledgeable as to its characteristics, yet at the same time, all the more determined to transcend it. Indeed, the glimpse we are afforded of Yecao's "real" life in the story reveals an attempt to move beyond a life dominated by the emotions toward one anchored in more intellectual and creative pursuits.

But if women's emotional tendencies—however problematic—are understood as the product of a particular social environment, why is Yecao so put off by their representation as such? And conversely, why, given her apparent disdain, does she nevertheless delineate her heroine in this way? One could of course argue, along contemporary theoretical lines, that as a social practice literature itself is inevitably implicated in the formation of female subjectivity—to inscribe women as excessively passionate, emotional beings is thus to somehow be complicitous in perpetuating this social reality. That Ding Ling foregrounds her heroine's apprehension about representing femininity in this way suggests, perhaps, that she was not unaware of this potential dilemma of realistic representation. But rather than simply deplore the crippling effects of such inscriptions of woman on women, Ding Ling's text proposes a somewhat different perspective on this issue than explored by contemporary scholars in critiques of the "female victim"; namely, the confessional text as a medium for personal change and self-actualization. Much like the figure of the female confidante we have seen in earlier stories, who functions both as the alibi and sympathetic listener for the beleaguered modern woman, here the text itself assumes the function of consoling the heroine. We are told, for instance, that in addition to daydreaming, Yecao "found comfort only in her writing" in which she "often alluded to her magnificent lonely heart" (105). Instead of allowing herself to be defeated by the despair and self-pity borne of former personal experience, in other words, literary self-examination affords her a creative outlet through which to alleviate private inner turmoil. Toward the end of the story, as Yecao heads back home after her date it is evident that she also relies on her writing to sustain her newfound self-discipline and autonomy, and thus to avoid reproducing the past. In short, writing is conceived here as the catalyst for personal female transformation: to write femininity as emotional, vulnerable, or weak is to somehow help overcome (and thereby *re*write) this imposed cultural script.

Yecao vacillates over the question of how to best represent her heroine, torn between her attraction to its cathartic emotional function and her aversion to the stereotype it might reinforce; in the end, however, Ding Ling herself reveals no such ambivalence in depicting her own heroine as an empowered (literary) woman. Perhaps this highly self-reflexive contrast is an indication of Ding Ling's reassessment of herself as a writer for, as other scholars have noted, "Yecao" marks a turning point in her literary career as she increasingly turned her attention to other subject matter.[92] On the other hand, it is difficult to deny that in this work, as Feuerwerker comments, "Ding Ling is expressing her confidence in the efficacy of writing as a means for handling the problems of living."[93]

Despite the significant critical acclaim she won for her early fiction, Ding Ling's legacy in canonical literary history, interestingly, would appear to have as much to do with her contribution to the May Fourth feminist discourse on the New Woman as with her subsequent disavowal of that discourse: in the context of intensifying revolutionary fervor and personal tragedy (her husband was executed by the KMT), by the early 1930s Ding Ling embraced leftist politics and its literary agenda of socialist realism. Experimental works such as "Shui" (Flood, 1931), which attempts to represent mass identity, established

Ding Ling's reputation as a vanguard revolutionary writer but also, as accounts almost invariably emphasize, marked the end of her engagement with feminist issues. That Ding Ling's literary career took such a turn is not in dispute; the highly symbolic role her evolution as a woman writer has come to assume in the narrative of feminism and Chinese literary modernity, however, needs correction. For whether she is invoked to illustrate the (alleged) triumph of a more mature revolutionary vision over May Fourth bourgeois ideology or to lament the (alleged) eclipse of a feminist perspective under the new rubric of class analysis, Ding Ling's example has worked to obscure the fact that New Women's writing continued to flourish alongside leftist culture throughout the 1930s.

High-profile writers such as Lu Yin and Chen Xuezhao, joined by relative newcomers like Chen Ying (1907–1986), continued publishing so-called New Women fiction that revolved around the aspirations of middle-class heroines, unfazed by the ever-more urgent call by cultural radicals for revolutionary fiction. While the short story would remain their preferred fictional form, there is some experimentation with longer narrative forms: Chen Xuezhao published her first novel *Nanfeng de meng*[94] in 1929 and in the next few years went on to write several more novellas including *Xingfu*. Lu Yin, who had already published several novellas in the twenties, completed her first full-length novel *Xiangya jiezhi* in 1931 (the novel was serialized starting that year in *Xiaoshuo yuebao*, although due to the Japanese attack on Shanghai in 1932, the serialization was interrupted. In 1934, the Commercial Press published the complete work in book form). Notably, both autobiographical content and the conventions of self-disclosure, in the form of inserted diary entries and excerpted letters, remain salient features. Quite a few New Women writers, including several with leftist leanings, also published full-fledged autobiographies in the 1930s, a topic I take up in the next chapter.

There is additional evidence as well that far from marking a silencing of women's feminist voices (or a disappearance of "gendered" writing), as is often suggested, this decade actually witnessed a surge of liberal activism around what some started calling women's culture (*funü wenhua*). This included newly launched feminist magazines in the early nineteen-thirties, such as *Nüsheng* (Women's voice) edited by Wang Yiwei (1905–1993) and *Nüzi yuekan*, issued by the Women's Bookstore in Shanghai—examples that are described in greater detail in the following chapter. As we continue to rethink this critical juncture in modern cultural history, then, it is important to bear in mind that, despite the political polarization that occurs during this moment, feminist literary discourse still encompassed a variety of perspectives.

*   *   *

As noted at the beginning of this chapter, contemporary critics of modern Chinese literature have expressed certain reservations about May Fourth realist representations of women's oppression. The progressive "content" of many works about women from this period, they have pointed out, is often undermined by the discursive effects of a narrative logic that seems to reinscribe masculinist values. Fictional realism in the May Fourth era, however, was neither a monologic nor static discourse, and the patterns discerned in works by leading male authors need not be taken as necessarily representative of all literary inscriptions of woman of this period. Indeed, implicit throughout this chapter has been an argument for a more nuanced approach to the question of feminism and realism, one that actually attends to the realist practices of women writers in the historical context of their own moment and their specific formal attributes.

CHAPTER 3

LOVE AND/OR REVOLUTION?: FICTIONS OF THE FEMININE SELF IN THE 1930S CULTURAL LEFT

> Women and Revolution! What tragic, unsung epics of courage lie silent in the world's history!
>
> Yang Gang, 1936

When Bai Wei (1894–1987) and Xie Bingying (1906–2000) both published autobiographies in 1936, their literary careers appeared to have already undergone the "political" transformation that modern Chinese literary histories often characterize as the shift from romanticism to revolution. As early as the late 1920s, with the breakdown of the first national alliance between the Guomindang (KMT) and the Gongchandang (CCP), the resurgence of concern over China's political future precipitated dramatic change in the literary practices of many progressive Chinese writers, as they turned their narrative gaze from the realm of subjective experience to the arena of social emergency. By the early 1930s, the looming threat of Japanese invasion, coupled with political persecution and the repressive cultural policies of the KMT finally galvanized disparate elements of the cultural left to join forces and form the League of Left-Wing Writers (*Zuoyi zuojia lianmeng*), and over the next few years the League aggressively promoted a prescriptive aesthetic that accorded primacy to class issues and the national crisis. Along with their better-known (and fellow Hunanese) colleague Ding Ling, both Bai Wei and Xie Bingying were among the small handful of women writers to win critical praise in the early 1930s for "living up" to the aesthetic challenges of the new era, having transcended the allegedly narrow personal focus that was now seen to limit other "women's writing," and assuming the responsibilities of the socially-engaged writer. In a 1933 account, the critic Fang Ying divided Bai Wei's literary work into two hierarchical stages: her early "ivory tower" writing, epitomized by her romantic tragedy *Linli* (1926), which explored themes of love and emotional betrayal, and her subsequent works which took on the more weighty issues of class conflict (*Dachu youlingta* [Fighting out of the dark pagoda of spirits], 1928) and national revolution (*Gemingshen shounan* [The suffering of the god of revolution], 1928).[1] The outspoken Marxist critic A Ying (Qian Xingcun) apparently considered her the most revolutionary woman writer of her generation.[2] Similarly, writing in reference to her hugely popular *Congjun riji* (War diary, 1928) critics hailed Xie Bingying's "unfeminine" and "revolutionary" style as the latest wave in women's writing, superseding what they considered the passé "sentimentality" (*duobing duochou*, literally to be laden with sorrow and illness) of established writers like Bing Xin.

Yet *Beiju shengya* (My tragic life, 1936) and *Nübing zizhuan* (Autobiography of a woman soldier, 1936) seem to defy this neat schema.[3] The former is a highly confessional autobiographical novel, which charts neither Bai Wei's political conversion nor her participation in leftist cultural spheres, but rather focuses on the author's traumatic entanglement with her lover, the poet Yang Sao (1900–1957), and a protracted battle with venereal disease. The latter retraces the author's personal odyssey as young woman as she struggled to extricate herself from the restrictive feminine roles and obligations of a conservative Confucian family. Why, the question thus arises, did these two writers revert to the project of writing the (feminine) "self" at the very moment when so many of their leftist colleagues were now repudiating autobiographical content as complicit with the (now suspect) May Fourth ideology of individualism? And why, given their public status as committed activists, do they continue to dwell on the intimate details of their own private histories? As this chapter explores, the answer to these questions lies in the authors' insight that, to borrow the axiom later popularized by American feminism, the personal *is* political. Their autobiographical writing thus represents not so much a naive retreat to the realm of self and private experience of early May Fourth romanticism as it is a conscious reclamation of that realm as relevant subject matter for revolutionary writing. As such, these texts not only challenged the dichotomies between self/society, personal/political, private/public that were coming to regulate the leftist discourse on revolutionary writing of the 1930s but, more specifically, the ways those dichotomies threatened to marginalize gender issues.

The following chapter is divided into three parts: in the first section, I review some of the critical scholarship on women's autobiography in China as a way of highlighting key theoretical issues at stake in evaluating the feminist implications of women's literary self-expression. In part two, I locate *Beiju shengya* and *Nübing zizhuan* more specifically in the context of leftist cultural debates of the 1930s, and suggest that, despite increasingly hostile attacks by male critics, women literary radicals did not simply abandon "gendered" writing in the way orthodox literary historical accounts would lead us to believe. To appreciate the kind of intervention these two authors make, however, it is important to understand the changes that were occurring under the newly radicalized literary climate; to that end I briefly discuss the "romance plus revolution" (*aiqing jia geming*) genre, a fictional genre that gained brief popularity among many leftist writers as they made the transition from subjective sentiment to political duty. And finally, part three performs a close reading of *Beiju shengya*, a fascinating yet disturbing work that resonated deeply with the female reading public at the time but which is virtually unknown today.[4] Here, the question I am most interested in examining is how Bai Wei appropriated the autobiographical form to examine the contradictory experiences of the radical female intellectual subject in relation to both desire and history.

WOMEN'S AUTOBIOGRAPHICAL PRACTICES IN THE 1920S AND 1930S

As noted in the previous chapter, if there is one salient characteristic that stands out above all others in Chinese women's writing of the early twentieth century, it is the preponderance of autobiographical and semi-autobiographical forms. Taking a sharp turn inward from the sociopolitical orientation of late Qing radical women writers with their sweeping and overtly didactic narratives of the *nüjie*, women writers in the 1920s and 1930s participated in the "imagining of modern selfhood" by narrating themselves and, in particular, the problems of personal gendered experience.[5] Even in the more explicitly fictional forms of May Fourth women's writing—for example, short stories, novellas, and novels—subjective narrative genres and conventions abound: Ding's Ling's acclaimed "Shafei nüshi de riji" (1928) is but of one of countless stories in which the heroine's intimate thoughts and desires are revealed in diary form, while epistolary fiction such as Lu Yin's "Shengli yihou" (1925) was also a favorite narrative mode among women writers of this period.[6] Nearly every major woman writer of the period also published personal accounts of her own life or parts of her life, in the form of autobiographies, memoirs, personal correspondences, and diaries. In addition to those considered in the present chapter, these include full-fledged autobiographies such as Lu Yin's *Lu Yin zizhuan* (Autobiography of Lu Yin, 1934) and Xiao Hong's *Shangshi jie* (Market street, 1936); autobiographical novels such as Chen Xuezhao's *Nanfeng de meng* (Dream of southern winds, 1928) and Su Xuelin's *Jixin* (Bitter heart, 1929); memoirs such as Lu Jingqing's *Liulangji* (Wanderings, 1932) and Chen Xuezhao's *Juanlu* (Weary travels, 1925); published private correspondence such as Lu Yin and Shi Pingmei's intimate lyrical exchanges in the *Qiangwei* (Wild rose) Journal (mid-1920s) and Bai Wei and Yang Sao's love letters *Zuoye* (Last night, 1933); and diaries such as Xie Bingying's *Congjun riji* and Lu Xiaoman and Xu Zhimo's coauthored *Aimei xiaozha* (Love letters to Mei, 1935).[7]

Yet, if it has long been observed that women writers of the 1920s and 1930s evince strong autobiographical proclivities, it is a topic that has been sorely neglected within mainstream Chinese literary studies. The two most important English-language studies to deal comprehensively with the role of subjectivity and autobiographical tendencies in modern Chinese literature, Leo Lee's account of May Fourth romanticism (1973) and Wendy Larson's study of literary authority (1991) are conspicuously reticent when it comes to women writers. Considerable differences notwithstanding, both link self-reflexive writing of this period to the "alienation" of the modern Chinese intellectual following the demise of the imperial state system and with it an end to the exam system that had formerly guaranteed a close affiliation between the literati class and the state. This loss of intellectual hegemony, according to both Lee and Larson, underwrites modern literary productions of the self. Clearly, whatever else one may make of this explanatory model, it has limited applicability as far as understanding women literary intellectuals, for whom this period was marked not by a loss but an expansion of cultural authority stemming from formal education and its attendant privileges.

In the scant research that has taken up the topic of women's autobiographical practice, none has been more influential than Yi-tsi Feuerwerker's pioneering essay "Women as Writers in the 1920s and 1930s" (1975).[8] The essay contends that the subjective orientation of May Fourth women's writing reflects the highly circumscribed perspective of its inexperienced authors, young women who failed to embrace the "whole range of literary subjects" that they could have (and should have, in Feuerwerker's critical view) potentially explored in their writing.[9] Preoccupied with themselves and, in particular, Feuerwerker emphasizes, themselves "as female," most literary women in the May Fourth never managed to mature into seasoned writers capable of dealing with the broader social themes of their day and instead wrote, "over and over, the stories of their own lives."[10] They did not just write about themselves, Feuerwerker maintains, they wrote primarily *for* themselves, relying on literary self-expression as a means of existential self-justification, a way of convincing themselves of their own new-found identities. The basic explanation (or apology) Feuerwerker offers for this allegedly deficient literary output is historical in nature: deep psychological anxieties and insecurities arising from the new roles urban intellectual women in early-twentieth-century China had begun to assume, often through prolonged and bitter personal struggle, compelled many to turn to writing as a mode of "self-affirmation." But ultimately, for Feuerwerker, this does not excuse the fact that, in her final estimation, May Fourth women's self-obsession resulted in writing which "lacked the balance, the mature detachment, the finality, that make for great works of literature."[11]

Like all pioneering studies, it is not difficult in hindsight to find fault with parts of Feuerwerker's essay. Now that the archive has been more fully excavated, for example, it is obvious that both women's literary output and the scope of women's literary practices of this period was far broader than she suggests. More problematic perhaps, as Rey Chow has pointed out, her analysis proceeds from an *a priori* definition of literature, which obviates a full critical engagement with the particular writing at hand.[12] Feuerwerker is unable to offer a fair assessment of the textual practices of May Fourth women writers because her presuppositions about what qualifies as "literary" already preclude an analysis of the style of writing Chinese women were in fact producing at the time. Curiously, what Chow herself does not challenge is the double critical standard at work in the evaluation of May Fourth liter-ature in general, whereby male-authored subjective writing of the same period has been analyzed in terms of self-conscious aesthetic movements such as romanticism, while for women it continues to be dismissed as naively narcissistic.[13]

The issue of greater relevance here, however, is Feuerwerker's conception of autobiography as a mode of "self-affirmation" and the theoretical assump-tions upon which the "self" implied in this formulation are based. The essay opens with a lengthy preamble in which Feuerwerker acknowledges the various ways in which traditional (by which she means pre-twentieth century) women writers' (self)-representations of femininity were inevitably textually mediated—inextricably embedded in conventionalized "modes of thinking and feeling ascribed *to* women in the literary tradition" (151). Rather than extend this logic to her consideration of women's writing in the modern era, however (by examining, for instance, how new or emergent gender ideologies—not to mention the theories of realism valorized at this time—also invariably mediated women writers' self-portraits), Feuerwerker appears on some level to subscribe to the May Fourth generation's view of modern literature as a "reflection of life." To put it another way, her own conception of literature concurs with the prescribed ideal of the May Fourth generation of a direct, transparent medium through which life and self could be expressed (in their case a goal to be achieved by virtue of the writer's iconoclastic adoption of the modern vernacular). From this, she contends that women writing in modern times had not just been liberated from their traditionally appointed social roles, they had been liberated from the shack-les of stale literary convention. Hence unlike their literary foresisters, who were dominated by the formulas, conventions, and masculinist values embedded within the literary tradition, modern women writers were free, or so she maintains, to "confront reality head on."[14] In short, for Feuerwerker, the female self that is allegedly being affirmed in autobiographies of this period is one which, having been emancipated from social as well as aesthetic constraints, is now simply being transcribed in textual form.[15]

If Feuerwerker finds fault with the autobiographical proclivities in women's writing on the grounds that all such texts convey is the bare "truth" of women's lives, British historian Elizabeth Croll valorizes them for precisely this reason. In her recent full-length study of personal narratives by twentieth-century women, *Changing Identities of Chinese Women: Rhetoric, Experience, and Self-Perception* (1995), Croll adopts an empiricist historical approach to explore how twentieth-century Chinese women experienced gender rhetoric.[16] In terms of the range of authors she covers, which include literary as well as nonliterary writers, this study has much to offer; from the point of view of contemporary feminist literary theory, however, its approach lacks nuance. Sidestepping the fraught issue of autobiography as form, she reduces personal narrative to direct documentation of lived experience, which supposedly provides "special access" into those spheres of female life and experience long marginalized if not occluded altogether in the official historical record.

Not unlike the opposition Feuerwerker posits between the highly conventionalized nature of traditional literary discourse, on the one hand, and the supposedly unfettered, direct medium of modern language/literature on the other, Croll draws an overly simplified distinction between what she calls the "rhetoric" about women and women's own self-expressions. And once again, rhetoric here is associated primarily with an outmoded "tradition," which is said to have been transcended with the advent of modernity. Despite having noted the flurry of intellectual and political discussion surrounding the Woman Question (*funü wenti*) in the twentieth century in her preface, what Croll emphasizes in the course of her analysis of modern female autobiographers is the "dissonance between their lives as new women in the early twentieth century and Confucian prescriptive codes or expectations" (12). To her credit, Croll's reference to emergent modern "rhetorics" early on in the book invites the reader to consider their bearing on the gendered self-perceptions and self-representations of her subjects; however, in the actual analysis of specific autobiographical texts,[17] experience and rhetoric are treated as discrete categories, as though the two can in fact ever be disentangled. In particular, Croll is interested in how the modern woman's experience contradicted increasingly obsolete Confucian gender prescriptions. Thus, the prevalent theme of daughterly rebellion she astutely discerns in women's autobiography, for instance, is said to spring from the collision of novel social experience and defunct rhetoric: in the absence of newly codified gender roles in the early twentieth century and an accompanying rhetoric to lend them legitimacy, Croll contends, young women increasingly came to see themselves as "rebels," and to perceive their lives largely in terms of defiance of traditional values and norms.

Croll's study identifies a number of salient patterns in women's autobiographical writings in early-twentieth-century China—the recurring narrative of rebellion and the importance of the gendered category of daughters, for instance. However, the key terms of her analysis (rhetoric, experience, and self-perception) derive from a critical discourse on female autobiography which has come increasingly under fire within certain strands of feminist literary theory.[18] Like Croll, contemporary feminist theorists admittedly value autobiographical writings for what they express about women who authored them; at issue, though, is *what* the autobiographical text can reveal and *how*. Whereas Croll maintains a view of personal narratives as neutral, unmediated documents that offer the reader "special entry to the secluded world of women,"[19] or as true-to-life reflections of real events and experience, the feminist theorization of autobiography has begun, as one critic aptly puts it, to complicate the "graphia" in women's autobiography—that is, to explore such writing as a particular mode of *textual practice*.[20] For autobiography, like fiction, not only relies on specific narrative conventions and formal rhetorical strategies, but is subject to the ideological constraints of the historical moment in which it is produced—including the very constructs of "self" and "femininity" which the woman autobiographer may embrace or, as the case may be, actively and creatively resist.[21]

Feuerwerker and Croll have drawn much needed attention to the complex historical context in which the subjective tendencies within Chinese women's writing of the period must be situated; however, by treating women's auto-biography as a spontaneous outpouring of personal detail or, alternatively, as a therapeutic exercise for coping with an unstable external world, many important questions remain unanswered. Above all, by ignoring the politics of form, they neglect the crucial issue of how women's autobiographical practices were specifically related to and shaped by developments in main-stream modern literary discourse itself: To what extent was the surge of self-writings driven by the cultural fascination (read market demand) with the so-called New Women? How do women's autobiographical writings intersect with shifting conceptions of the "self" during this period? For instance, how did early May Fourth notions of authentic individuality or the new importance attached to class identity by the cultural left in the 1930s inform (or constrain) modern women writers' constructions of their lives? What is the relationship between the "fictions of subjectivity" explored in the previous chapter and autobiography *per se*? Did these life-stories assume particular narrative patterns, and how did such forms help define, shape, or organize female "experience"? These and other questions underline that the parameters of the issue of women's autobiographical practice are much broader than either Feuerwerker or Croll admit and, clearly, warrant further consideration if we are to fully appreciate how Chinese women writers of this era deployed autobiography not just to describe but to actively and creatively redefine their lives.

* * *

GENDERING THE CULTURAL LEFT—PERSONAL LIFE AS POLITICAL CRITIQUE

If Bai Wei and Xie Bingying's autobiographical writings belong to one of the most prominent genres of Chinese women's literary modernity, they also need to be anchored in the specific context of 1930s culture. For, contrary to the critical assumption that the prevalence of personal genres reflected an inability and failure on the part of women writers to progress to a "broader vision of reality," both women were authors who had demonstrated an unmistakable commitment to the revolutionary literature now hailed by the cultural left: writing the self, in other words, can not be explained as arising from some immature preoccupation on their part but seems to represent a deliberate literary—and political—choice. It was a choice that did not sit well with the radical literary camp with which they were aligned and that, as Lydia Liu comments, "decided to reject the self in order to implement the project of modernity on a collective basis."[22] Neither Bai Wei nor Xie Bingying's works, as I will show, endorsed the romantic individualism that so troubled some of their comrades, although this fact seems to have eluded most of their interpreters.

By the mid-1930s, both Xie Bingying and Bai Wei had firmly established credentials, both through their literary publications as well as their direct involvement in radical cultural activities, as leftist writers. After having achieved (inter)national fame for her celebrated *Congjun riji* (1928)[23] Xie Bingying joined Yang Gang, Pan Mohua (1902–1934) and others in founding the Beijing League of Left-Wing Writers (*Beifang zuolian*). For reasons that are not entirely clear, she withdrew from that organization in 1931, although her publications reveal a continuing commitment to a leftist ideological framework. Her first full-length novel *Qingnian Wang Guocai* (The young Wang Guocai, 1931), for instance, examines the decisive role of money and social status in bourgeois love, while her short story collection *Qianlu* (The road ahead, 1932) included stories concerning the plight of working-class women and female revolutionaries. Among the best is the novella "Paoqi" (Abandoned), which centers on an impoverished labor activist who struggles to reconcile the maternal feelings newly awakened by the birth of her baby and the life of revolutionary action she has chosen. In 1932, in the wake of the Japanese occupation of Manchuria, Xie took on the editorship of *Funü zhi guang* (Women's light) a journal sponsored by the Women's National Resistance and Salvation Alliance (*Zhongguo funü fanri jiuguo datongmeng*).[24]

As for Bai Wei, like her friend and colleague Ding Ling, her work was often applauded for having evolved from an early May Fourth style to a later revolutionary mode, a shift attributed to the author's ideological maturation in the late 1920s.[25] She was a regular contributor to left-leaning journals in Shanghai, including *Beidou* (Big dipper), a journal sponsored by the League of Left-Wing Writers which came under Ding Ling's editorship in 1931, *Xindi yuekan* (New earth monthly), and Lu Xun's slightly more nonpartisan journal *Benliu* (Torrents). In the aftermath of the September 18 incident, when Japan launched its military campaign in Northeast China, she was among the first to publish works protesting Japanese aggression, including her one-act play "Beining lu mouzhan" (A certain stop on Beining road, 1932). Bai Wei also actively joined efforts to mobilize progressive artists and writers in Shanghai in the early 1930s as the anti-imperialist movement heated up, working tirelessly in progressive drama and film circles.[26] In 1932, along with Lou Shiyi and Yuan Shu, she founded the Shuxing Drama Troupe, which staged a number of overtly political plays in Shanghai. For these reasons, her apparent relapse to the subjective literary style associated with the increasingly suspect May Fourth era and, in particular, the primacy Bai Wei's accords in her autobiography to the private realm of the emotions and sexuality confounded some of her contemporaries. Did this autobiography mark a regrettable solipsistic lapse from the author's otherwise politically engaged writing? If not, why had Bai Wei chosen to focus exclusively on the apparently narrow realm of intimate personal experience despite heightened cries for a "relevant" revolutionary literature that could better propel social change?[27]

Guan Lu (1907–1982), for instance, a prominent woman poet with leftist ties, was both perplexed and disappointed by the thematic focus of *Beiju shengya* given what she knew of Bai Wei's deep involvement in progressive politics, including her efforts in promoting women's liberation. Although she applauded Bai Wei for the brutal honesty of her account, in a review she also expressed certain reservations about the appropriateness of Bai Wei's self-portrait:

> As far as I know, the author is a social activist, a woman who has continually struggled for social and political emancipation and who has not devoted most of her life to her private romantic life. But this work is entirely about love; it depicts her romantic entanglements as if they were the major aspect of her life. Reflections on society are only inserted at the margins . . . Miss Bai Wei is clearly a woman who stands on the front lines of [the socio-political] struggle and has devoted much effort to that end. Therefore, her writing ought to center on society, while her private life ought to occupy merely one part. For the private love life is but a tiny part of life as a whole and shouldn't be overemphasized.[28]

Typical of the sorts of injunctions being issued in 1930s radical circles for sociopolitically engaged literature, what this statement also belies is the growing tendency within leftist discourse to depoliticize the patriarchal domestic sphere altogether. Women writers in particular, many of whom continued to grapple with issues of female subjectivity and gendered experience (including topics of marriage, pregnancy, motherhood, and abortion) now became the targets of disparaging left-wing criticism because their subject matter was deemed to be "narrow," "decadent," and "bourgeois." Despite the author's repeated reminders in *Beiju shengya* that Wei's physical, emotional, and psychological experience is not unique (and therefore not purely private) but the product of the systematic patriarchal logic that permeates Chinese society as a whole, the sociopolitical relevance of the narrative apparently eludes Guan Lu who instead chastises the author for privileging her private life above her political work. And, failing to grasp the way in which Bai Wei critiques heterosexual romance as an arena of unequal power relations, Guan Lu misinterprets the text as one that is simply about love.

The assumptions underlying Guan Lu's critical ambivalence—assumptions *against* which Bai Wei and Xie Bingying were consciously writing—are tightly bound up with shifting conceptions of "the political" in 1930s revolutionary culture. In particular, they reflect the devaluation of gender as a political problem, or at least as one that deserved immediate and continuing attention. Whereas women's liberation from traditional domestic roles had, in the 1920s, been at the fore of leftist theoretical debate and stratagems for social revolution (something that distinguishes early Chinese Marxism from movements elsewhere), the relationship between the women's movement and socialist politics showed signs of tension and fissure by

1930.[29] In addition to the fear and disillusionment many activists suffered, the backlash against grassroots feminist activism following the revolutionary upsurge of 1926–1927 seemed to prove that a radical challenge to the male-dominated social order could be potentially divisive. Thus, although the CCP would continue to endorse gender equality as a long-term objective, it came to be widely believed that it could not and should not be accorded primacy within the immediate revolutionary agenda. As Christina Gilmartin notes in her well-documented study of the role of feminist politics within early Chinese communism, the "Resolution on the Women's Movement" adopted at the Sixth Congress of the Chinese Communist Party (convened in Moscow in 1928) marked the beginning of an official downgrading of gender politics within Chinese socialism in that it "facilitated a clear departure from the feminist program and the subsequent adoption of an orthodox position on the primacy of economic class oppression over gender exploitation."[30] The resolution, which vehemently denounced the "independent" and "bourgeois" nature of the Chinese feminist movement, called for leadership by urban working-class and peasant women in directing the struggle against gender oppression. What the resolution also clearly implied, however, was that in the future any feminist agenda that might deflect attention (or vital resources) away from the CCP's primary agenda of class revolution would not be tolerated.

To be sure, in the early 1930s, official party doctrine can hardly be said to have dictated leftist cultural practice in any absolute or systematic manner. Indeed, there were considerable differences in the theories and practices of progressive male critics and writers about what a politically-engaged literature should entail, as revisionist scholarship of this period in literary history has begun to reveal.[31] Nevertheless, the marginalization of gender within revolutionary discourse does appear to have produced discernible effects in the leftist literary representations of women. Yushi Chen, for instance, has observed that the 1930s witnessed nothing less than a paradigm shift in the cultural inscription of revolution: as the emancipation of women ceased to function as a rallying point for political action, exploited laborers came to replace oppressed women as the paradigmatic symbol of social oppression in fiction. The figure of the female victim did not disappear entirely from the literary landscape, but what now often took precedence in fictional narratives was her socioeconomic plight under class-based (rather than specifically gender-based) forms of exploitation.[32]

More disturbing, whereas women writers had only recently been celebrated for their insights into the Woman Question, they now risked being discredited for continuing to dwell "narrowly" on domestic subjects, including issues of gender and sexuality. According to Wendy Larson's research on the subject, as leftist critics began to call with greater urgency for a new literature more attuned to the current social realities of class and nation, they often singled out women writers for their "individualism, an excessive narrow scope and framework, a mystifying approach to experience, a lack of social knowledge and awareness, extreme emotionalism, pessimism and doubt, escapism, a poetic and romantic mentality, decadence, emphasis on individual (and especially female) psychology and on various kinds of love and love conflicts."[33] While this critique arose as part of an overall reaction against the (perceived) romantic excesses of May Fourth literary style, Larson argues that the discussion was gendered in such a way as to associate such excesses primarily with women writers and that, as a result, the category of *funü wenxue* as a whole was constructed as "out-dated and unprogressive" (69). At the same time, the fierce debates that now erupted over, for instance, proletarian literature and national forms, seemed for the most part gender-blind. Even if it is true that many male radicals continued to support feminist principles in theory, literary radicalism no longer seemed to offer any clear direction as to how to address women's predicament as part of the broader social struggle.

Before going further, let me pause here to note that for a number of women writers leftist polemics actually seemed to have made little imprint on their literary output. Lu Yin (1898–1934) and Chen Xuezhao (1906–1991), both of whom had made their debuts at the height of the May Fourth movement remained prolific in the 1930s: prior to her premature death in 1934, the former completed, among other works, four full-length novels *Guiyan* (Returning geese, 1930); *Nüren de xin* (Heart of a woman, 1933); *Xiangya jiezhi* (Ivory rings, 1934); *Huoyan* (Flames, 1935, published posthumously) and an autobiography (*Lu Yin zizhuan*, 1935), and her fiction would remain available to readers throughout the thirties and forties in reissued collections of her work. With the major exception of her experimental novel *Huoyan*, which recounts the events following Japan's bombing of Shanghai in January of 1932 through the eyes of a young soldier in the Nineteenth Route Army, these works continued to explore the theme of the modern woman's (thwarted) search for meaning and happiness.[34] The latter, who returned from France in 1934 after completing a Ph.D. in literature, published two collections of essays which addressed the condition of women in 1932 (*Shidai funü* [Women of the age] and *Baixu ji* [Withering wisps]) as well as such works of fiction as her feminist novella *Xingfu* (Happiness, 1933). Relative newcomers to the literary scene such as Chen Ying (1909–1986) achieved popularity with urban readers in the 1930s with fictional works that, continuing in the vein of May Fourth New Women fiction, examined the domestic and sexual dilemmas of educated, middle-class heroines.[35]

It was also during this time that Women's Bookstore (*Nüzi shudian*) opened its doors in the French concession district of Shanghai (1933–1936) to launch an avowedly nonpartisan magazine and a press devoted to promoting women's writing. The bookstore was founded by Huang Xinmian and her husband Yao Mingda, a professor at Fudan University, and affiliated members included Chen Baiping, who served as editor of *Nüzi yuekan* in 1934; and writers Zhao Qingge (1914–) and Fengzi (1912–1996). In addition to numerous monographs on gender-related subjects and the international feminist movement,[36] the press also issued many literary volumes by modern Chinese women authors, including Chen Xuezhao, Feng Yuanjun,

Lu Yin, Zhao Qingge, and Wu Shutian. Another example that could be cited as evidence that feminists continued to use the print media as a public forum during this period is the magazine *Nüsheng* (Women's voice) edited by Wang Yiwei (1905–1993), which ran from 1932–1935, and featured polemical articles by progressive women scholars on gender-related topics as well as literary works by contemporary women writers.[37] Numerous feminist cultural organizations also sprang up in the early 1930s, including *Funü gongming she* (Women's sympathetic understanding society); *Tianjin shi funü wenhua cujin hui* (Tianjin society for the advancement of women's culture); and the *Shanghai Zhonghua funü hui* (Shanghai Chinese women's society), which sponsored a host of educational and cultural activities and programs for women.[38]

At issue here, however, is what did the devaluation of sexual politics mean for feminist writers with leftist sympathies? Much has been made of the fact that Ding Ling, whose early May Fourth fiction evinced keen insight into the specific psycho-sexual burdens of the new urban woman, basically abandoned such feminist concerns in her revolutionary fiction of the 1930s.[39] Sharply contrasting the women-centered stories of her first published collection *Zai hei'anzhong* (In the darkness, 1928), for instance, the short stories she published in *Yiwaiji* (Unexpected collection) in 1936 (the same year Bai Wei and Xie Bingying's autobiographies appeared) foregrounded the economic struggles of laborers, peasants, and the urban poor. Among her fictional characters are women, to be sure, but it is their classed positioning that occupies her concern. But if Ding Ling's literary career presents an intriguing (if discouraging) illustration of the difficulties entailed in sustaining a feminist agenda *within* Chinese leftist culture, she is certainly not the only example worth examining. Yang Gang (1909–1957), for instance, who joined the Communist Party in 1930 and participated as a member of the Beijing branch of the League of Left-Wing Writers (*Beifang zuolian*), gave voice to specifically gendered concerns of female revolutionaries in a story addressing motherhood and political commitment ("Riji shiyi" [Fragment from a lost diary], 1936). Her later semi-autobiographical English-language novel *Daughter* (written while the author was in the United States between 1944–1948) depicts the sexual/political awakening of a young heroine Li Pingsheng whose class-consciousness is sharpened by, among other things, a romance with a working-class man.[40] Feng Keng (1907–1931) and Guan Lu (1907–1982), both literary activists based in Shanghai, published short stories exploring women's sexual objectification as a function of capitalism.[41] Other women writers without formal allegiance to socialism yet who were nevertheless influenced by leftist literary trends include Luo Shu (1903–1938) and Xiao Hong (1911–1942), both of whom wrote fiction centered on the lives of working class and peasant women.[42]

Bai Wei and Xie Bingying also offer striking counterexamples to the way this period in literary history has been read in that they persisted in their critique of patriarchal domestic arrangements, in spite of the emerging prescriptions of what constituted a progressive literary orientation.

Moreover, I would propose here that in availing themselves of the personal literary mode of autobiography bot. when and in the manner in which they did, they consciously resisted the erasure of woman as a gendered subject under the terms of leftist discourse of the 1930s. Bai Wei says as much in an unapologetic defense of her motivations for writing *Beiju shengya* that appeared in *Funü shenghuo*:[43]

> A few years ago, revolutionary literature was all the rage in China; everyone devoted themselves to decrying the plight of the working classes, though only very few paid attention to the even worse plight of women. Right now, the wheels of history are moving backwards: the women who lifted their heads after the May Fourth movement are being forced back into the home, into that grave, by the dark hands of the era. At the same time, the corrupt feudal patriarchy has reasserted itself within that grave, demonstrating its force, wreaking havoc . . . I wanted to use the opportunity to highlight as well as I could some of the innermost sufferings of women.[44]

Defiantly reversing the hierarchy of values implicit in Guan Lu's review, which assigns to the domestic/private terrain of female suffering a lesser value of importance than allegedly "broader" or more political arenas, Bai Wei not only claims the utmost political urgency for the theme she addresses—"the innermost sufferings of women"—but subversively insists that her subject is even more political than the political topic *par excellence* of 1930s cultural left: class. The latter point regarding the relative importance of gender versus class politics is obviously suspect; the challenge, after all, is not to rank forms of oppression, but to understand how they operate and intersect in their own specific ways and to negotiate means of articulating women's gendered oppression without eliding the question of economic forms of injustice, and vice versa. That Bai Wei ultimately failed to do so, at least in the eyes of her contemporaries, may well be an indication of the limits of her own understanding of the connections between personal gendered experience and class-based forms of exploitation. Bai Wei's explanation here, however, also points to an alternative explanation whereby her text can be seen as a strategic intervention against a leftist cultural discourse, which refused to take seriously the politics of gender in general. As her comments seem to reveal, the principle agenda of her autobiographical project is to (re)politicize women's personal, subjective experience in a cultural context in which revolutionary politics and traditional modes of patriarchy seemed to coexist all too easily.

It was not just that leftist literary intellectuals were themselves often guilty of sexist attitudes and behavior within their ranks (as several episodes in *Beiju shengya* reveal), but that, in turning their attention to issues of class and proletarian revolution in the 1930s, they had seemingly abandoned their earlier commitment to eradicating gender subordination within the family and the domestic sphere (topics which are of course closely tied to the politics of gender). Xie Bingying's emphasis on her rebellion from a traditional family and Bai Wei's privileging of her romantic failure over their more public careers in cultural politics of those years, in other words, can and should be read as a deliberate *choice*; a textual strategy rather than a spontaneous overflowing of (feminine) emotionalism (as some critics would have it) or a relapse into "bourgeois" solipsism. They are, in short, self-conscious attempts by high-profile, politically active female intellectuals to show first how, because of their positioning as women in a patriarchal culture, personal life itself remains the scene of political struggle; and second, to (re)direct attention back to the urgent terrain of domestic revolution. And, in light of the immense popularity of both of these texts (*Beiju shengya* sparked a flood of fan mail, while *Nübing zizhuan* went into its second printing within six months), it is clear that this kind of writing still held great appeal for urban audiences.

The genre that perhaps best exemplifies the narrowing parameters of the "political" under leftist cultural discourse, and in particular the marginalization of domestic, sexual politics that *Beiju shengya* and *Nübing zizhuan* contest is the so-called love plus revolution genre (*aiqing jia geming*) that flourished briefly in the late May Fourth era. The formula reflects an attempt on the part of leftist writers (including otherwise diverse writers such as Jiang Guangci, Mao Dun, and Ding Ling) to renegotiate the boundaries between private and public forms of desire at a moment when revolutionary commitment increasingly dictated the personal lifestyles of radical intellectuals. Could the political activist reconcile his/her romantic and revolutionary aspirations? Would the pursuit of individual passion diminish one's public/political will to transform the collective society at large? These were the (rather predictable) questions "love plus revolution" narratives posed in one form or another and, judging from the fictional resolutions they offered, it appears that most radicals at the time took a fairly ascetic view of political life. Whether squandering away precious time and energy in frivolous "bourgeois" flings or finding temporary romantic bliss in the arms of a fellow comrade, the hero/heroine almost inevitably has to transcend the seduction of love in order to realize his/her even greater aspirations for China's political transformation. Significantly, however, in polarizing private, personal experience (love) on the one hand, and public, political life (revolution) on the other, the *aiqing jia geming* genre clearly participated in the de-politicization of issues of gender: not only is the political defined quite specifically as that which takes place beyond the domestic space where women were still predominately located (whether in protest demonstrations, picket lines, or war zones), but oftentimes in order to further elevate the revolutionary "cause" the home and family are constructed as a relatively conflict-free, self-fulfilling arena. Indeed, in many cases, the "choice" such narratives render requires the protagonist to decide between the selfish pursuit of individual contentment and happiness and the more noble, self-sacrificing struggle for the greater good of society.[45] As such, this genre can be seen as an example of the way in which personal subjective experience, a terrain fraught with political meaning in literary texts of the 1920s, was effectively removed from the domain of politically engaged literature of the 1930s.

Consider, for example, Ding Ling's "Yijiusanlingnian chun Shanghai" (Shanghai, spring 1930), one of two "love plus revolution" stories Ding Ling published in 1930 just as she began to assume a more active role in leftist cultural circles.[46] A two-part novella, the story features two separate but parallel narratives that trace the protagonists' transformation from romantic partner to revolutionary activist. Part One details the domestic life of two fashionable members of the Shanghai culturati, an attractive modern woman named Meilin and her partner Zibin, a sentimental poet whose literary celebrity has begun to wane. His career, we are told, has been driven by a quest for fame and fortune, a stance that has now begun to alienate him from his more politically inclined intellectual friends. Once a devoted fan with a romantic disposition herself (nurtured, significantly, through westernized romantic literature like Zibin's), Mei Lin, as we find her at the beginning of the story, has grown increasingly disenchanted with her frivolous life of imported chocolate, foreign films, and fashionable attire. No longer an impressionable young woman content with the doting affections of her paternalistic lover and the material luxuries he provides, Meilin now realizes the relationship affords her little autonomy: "she seemed to feel that he oppressed her, invisibly, in every manner. He did not permit her any freedom; it was worse than in a traditional family. He coddled her, humored her, provided her with all types of material satisfactions. But in his thinking there was only the one idea: that she should love him and love that which he loved."[47] Despite the seemingly feminist implications of this insight, what the narrative goes on to emphasize is not the heroine's burgeoning awareness of (or indeed resistance against) masculinist sexual politics but her budding class consciousness: with encouragement from a leftist intellectual (who, incidentally, seems more captivated by Meilin's sexy high-heel shoes than her political ideas), she attends a meeting with workers and activists. By the end of Part One, she has left behind her lover to devote herself to revolution. The "choices" Ding Ling contructs for her heroine are thus limited to two: either sacrificing her personal autonomy to an egotistical man in exchange for material comfort, or sacrificing herself to revolutionary causes for the more abstract goals of economic justice. (The story apparently sides with the latter, although it's worth pointing out that since the objectifying male gaze seems to transcend ideology the narrative does raise the question, however subtly, about what the future has in store for the "new" Meilin.)

Part Two features a second urban couple who, like Zibin and Meilin, will eventually part ways over differences vis-à-vis "revolution," only in this case it is the male character who aligns himself with radical politics. The hero Wang Wei, a new convert to the revolutionary cause, finds himself caught between the demands of his glamorous girlfriend Mary, who has recently moved to Shanghai so they can be together, and the underground political work in which he is now involved in the city. Despite his efforts to reconcile the two sides of his life by urging Mary to join the "cause," she shares little of her lover's political idealism and in fact loses a certain degree of respect for him after witnessing firsthand what his work actually entails (what exactly she objects to is an interesting question that the narrative does not pursue). Nevertheless, it is evident that were it not for Wang Wei's political obligations, their relationship would be mutually satisfying. Thus when Mary issues Wang Wei an ultimatum—loving either her or the revolution—he chooses the latter, but not without suffering pangs of loneliness and longing in her absence.

In both versions of the "love and revolution" dilemma explored in this narrative, the issue of sexual politics gets suppressed: in the first, domestic dissatisfaction inspires the heroine's ideological awakening, but her specific gendered concerns are displaced onto the struggle for class equality; in the second, by idealizing modern romance, political struggle is defined in opposition to the private and domestic spheres.

*   *   *

By contrast, Xie Bingying's *Nübing zizhuan* clearly plays upon the opposition between love and revolution in establishing the political credentials of her autobiographical persona, only to go on to introduce a significant twist. In recalling her days as a young student in Changsha in the early 1920s in the first part of the narrative, the author confesses how she too had been nearly swept away by the romantic delirium that engulfed her youthful generation: she admits, for instance, to having been "deeply influenced" by Goethe's *Die Leiden des Jungen Werther* (a book which came to epitomize the self-indulgent romanticism of the May Fourth generation for leftist intellectuals in the 1930s)[48] and to having fallen in love for the first time just as China's national crisis took a turn for the worse in 1925. Immediately following a reference to the massive student protests in the wake of the May 30 Incident, in which Chinese demonstrators were fired upon by British and Japanese police in Shanghai, the author includes a brief excerpt from her diary to expose her own emotional (as opposed to political) preoccupations at the time. But all this of course is a prelude to Xie's revolutionary conversion when, as readers familiar with her acclaimed *Congjun riji* would know, she enrolls in the Wuchang Central Political and Military School in hopes of enlisting in the nationalist revolutionary campaign as a woman soldier. Interestingly, the author articulates her political motive again in terms of reading practices:[49] her initial awakening occurs when an older brother urges her to stop reading sentimental romances and sends her some works of Marxist literature.[50] The inspiring ideas she finds in these works, coupled with her later first-hand experiences working with rural women at the grassroots level convince her (along with her sister comrades) that the commitment to social change offers a far more noble undertaking than the pursuit of "modern" love. Thus the author writes:

> [We] knew that unless the old system was completely shattered, womankind could never be freed. To create a happiness which would be enjoyed by all members of society was the most urgent need of mankind. Personal love is a

private and selfish affair and is of no consequence. While we were all quite ready to sacrifice our lives for the welfare of the masses, we considered love a plaything entirely belonging to the idle rich. (111)

But the central conflict explored in this autobiography, as it turns out, is not between politics and romantic love at all, but between politics and maternal love. The dominant figure in the narrative, against whom Xie most vigorously rebels but also whose love and approval she most desperately seeks, is that of her mother. An old-style Confucian matriarch, Xie's mother stands for values and a way of life to which the author is both morally and politically opposed: it is she who "lovingly" betroths her daughter at the age of three, binds her feet, and attempts to inculcate in her the virtues of feminine submission from the classical Confucian texts for women, all in hope of securing her daughter's future happiness (i.e., in marriage).[51] Xie's rejection of this love, as she attempts to fashion a new feminine script for herself, naturally puts a tremendous strain on the mother–daughter bond and leads eventually to their virtual estrangement. As the narrative also shows, however, this comes at a tremendous personal cost for the heroine.

Xie Bingying's political career, insofar as it is represented in this autobiography, has everything to do with her mother. The reader learns, for example, that while the heroine's ideological conversion makes her sympathetic to the Revolution, her *primary* motivation in joining is to avoid the arranged marriage her mother had been planning for her since she was a young girl. As she writes, "I believe that all the girl students who wanted to join the army had as their motive, in nine cases out of ten, to get away from their families, by whom they were suppressed. They all wanted to find their own way out" (93). A highly suggestive statement, Xie's testimony again complicates the common assumption that radical women of this generation simply "subordinated" their gendered interests to the revolution: here, political action is understood *precisely* as a personal act of resistance to normative feminine roles.[52] In this sense, it might also be noted, *Nübing zizhuan* constitutes a rewriting of her earlier *Congjun riji*, the highly acclaimed work that launched Xie's literary career. A series of first-hand reports written during her brief career as a woman "soldier" (or propagandist) on the Northern Expedition, the text paints a rosy picture of revolutionary politics, particularly the efforts to eradicate feudal patriarchy. By contextualizing this experience in relation to her life both prior to and after 1926, Xie's *Nübing zizhuan* presents a very different view of this historical moment.

Xie's deeply personal stake in the revolution becomes most apparent when, as she describes, the political coalition by which it was driven fell apart in the spring of 1927 and her all-female brigade was demobilized.[53] Despite the impending marriage that awaits her, she is forced to take refuge at home, partially because she needs a safe haven to hide from the authorities but more importantly because she desperately wants her mother's blessing for the new life she has carved out for herself (and permission to annul her engagement). As if to accord equal status between social revolution and the domestic dispute that ensues over the matter of her marriage the author couches this encounter in militant terms: ". . . I decided to come back and fight the old system with its own weapons and on its own ground, and I have the firm resolution that until my aim is achieved I will never stop. I would rather sacrifice my life in this fight than surrender to dark old system" (145). The contest of wills in which she and her mother soon become deadlocked, however, prove even more challenging than the military campaigns she had joined in rural Hubei and Hebei. Her mother, to whom she darkly refers as her "enemy," refuses to negotiate, forbids her any contact with the outside world, and even deprives her of the opportunity to read or write in the room where she is virtually imprisoned while final preparations are made for her wedding. But for Xie, the principle source of pain and distress throughout this ordeal is the discovery she makes about the nature of her mother's love: "I had always thought that a mother's feelings for her child were above all things on the earth, and now that I realized that such a philosophy was all wrong, my heart was broken. My mother, who had loved me, now loved nobody but herself. What was there to live for?" (150). So distressed is she that she even contemplates suicide—a fate not at all uncommon in fictional narratives of women in her predicament.[54] As the narrator emphasizes, this is quickly ruled out after she reminds herself of her revolutionary aspirations. Note the marked shift in narrative address in the following passage, as if the narrator/protagonist were attempting to persuade herself (and undoubtedly her readers) not to give up in despair:

> You were baptized in the revolution; you are a soldier; you have been in the line of fire . . . you have sworn to fight for the liberation of the toiling masses of the world . . . You refused to consider yourself a weak and common girl, but rather a girl with determination, courage and hot-blood. You are pledged to war against the old system."[55]

Xie Bingying finally does give up trying to resolve the conflict amicably and resolves to escape to Changsha (which, after several failed attempts, she eventually succeeds in doing). Interestingly, though, she remains to the end concerned (and guilt-ridden) about the pain her rebellion causes her mother.

In 1940, Xie Bingying wrote several additional chapters for the English translation of *Nübing zizhuan* (which were subsequently included in Chinese editions).[56] Contained in them is a particularly poignant scene describing a strained reunion that reportedly took place between mother and daughter when Xie (by this point a mother herself) had occasion to return home several years after her "escape." Although her mother still refused to speak to her, she recalls, late one night she slipped quietly into Xie's bedroom to cover her up. Xie pretends to be asleep, but is moved by the tears she can feel dripping on her face. She yearns to confide in her mother about the tremendous suffering she has endured in the intervening years but, she claims, to spare her mother further sorrow, she holds herself back. While the scene captures the painful distance that separates the traditional mother and the emancipated daughter, it also gives powerful expression to an unspoken desire for reconciliation.

Xie Bingying's thematization of maternal love draws attention to the profound implications of revolutionary social change on relationships between women. And it is thus further testimony to the turbulent times in which she lived that the author's relationship to her own daughter (born after a short-lived romance with a fellow comrade who winds up in jail) is fraught with difficulty. Persecuted for her political convictions, and barely able to eke out a living as a leftist writer, Xie reluctantly left her infant daughter in the care of the father's mother in Wuchang. In the final scene in her autobiography, which depicts the author's subsequent return for the child, however, the family refused to hand her over, maintaining that Xie is unfit to raise the daughter properly. There is little doubt that this actually occurred; in a narrative that has foregrounded the absence of a positive maternal model in the author's own life, this takes on a deeper symbolic resonance with the difficulties of transmitting the new revolutionary ideal because of very real and systemic limits on such social consciousness.[57]

* * *

In *Beiju shengya*, Bai Wei can also be said to deconstruct the "choices" implied by the love-plus-revolution formula from a gendered perspective by interrogating the simplistic split between the private and political spheres.[58] Putting paid to the (emergent) construction of the domestic arena as the idyllic "other" of public, political struggle, she focuses relentlessly on the oppressive—almost lethal—effects of "love" on the life of her politically awakened autobiographical protagonist Wei. Sharply critical of the utopian vision of modern romance as a heterosexual relationship based on mutual respect, emotional fulfilment, and pursuit of common social/political aspirations, Bai Wei's position is consistent with that of the New Women writers described in chapter 2: here romance unfolds as an unequal battle between a man and a woman whose respective roles have been largely predetermined by their gendered socialization. Beneath his veneer as a sensitive "new man," Zhan's domineering and degenerate behavior belies an all-too conventional pattern of male authority. For her part, Wei clings to an illusive ideal of equality and reciprocity and, as the narrative shows, again and again capitulates to Zhan's self-serving needs and demands. Always on the losing end of that grim battle, Wei experiences love as a form of personal subjugation and *disease*, limiting rather than liberating the self's potential.

But in illustrating how patriarchy saturates the emotional life of her autobiographical subject, Bai Wei also reveals the naiveté of the narrative of transcending romance through revolution. Whereas Ding Ling's Meilin appears to undergo no internal struggle whatsoever in disentangling herself from bourgeois domestic life, Wei is incapable of simply sublimating her lack of personal fulfillment in her romantic life with political purpose. Her emotional and erotic bonds to Zhan, however contradictory and self-destructive, often override her own convictions, and in effect keep her locked into an oppressive relationship. The remainder of this chapter explores in more depth Bai Wei's fascinating engagement with the autobiographical form to articulate these, and other, dilemmas of the modern female self.

ROMANCE AND THE QUEST FOR THE FEMALE SELF

Bai Wei prefaces *Beiju shengya* with an intriguing, yet seemingly paradoxical, disclaimer. On the one hand, she offers the conventional claim of the autobiographer by asserting the "absolute truth" of her personal narrative. Composed in candid, unadorned prose, this epic nine-hundred-page tome is said to have been produced in a frantic effort to inscribe an authentic "record" (*jilu*) of her life before undergoing a risky surgery to treat the venereal disease she contracted from her lover (who himself had apparently become infected at a brothel in Singapore). As she emphatically states, "I have exerted my utmost to get down to the essence of the repetitious facts of the tragic unfolding of daily life, and to record them in simplified, objective, and unembellished form, in order to express the truth (*zhenshi*) of these facts, the truth, the absolute truth."[59] On the other hand, Bai Wei distances herself from the autobiographical subject at the center of her text "Wei" who, as she informs the reader, is not identical with her true self. This is not due to any modest aversion to self-revelation, however, but (and herein lies the apparent paradox) because there is no such self to reveal:

> In this decrepit, moribund society, this nefarious society permeated by patriarchy, women lack an authentic nature (*zhenxiang*). Their true nature has been falsified to such a degree that they have sacrificed every single aspect of themselves. Women are completely determined by society, their environment, men, reputation, and rumor. (5)

Contrasting the declaration of her contemporary Yu Dafu that "the greatest success of the May Fourth period lay, first of all, in the discovery of the individual" (1935), Bai Wei here proposes an alternative gendered formulation of the self, by openly decrying the continued presence of a masculinist social–cultural order in which to be/come a woman is to undergo a process of self-alienation. *Beiju shengya* proceeds, accordingly, not so much as a romantic revelation of authentic selfhood or unique individuality but as a critical exposé of the multiple forces which have defined and *disfigured* the author as a feminine subject. The text is, in this sense, an autobiography as biography, the portrait of a self with whom Bai Wei as the authorial subject of the text does not identify.

According to the classic definition proposed by Philippe Lejeune, one of the most influential western theorists of autobiographical discourse, a work qualifies as autobiographical when the conditions of what he calls the "autobiographical pact" are met: namely, when the reader can assume an equivalence or coherence between the author, narrator, and autobiographical protagonist. For Lejeune, this pact depends on certain conventional formal markers, most typically the overt declaration by the author that the text in question is autobiographical and/or the congruence of author/ protagonist's name. On one level, Bai Wei seemingly enters into just such a contract by promising her readers a truthful account of her personal experience—and indeed, the evidence indicates that the text was in fact interpreted as an autobiographical account by readers at the time. On a more important level, however, writing as a feminist who has embraced a non-identificatory relation to the subject of subjection in her patriarchal culture, Bai Wei also radically destabilizes the generic conventions of autobiographical identity. The autobiographical protagonist "Wei" (a homophone of the author's name) who occupies the center of her text is not presented as simply an embodiment of the self at a prior moment in life but rather as a figure of the self rendered as other by masculinist culture. The identity she signifies, therefore, is precisely one which the authorial voice actively attempts to disavow.

Eschewing such conventional adornments of autobiographical introduction as family genealogy, date and place of birth, and early childhood experience, *Beiju shengya* begins, as it were, *en media res*, during the author's financially strapped days of self-exile as a young woman in the mid-1920s in Japan.[60] Over the course of the narrative, certain details of the circumstances of her life prior to this time sporadically surface, but in general the past here is associated with excruciating memories of personal violence and violation from which Bai Wei is clearly at pains to distance herself. Indeed, far from being primarily a source of identity/identification (as it was for most male autobiographers, both traditional and modern), the past is something to be excised. The following passage, for instance, one of the rare occasions on which the narrator breaks her silence about "Wei's" previous life, consists of a flashback to the horrific ordeal Wei endured as a young bride and her eventual escape from what the narrator calls simply "a living hell":

> . . . when she was sixteen, her parents banished her to the household of a tyrannical widow. There, she endured countless beratings and beatings; her eyes were punched, her legs broken, her clothes torn off her body. She was beaten until the wounds covering her body dripped with blood and she ran naked to throw herself in the river to escape. The widow goaded her son on and together they abused Wei; for days they would deny her food, and during the winter the son would kick her out of the bed at night and make her sleep on the cold floor weeping in silence. But the widow would still sit there and curse her for not producing a baby. The reason for this abuse: they blamed Wei for having studied. That is why, in the middle of one night she ran away from the living hell (*renjian diyu*) and enrolled in a teachers school, and that is why, after she graduated from the school, she again struggled to break free of those chains and, with only six dollars to her name, fled to Japan. (51)

Notably, this passage occurs in a scene in which Wei is engaged in conversation about her background; rather than convey the memory through direct dialogue (a technique often applied in this text), however, Bai Wei switches narrative modes to report it as a self-contained flashback. The conspicuous lack of any mediating commentary from the narrator, coupled with the highly dispassionate tone of the description underscore the sense of detachment she now feels in relation to this former experience. Like the rupture inscribed in this autobiographical "self"-portrait as a whole, Wei's identity as a traditional daughter and daughter-in-law belongs to a now repudiated personal history, split off from the present self.

In an earlier autobiographical essay, Bai Wei had provided a fuller—if still decidedly pained—account of the chain of events that landed her in Japan.[61] Forced into an arranged marriage at the age of sixteen, she eventually ran away from her in-law's household and made her way to the town of Hengyang, where she enrolled in school; later, because of her student activism during the early May Fourth movement, she was asked to transfer to the Changsha First Provincial Women's Teacher Training School in the provincial capital.[62] Shortly before she was due to graduate in 1918, however, she learned that her father had conspired with school officials to have her sent back to her husband—a fate to which she was not about to acquiesce for a second time. With help from sympathetic classmates, she managed to elude the school guards by sneaking out through an old sewage duct and, having borrowed enough money for a third-class berth, sailed for Japan, arriving with just two *mao* in her pocket. This decisive action effectively brought an end to Bai Wei's battle with the traditional familial order. Bai Wei's new life in Japan was from the outset beset with adversity: too poor to afford tuition for college, she was obliged to take up work as a maid for British missionaries in Tokyo, and later, after having won a scholarship to attend the prestigious Higher Normal School for Women of Tokyo, the unexpected arrival of her younger brother (also estranged from the family) put her under a financial strain she could scarcely handle. On one occasion, when her brother was taken ill, she was forced to sell off her textbooks and best clothing and to survive on a meager diet of yams and miso soup in order to pay his medical bills. Unfortunately, Bai Wei's own health took a turn for the worse as a result of these hardships and she ultimately had no choice but to drop out of college.

As dramatic a personal saga this may be, however, it is not the one Bai Wei chooses to foreground in *Beiju shengya*. In 1924, approximately six years after she first moved to Japan to begin her new life, Bai Wei was introduced to and subsequently became romantically involved with the young poet Yang Sao (or Zhan, as he is referred to in the text). It is the history of their ill-fated "modern" affair that provides both the temporal boundaries and central thematic content of her autobiography.[63] Unfolding in unglamourous and at times gruesome detail, the narrative painstakingly delineates the devastating emotional, psychological, and physical toll the relationship takes on the heroine: the exuberant and ambitious young Wei who appears in the first part of the text becomes, by the end of the saga, a deeply disillusioned woman with a disease-ridden body and shattered sense of identity. The romantic love she so ardently embraces, love which she, as a member of the "Romantic" generation, idealistically views as the key to personal, political, and artistic fulfilment, proves the opposite: it is a dangerous illusion, which lures her into a life-consuming tangle of emotional dependency, betrayal, and physical destruction. Wei's hospitalization in the final segment of the narrative, as she prepares for and reluctantly undergoes a radical hysterectomy (to treat the severe gynecological complications resulting from the venereal disease contracted from her lover) joins the story to the narrative occasion of the text: as Bai Wei writes in her preface, it was in 1936 that she composed her autobiography from a hospital bed, in the face of what she felt sure at the time was to be a race against death.

To register the problematic nature (indeed, the absence) of the solid authentic female "self" alluded to in her preface, Bai Wei eschews the first-person "I" that had come to dominate May Fourth writing in the 1920s and had continued to ring loud in the din of autobiographical texts in the 1930s. She adopts, instead, the more distanced third-person narrative voice to construct the story of her autobiographical subject Wei. Significantly, it is a voice that shifts constantly in the text, oscillating between the relatively impartial stance of an omniscient narrator (with access not only to Wei's interior thoughts and emotions but those of the other central actor in this anti-romance, her lover Zhan), to that of an intimate, sympathetic observer of Wei's struggles, to that of ironic critic who zeroes in on the heroine's contradictory and often self-defeating behavior. During several important interludes (e.g., section two, which is comprised entirely of entries from a diary Bai Wei kept in 1927), the narrative voice even reverts to the more standard "I"—although, within the context of the narrative, even this "I" is subjected to critical scrutiny and thus differs from the subjective voice explored in the previous chapter. Finally, further fragmenting Wei's story, the narrative is also interspersed with poems and letters written, we are told, by both the author and her lover over the course of their tumultuous love affair.

The fragmented narrative voice constitutes a key textual strategy that is centrally linked to Bai Wei's feminist exploration of selfhood. Perhaps most importantly, it enables Bai Wei to reconstruct her personal history in such a way that avoids (and therefore implicitly challenges) the fiction of autonomous, authentic subjectivity which underpinned the self-centered writings of May Fourth intellectuals in the 1920s. According to Jaroslav Průšek, among others, the idea of the self as possessing a unique personality, an inner core of being from which flowed the highest forms of truth and knowledge about human existence, began to find expression in Chinese literature as early as the Late Qing, with the emergence of a more individualized type of narrator whose own attitudes and personal idiosyncrasies asserted a conspicuous new presence in texts. Most scholars agree, however, that such a redefined vision of subjectivity achieved it fullest articulation in the explosion of first-person literary texts in the 1920s, in which "the individual takes himself or herself most seriously, asserts his or her absolute rights against society, and possesses an interiority fully representable in narrative."[64]

Since the complex matrix of historical and ideological factors that informs the literary introspection of the May Fourth has been amply dealt with elsewhere, it need not concern us here.[65] What is more pertinent on this occasion is the sense of self it represented. Pointing to the "new emphasis on sincerity, spontaneity, passion, imagination, and the release of individual energies" (292), Leo Lee has convincingly argued that the new textual "I" represents the consolidation of a fundamentally Romantic conception of self-identity. The typical I-narrator, whose own subjective consciousness now often functioned not only as the mediating lens through which the external social reality in a given narrative was presented, but also as the focal issue itself, reflects a redefined vision of the self as endowed with "inner" depth. Emotionally and psychologically complex, the intense "I" authorizes his/her individual identity through reference to the realm of private subjective experience of feeling. What is revealed through such introspection is not always flattering or glamorous, but it is nevertheless implicitly assumed to reflect "the preciousness and uniqueness of his [or her] own life experience" (251). Accompanying the construction of unique individuality was of course also new confidence in the expressive potential of writing itself: whereas the dominant traditional literary paradigm held writing to be a vehicle of metaphysical truth (*wenyi zaidao*), writing was now to be a medium of self-revelation.[66]

But if May Fourth Romantic literary discourse assumed both an unproblematic and privileged relation between the self (with its authentic personality and experience) and its textual representation, Bai Wei reformulates the project of literary self-disclosure by conceptualizing feminine subjectivity as a form of impersonation. For if, as she proposes, under contemporary conditions there had yet to exist an authentic female "I," but only various imposed modes of femininity, then how can the female self be represented? Rather than make claims to special knowledge about the "real truth" of feminine nature or purport to uncover an "essential" self buried beneath woman's myriad social guises, what Bai Wei strives to represent in this work is how the female self is constructed in social interactions but also how these constructions can render the self as other to itself.

In particular, Bai Wei's concern lies with the problematic female self engendered within modern romance, and it is perhaps here that she departs most dramatically from the assumptions of early May Fourth literary culture. For Bai Wei, the interior realm of the emotions, erotic desire, and imagination, far from representing the essential core of true identity, are instead shown to be social in nature and deeply implicated in women's continued subordination to male authority. But representing this presents its own challenges: how can the pseudo-self be portrayed? How can the distance—indeed, the non-identification—between the narrating subject and her auto-biographical persona be conveyed?

Abandoning the unified voice of the "I," Bai Wei presents Wei through a myriad of different lenses, juxtaposing objective and subjective visions of the self, refracting the personal story from shifting temporal and narrative perspectives. Wei thus emerges neither as the central controlling consciousness of the autobiography nor as a fixed character but as a composite of multiple fluctuating and discontinuous representations, which inhibit any attempt to reduce or fix Wei to any one single identity. The reason for incorporating private poetry, diary entries, and love letters in the text, for instance, is not so much to bear witness to the depth of Wei's "true" self or to naively celebrate the intensity of past emotional experience, but instead to underline the irony or critical distance between the narrator's retrospective knowledge and Wei's former subjective states.[67] On one level, the reader is thus made painfully aware of the limits (and the illusion) of Wei's agency as an autonomous subject as the text charts the patriarchal social dynamics that ineluctably shaped the heroine's personal experience. On another level, however, the very premise of subjectivity as the locus of "truth" and meaning unravels as the heroine's inner realities are relativized through the presence of alternative and at times conflicting points of view.

While the text enacts a discursive resistance to the ideology of authentic selfhood, it also explicitly challenges that ideology on the level of manifest narrative content through its scathing critique of modern romance. True to her generation, Wei is shown to be thoroughly romantic in her initial expectations that her "modern" relationship with Zhan would enable "the fullest possible realization of the self" (Lee). Recalling her former idealistic view of love, the narrator remarks:

> I believed that love was the bridge of progress (*jinbu de qiao*) during one's youth, that once I had found love, my solitude and ennui would be like the grass that receives rain and sunlight, that love would invigorate my life, fortify my strength, provide a solid bridge spanning across the gullies and rivers that I hadn't been able to cross before, and enable me to move forward . . . therefore, I always regarded love as the bridge of human life (*rensheng de qiao*). (196)

Crucially, what the narrator goes on to add is that such a romantic vision was an illusion—in reality, "love was a chasm, a trap into which I fell, like an ignorant small wild creature with no one to rescue me" (196). Far from simply a personal tragedy, however, Wei's thwarted quest for liberation and self-fulfillment in romance is shown to be a consequence of the asymmetrical relations of power that structure male–female interaction. Unlike the typical May Fourth (self) portraits of the romantic hero Leo Lee has examined, therefore, whose suffering in love registers (and valorizes) the extreme sensitivity of his personality, his "capacity for heightened emotional response" (251), here the author's examination of the high physical and psychological cost of love is an attempt to demystify romantic love itself.

Like a number of other prominent literary couples, Bai Wei and Yang Sao's "romance" had achieved a certain notoriety even before the publication of *Beiju shengya*. In 1933, a collection of their love letters, apparently coedited, was published under the title *Zuoye* (Last night)—one of numerous such textual contributions to the "whirlpool of love," which swept through the contemporary literary scene.[68] Given the alignment of love with sincerity and freedom, along with what Leo Lee aptly describes as a "vogue of self-exposé" (263), many leading figures of the intelligentsia (Lu Xun and Xu Guangping, Jiang Guangci and Song Ruoyu, Xu Zhimo and Lu Xiaoman, Lu Yin and Li Weijian, to name just a few illustrious pairs) published personal correspondences in celebration of romantic sentiments. Such public displays of private passion were often justified as evidence of the emotional sincerity and authentic affection that were thought to be defining marks of modern identity.[69] For example, in the preface to *Aimei xiaozha* (Love letters to Mei), a slim volume of intimate letters and diaries that Lu Xiaoman assembled in 1936 to commemorate her relationship with Xu Zhimo (who had died in a plane crash five years earlier), she contrasts the superficial nature of her first marriage, which had been arranged for her according to traditional custom, to the genuine love she and the famous poet apparently shared.[70] Neither "her family nor society" approved of their liaison, she writes, obviously referring to the tremendous scandal that erupted when she (a married woman) became romantically involved with Xu Zhimo, but the couple was willing to defy convention to be true to their hearts.

On the surface, *Zuoye* seems consistent with this outpouring of authentic feeling. Even though their relationship was over, as Yang Sao readily admits in his introductory remarks to the volume, their love letters "whether happy, remorseful, tormented, hateful, or hysterical, reveal the genuine feelings (*zhenxin zhenxie*) the authors felt at the time" (2). Bai Wei, too, invokes a certain Romantic ethos when she suggests in the poem she composed in lieu of a preface that, if anything, it was the very intensity of her sentiments and passion that invests the failure of their relationship with such poignancy: "I shouldn't have loved so passionately/for my lover didn't give me a warm garden, only the irons chains of death/our joy was but a flash in the pan!/ I shouldn't have harbored such ambitions for progress/for love destroyed my soaring heart and gave me nothing but endless sorrow" (2). But Bai Wei also goes on to openly undercut this lofty rhetoric by highlighting the commodity status of the text and insisting that her own motivations in publishing the volume were strictly financial. As she candidly announces, "In *The Jungle*, Sinclair used the voice of Maria to say/when people are poor, there is nothing they won't sell/this explains the reason behind this volume *Zuoye*" (1). By invoking the image of the destitute woman who prostitutes her body, Bai Wei's analogy not only deflates the discourse of romantic love by insinuating that even "free love" was subject to the crass forces of the market (like everything, the emotions can be packaged and sold), but subtly implicates the readers who purchase the "thrill" of romantic revelation. Although *The Jungle* is by all means an emotional work, it is clearly not a work of romance. Given the fact that Sinclair's novel was a bold work of social critique with a direct effect on American political life (the reform of the meat-packing industry) this is not an innocent reference.

Bai Wei goes on to bluntly disavow *Zuoye* in her autobiography, claiming it represented a distorted picture of their romantic history, and that it had come about as a result of Yang Sao's desire to conceal the evidence of his less than romantic partnership. As she recounts, during her hospitalization in 1933 at which point there seemed little hope of recovery, Yang Sao seized the opportunity to pry through her private correspondence in order to edit a carefully censored version of their romance for the public eye. Although she went along with the project at the time for financial reasons, later she was to discover an appalling "diary" he had fabricated as a companion volume to *Zuoye* to be published after her death. In this diary, Yang Sao went even further in rewriting their romance, reversing in effect its dynamics by casting himself in the role of self-sacrificing, considerate, and loyal lover while insinuating that it was Bai Wei's deception and sexual promiscuity that had undone their relationship. Unlike *Zuoye*, this pseudo-diary never made it into print because Bai Wei eventually destroyed most of the manuscript (all except for the brief excerpt she saved and reprinted in her autobiography [708–717] as evidence of his deceit). Bai Wei's allusion to both of these texts, however, provides a number of important clues to understanding *Beiju shengya* and the kind of feminist intervention it attempts to make. For one, it sets up a comparison between Yang Sao's pseudo-diary and love letter collection and Bai Wei's pseudo-autobiography. The former exemplifies the deceit of self: namely, the projection of an idealized romantic male self designed to write out or rewrite his subjective relation to women. The latter seems to be designed to identify precisely the processes that allow these gross projections: to show, as it were, how the self may be falsely "prescribed" or coded in alienating and distorted ways. Above all, however, if *Zuoye* exemplifies the collusion between the discourse of romance and modern patriarchy, *Beiju shengya* can be seen as an attempt to critically explore and expose that complicity—to debunk the myth of true romance as the locus of sexual liberation and individual freedom.

This is not to say that Bai Wei denies the importance or value of love *per se*—indeed, Wei's "tragedy" as it is depicted in this text is not so much that she desires the intimacy of romantic companionship but that, given the sociohistorical realities of male hegemony that saturate even the most personal dimensions of male–female relations, what she desires is practically impossible. Interestingly, in a recent discussion of the genre of Western feminist confession Rita Felski argues that the impulse shared by many feminist autobiographers to disclose the often harrowing details of personal relationships stems precisely from a "longing for [the] intimacy" (108) that is found to be lacking in heterosexual liaisons under patriarchy. Failing to achieve the desired bond with a man, the feminist confessor seeks compensatory sympathy, understanding, and identification from her (implied female) audience. While the sheer magnitude of *Beiju shengya*, with its over-whelmingly excessive recounting of Wei's frustrated attempts to secure hap-piness with Zhan, is no doubt partially a function of the economics of May Fourth publishing (since authors at the time were typically paid according to the length of their manuscripts), Felski's argument may well be pertinent here in understanding Bai Wei's autobiographical motivation.[71] That is, *Beiju shengya* may not just be a text about the failure of romance but an attempt to compensate for its lack.[72]

As if to underscore the masculinism of the romance she will depict, Bai Wei chooses a rather unusual (even for an unconventional autobiography such as this) point of departure for her autobiographical narrative—at the tumultuous end of a romantic affair in which Zhan was involved prior to his acquaintance with Wei. The narrative focus soon shifts (beginning in chapter two) to Wei herself, but this circuitous beginning ominously foreshadows that the romance is to be *his* story and that it is he who will control the course it will take. Revealingly, Wei enters the narrative as the one who will restore *Zhan*'s desire and will to live, and indeed it is within this supporting role that she remains. For as is soon borne out by the narrative, Zhan's fickle needs alone drive the relationship, dictating its mood and pace, and what Wei mistakes as an equal role in a modern partnership of mutual under-standing is revealed in fact to be a subservient relation to an utterly self-absorbed man.

Initially, Wei appears seduced by the "modern" language of courtship that Zhan deploys—from his proclamations of love based on his spiritual (as opposed to purely physical) attractions to Wei, to his declarations of admiration and esteem for Wei's creative abilities and her "resolute and fight-ing personality (*gexing*)." But language, as it is construed in the context of Bai Wei's narrative, is no guarantee of truth, especially in the power of a self-serving scoundrel like Zhan. Depicted with unsparing detail as an over-possessive, spoiled, arrogant, jealous, morally irresponsible, and manipulative man, Zhan's actions reveal him to be one of the most callous villains of May Fourth literature, with few if indeed any redeeming qualities. Far from providing the intellectual support, emotional intimacy, and sexual fulfilment Wei craves (and expects from a "new man" such as Zhan claims to be), the narrative unfolds a harrowing account of Zhan's abusive and self-indulgent behavior over the course of their involvement.[73] On the one hand, he is the classic domineering lover who believes that Wei "belongs" to him (408): he jealously monitors her life outside of their relationship, reading her mail for instance, and disapproves of any activity that might detract from her devo-tions to him. In addition to constantly belittling Bai Wei's political views, for instance, he also guilt-trips her for being interested in things besides him. Consider the passage in the following letter Zhan sends when Bai Wei becomes increasingly serious about radical politics: "My lover is a cruel hero-ine; in her view, she needn't care about a single individual but only about her career, the revolution, and the future of humanity . . . My lover stubbornly clings to her convictions while cruelly abandoning the person who cares about her the most. This makes me feels infinitely lonely, uncertain and empty!" (536) On the other hand, Zhan can also be a ruthless chauvinist, demonstrating a flagrant lack of regard for the woman he claims to love. He betrays her with his inveterate philandering; he is verbally and physically abusive to her;[74] and he has a cruel habit of conveniently disappearing at precisely the moments Wei most needs him. And, the longer Wei remains under the spell of his authority, the more the "free and full self" described by Leo Lee as the aim of modern romance eludes her.

At the center of Bai Wei's own reconstruction of the relationship is the physical ordeal she undergoes after becoming infected with a sexually transmitted disease. The narrative dwells at length and in often gruesome detail on how the disease takes over Wei's body and her life. Never truly at home in her body (she constantly worries about whether it conforms to contemporary sensibilities of feminine beauty, on conspicuous display in urban advertising and visual culture),[75] Wei is now even further alienated from her physical self. Abandoned by her lover (who denies responsibility for her condition) and unable to shoulder the costly medical treatment herself, she suffers as the advancing illness robs her of health and sexual drive, and renders her intellectually and politically incapacitated.

The candid examination of this intimate condition is, one could argue, in and of itself provocative: sexual discourse of the 1920s–1930s had raised public awareness and concern about the spread of sexually transmitted diseases (*hualiu bing*) but, as the term itself implies, they were generally thought of (and publically discussed) as an affliction of prostitutes.[76] The stigma attached to venereal disease was appropriated by writers at the time who (taking their cue from Ibsen and other fin-de-siècle European writers they read) exploited it figuratively to denote modern social malaise, whether in terms of the burden of tradition (Lu Xun), capitalist depravity (Lao She), or the alarming unruliness of liberated New Women (Mao Dun).[77] By disclosing that she, a prominent female intellectual, was infected, Bai Wei no doubt hoped to destigmatize sexual disease and expose the potential health threat to all women, regardless of their walk of life or class status.[78] At the same time, disease permeates the narrative as a metonymic projection of problematic gendered subjectivity.[79] Throughout, her infected body bears witness to the ways in which hegemonic culture deprives the female subject control over her own destiny and renders the experience of self one of profound alienation. Again, I would suggest that in formulating her physical (as well as emotional and psychological) experience not as the private history of one unique individual but as the product of an endemic patriarchy plaguing modern Chinese society as a whole, Bai Wei presented her text as social critique.

Bai Wei's account, however, is no banal tale of female victimization. As ruthless and depraved as he comes across, the narrative is ultimately less interested in Yang Sao's masculinist misconduct than in exploring the conflicts and contradictions of the female sexual body. On the one hand, the text explicitly establishes Wei's identification as a "New Woman" by representing her as a subject who experiences, and acts upon, erotic desire. (In this last respect, incidentally, she is clearly more emancipated than Ding Ling's Sophie, another ailing new woman, whose moral inhibitions and fear prevent her from living out her sexual fantasies.) She is a woman who imagines physical passion as an essential dimension not only of love, but of a creative and politically active life in general, as the reader is shown through Wei's erotic dreams. On the other hand, sexuality is actually experienced as a self-estrangement: the sensation of losing control over her own body occurs not just with the devastating deterioration of her health, but time and again, from the harassment she encounters from male employers and comrades, to the gossip columns that circulate rumors about her affairs, to women who offer unsolicited beauty tips on how to look more "feminine" and, finally, to a modern medical establishment which seeks to "cure" her through the surgical removal of her reproductive organs.

Nowhere is Bai Wei's critique of sexual desire more powerful than in her self-analysis of her masochistic attachment to Yang Sao, the man she considers her lover and comrade and who repeatedly fails her on both fronts. Echoing May Fourth confessional narratives of female disillusionment with the sphere of "free love," the autobiographical protagonist experiences a painful contradiction between her desires and a domestic reality that subsumes those desires. Whereas writers like Lu Yin strive to elicit the reader's sympathy for their heroine's tragedy, Bai Wei grapples with the reasons *why* the protagonist remains entrapped in such an obviously self-destructive relationship.[80] Having already once decisively "liberated" herself from an arranged marriage, why doesn't this would-be Nora (whose figure the author deliberately invokes in the preface) take control again and simply leave her unworthy lover? And what does her inability to do so reveal about the ideology of romantic love and its complicitous role in the consolidation of modern patriarchies? The text offers several answers to these difficult questions, the first being that the protagonist's internalization of romantic scripts prevents her from apprehending the actual nature of her attachment to Zhan. Yet the disillusionment that eventually comes from lived experience fails to have the effect we might expect. Conspicuously absent is the pivotal moment of "awakening" which enables the tormented heroine to "move beyond" her debilitating private existence and decisively into the realm of autonomous selfhood. Instead, inclusion of journal entries reveal that even though past betrayals warn her against this fatal attraction, she is unable to resist the deep infatuation she feels for him.

The predicament, we might note, resonates sharply with contemporary feminist theorization of subjectivity in terms of a struggle to divest the (female) self of imposed identities and cultural imperatives that inhibit an independent sense of self. In Bai Wei's critical account, Wei's very sense of identity and personal worth as a woman is so anchored in having a man in her life that her romantic delusions, while totally misguided, serve as an inevitable form of self-validation. Accordingly, she continually allows herself to fall for Zhan's hollow declarations of love and commitment and rationalizes his infidelities and abuse. As often as not, however, the protagonist is shown to be painfully aware of the contradictions of her behavior yet nevertheless at a loss to change: Will (*yizhi*) and reason (*zhi*), to use the terms the narrator provides, are apparently no match for the power of love (or control) that Zhan embodies. But rather than simply assign blame to the heroine for her "weakness" (or to Zhan for his "villainy"), what is at issue here is the inordinate difficulty, even for a politically self-conscious intellectual like Wei, to overcome the structures of desire and internalized emotional dependence that sustain the imbalance of power in conventional male–female relations. Thus while Wei intellectually rejects the *idea* of feminine subordination and self-sacrifice, her own compliance with such norms is exposed in the way she assumes the burden of guilt for the relationship's failure. Consider, for example, the following passage:

> I was absolutely incapable of being virtuous like those "wise wives and loyal mothers" who only know how to serve men with their obedient natures. I felt I was the same as a man in that, in this deformed society, I wanted equality with men in all those things that I could do equally; I felt no one should control or obey the other but instead there should be mutual understanding and compromise. Furthermore, I didn't believe in one partner taking care of the domestic sphere while the other deals with the public affairs; both needed to step into the great fold of society. In short, there was nothing about me he could love. (206)

The culpable party, from Wei's anguished point of view, is not the chauvinistic Zhan but Wei herself, whose inadequacies make her feel "unworthy" of his love.

In many respects, indeed, Bai Wei represents the role Wei assumes in her relationship as precisely one of conventional feminine self-sacrifice and acquiescence. Not only does she repeatedly subordinate her own emotional needs by forgiving Zhan for his endless acts of cruelty, but she even willingly compromises her intense artistic and revolutionary aspirations. For example, soon after they begin living together, Wei's romantic enthrallment overwhelms her ability to write, absorbing her entire consciousness. "What's difficult is not all the housework," she writes in her diary, "but the fact that he gets into my head and dissolves my will to create and to exert myself; he fills my entire mind" (261). That Zhan openly objects to her activism (preferring that she conform to a more conventional domestic role) places additional pressure on the heroine, and is an important narrative detail that the author uses to elaborate themes of the embeddedness of personal and political experience.

Wei's difficulty in extricating herself from romantic entanglement brings on feelings of guilt and profound psychological stress. Lacking an explanation for why she continues to love someone who causes her such pain, she experiences not only a devastating loss of self-control and vulnerability but a disturbing sense of self-loathing: "she started to hate herself for being so weak and useless; she was, in the end, a woman, submitting to the control of love and men" (277). In the final section of the text, entitled simply "Her Laugh," the author chronicles Wei's psychic and physical collapse, a condition for which, according to the narrator, there is no language to describe.

In depicting Wei's struggle as a series of repetitious, internal battles which must be waged, over and over again, at the level of Wei own's conflicted psyche, *Beiju shengya* departs significantly from the narrative model of female/feminist awakening that characterizes so many modern women's life stories (both fictional and autobiographical), including those described in the first chapter of this study. This model typically posits the acquisition of knowledge or consciousness as the pivotal factor that enables the tormented heroine to move out of her oppressed domestic role and decisively into the realm of autonomous selfhood. In Bai Wei's much less sanguine rendering of subjective transformation, the collision between the heroine's intense desires for Zhan and her intellectual repugnance of the hegemonic power he embodies do not easily translate into self-empowering knowledge, but rather heighten her sense of self-alienation and disorientation.

In the final and most grim section of *Beiju shengya*, the cumulative effects of Wei's "romantic" experience—her emotional demoralization, her raging anger toward Zhan, and above all her rapidly deteriorating state of health, bring her to the verge of mental collapse. Wei's disintegrating mental world is captured in the disjointed narrative style Bai Wei employs in this section, such as in the following passage, one of numerous bouts of madness:

> She thought and thought, her mind was confused. How she wanted to destroy everything in the room, just as Zhan had destroyed her. She struck the table hard and tore up her books and clothes . . . Mad eyes protruding, beating her chest. She grabbed her hair and pulled it out in clumps . . . Laughing loudly, limping, eyes glaring . . . Zhan's cruel face looking at her; Zhan's smiling face as he embraced and eloped with his lover . . . the scene of Zhan sitting at his lover's feet having his hair curled and forcing her, after she had a relapse of her illness, out again onto the street . . . the scene of Mrs. K in the alley insulting her . . . the scene of thick hairy hands pressing her down and the sounds of teacups breaking . . . the scene of Zhan boarding the steamboat with his lover, leaving her critically ill, crawling on the floor to take care of herself . . . these scenes flashed before her eyes, lifelike and rapidly. She laughed loudly, beat her chest, and wiped away the beads of sweat. (845–846)

Unable to cope rationally with the painful reality around her, throughout this section Wei frequently breaks into hysterical fits of laughter because, as the narrator explains, language itself was no longer adequate to express the utter despair she now feels.

In foregrounding Wei's relationship to Zhan as a form of emotional and physical bondage which exerts a crippling rather than liberating influence on her life, *Beiju shengya* of course radically demystifies the romantic notion of love as the ultimate act of individual freedom. But, more importantly, it calls into question the stylistic and social conventions that allow Zhan to dictate the terms of the relationship. In stunning and harrowing detail, Bai Wei's narrative reveals the ideological underpinnings of "romance" to be thoroughly masculinist and hegemonic, the latter showing how Wei in this instance actively becomes complicit with the structure of power that otherwise alienates her.

Significantly, the narrative itself offers no simple resolution to Wei's predicament, either through a final act of separation from Zhan or in the discovery of an alternative outlet for her desires. The autobiography instead ends with a description of the unsuccessful medical surgery Wei underwent (the doctors decide her case is hopeless and stitch her back up), and an enigmatic final comment by the narrator: "Did she get better or not? The outcome is uncertain. But if she is still living, I hope that her future life is the beginning of a new and glorious history (*guangmingshi*) rather than the continuation of that tragedy" (907). Bai Wei, of course, did survive her surgery, as the very completion of her autobiography testifies, and interestingly enough the material text played no small role in her final recovery. In 1937, shortly after *Beiju shengya* was published, the editor of the Shanghai magazine *Funü shenghuo* (Women's life) Shen Zijiu was flooded with letters of support from sympathetic readers and decided, along with a group of prominent leftist female intellectuals, writers, and activists (including Chen Bo'er, Wang Ying, Guan Lu, Du Junhui, and Li Lan), to issue a public letter soliciting donations for Bai Wei's medical bills.[81] Money poured in from fans of Bai Wei's work in and outside China, thus enabling her to go to Beiping for further treatment.[82] But it may be in the creative— and cathartic—act itself that we can locate a more provocative remedy for the social ills named in this text; for by inscribing the *socialization* of the woman's body Bai Wei confronts her personal objectification, and this is a lesson that *exceeds* her individual history.

CHAPTER 4

Outwitting Patriarchy: Comic Narrative Strategies in the Works of Yang Jiang, Su Qing, and Zhang Ailing

We have come to a moment in history when we are surrounded on all sides and oppressed by the absurd . . . the rhetoric of our times should persuade us to contemplate the ridiculous nature of the reality before us, and teach us to mock it.

Muriel Spark

Laughter demolishes fear and piety before an object, before a world, making of it an object of familiar contact and thus clearing the ground for an absolutely free investigation of it.

M.M. Bakhtin

In depicting Wei's descent into poverty, illness, and mental disequilibrium, Bai Wei uses laughter to call attention to the female subject's problematic relationship to language itself. Driven precariously to the brink of rage and hysteria by a world of patriarchal privilege and power, Wei is rendered speechless, reduced in the end to a state of irrepressible mad laughter. On another level, as a mechanism of survival her laughter also signifies a subversive resistance to the stereotyped image of the passively suffering female and the tragic narrative ending to which she is habitually consigned. In this chapter, I am interested in further exploring the role of laughter in Chinese feminist narratives. Specifically, I will focus on the works of three popular women writers who came to prominence during the Shanghai Occupation period (1937–1945), all of whom draw on comic devices to critique modern gender relations. Yang Jiang (1911–) appropriated the European comedy of manners genre to expose the absurdities of bourgeois patriarchy in her two plays, *Chenxin ruyi* (As you desire, 1943) and *Nongzhen chengjia* (Forging the truth, 1944).[1] In her best-selling novel *Jiehun shinian* (Ten years of marriage, 1944), Su Qing (1914–1982) incorporates satire into a scathing analysis of the contemporary institutions of marriage and motherhood.[2] And in her novella "Qingcheng zhi lian" (Love in a fallen city, 1943), Zhang Ailing (1920–1995) subtly mocks the traditional *femme-fatale* paradigm to depict her heroine's quest for love and marriage amid national crisis.[3] Different in numerous respects, what Yang Jiang, Su Qing, and Zhang Ailing all share is a blatant eschewal of the tearful sensibility that, as I have explored in earlier chapters, characterized much of the feminist creative literature of the 1920s and 1930s.[4] Like their predecessors Lu Yin, Shi Pingmei, Bai Wei and others, these writers interrogate patriarchal ideology and its social practices, but adopt a markedly more detached cynical stance from which to do so.

Yang Jiang, Su Qing, and Zhang Ailing emerged onto the Shanghai literary scene in the midst of the Sino-Japanese war, at a moment when escalating tensions between the Communist Party and the KMT threatened the fragile United Front (established in 1938) and rendered their joint resistance against Japanese aggression increasingly ineffectual. China's eastern coast, which had fallen hostage to enemy forces in the first year of the war, bore the brunt of the invasion and remained at the mercy of Japanese military policies; in Nanjing alone, an estimated 200,000 people lost their lives in the first year of the war. A virtual island in this sea of national turmoil, the cosmopolitan city of Shanghai nevertheless managed to sustain a relatively prosperous cultural life. A new crop of publishing houses, newspapers, and literary magazines, including the journal Su Qing launched and edited *Tiandi* (Heaven and earth), soon filled the void left by those that were either destroyed during the bombing in 1937 or closed and relocated to the Chinese interior along with the major exodus of intellectuals and writers after the onset of war. The ban on Hollywood film, previously a staple of popular urban entertainment, sparked an unprecedented boom of interest in Chinese drama, thus paving the way for the founding of several major commercial theater companies.[5] Periodic arrests and assassinations of artists and intellectuals and the constant, if unsystematic, surveillance and censorship by Japanese authorities imposed serious constraints (including that of self-censorship) on the cultural production of many of those who, for whatever reason, choose not to join the exodus to Chongqing, Yan'an, or Hong Kong.[6] Despite these factors, and in part because of them, the Shanghai occupation era produced significant culture.

According to Edward Gunn in his book *Unwelcome Muse*,[7] because of the dangers of political expression during the war years, the once highly politicized Shanghai cultural arena became increasingly geared toward providing popular entertainment for the sake of diversion or distraction. Tightened restrictions on both political and foreign imported art, coupled with the hedonistic mood that engulfed the isolated city, fueled a thriving market for popular drama, fiction, and film with subject matter not pertaining to the historical calamity unfolding in Shanghai and the Chinese nation at large. To be sure, the vocal contingent of radical left-wing intellectuals, writers, and critics of the Shanghai "underground" that based itself in the foreign settlement area continued to develop ways of voicing anti-Japanese and patriotic sentiments (through the veil of historical drama, for instance). But notably, the cultural–political circumstances that prevailed encouraged in their work a subtlety of expression less common in the so-called national resistance literature being produced in the interior of China. But one could also argue that for some writers in Shanghai, including the women writers examined here, the virtual outlawing of overt forms of nationalistic literature during the occupation freed them to take up issues and perspectives marginalized by the intellectual movement underway since the early 1930s to mobilize cultural forces for patriotic and/or revolutionary purposes. Indeed, this and the fact that many leading male literary intellectuals choose to withdraw from public culture as a form of anti-Japanese political protest may very well help explain why so many women writers prevailed in the literary scene of the time.[8]

Judging from their immense popular success, Yang Jiang, Su Qing and Zhang Ailing's comic writings clearly resonated with the public's desire for amusing entertainment. Despite the fact that she was a virtual novice as a playwright, Yang Jiang's *Chenxin ruyi* and *Nongzhen chengjia* were box-office hits when they were produced by major commercial theaters in Shanghai in 1943 and 1944, respectively, and were soon available in print both in a single volume as well as in the multivolume compendium of Shanghai drama assembled by Kong Lingjing.[9] Su Qing's *Jiehun shinian* ranked as the top best-seller of its day, going into more than thirty consecutive reprintings after its initial publication in 1944.[10] And Zhang Ailing's "Qingcheng zhi lian" so delighted Shanghai readers that she was asked to turn it into a play in 1945 (directed by Zhu Duanjun).[11] Yet, while it is true none of these writers dealt directly with contemporary wartime politics, it would be misleading to characterize their works as politically disengaged literature. Their comedies do not fit neatly into either of the categories typically assigned to this period of literature, constituting neither purely escapist wartime entertainment nor politically correct "resistance" literature; instead, as I shall show, their writing combines popular conventions that obviously held appeal to contemporary urban consumers but at the same time articulated an incisive feminist perspective on the embattled terrain of domestic relations.

In some sense, Yang Jiang, Su Qing, and Zhang Ailing can be said to have carried on the legacy of the highly self-conscious critique of patriarchal culture that had concerned feminist intellectuals and artists in the previous decades.[12] According to Meng Yue and Dai Jinhua in their survey of women's writing in twentieth-century China, the Shanghai Occupation marked one of the high points of the modern women's literary tradition, and they cite as a primary reason the unique "discursive space" (*huayu kongxi*) that opened up to women during the war.[13] For all the horrors imposed on Shanghai (not to mention the rest of China), the Japanese occupation also ushered in a temporary suspension of the male-centered discourses of national salvation and revolution that, as other literary scholars have noted, had often worked against the gendered discourse of feminist writers. This condition no doubt has much to do with the significant literary output of Shanghai women writers during this era: in addition to those figures examined in the present chapter, other women writers who made a name for themselves at the time and whose work reveals a certain continuity with feminist literary discourse from the pre-war era include Guan Lu (1907–1982) who published, among other works, a significant autobiographical novel in 1939 entitled *Xinjiu shidai* (The era of old and new);[14] Shi Jimei (1920–1968); and Wu Guifang (1915–1990).[15]

The comic vision that informs Yang Jiang, Su Qing, and Zhang Ailing's take on the arena of contemporary gender relations, however, also marks a fundamental departure from the "tearful realism" that to a greater or lesser degree had informed feminist literary discourse in the preceeding decades. The May Fourth legacy, in general, generated a vast assembly of somber literary texts populated with exploited and suffering women, some heroically defying conventional gender roles and expectations, others despairing at their inability (whether for economic, domestic, or psychological reasons) to do so. The reader of modern Chinese literature thus may be prone to ask, as women writers clearly alert to the plight of Chinese women in a sexist culture, where are Yang Jiang, Su Qing, and Zhang Ailing's feminist outrage and indignation? Why do their heroines laugh, rather than cry, at their domestic ordeals and social marginalization?

Just as the particular cultural–political milieu of the Shanghai Occupation helps to explain the continued presence of feminist concerns, this unique historical moment no doubt also conditioned the new developments in women's literary production, including the marked shift from sentiment to irony, and from tears to laughter. For one thing, these three writers clearly belong to what Edward Gunn has incisively characterized as the "anti-romantic" trend in Shanghai literary culture beginning in the late 1930s. This trend, a reaction in part to the moral ambiguity of contemporary realities under the occupation, exhibits a profound intellectual cynicism that stands in sharp contrast to the impassioned, idealistic, and often deeply emotional visions of political struggle and social liberation prevalent in literature just a generation earlier. Whereas didactic and sentimental modes had dominated that literature, now ironic modes came to the fore. Yet to understand the complexities and force of the gendered comic voice of writers like Yang Jiang, Su Qing, and Zhang Ailing, one needs to go further. As I hope to elucidate in the course of this chapter, Shanghai women writers' use of comedy is also related in several important ways to a specific juncture within Chinese feminism itself and should be seen as a new type of narrative response to this moment.

This chapter is divided into four parts: in part one, I briefly consider the theoretical implications of the persistent representation of female suffering in modern Chinese literature in order to set the stage for my discussion of the emergence of an alternative comic feminist voice in Shanghai literary culture in the 1940s. While feminist scholarship has drawn attention to the overinscription of the oppressed woman within modern Chinese gender discourse in terms of reification, I point out that there may be another kind of rhetorical violence at work that also warrants consideration: namely, how the ritual invocation of woman-as-victim may actually empty representation of meaning, rendering complex realities of female experience under patriarchy banal through sheer repetition. As an alternative representational mode (defined by strategies of parody, understatement, literalization and so forth), I suggest that comedy was adopted by feminist writers to offer relief from the relent-lessly serious fare and, at the same time, to attack the ridiculous discrepan-cies between the dominant discourse and current gender realities. In the second part, I shift my attention to a textual analysis of Yang Jiang's rework-ing of the Western genre of comedy of manners into feminist drama. My par-ticular focus here is on how she rewrites the most conventionalized female character types of early-twentieth-century Chinese literature (the oppressed female victim and the self-emancipated Chinese Nora) into what I term the laughing heroine; I also explore her parody of the stereotyped figure of the "patriarch." A discussion of these points will elucidate the complex web of signification of the comic (interconnections, for example, between anger, tears, and laughter) in Yang Jiang's drama. Next, I turn to Su Qing's powerful novel *Jiehun shinian*, which I analyze as a satirical rewriting of the sentimental tradition of women's confessions. Here self-pity is replaced by cynicism, with an innovative first-person narrator who laughs at her own follies as a modern woman trapped (at least temporarily) in an absurdly old-fashioned family, as well as the silly sexist views that contribute to her subordination. And in the final section, I examine Zhang Ailing's ironic tale of a modern day *femme-fatale*, "Qingcheng zhi lian," in relation to questions of female desire and historical change.

* * *

"[W]hat distinguishes modern Chinese writings," Rey Chow has remarked, "is an investment in suffering, an investment that aims at exposing social injustice."[16] The operative term in this statement is, of course, investment: according to Chow's intriguing hypothesis, the self-appointed mission of twentieth-century Chinese literary intellectuals to bear witness to the wrongs their culture inflicts upon the weak and marginalized has in practice estab-lished a profoundly problematic *dependence* on the oppressed. Speaking on behalf of "the oppressed" has come to represent such an indispensable basis of identity and authority for modern intellectuals and writers that, paradox-ically, their interests have seemingly become staked not to the eradication of the suffering of society's victims but to its ongoing operation: "the conscious representation of the minor as such also leads to a situation in which it is locked in opposition to the hegemonic in a permanent bind . . . support for the minor, however sincere, always becomes support for the center."[17]

Although by no means the only subaltern group to have received sustained attention as a subject in modern Chinese literature, women have occupied a major place, thus prompting Chow to urge particular caution when it comes to investigating cultural representations of their subjugated condition. For to perpetually invoke women as "the suppressed and victimized other" is, in her view, to run the risk of reproducing the "violence of rhetoric"[18] in which Chinese literature is allegedly already implicated. Given the discursive predicament she discerns, Chow ultimately proposes that for feminist critics today "the first critical task is to break alliance with this kind of official sponsorship of minority discourse."[19]

One way contemporary feminist literary critics have begun to make the break Chow calls for is to scrutinize and expose the limits of the "enlightened" gender discourse of Chinese literature. Yue Ming-Bao, for example, in a critical rereading of May Fourth writing, suggests that the obsessive "narrativization of oppressed women," in fiction and nonfiction genres alike, exhibits clearly "the discursive habits of a patriarchal tradition."[20] By construing women's oppression as a sociological "problem" that had to be resolved along with multiple other obstacles to national salvation, modern male intellectuals (unwittingly, perhaps) carried on the tradition of male hegemony by (re)inscribing woman as the passive object of, rather than productive subject of, discourse. For example, the numerous "case-studies" of women featured in the progressive periodical press in the 1920s (such as the young Mao Zedong's reportage on female suicide) and the genre of realist fiction modeled after them typically relied on a split between a conscious (male) narrator/investigator and a female victim. The latter, often an illiterate peasant, seldom testifies on her own behalf in the text and gets delineated primarily in terms of her physical (often sexualized) attributes. A figure of pity, she is simultaneously rendered a pathetic and inert object, the antithesis of the energetic male mind who encounters and observes her. Thus, despite the overtly progressive political stance of the narrative toward social oppression, Yue observes, such writing would appear to reproduce a discursive logic akin to that evinced by traditional genres reserved for writing about women. In particular, it bears a certain resemblance to the conservative *lienü zhuan* (biographies of women) genre traditionally used to inculcate the proper codes of feminine conduct in female readers. In the *lienü* tradition, female self-sacrifice (committing suicide to preserve chastity, for instance) was celebrated as the pinnacle of virtue and a tribute to the triumph of Confucian morality. In modern literature, an analogous notion of femininity (i.e., one that upholds the "construction of female virtue as self-immolation") is produced when representations of female sacrifice are enlisted to promote reigning ideological agendas of modernity.[21]

In the present study I have attempted to complement and expand the contemporary critical discussion on gender representation, specifically, by reframing these issues in terms of women's feminist literary practices. For the writers explored in Chapters 2 and 3, for example, suffering was examined as a central motif in their realist depictions of the New Woman yet, as I attempted to show, the strategies (and effects) of their representation differ in rather significant ways from those Yue suggests. By the 1940s, however, for many writers the figure of the female victim had clearly run its course. Here, therefore, I would like to pick up on another mode of rhetorical violence (to which Rey Chow alludes in her earlier study *Women and Chinese*

Modernity); namely, the trivialization of women's suffering through its sheer excessive representation. If monotonous repetition can transform even the most profound message to banality or cliché, then we would do well to ask what effect did the surfeit of tearful tales dwelling on female oppression have on Chinese writers and readers at the time?

At the very least, it would be safe to surmise that the novelty of such representations had worn off and no longer resonated in the same way. If many of the underlying problems facing contemporary Chinese women remained the same, writers who sought to illuminate these concerns had a new challenge to consider: namely, how to reanimate a discourse whose rhetoric and imagery had begun to grow stale and conventional. The issue is prefigured, interestingly, in Lu Xun's "Zhufu" (New year's sacrifice, 1924), a story that on the surface centers in classic May Fourth fashion on the tragic spectacle of female suffering.[22] But the figure at the center of the text, Xianglin Sao, represents not just as an embodiment of pity, but an object of ridicule. As will be recalled, Xianglin Sao's string of misfortunes—being forced to remarry, the fatal illness of her husband, the violent death of her young son in the jaws of a hungry wolf, her loss of employment—initially elicit a sympathetic response from those who hear of them. In time, however, her incessant retelling of these travails reduces her experience to a village joke, or what Rey Chow aptly describes as a "ridiculous psychosis [that] no one bothers to investigate."[23] Neurotically rehashed, her tragic testimony is thus divested of its affective intensity, no longer capable of moving listeners in the village to contemplate the details of the poor woman's misfortune. And in the end even Xianglin Sao herself seems desensitized, and "looks as though she were carved out wood" as she mechanically chants her story by rote.

By invoking this example, I do not mean to suggest that the cultural representations of women's oppression in China had somehow deteriorated into a collective public joke by the 1940s; nor for that matter can the intellectuals, writers, and activists committed to protesting sexism be accused of monotonous redundancy. As a text that calls attention to the narrative act, and specifically, the gradual loss of a story's ability to communicate the experience of ordeal, however, it accentuates a critical dilemma of post-May Fourth feminism; namely, how to sharpen the edge of a critique that was rapidly being dulled through excessive repetition and ritual invocation of stories and images of women's suffering and exploitation?

The construction of radically new narratives of female subjugation from a comic perspective by writers like Yang Jiang, Su Qing, and Zhang Ailing can be read, I believe, as one attempt to resist this drift toward banality. By endowing their heroines with an ability to laugh in the face of adversity, and by exposing the absurd conventions of patriarchy, these texts employ comedy as a kind of defamiliarizing tactic to reinvigorate a discourse on gender whose imagery and language was well on its way to becoming overly predictable and commonplace. At the same time their vision refuses the facile and false conception of patriarchy as a dichotomous battle between male villains and female victims. And finally, it throws into relief the limits of the supposedly enlightened contemporary inscriptions of gender by mocking modern stereotypes and implicitly critiquing the conservative ideological function they serve. While it must be recognized that to some extent representation ultimately always involves reconfiguration or disfiguration (thereby enacting a sort of "violence"), the comic feminist texts such as those discussed here appear to provide an important alternative to the particular violences of representation noted above.

* * *

YANG JIANG'S FEMINIST COMEDY OF MANNERS

Concerned about the prospect of war in Europe and about the welfare of their families back home, Yang Jiang and her husband Qian Zhongshu set sail on a French ocean liner bound for China in November 1938. Qian disembarked in Hong Kong and headed out to Kunming to assume a teaching position in the foreign languages program of Southwest Associated University, a coalition of universities from the Beijing-Tianjin area that merged during the war; Yang Jiang continued on to Shanghai where her elderly father had taken refuge in the Foreign Settlement (an area of the city which would remain unoccupied until the beginning of the Pacific war in 1941). The couple, having met when Yang Jiang was pursuing graduate studies in foreign literature at Qinghua University, had spent the last few years taking classes at Oxford and had recently moved to Paris where they hoped to continue their studies in literature. Compared with their serene years in Europe, adjusting to wartime conditions in Shanghai was not easy. Yang accepted a position as principal at her alma mater the Zhenhua Highschool for Girls, which had recently opened a new campus in the foreign concession, although the school shut down after the Japanese annexed the foreign areas in December 1941 and she was forced to scrounge for tutoring jobs. The new phase of the Occupation, bringing heightened military presence and stricter censorship, as well as rampant inflation, made everyday urban life all the more perilous, although for Yang Jiang there was a silver lining in what Shanghai residents popularly referred to as "the dark world" (*hei'an shijie*): Qian, having returned for a holiday visit earlier that year, was now stranded in Shanghai, thus reuniting the family for the duration of the war.

Among Yang Jiang's neighbors in the French Concession where she lived on Avenue Joffre were the playwright and academic Chen Linrui and his wife who introduced her to noted literary critic, playwright, and translator Li Jianwu. A graduate of the foreign languages department of Qinghua University who had spent several years abroad doing graduate work at the University of Paris, Li found he had much in common with Yang Jiang and Qian Zhongshu and soon spent a great deal of time with them, together with Chen Linrui, discussing drama and foreign literature.[24] Aware of Yang's literary aspirations (she had published several essays and short stories in the late

1930s, at the encouragement of Zhu Ziqing, under whom she studied creative writing at Qinghua University) and perhaps also her need for a new source of income, he encouraged her to try her hand at writing drama. The result was four plays written between 1942–1946, beginning with two European-style comedies of manners.[25] Li Jianwu was reportedly so impressed by the quality of her first play *Chenxin ruyi* that he helped arranged for the prominent director Huang Zuolin to stage its production at the Shanghai Golden Capital Theater, and even played the part of Xu Langzhai himself.[26] He was even more enthusiastic about *Nongzhen chengjia*, which she completed the following year, writing in a review at the time that it marked a milestone in modern Chinese literature, second only to the comedies of Ding Xilin.[27]

At its peak in eighteenth-century Europe with such plays as Richard Sheridan's *The School for Scandal* (1777), the comedy of manners (known also as domestic comedy or parlor-room drama) was a dramatic genre featuring light-hearted mockery of the private life of the *beau monde*. Set in the drawing room, the early manners play typically refrained from overt moral or political criticism of the class it depicted, instead offering humor in the *bon repartee* of aristocratic characters, witty observations, and the comic misunderstandings that invariably arise in the domestic scenarios through which the drama unfolds. Sociopolitical realities of class privilege are taken for granted: in the words of one scholar, the genre is typified by "an air of amused tolerance with life and unconcern for the moral consequences of action . . ."[28] In short, the comedy of manners originated as a mild form of amusing entertainment that preserved rather than challenged the status quo.

Chenxin ruyi and *Nongzhen chengjia*'s debt to the manners genre is immediately evident, and critics of Yang's drama often note the influence of foreign dramatists on her work.[29] First of all, both plays are set, consistent with generic convention, in the drawing rooms of wealthy Shanghai families: in *Chenxin ruyi*, each of the four acts takes place in a different parlor as the heroine Li Junyu is tossed from the home of one relative to the next. In *Nongzhen chengjia*, a five-act play, the setting alternates between the luxurious parlor of the Zhang residence and the shabby storefront/flat of Zhou Dazhang's family. Both plays adhere to generic convention as well by dramatizing the lives of members of the *beau monde*, here the contemporary Shanghai bourgeoisie. Although her central heroines are peripheral members of that class, the majority of characters who populate these plays are privileged members of the ruling elite: among the Zhao relatives with whom Li Junyu resides in *Chenxin ruyi*, there is the fastidious banker Zhao Zuyin, his scheming wife, Lady Zhao Zuyin, the hen-pecked factory boss, Zhao Zumao, his do-gooder "modern" wife, and the pretentious Zhao Zuyi, a retired foreign diplomat. Similarly, the subjects of *Nongzhen chengjia* are the affluent Zhang family, headed by the calculating capitalist patriarch, Zhang Xiangfu. In both plays the comic predicament revolves around the themes of love and marriage, another typical feature of the comedy of manners. And finally, both plays masterfully capture the refined tone generally associated with the genre: here, by avoiding explicit reference to the war, the Japanese occupation, or social crisis, they seem to offer a detached, almost disinterested, vision of contemporary society.

But if both plays are constructed on the surface as comedies of manners, it does not take long to realize that they would be more accurately classified as parodies of that genre. The opening scene of *Chenxin ruyi* begins, for instance, just beyond the parlor, as an arrogant servant at the Zhang residence bars the lead character Junyu and her shabbily dressed boyfriend Binru from entry. The two eventually *barge* their way in, but already the atmosphere of gentility and harmony central to the genre has been shattered. A seemingly insignificant scene, this initial episode is symptomatic of Yang Jiang's rewriting of the genre: what was previously the exclusive and unquestioned realm of upper-class domesticity has become contested territory, a site of confrontation not just between social classes but, as I will show, a terrain on which traditional and emergent gender roles will collide.

Yang Jiang's subversion of the manners genre is of course not entirely her own innovation. In Europe, the politicization of the comedy of manners had long been underway by the time Western dramatic forms came in vogue in China in the early twentieth century.[30] With the advent of realism in the Western tradition and its concomitant moral and political agendas, the "pure" comedy of manners in the tradition of eighteenth-century writers was gradually transformed. Oscar Wilde's *The Importance of Being Earnest* (1895), for example, carried on the convention of witty dialogue, but the *beau monde* itself had now become the subject of ridicule: now the upper-class is depicted as more decadent than decent, more pompous than principled. The once-aristocratic genre was turned, as it were, against the ruling class.

But if Yang Jiang inherited the legacy of an already politicized comedy of manners (and indeed she follows the example of Shaw and Wilde by ridiculing the bourgeoisie), she refashions the genre yet again in adapting it to address contemporary Chinese debates about gender: that is to say, she invents a feminist comedy of manners. Not only does she transform the parlor setting from an arena of domestic mischief and romantic intrigue into a site of female exploitation and objectification, but she uses it as a space of negotiation over the meaning of the familiar modern concepts of gender oppression and emancipation.

One way she achieves this is by populating her dramas with characters who represent send-ups or at least amusing spin-offs of well-established "types" of modern women and men in fiction and drama: the persecuted female victim, the emancipated Chinese Nora, the evil capitalist patriarch, the modern romantic lover, as well as other familiar types all make appearances in her plays. Instead of valorizing such stock figures, however, Yang Jiang subtly rewrites them—throwing into relief the limitations and ideological content of "modern" gender roles of mainstream literature. In each case the basic strategy is that of mimicry, a textual strategy that has been frequently discussed in relation to Western feminist writing. Luce Irigaray, in

This Sex Which Is Not One, identifies the manipulation of well-known images or narratives as a fundamental strategy in feminist literary practice:

> To play with mimesis is thus, for a woman, to try to recover the place of her exploitation by discourse, without allowing herself to be simply reduced to it. It means to resubmit herself—inasmuch as she is on the side of the "perceptible" of "matter"—to "ideas," in particular to ideas about herself, that are elaborated in/by a masculine logic, but so as to make "visible" by an effect of playful repetition, what was supposed to remain invisible.[31]

Given the complicity of language and patriarchy, this internal disruption of masculine logic is, for Irigaray, the only productive (i.e., nonpatriarchal) textual practice available to the woman writer. While this last point is debatable, the identification of mimicry as an important formal strategy in feminist writing is, I think, a useful starting point in the case of Yang Jiang's literary project.[32]

The heroines of Yang Jiang's plays bear an unmistakable resemblance to their fictional predecessors. They are basically enlightened New Women with wills and desires of their own though, again true to type, they are socially powerless to overcome the various obstacles they encounter. Also in keeping with the dominant discourse of female oppression evolving since the May Fourth Movement, the heroines' plight is examined in relation to the realms of romance, marriage, and family. *Chenxin ruyi*, for instance, revolves around the trials and tribulations of a proud but penniless young woman Li Junyu whose parents have died and who has come to seek the support of her rich Shanghai relatives. Years earlier, these same relatives disowned her mother for having defiantly married a struggling painter.[33] While many of the heroine's troubles stem from her economic dependence upon her relatives (shunted from family to family, Junyu literally moves from one site of exploitation to the next as she is conscripted as secretary, nanny, typist, and maid), the force that drives the action of the play is romance. What precipitates Junyu's repeated expulsion from the homes of her relatives is in each case linked to her alleged liaisons with two young bachelors, Binru and Jingsun. *Nongzhen chengjia* dramatizes the hypocrisy and fraud of marriage, another popular topic of May Fourth fiction: in this play, a gold-digging trickster named Dazhang attempts to seduce the unsuspecting daughter of a wealthy Shanghai businessman. Meanwhile, the heroine of the play Yanhua, once again a poor relative on the margins of the family, narrowly escapes an unsuitable and potentially disastrous match with a pedantic buffoon selected by her self-serving relatives, only to unwittingly wed the imposter. Ultimately, Yang Jiang's comic vision significantly disrupts the conventional handling of such themes and thus marks a sharp departure from the May Fourth tradition; still, the central themes of both plays and the predicaments of their female characters are certainly familiar enough ones for readers of Chinese women's and feminist literature produced during the early decades of the twentieth century.

One important intervention in the plays under discussion here is Yang's comic revision of the trope of the suffering woman immortalized by such figures as Lu Xun's Xianglin Sao ("Zhufu," 1924) and Ba Jin's Mingfeng (*Jia*, 1933), or, from the theater world itself, Cao Yu's tragic heroines Sifeng and Fanyi (*Leiyu*, 1934).[34] These are all female victims who inhabit worlds of tears, self-sacrifice, and despair and who are driven eventually to madness, suicide, and death by stifling domestic or marital circumstances. Strong characters such as Junyu in *Chenxin ruyi* and Yanhua in *Nongzhen chengjia*, by contrast, mark a new breed of modern heroine who, rather than respond with the customary flood of tears, resist and struggle against their oppressors with laughter. Junyu and Yanhua may not be immune to the cruel hypocrisies of bourgeois patriarchy but in their characterization as survivors they debunk the tragic plotting of the modern woman's life.

Rather than a tragic casualty of the traditional family, Li Junyu is portrayed as a disarmingly resilient young woman who refuses to play the part of the helpless victim; in so doing she constantly defies the expectations of the relatives she meets (not to mention Yang's audience). In a revealing scene near the end of the play, for example, the benign but hopelessly self-centered male lead Jingsun presses her to accept his hand in marriage. Until that point he has mistakenly assumed that his "less fortunate" cousin is madly in love with him. In a typically presumptuous manner, he reasons "you think you're not good enough for me, but you mustn't sacrifice yourself. You keep saying that I shouldn't hurt my fiancée, but think for a minute, how could I ever break your heart, how could I ever torment you? (99)" To Junyu, who neither considers herself a pitiful, vulnerable victim in need of male rescue nor has any romantic interest in Jingsun whatsoever, this notion strikes her as absolutely ludicrous and, in response, she laughs in his face.

In fact, from the moment she bursts into the Zhao family parlor in Act I, Junyu appears less intimidated by the affluent world of her pretentious relatives and the marginal position she occupies within it than amused by it all. Significantly, her laughter (laughter specified by the stage direction) tends to erupt when we least expect it: in the first scene, Junyu returns to the parlor just in time to overhear her Aunt and Uncle discussing how to get rid of her. Junyu reacts by laughing. In Act II, she giggles when Second Uncle saddles her with yet another onerous job (on top of her steadily mounting duties as First Uncle's personal secretary and tutor to Second Aunt's children)—this time to transcribe his prized (and jealously guarded) manuscript, "research" collected on his travels abroad. In Act III, Junyu again chuckles as she admits that Fourth Aunt despises her, and so on. Coming from the "victim," this seemingly incongruous response is made to signify a multitude of meanings; frequently, though, it serves the double function of both a strategy for survival and an act of defiance. "Comedy," writes one leading scholar on the subject, "is a defense as well as a weapon" and this is certainly true of Junyu's laughter.[35] On the one hand, it fortifies her against the belittling scorn that surrounds, enabling the embattled heroine to avoid being defeated by anger or self-pity; on the other, it can be seen as a subversive tool with which the author arms her heroine to strike back at her would-be oppressors.

Yanhua, the feisty young protagonist of *Nongzhen chengjia* is similarly disinclined to shed tears over her predicament. Although the frequent stage direction to laugh, as in Junyu's case, is not given to this character, her actions bespeak a definite sense of humor. Like Junyu, Yanhua is a young single woman: her father has remarried and for all intents and purposes left her to the mercy of wealthy relatives. When she makes her first appearance in Act I, she could easily be mistaken for the domestic help as she mechanically follows Master Zhang's order to fetch his slippers—though in fact she is his niece. The play's central plot, to summarize briefly, hinges on a typical love triangle: both Yanhua and her spoiled cousin Wanru are in love with Zhou Dazhang, a sophisticated gentleman who, unbeknownst to the either young lady, is actually an ambitious imposter scheming to marry his way into social status and wealth. Despite the fact that he secretly harbors feelings for Yanhua, he courts Wanru with his sights set on her inheritance. To further complicate matters, Feng Guangzu, a bumbling academic who resides with the Zhangs, has taken a fancy to Yanhua, a match that Lady Zhang and her husband actively encourage for their own selfish reasons. Rather than wallow in despair over unrequited love (as the scorned lover in a Cao Yu play might, for example), or humbly settle for the uninspiring Feng, Yanhua takes matters into her own hands. Herein lies the comedy. First, she dodges Feng's offer of marriage by facetiously claiming that the best way she can repay his kindness is to *not* marry him. In a transparently tongue-in-cheek explanation, she insists she has a fiery temper and would make a terrible wife: "As I think about it now, in order to express my gratitude and repay you, I actually ought to promise not to marry you—you know my disposition; whoever marries me will have plenty to cope with . . . you wouldn't be able to put up with me. For sure, I would tyrannize you, trample all over you, bully you . . ." (163).

Even more ingenious is the way she tricks Dazhang into believing that Wanru has broken off their engagement. Having "borrowed" Wanru's engagement ring on the pretext of arranging a rendevous for the two lovers, Yanhua then uses it to fool Dazhang into thinking that Wanru has eloped with none other than the foolish Feng. Dazhang not only takes her word for it, but offers her the ring in an impulsive marriage proposal. In short, by playing the female trickster—by subversively laughing and playing jokes on the men who would manipulate her—Yanhua turns her station as a powerless and dependent relative into a situation of control, or so it would at first seem.[36]

It is important to emphasize that in both cases the heroine's laughter registers a complex response to social marginality, signifying a range of different and sometimes conflicting emotions, from anguish over perceived inequities to a stubborn determination to survive. Junyu's ambiguous laughter, for example, is clearly inflected with despair and anger. This is manifest in a key scene in Act II, which unfolds during Junyu's brief stay at Second Uncle's house. Uncle Zuyi has just exited after having subjected Junyu to a patronizing lecture about how to type his manuscript, leaving her sitting alone giggling uncontrollably, as the stage direction specifies (*du chixiao*). But when

Jingsun enters and demands to know what she finds so funny, she is puzzled herself, protesting that she actually feels sad:

JINGSUN   Are you laughing at me?
JUNYU   Was I laughing?
JINGSUN   You can't hide it from me, I saw you laughing.
JUNYU   That's unfair! I actually feel like crying. (30)

The trickster Yanhua is a similarly ambiguous comic figure, whose mocking laughter often gives way to fits of rage. When, on one occasion, Feng advises her that she "should not" attempt to win Zhou Dazhang away from her rich cousin Wanru, she explodes into the following diatribe: "Why shouldn't I? Why should Wanru be the pampered little lady! Why should I be the suffering, slaving servant! Should Wanru enjoy all the wealth, while I have absolutely nothing! . . . should this! should that! All the fires of hell are burning in my heart!" (164–165) More revealing still is her own self-description as an angry young woman: "I'm like a big bomb. There is gunpowder buried in my heart, wrapped in layers of thick paper just waiting to be ignited. Pow! Pow! I'd explode in a second into so many fragments and go flying away, my whole body burnt to cinders. Only then could I be relaxed and carefree!" (163). And, as it turns out in this play, the final joke is on Yanhua herself— prince charming is in fact unmasked as a fake with desires for immense wealth and power but none in his own possession and it not until after the wedding that our "clever" heroine discovers her blunder.

Yang Jiang's innovative construction of a laughing heroine can be seen on one level as a rewriting of the long-suffering female victim who silently endures the indignities of male-dominated culture, and in particular that notorious patriarchal stronghold, the family. As a narrative strategy this re-vision calls attention to the patriarchal ideology that informs that fictional narrative and as such constitutes a subtle but significant feminist intervention against a potentially repressive female script. But if the oppressed female victim represents one modern literary stereotype of women, the figure of the Chinese Nora embodies another. Ever since the Chinese translation of Ibsen's celebrated play *A Doll's House* (1879) first appeared in *Xin qingnian* in 1918, the "Nora" paradigm exercised tremendous influence on literary treatments of women's oppression. One of the earliest examples of this influence can be found in Hu Shi's *Zhongshen dashi* (The greatest event in life, 1919), a one-act play clearly inspired by *A Doll's House*.[37] Hu Shi reincarnates Nora as a young woman named Tian Yamei whose independence (here, interpreted essentially as her desire to marry according to her own choice) is thwarted by traditional culture: Yamei's mother opposes her decision after consulting a fortune-teller, and her father objects because it would violate an ancestral taboo. But just as Ibsen's Nora triumphs by asserting her own will, captured in the famous finale in which she storms out the door, in the end so too does Yamei triumph over Confucian patriarchy: instead of acquiescing to her parents' wishes, she also walks out the door, presumably to elope with her lover. Although Hu Shi's play may lack nuance, his characterization of Yamei is typical of the self-emancipating Nora featured in fictional texts throughout this period.[38]

Rather than romanticize the Chinese Nora who (ostensibly) finds freedom and self-worth through romantic love, Yang Jiang ridicules this by-now all too formulaic tale of female emancipation in *Nongzhen chengjia*. Yanhua's refusal to be sacrificed to the academic boor, Feng Guangzu, and her aggressive scheme to marry the man she loves, Zhou Dazhang, a handsome, and supposedly well-educated and wealthy young man, are clear codes signifying the Noraesque "new woman" who strives for self-autonomy and sexual freedom. The comic twist is that while Yanhua prevails in getting the man of her "choice", he is ultimately exposed as a complete sham. Far from being the foreign-educated scion of an old and respectable scholarly family that he has claimed to be, he is actually the fast-talking son of a poverty-stricken Shanghai widow. Although the audience is privy to Dazhang's true identity early on in the play, it is not until too late, after having been tricked into a hastily arranged marriage ceremony that Yanhua discovers her blunder. Indeed, it is from this dramatic irony that much of the play's humor arises. Another major irony occurs in the final climax when our "victorious" heroine returns to Shanghai after attempting to elope with Dazhang, thus falling into the marriage trap set for them by their two families. A humorous, if deeply cynical, response to Lu Xun's 1923 question "What happens after Nora leaves home?," the lovers are forced to come back when they discover neither has brought (or indeed possesses) any money.[39] The wedding in the final act, fittingly, does not embody a joyous celebration of the modern ideals of free choice and romantic union we might expect, but becomes instead a grotesque imitation of the traditional marriage ritual.[40] Evidently, Yanhua has walked out the door of one bad situation only to fall straight into another. While we laugh at her folly and the futility of her self-initiative in the final act, the play concludes on a decidedly ambiguous note.[41] After the crowd of obnoxious relatives disperses, Yanhua and Dazhang, now legally married, are left alone on stage together for a moment. Yanhua seems resigned to accept her "fate" in good spirits, but the humor of the situation has dissipated: in fact, the dawning self-realization of the hand she has played in her own undoing has nearly tragic implications.

While some might object that the final downfall of the heroine is problematic, I believe that Yang Jiang's refusal to invent easy or idealistic textual resolutions—for instance, by making her laughing heroine impervious to or somehow removed from patriarchal culture—signals a very serious prognosis of the problem. Indeed, just as Yang Jiang deconstructed the figure of the passive victim, she is equally emphatic about the inadequacy of the other dominant literary image of woman, the heroic female rebel.

PARODY OF THE PATRIARCHS

Yang Jiang's comic revisions of the literary stereotypes of the "oppressed" woman on the one hand and the "emancipated" woman on the other are clearly indicative, as I have stressed, of a new textual approach to sexual politics. Although I have focused up to this point almost exclusively on the ways in which this author reconstructs female gender roles, her characterization of male figures also challenges prevailing gender stereotypes. Not surprisingly, while the men in Yang Jiang's plays clearly enjoy the privileges and power of patriarchal society, her fictional world does not allow for either tyrannical villains or noble heroes. Instead, Yang Jiang assigns to her male characters the drastically deflated role of buffoons who inspire laughter instead of terror or awe. Two types of clowns that take center stage in *Chenxin ruyi* and *Nongzhen chengjia*, and therefore deserve our close attention, are the capitalist patriarch and the modern romantic lover, both familiar enough character-types in early-twentieth-century Chinese fictions of women's emancipation.

Zhang Xiangfu, the wealthy capitalist in *Nongzhen chengjia*, represents an unmistakable parody of bourgeois masculinity. Self-important and chauvinistic, he lords over his family and spouts his superior wisdom every chance he gets. But rather than leave the economic self-interest that drives this character as an underlying, unspoken subtext, Yang Jiang undercuts his authority by over-exaggerating Zhang's capitalist rhetoric. The result is that he comes across sounding as though he were parroting lines that seem to be drawn directly from descriptions of the capitalist mentality in Marxist literature like Engels' treatise "Family, Private Property and the State." And, in this way, he is revealed as a callous but also silly fool who reductively views the world, his own daughter included, in terms of profit and loss. A key scene in Act I, in which Zhang and his wife discuss whether Dazhang would make an appropriate husband for their daughter, for instance, highlights his calculating attitude. For Zhang, his daughter's marriage is tantamount to a major financial venture. Explaining to his wife the reason why he objects to Wanru's suitor, he says "I have asked all over, and nobody knows anything about him. He's nothing more than a new brand-name, very risky business" (113). Yet, when his wife thus advises they take their time to become better acquainted with the young man, Mr. Zhang goes on to invoke the economic principles of supply and demand: "When you take a fancy to some product which is a sure money-maker, before you can bat an eyelid you've got to snatch it up. In today's market, how many girls are there waiting to get married. But how few quality sons-in-law there are!" (114). Yang Jiang uses this character to expose the economic imperatives that underlie bourgeois life; significantly, however, his argument hardly convinces his wife, who easily dismisses his facile approach to human relations and his equation of their daughter's marriage with a business transaction (*shengyi maimai*, 114). In short, Yang Jiang's caricature of Zhang Xiangfu denies him the more noble stature of a formidable arch-villain, and instead deflates him into something pitifully predictable.

A second important example of the way Yang Jiang rewrites conventional male scripts in these two plays is her characterization of the romantic male lover. Again, Yang Jiang's depiction of the male lover as a comic figure is a strategic move, in this case to debunk the patriarchal myth of romantic love, so it is worth examining more closely how she depicts such characters as

Feng Guangzu, Zhou Dazhang, and Zhao Jingsun. An impoverished scholar living off his relatives, Feng Guangzu is perhaps the most buffoonish of Yang Jiang's romantic suitors. In stark contrast to the ideal of the eloquent, sincere, and passionate suitor, Feng is a pretentious, stuttering fool who irritates and bores his would-be beloved. In one of the most hilarious scenes in the play, Feng turns his proposal of marriage to Yanhua into an exasperatingly tedious academic lecture. Consider, for example, the way he broaches the topic of marriage with the unsuspecting Yanhua:

> That's good, then I'll lay the whole matter out very clearly for you. There are five points: the first point is, that is to say, the basic issue is whether or not this is worth discussing at all. In the past, when young ladies were confronted with the topic of marriage, they would get embarrassed, and as for their own "important event" they would get so flustered they would let other people go and take care of it for them. (159)

When Yanhua appears bewildered, he makes a second, and even more stilted, attempt to get his point across:

> Let me first finish giving you the overall outline and then we can discuss the individual points one at a time. The third point is, why haven't I gotten married yet? There are several reasons for this, and I will tell you them gradually. The fourth point is, can I get married right now? There are two sub-points here: One is your perspective on this, the other is my perspective on this. The fifth point is the union of these two points, that is to say . . . (160)

And so on. Needless to say, Yanhua is not in the least bit impressed by Feng's scientific approach to romance, "Professor Feng's marriage proposal method" (*Feng jiaoshou de qiuhunfa*), as she disdainfully describes it, and she turns him down.

An equally inarticulate though different kind of romantic lover is Zhao Jingsun in *Chenxin ruyi*. When this comedy begins, Jingsun is happily engaged to be married to his cousin Lingxian. As the play progresses, however, his affections are drawn toward Junyu, with whom he believes to have discovered "true" love. A seemingly standard romantic plot, Yang Jiang deflates this lover by exposing his affair with Junyu to be nothing more than an egocentric fantasy on his part. From the outset, Junyu shows little romantic interest in her cousin, and in fact repeatedly sidesteps his flirtatious advances; Jingsun nevertheless simply assumes that the feelings he has for her are mutual. It is in the comic climax of the fourth act, during an awkward exchange between the two just moments before Jingsun's engagement party, that Jingsun's romantic illusion is finally shattered. As is evident in the following dialogue, at first Junyu doesn't quite know what he is talking about:

> JINGSUN   These are the final moments! In a minute, the banquet will commence, I'll sit in the place of honor, Uncle will make the announcement in the presence of everyone, and I'll be engaged to Lingxian.

JUNYU   My congratulations in advance.
JINGSUN   Junyu, as I said, we don't have time for such nonsense.
JUNYU   When have I ever had time for nonsense!
JINGSUN   Yes! We don't have any more time for nonsense. You might as well
            go ahead and give me an honest reply.
JUNYU   Brother Jingsun, everything I have said has always been honest.
JINGSUN   Junyu, I know about your difficulties.
JUNYU   What difficulties?
JINGSUN   Perhaps you don't understand yourself that well, but I completely
            understand.
JUNYU   [looks at watch] Aiya, Brother Jingsun.
JINGSUN   I know you're nervous, but, Junyu, we still have time, as long as
            that single sentence comes from your . . .
JUNYU   What sentence, please, get to the point. (98)

When Jingsun realizes that Junyu is not the vulnerable, helpless woman he
has imagined her to be and who, moreover, refuses his pity and his "generous"
offer of marriage, he changes his tune, declaring that what he feels is not love
but merely sympathy. A revealing shift, this reaction raises important questions about the nature of romantic discourse. Does romance depend upon
the construction of a vulnerable female whom the (older, wiser, richer)
"hero" can sweep off her feet? Does the romantic marriage plot require the
(male) rescue of a helpless woman? In short, is supposedly emancipatory
romantic love actually also constructed according to masculinist ideology?[42]

Closely related to Yang Jiang's comic rewriting of the romantic lover is
the romantic impostor. If Jingsun represents the male-centered nature of
romantic discourse, Dazhang exposes its underlying economic motive. Again,
we can read this as an implicit subversion of the heroic male lover featured
in earlier modern writing. For example, in Hu Shi's play, even though Tian
Yamei's lover Mr. Chen never actually makes an appearance, the author
leaves us in little doubt about his integrity or respect for Yamei. Apparently,
Hu Shi assumes that the "modern" man as embodied by the romantic lover
has automatically discarded his masculinist ideology along with the
Confucian classics. Yang Jiang, by contrast, constructs Zhou Dazhang as a
con-man (albeit a likable one) who imitates the external gestures and scripts
of romance for ulterior motives that have little to do with the values of personal choice, freedom, or emotional attachment celebrated in Hu Shi's play.
Indeed, there is no passion or emotional depth to his relationship with
Wanru; he seeks to marry the naive and pampered young lady solely to
acquire the Zhang family fortune. Although Dazhang successfully masquerades as many things he is not (a returned student, a well-connected entre-
peneur, the filial son of a strict Confucian family), his "true identity" as an
impostor is revealed, if only for a brief moment, in the first act. In one of several flirtation scenes (Act I, 131–134), Zhou clearly "misses" an important
romantic cue, which infuriates Wanru. Ironically, she accuses him of merely
following a formula and relying upon clichés, since of course that is precisely
what he is doing.

In short, Yang Jiang demonstrates an acute cynicism toward the dominant literary representations associated with modern discourses on female emancipation—the story of the persecuted woman with its tears and suffering, like that of Xianglin Sao at one extreme, and the aggressive, individualistic and self-emancipating Chinese Nora on the other. As I have argued, by re-presenting her female heroines as capable of laughter, Yang Jiang saves Junyu and Yanhua from the growing ranks of pathetic victims of patriarchy in modern Chinese literature portrayed as casualties of a misogynist culture. Yang Jiang also derides the superwomen who imply that female emancipation is simply a matter of romantic choice or an assertion of individual will. At the same time, these two plays are concerned with reexamining conventional male roles, particularly the capitalist patriarch and the modern romantic lover. Aside from the pure entertainment value of comedy, Yang uses it as a means of critiquing dominant inscriptions of gender, and for constructing a new kind of feminist laughter. As many critics have noted, comedy functions as a strategy of defamiliarization: that is, it jars the reader's sense of reality and throws into (comic) relief that which we assume to be true or natural or realistic. Although Yang Jiang's plays rely, as all good comedies do, upon clever use of language and intricately arranged scenarios, a good deal of Yang Jiang's comic strategy is to defamiliarize ways of dealing with the *funü wenti* as a way of injecting its still pertinent issues with new vitality.

* * *

DEMYSTIFYING MARRIAGE AND MOTHERHOOD

Much like Yang Jiang, Su Qing's comic style begins with a playful subversion of a well-known literary genre, in this case the prevalent genre of female autobiography. Described by Su Qing herself as a fictional autobiography *(zizhuanti xiaoshuo), Jiehun shinian* (1944) is constructed as a first-person narrative that chronicles the experience of a young college-educated woman Su Huaiqing in a disastrous decade-long marriage that eventually ends in divorce. Su Qing herself divorced her husband in 1944, supporting herself and three children on the income she earned writing, and these and other parallels with details in her novel fueled immediate speculation as to its factual basis. At a symposium of women writers later that same year, the author candidly acknowledged that certain material for the novel had indeed been drawn directly from her own life, but at the same time insisted that for the most part the story was purely fictional (*xugou de gushi*).[43]

Su Qing (born Feng Heyi in 1914), made her literary debut when her essay "Shengnan yu yunü" (Giving birth to a boy, giving birth to a girl) appeared in 1935 in *Lunyu* (The analects), the popular humor magazine run by Lin Yutang. A year earlier she had got married and withdrawn from her studies at National Central University in Nanjing to have her first child. The essay, reportedly written in an effort to alleviate the boredom of being cooped up at home, was a droll reflection on the Chinese family's obsessive preoccupation with male descendants.[44] A few months later *Lunyu's* editor Tao Kangde wrote to encourage her to submit her work to Lin Yutang's newly launched *Yuzhoufeng* (Cosmic wind), and over the next few years Su poured out a steady stream of humorous essays on topics ranging from contemporary female education to divorce to perming hair. Typical of the style of Lin Yutang and the "nonaligned" literature for which he and his protégés were known (and in leftist literary circles much maligned), her essay-writing assiduously eschews the serious and often self-righteous tone common to revolutionary literature of the day and instead muses on contemporary themes with wit and a sense of ironic detachment. After the outbreak of the Sino-Japanese war, Su Qing continued writing prolifically in this same vein, contributing to major Shanghai literary journals, including those associated with the Wang Jingwei regime such as *Gu Jin* (Reminiscences), *Fengyu tan* (Talks amid hardship) as well as *Zhonghua zhoukan* (China weekly). In 1943, she launched and began editing her own highly successful literary magazine, *Tiandi* (Heaven and earth), a venture that had the backing of several high level collaborationist city officials, including Chen Gongbo, the mayor of Shanghai from 1940–1944. (These connections, plus the fact that she accepted a cushy appointment in the Shanghai municipal government, would later be cited as evidence of Su Qing's reactionary crimes in the post-revolutionary era.) *Tiandi* featured work by Zhang Ailing, who had newly arrived on the Shanghai literary scene, as well as numerous other contemporary writers, though Su Qing also used *Tiandi* to showcase her own work: her essays appeared in virtually every issue until the magazine's demise in mid-1945 and she would also have the press issue several individual volumes of her work. In 1944, *Tiandi* issued a book version of *Jiehun shinian*, which had received an enthusiastic response from readers during its serialization the previous year in *Fengyu tan*. The novel was Su Qing's most successful creative work, and made her one of the most widely read authors in Shanghai in the 1940s.

In terms of both its central theme of modern marriage and the various narrative components of the story—a semi-old-fashioned marital arrangement, the heroine's conflict with conservative in-laws, a scoundrel of a husband, and the protagonist's frustrated desires for a meaningful vocation and economic autonomy—*Jiehun shinian* shares much in common with the autobiographies of other Chinese female intellectuals of her generation. But Su Qing defies the reader's expectations from the novel's first scene by introducing a satirical twist to this familiar story. The novel opens on the morning of the I-narrator's betrothal, and describes in detail the myriad rituals to which she is subjected over the course of the day, including of course the obligatory journey in a bridal sedan to the groom's home. Rather than depict such formalities as a traumatic ordeal that has been cruelly forced upon her against her volition, as was usually the case in twentieth-century women's autobiography,[45] however, the narrator admits that she was a willing participant who knowingly went through the motions. Described in a mildly self-mocking tone, the marital customs that were once so ardently contested by the May

Fourth generation here seem like so many ridiculous rituals, embarrassing and awkward to be sure, but certainly not cause for deep moral or personal offense. Strictly forbidden to get out of bed before the bridal sedan arrives, for instance, the narrator describes how in desperate need to relieve her bladder, she furtively urinates on the pillows. The dampness, as she cleverly calculates, will likely be mistaken for the tears of an unwilling bride.

Even more comical is her description of the custom of riding in the bridal sedan, a "privilege" that, according to village lore, was reserved for virgins (superstition had it that a non-virgin would be struck dead by the god of sedan chairs): although the narrator confesses her embarrassment over the incongruity of taking such a traditional mode of transport to the YMCA where the "modern" (*wenming*) wedding ceremony is to take place, she acquiesces lest her elderly mother imagine her reluctance is because she is not a virgin! And, on the wedding day itself, the scene of struggle that is so often represented in association with the bridal sedan is humorously revealed to be a completely staged event:

> After I was done dressing, the music started playing outside and my little brother came to carry me out to the bridal sedan. Apparently I was supposed to weep at that point to show that I didn't want to get in the sedan and that brother was forcing me to. But I didn't do this because I thought it wouldn't be fair to brother. The truth of the matter was, he wasn't forcing me at all to get into the sedan to get married. Nevertheless, he still had to abide by the custom of carrying me out, which so exhausted him that the veins on his forehead popped up and he gasped for breath as he lugged me out to the front of the carriage . . . (4)

The rest of the wedding day is recounted with equal amusement, down to the awkward first night together as husband and wife. Mistaking her performance as the traditional bashful bride for the real thing, her new husband keeps a respectful "modern" distance from her and thus, much to her dismay, the newlyweds pass a singularly uneventful evening!

To be sure, not all aspects of the narrator's ten-year-long marriage will be treated in such light-hearted terms. The profound frustration she is to experience as a young wife and mother, for example, surfaces in the narrative in ways that are more likely to have elicited pained chuckles of recognition from her readers than anything else. Whatever the comic register, however, the narrator assiduously avoids the sentimental and tragic modes so common to confessional May Fourth accounts of feminine experience by maintaining a cool sense of humor about herself and the story she is telling.

Interestingly, the ironic tone Su Qing adopts in *Jiehun shinian* in her portrait of a semi-modern woman's experience in marriage and motherhood proved too subtle for some readers and critics of her day. Unlike Yang Jiang, who was immediately hailed by her contemporaries as the second Ding Xilin and who has enjoyed an undisputed place in the comic tradition in modern Chinese drama since her "rediscovery" in the post-Mao era,[46] Su Qing's novel was labeled by influential critics in the postwar era as pornography, a stigma that it has never quite lived down, despite the strong defense Su Qing's contemporary Zhang Ailing mounted on her behalf at the time (and, more recently, by another Shanghai woman writer Wang Anyi).[47] The *Wenhui bao*, for instance, denounced the novel as pornography (*seqing duwu*) while the Shanghai magazine *Qianjin funü* (The progressive woman) branded Su Qing a "literary prostitute" (*wenji*), accusing her of "enslaving the minds of Shanghai women and numbing their consciousness of resistance, making people forget oppression and the bloodiness of reality."[48] According to Edward Gunn, one of the few western Sinologists who has evaluated Su Qing's writing in any depth, such blatant critical hostility toward her work (and Su Qing personally) stemmed from rumors of her romantic involvement with a leading collaborator in the Nanjing regime and of her own pro-Japanese sympathies.[49] Su Qing herself adamantly denied such charges in the preface to the sequel she wrote to *Jiehun shinian* in 1947 and defended the validity of the themes addressed in the novel.[50] To those who were of the opinion that anything less than virtual silence on the part of writers of the occupied territories had been tantamount to collusion, moreover, she also pointed out that as the sole bread-winner of her family writing was not a political choice but an economic necessity and a matter of personal survival. Gunn, who includes Su Qing as part his discussion of the "anti-romantic" trend in literature of this period, offers a more sympathetic and insightful reading of the novel; but he too ultimately appears to overlook a crucial dynamic of the text when he applauds Su Qing as "an accomplished writer in the style of *unaffected sincerity* [my emphases]."[51]

According to recent feminist studies of comedy, neither misreading is all that surprising, since women's comic voices have long been misinterpreted by the (male) literary critical establishment. Whether because of the stereotype that women lack a sense of humor or because women's humor often defies conventional definitions of what is deemed "funny," the comic elements of women's/feminist writing have frequently eluded critical detection. "A joke," one scholar reminds us, "depends on the teller and the told," and clearly what makes women laugh in a male-centered society may provoke a very different reaction from men.[52] One cannot help but wonder in this case how much Su Qing's mild caricatures of men and, in particular, the sacred institutions of marriage and motherhood may have had to do with the dismissive reactions (and later, conspicuous indifference) her work seemed to elicit from male critics.[53]

Much in the same way as Yang Jiang, Su Qing focuses her comic attention in *Jiehun shinian* not on the atrocities but on the absurdities of patriarchal culture. Both writers evince a highly cynical vision of male power and privilege, and suggest that when we look beneath its imposing veneer patriarchy is run—at least in part—by self-important buffoons, empty rhetoric, and highly dubious assumptions and values. But whereas Yang Jiang's laughter tends to concentrate on the modern gender roles assigned to men and woman, for Su Qing, it is the curious commingling of old and new conventions of gender that provides the opportunity to mock the follies of male domination and the fools who keep falling for them. Many of the patriarchal practices represented here appear ridiculously anachronistic and impractical, even as they continue out of sheer force of habit to exert influence over members of society.

Thus, far from the usual tearful confession of a disenchanted wife, this narrator's account of marital misadventure ripples with mocking laughter at the various "forces" with which she must battle—she laughs, for instance, at the silly antiquated customs that govern life in the quasi-Confucian family she marries into, the ludicrous misogyny of her parents-in-law, the excruciating banality of the domesticity expected of her, as a childbearer and housewife, and the bogus authority of her husband. Bakhtin once wrote that "laughter demolishes fear and piety before an object"[54] and here I would suggest that the aim of Su Qing's satirical style is precisely to deride, and thereby diminish, the already dwindling authority of traditional structures (both practices and rhetoric) of male domination. She does this not through a full-fledged carnivalesque vision of a new social (dis)order with women on top, however, but through the narrator's relentlessly irreverent treatment of the values, manners, and mores of the prevailing gender order.

This comic subversion is perhaps best exemplified in Su Qing's treatment of one of the novel's central themes: namely, the narrator's experience of motherhood. Early on in her marriage the narrator is confronted with the age-old assumption that her primary duty as a wife and daughter-in-law is to produce a male heir to carry on her *husband*'s family line (*ta de zong ta de dai*). That she fails to give birth to the requisite male offspring the first time, and the next, and the time after eventually leads to the narrator/protagonist's ostracism from the family; it also, as a recurring pattern in the novel, comically underscores the Confucian family's obsession with male progeny. But the narrator's humor extends not just to the traditional preference for sons over daughters, but to conventional views of motherhood itself. In particular, she satirizes the way the cultural preoccupation with (patri)lineage itself reduces women to a merely utilitarian, reproductive function, valuable to the family only in the way a particulaly useful machine or prized livestock might be.

During her first pregnancy, this can be seen in the way Su's body— particularly the size and shape of the region "from her belly to her feet" (58)— becomes the object of intense scrutiny and discussion as observers anxiously try to ascertain whether or not she'll give birth to a son. For Su, of course, having only recently returned from college herself where she was accustomed to being the subject, not target, of examination, this sudden reversal of roles is quite disconcerting. And when her mother-in-law arrives at the crucial affirmative verdict, based on the supposedly revealing contour of Su's stomach and the firmness of her belly-button, her body also suddenly becomes the object of intense devotion. Consider, for example, how the narrator describes the excessive attention now lavished upon her by her husband's parents, who fatten her up in anticipation of the birth of their grandson:

> After Xian left, my parents-in-law treated me exceedingly well. Everyday they would prepare my food, tendons of pork, stewed duck, carp broth, anxiously

feeding me like a little Buddha. When it was time to eat and the dishes had
been brought to the table, my father-in-law would announce, "This is to enrich
your blood," and then my mother-in-law would move them all in front of me
so I wouldn't have to reach and accidentally shift his umbilical cord. (46)

Needless to say, the special attention Su receives comes to an abrupt halt
when she gives birth to a girl (so much so that she undergoes hunger with-
drawals), another reversal that seems to underscore her utter lack of value to
the family except as a producer of male heirs.

The image of the maternal body as simply a medium for breeding (boy)
babies surfaces in even balder terms when her husband takes charge of her
diet upon the birth of their third daughter. Whereas previously Su had been
strictly forbidden to breast-feed (another instance of her own lack of control
over her maternal body), her husband now adopts a different view on the
subject and insists that she do so. When Su fails to lactate, he attempts to
take control: "Xian would often buy things for me to eat, although he wasn't
interested in what they tasted like, just their nutritional value. He believed
they would improve my breast milk, increasing both its quantity and quality"
(188). That she has neither the appetite nor the inclination to consume these
endless treats is irrelevant, and he even grow impatient when his measures
fail to achieve the desired effect: "One day he said to me quite unhappily,
"How is it that you've been eating so much yet you're still not producing
any milk? Your body, however, keeps getting fatter and fatter—what a selfish
mother you are!" (188).

By bluntly portraying motherhood as simply a physical service expected of
women, a process whereby the female body is usurped as a "tool" (*gongju*,
79) of the patriarchal family, Su Qing taps into what Bergson describes as
one of the key comic tropes: namely, by projecting an image of "something
mechanical encrusted on something living."[55] As Bergson explains in his
famous essay on comedy, "[t]he attitudes, gestures and movements of the
human body are laughable in exact proportion as that body reminds us of a
mere machine." Ultimately of course the target of the author's parody here
is not the maternal body *per se* but the traditional institution of motherhood
that renders women into such ridiculous automatons.

Another specific problem Su Qing explores as part of her comic critique
of traditional motherhood is the threat women's reproductive roles pose to
female sexuality. Perhaps to deflect the conservative opposition such a
"risque" topic of discourse might provoke, but also clearly to challenge the
very taboo against expressing views on sexuality, Su Qing tackles the question of female sexual desire from a humorous perspective.[56] For example,
when the young narrator comes to realize not long after her wedding that
she has been brought into the family essentially as good breeding stock and
that her husband is romantically involved with another (much prettier)
woman, she defiantly heads back to college in Shanghai, declaring the marriage annulled and vowing never to return. Treating the fiasco more as a
minor mishap than a major tragedy, she even manages to muster a sense of

humor about what she has gotten in lieu of the honeymoon she obviously anticipated:

> Before, my understanding of love was quite vague; I didn't know how to love or what love was like, though now I understood it completely. I wanted a young, handsome, passionate man with whom I could snuggle up every night. We would have no need to talk since our hearts, souls and bodies would be like one, joined in an eternal embrace. But in reality here I was now sleeping alone in a lonely dormitory with nothing but a big empty bed around me. It took me a long time to drift off to sleep in the dark as a number of bedbugs crawled up through the cracks in the bed onto my pillow to give me furtive kisses on my neck and ears. (30)

Couched skillfully in comic imagery in this passage is a rather bold acknowledgment of the narrator's sexual desire. Indeed, the joke about the amorous bedbugs is funny precisely because of the contrast they offer to what she actually longs for—a lover with whom to share her bed. Ultimately, however, the comical disparity between her erotic desires and the present reality captured in this passage also foreshadows the disappointment that lies in store for the narrator in her marriage.

Full of newly awakened sexual desire and believing herself to be a free woman, the ex-"newlywed" at this point proceeds to pursue an affair with Yang Qimin, a mild-mannered engineering student she notices one day at the college library. While not exactly the Adonis of Su's fantasies, the feelings he arouses in her are enough to distract her from the Chaucer she is reading and before long the two begin spending all their time together. But storybook romance has no place in the cynical vision of this author and thus it comes as little surprise that the relationship is derailed by what proves to be an unsurmountable obstacle in the heroine's path to happiness: Su finds out that, as a result of her short-lived conjugal relationship, she is pregnant. Still, what in earlier fiction would have been an occasion for much mental anguish, here becomes an occasion to laugh cynically at the limited abilities and options of the two lovers.[57] For example, when Su, assuming her new boyfriend to be distraught by the revelation, tries to console him, she clearly over-estimates the impact of the news: " 'You won't . . . will you?' I stammered. He answered very candidly 'I definitely won't hate you.' 'No' I continued, 'What I meant was you . . . you won't kill yourself, will you?' 'Why would I kill myself?' He started laughing loudly, which at once terrified and mortified me" (41). More serious perhaps than his "failure" to become suicidal, Yang Qiming does little to help Su (who secretly contemplates having an abortion) avoid returning to her so-called husband and in fact only accelerates that process by supplying her with books on pregnancy and childbirth.

Although the narrator's maternal urges, coupled with a seeming lack of other viable options, send her back to the husband she doesn't love, the immense cost of her brief sexual encounter with him is not lost on her. Reflecting sarcastically on the marriage in which she became trapped as a result of that brief encounter, the narrator comments: "Marriage really was no fun at all—in terms of our feelings, we were still far apart; as far as our sexual relationship, it was over in a flash, less than ten minutes cost me ten months of pregnancy and ten years of suffering raising children" (57). While Su Qing laughs bitterly at the devastating consequences of sex for women during an era when neither birth-control nor abortion were readily available, she also demystifies the role of sex in marriage, mocking in particular the way women resort to using sex as an instrument of power. For instance, as much as Su detests her husband, her financial dependence on him requires her to calculate carefully: "on the one hand I wanted to just please him, but then again I was scared of getting pregnant; but on the other hand, if I didn't satisfy him I was afraid someone else would. It wasn't that I loved him, but I certainly didn't want him to love someone else!" (77).

Throughout the novel, Su Qing also deploys comedy to explore the neo-conservative notion that women's proper place is in the domestic sphere. Through a number of humorous domestic debacles highlighting the heroine's utter lack of interest and aptitude for housekeeping, for instance, the narrative quickly debunks the myth that becoming a housewife is somehow the most natural or meaningful vocation available to the modern woman. Characteristically, rather than stridently attack the prevailing system by creating an insurgent heroine who mutinies against the bonds of marriage and family, Su Qing takes more of a Swiftian tack to the problem, offering preposterous solutions to the troubles in contemporary marriage and relationships between women and men that work to throw into relief the limits of conventional feminine gender roles. Reflecting on the current trend of high divorce rates in Chinese society in a postscript to the novel, for instance, the narrator draws an obviously ironic conclusion about competent women. The passage is worth quoting in full to capture its mocking undertone:

> I believe that men don't really mind if their wife is vulgar or boring; they don't mind if she's a spendthrift and they can even put up with her if she's somewhat ugly. But what they do mind is if she's competent and stronger than they are. According to general social belief, women are supposed to be weaker than men, or at the very least they should pretend to be so. An incredibly healthy woman seems like an insult to men, and there isn't a single man who would publicly admit that he is physically weaker than his wife. This is why the sickly beauty Lin Daiyu inevitably garnered people's sympathy and love while the sturdy Baochai never caught people's fancy. It's alright for a woman to be intelligent but she must not be competent. She might be forgiven if she's competent in domestic matters, but if she displays her talent in a public career it'll make men shake their heads and sigh. In addition, women must not have any scholarly achievements, because most men don't have any and they hate it when their wives are able to discuss things with more brilliance than themselves. Of course the men who really do have intelligence aren't scared of their wives being competent but this category of men doesn't seem to be very big. Therefore it's better for a woman to be a little bit shallow. (231)

Obviously tongue-in-cheek, this commentary is not an endorsement of the prevailing order but an ironic indictment of the cultural prescriptions of feminine inferiority.

Throughout the novel the narrator mocks the contemporary gender roles assigned to both women and men as scripts—a strategy that, for one thing, negates the conservative assumption that female and male behavior derives from natural or inherent gender attributes. Early on in the novel, for instance, the I-narrator laughs at the lengths to which she goes to conform to masculinist ideals, doing her best to play the subordinate role expected of her by, for example, hiding from her husband Xian the fact that she has both intellectual interests and literary ambitions. Indeed, despite having discovered that her true calling lies in writing and that she could make a career of it, she nevertheless struggles to maintain the appearance of a devoted housewife. The reason she does this, aside from her vague need for social approval, is to protect her husband's sense of pride. According to the narrator, he believed "that a man with ambition would rather work himself to the bone earning money for his wife to spend, even if it's only to play mah-jongg, than to have a wife who seemed more competent than him" (143). In time, as Xian grows suspicious about Su's secretive literary activities, he attempts to undermine her projects by confiscating the daily newspaper that is delivered to their home, jealously safeguarding it under his pillow each morning and then taking it with him to work, even though he himself is not in the habit of reading the paper. Still, in a funny spin on the battle of the sexes, Su still doesn't confront him about it but simply outwits him by sneaking money from the grocery budget to buy her own. In public, the narrator also reports, she plays the stereotypical dumb wife, even though this means concealing her true intellect: "I understood him and knew that to get on his good side I had to ask him ridiculously childish questions. Proudly, he would show off by explaining everything to me. Sometimes he would seem even more ridiculous than me, but I still had to pretend as though I were utterly convinced by everything he said" (144). The patriarchal myth that women are inferior intellectual beings is here debunked as a preposterous lie, a charade that women themselves often go along with simply to stroke the sensitive male ego

Women of course are not the only ones who "perform," as Judith Butler would say, their respective gender roles.[58] As the narrator wryly observes, her husband's masculine bravado is also a bogus act that has more to do with the image of authority he wants to project than a reflection of his "real" self. After years of eking out a living as a teacher, Chongxian finally decides to change careers and become a lawyer. In the process he also radically makes over his self-image, now parading around with affected air of erudition:

Now, he'd taken to decking himself out in a long Chinese style black robe. Even when he wore a western suit, as he used to, he would choose one that was big and plain, and for no reason whatsoever perch a pair of tortoise-rim eye-glasses on his nose, put a pipe in his mouth, and carry around a walking stick.

> I thought: why does he goes to so much trouble? Chongxian would always be
> Chongxian. Did he think people would change their opinion of him with an
> act like this . . .? (187)

The narrator's ability to laugh at her pretentious husband ultimately empowers her to extricate herself from her unhappy marriage, something which sets her far apart from the long-suffering heroines of May Fourth culture.[59] She too is a victim of male chauvinism—as much of a buffoon as she reveals him to be, we also learn that her husband beats her, cheats on her, and maintains the upper hand in their marriage with constant economic threats. But through its subtle humor, the narrative refuses to grant the figure of the patriarch the status of an omnipotent power capable of dictating, let alone destroying, the heroine's life. By the same token, the narrative also underscores the points showing that male power is merely a posture, a pathetic con that the narrator can easily see through. In both ways, the text exposes an ironic disparity between the pretense of patriarchy and its present reality, thus affording the reader a critical distance from which to judge the problem of contemporary women's struggles.

Finally, much in the same way Yang Jiang's female characters introduced a new, namely comic, heroine to Chinese literature, Su Qing's narrator possesses a self-irony that undercuts the romantic female identity popularized in the fiction of previous decades. In both cases, these characters seem to reflect a new level of self-confidence that enables them to laugh, even at themselves. Neither a heroic rebel nor pathetic victim, Su Qing's narrator presents herself as just an ordinary woman with fairly ordinary foibles. On occasion, when she catches herself slipping into the mode of self-aggrandizement she finds so pretentious in her husband, she does not hesitate to poke fun at herself. For example, when her first essay is accepted for publication, she describes self-mockingly how she strutted down the street thinking how awestruck the public must be upon seeing her, the "woman writer." Eventually, it *is* her writing that affords the I-narrator (like Su Qing herself in real life) a ticket out of her miserable marriage, enabling her to take what was still a radical step for a woman in the 1940s and divorce her good-for-nothing husband. In her typical under-stated way, however, writing is presented more as an expedient way to make a living than a grand emancipatory action.

Edward Gunn has argued that what makes this novel so effective as a critique of contemporary gender relations is precisely the "conventional" identity of the central protagonist; I agree with this assessment but would add that its force derives in large part from the fact that the narrator does not exempt herself from the system she indicts. Unlike the self-righteous narrators so often encountered in twentieth century Chinese literature, and the moral high ground they claim in denouncing the cruel injustice of contemporary society, this narrator scornfully laughs at her foibles and her own duplicity in perpetuating the system. Nor does Su Qing's narrator simply blame male domination for her predicament but, from the beginning, faults her own stupidity for having fallen for its ruses. The suggestion, ultimately, is that she should have known better than to be duped by the bogus myths and lies that prop it up.

After having muddled through ten years of marriage, the narrator finally has grounds for a divorce when her husband has an extramarital affair with one of her close friends. Funnily enough, she discovers his infidelity not long after giving birth to the son he and his family have long awaited. The shocking news, which she reports to her father-in-law in a letter, proves too much for the old man, who dies before he has a chance to even see the grandson who will carry on his name. The novel ends, however, not on this dark note of comic revenge but on an exaggerated upbeat tone as the narrator finds a new lease on life through a friendship with a woman doctor and the legal divorce from her husband. In some ways, the ending seems to mock the traditional comic ending. For what is celebrated here is of course not the union or consummation of heterosexual love, but liberation from a bond that brought little joy to begin with. Nor does Su Qing give in to convention by allowing the heroine to find meaning in a budding romance elsewhere: despite having dangled just such a possibility at the beginning of the novel in the figure of Yang Qimin (the narrator's college sweetheart), no such *deus ex machina* is to be found in the resolution of the novel.

The postscript that Su Qing appended to the novel when it was published in book form in 1944 sheds further light on the "forgiving" tone some critics have claimed characterizes its ending.[60] Delivered in a deadpan manner that invites the reader to reject the statement at face value, the author offers the following commentary on the divorce her heroine has finally achieved: "Actually neither the female nor male protagonist in the book are bad people, and there was actually no reason why they had to get divorced; but today's social environment makes it too easy for young people to divorce, and so they did" (232). Although it is certainly true that the novel eschews unsavory villains of the sort that populate May Fourth narratives of women's oppression in marriage, the novel's critical exposé of that institution flatly belies this assessment of the ultimate demise of Su's marriage. Of her heroine, the author/narrator concludes with the final cynical remark about the no-win situation for contemporary women: "After this I don't believe it will get any better for her. Women born in today's world are really tragic. For them it's no use getting married, but it's no use not getting marred either; getting married and then getting divorced is no use, but getting married and not getting divorced is no use either . . ." (230).

* * *

To conclude this chapter, I turn finally to the work of the most well-known woman writer to emerge as a powerful new literary voice in Shanghai during the Japanese occupation era. I refer, of course, to Zhang Ailing (Eileen Chang, 1920–1995).[61] Unlike her contemporaries Yang Jiang and Su Qing, writers who have received minimal attention within mainstream literary history,

Zhang Ailing's essays and fiction have long been deemed by critics to rank among the "great" works of modern Chinese literature. C.T. Hsia, for example, reserved his highest praise for Zhang in his pioneering study *A History of Modern Chinese Fiction* (1961) dubbing her the "most important" writer of twentieth-century China. Of Zhang's fiction, the work most typically cited as evidence of her literary genius and illustrative of her signature vision of "desolation" (*cangliang*) is *Jinsuoji* (The golden cangue, 1943). A grim tale with gothic undercurrents, this brilliant novella delves into the warped world of an old-style Confucian family to divulge the terrible toll it exacts on several of its female members.[62] In a reading that emphasizes the feminist implications of this disturbing tragedy, Lim Chin-chown writes that Zhang's "gloomy and bleak narrative style reflects the manner in which the female Self is repressed within the prison of Confucian femininity, where each woman dwells within her personal 'Iron Boudoir.' "[63]

What I would like to briefly examine here, however, is a significant countercurrent within Zhang's narrative approach to Confucian femininity, one which partakes of a far more detached, cynical style in exploring the constraints on women in Chinese society. Like Yang Jiang and Su Qing, Zhang tends not to envision sweeping social changes for women but, in some of her creative writing, relies on subtle comic techniques to articulate the gaps and weaknesses in the everyday patriarchal order. Here, my discussion focuses on a work published a few months prior to her classic *Jinsuoji*, Zhang's hugely popular 1943 novella "Qingcheng zhi lian" (City toppling love/Love in a fallen city). If Cai Qiqiao would come to symbolize the tragic self-annihilation of the Confucian woman, the heroine of this work, Bai Liusu, represents the resilience and resourcefulness of a woman who refuses to succumb to such a fate. An attractive divorcee, Bai Liusu flouts family pressure to return to the home of her (now deceased) husband to fulfill her "proper" duties as a widow, embarks on a risky romance with an overseas Chinese playboy and, through a combination of subtle calculation and circumstance, lands herself a new husband by the end of the story. Rather than cast the narrative in the emancipatory rhetoric of female sexual liberation, however, Zhang parodies the traditional paradigm of the *femme-fatale* to produce an ironic tale of modern female desire.

The title itself establishes the initial connection between Liusu and the age-old motif of the *femme-fatale* from classical Chinese literature: the "*qingcheng*," or city-toppler, from the stock phrase "*qingcheng qingguo*" describing a woman of exceeding beauty and sensual allure, recalls ancient tales of havoc wreaked upon kingdoms and dynasties by the alleged power of feminine sexuality.[64] In the popular fiction tradition, the sexually active *femme-fatale's* path of destruction often extended only as far as her own family or the lives of men she encounters but the underlying lesson is always the same: women who openly express desire constitute a destabilizing force, a threat to the moral and social order itself.[65]

Zhang Ailing further invites the reader to identify her heroine as a modern-day *femme-fatale* by specifically aligning the character with the most famous traditional "kingdom-toppler" of them all, Yang Guifei, the legendary beauty popularly implicated in the upheaval and near collapse of the Tang dynasty in the eighth century. Immortalized in Bo Zhuyi's famous poem *Changhen ge* ("Song of everlasting pain"), Yang Guifei's fateful seduction of the Tang emperor Xuanzong is achieved in large part through the erotic "foreign" dances she was said to have performed for him, thus causing him to neglect the affairs of state: "Songs so slow and stately dances / notes sustained on flutes and strings / and all day long the king and lord / could never take his fill." In Zhang's story, dancing similarly constitutes a key strategy in Liusu's panoply of physical charms, a skill which the narrator subtly links to the past: "As she performed in the mirror, the *huqin* no longer sounded like a *huqin*, but like the strings and flute intoning a solemn court dance. She turned toward the right a few steps, then turned again to the left. Her steps seemed to trace the lost rhythms of an ancient melody" (67). And significantly, foreign-style dancing proves to be precisely the talent that helps Liusu first capture the attentions of Fan Liuyuan, an eligible overseas Chinese bachelor who represents her ticket out of the stifling circumstances in which she finds herself at the beginning of the story. Part of an entourage of chaperons on an introductory date between the younger Bai sister and the worldly playboy, Liusu happens to be the only one sufficiently skilled to dance with Liuyuan at the nightclub they visit. This naturally provokes the disapproval of Liusu's relatives (who, predictably, already blame the divorcee for the family's declining fortunes), but soon it also procures her an invitation to Hong Kong where the romance will unfold.

The historical setting of this romance—in Hong Kong as the glittering city falls to Japanese forces during World War II—provides yet another obvious reference to the paradigmatic *femme-fatale* narrative. A figure of excess and transgression, the sexualized woman traditionally stood at once as the physical manifestation of and the causal force behind historical upheaval. *Shuihu zhuan* (Water margin), for instance, the classical novel strewn with dozens of memorably wicked women, including the conniving temptress Pan Jinlian, takes place during the chaotic and corrupt reign of the Song dynasty emperor Hui Zong. Female sexuality in this narrative represents the primary obstacle, and hence object of intense resistance and eventual expulsion, in the heroes' quest for a new (masculine) order. In early-twentieth-century fiction, the powerful correlation between sociopolitical decline and the figure of the erotic woman resurfaced, perhaps not surprisingly in light of the tumultuous events of this historical era. Of particular note is Mao Dun's 1933 novel *Ziye* (Midnight), a narrative that draws heavily on the imagery of erotic femininity to denote the moral and social bankruptcy of a decadent and capitalist Shanghai. In that novel, characters like the bewitching Xu Manli and Liu Yuying, who unleash the passions of men around them, epitomize the depraved indifference and greed of the contemporary city.

But Zhang Ailing's overt allusions to the *femme-fatale* motif work against this profoundly patriarchal construct, uncovering its disturbing logic. By conspicuously juxtaposing the mundane romance of an ordinary woman with the major historical calamity that befell Hong Kong in 1941, the narrative clearly (and rather cleverly) underscores the utter lack of causality between the two. There is, as Rey Chow remarks on Zhang's literary technique in general, an "incongruity between the details and what they are supposed to describe."[66] For all her trappings as a *femme-fatale*, Liusu is hardly the embodiment of moral depravity that must be overcome by a patriotic hero (in this case, the male protagonist Bai Liuyuan exhibits no political ambitions whatsoever), and even less the cause in the narrative of the downfall of the Chinese nation. In fact, her romantic pursuits pose no threat to family or the social order, but are in the end merely an expedient means of personal survival.

While Zhang Ailing refuses to implicate feminine sexuality in historical disorder, she does represent it as a source of personal agency for her heroine: it is through the careful manipulation of her erotic appeal (her sole remaining asset after her brothers squander her savings) that Liusu is able to escape her restrictive life in the Bai residence and the insecurity of life as a divorcee. As if to foreshadow the seduction that lies ahead, we first find Liusu smiling a "private, malevolent smile" (67) after gazing at herself in the mirror. But Zhang plays on conventional expectation here too: far from a steamy seduction, the heroine quickly perceives that what Liuyuan is after is, as he puts it, "a genuine Chinese woman," and so she performs accordingly. On a flirtatious evening stroll with Liuyuan in Hong Kong, for example, she plays along with his yearning for a "spiritual" confidante, all the while keenly aware of her appearance: "She leaned her head toward him, and answered softly, 'I do understand, I do.' But while comforting him, she thought of her moonlit face. That dedicate profile, her eyes, her brow, all of an irrational, ethereal beauty. She slightly bowed her head" (77). Ironically, then, the only feminine wiles here are those that furnish her image as a demure maiden.

Critics have often commented on Zhang Ailing's thoroughly cynical vision of "civilization." In a summary of Zhang's fictional world, Zhang Yingjin, for instance, notes "It is 'a dead world' concealed by the 'black curtains,' 'a place without light,'or a pure presence of desolation and darkness."[67] Certainly, "Qingcheng zhi lian" is devoid of the optimistic faith in the historical progress that is to deliver China to a new era that other contemporary fiction evinces; in fact, what the narrative details accentuate is the inability of the heroine to look ahead toward any future whatsoever: metaphors of broken clocks, feelings of being trapped in the past, and references to blocked vision all reinforce a sense of the heroine's distance from the flow of historical change—and the bleak image of "desolation" much of Zhang's writing is said to evoke.

But this particular novella also ends with a classic comic reversal, one which may reveal something new about Zhang's fascination with destruction. In the end Liusu does not, as the author herself stresses, develop into a "revolutionary woman" to participate in saving China from historical calamity;[68] on the contrary, the calamity saves her. After several rounds of delicate (and not always successful) maneuvers to win Liuyuan's heart, Liusu appears to have settled for the prize of becoming his mistress—a better option than Confucian widowhood, but still short of the solid victory of marriage for which she had aimed. It is at this very moment, however, that the Japanese forces attack Hong Kong, forcing Liuyuan to delay his return to England. Amid the ruin and upheaval of the fallen city the lovers are finally forced (or freed) to strip away their insincere facades and, if only temporarily, expose their true feelings for each other. The real revelation of the story (and the second more literal meaning of the title) is thus the following: it is not the passionate love emanating from the beautiful woman that produces social upheaval, but rather social upheaval that produces the conditions for passionate love.

Whether or not this is simply another joke on Zhang Ailing's part (is there room in her cynical vision for a belief in true romance?) is uncertain: what is certain is that the experience finally convinces Liuyuan to marry Liusu. Hence, for Liusu the surrounding turmoil is not cause for mental anguish, guilt, or trauma, as it would be in a more patriotic literary text, but rather offers a rare window of opportunity to improve the circumstances of her life. She is, in short, a woman whose desire is fulfilled *because* of the temporary social disorder and displacement that reign due to China's historical crisis of the 1930s and 1940s.

In foregrounding the unexpected reversal of fortune of her heroine against the backdrop of national "tragedy," Zhang Ailing's fictional narrative proposes an interestingly feminist view of historiography, one which uses gender to challenge the notion of History as a singular, objective narrative of change. The story shows how the meaning of particular historical events, in this case the Japanese invasion of Hong Kong in 1941, is open to multiple interpretations. From the point of view of our heroine, for instance, what might seem a moment of national chaos and disorder paradoxically offers a glimpse of personal liberation.

Interestingly, the same may be said of Zhang Ailing's extraordinary literary success itself during the 1940s, as indeed the critic Ke Ling once pointed out. Commenting on the dominant political trends in modern Chinese literature in the twentieth century (the anti-imperialist/antifeudal mission of May Fourth literature, the literature of class struggle in the 1930s, and the patriotic resistance literature of the war period) he writes: "[Even] in such a big literary world, there was not one phase which would have accommodated a Zhang Ailing: only the occupation of Shanghai gave her the opportunity . . . With Heaven high above and the Emperor far away, this provided Zhang Ailing with the stage on which to distinguish herself."[69]

In a broader sense, it could be said that the historical interlude covered in this inquiry as a whole—from the end of the traditional imperial order to the eve of the People's Republic—provided the conditions of disorder that made possible the feminist imaginings of all of the women writers I have examined. For it was within that very moment of breakdown of established cultural assumptions and practices (the ingrained modes of reality Qiu Jin once named the "darkness") that new feminine scripts could emerge in life and in literature. And only by understanding the conditions of that emergence will we fully appreciate such literature and the central importance of women's creative and historical struggle in producing it.

CHAPTER 5

A WORLD STILL TO WIN

It's really not surprising that women don't care for history. They don't know how many of their commendable heroic accomplishments there are in history, and they don't know how to find themselves in a history that has submerged women. It's as though women's history has been artificially severed, in the history books, in museums, and in people's minds.

Li Xiaojiang (1993)

Most scholars tend to agree that the nascent feminist literary imaginary that had begun to animate the public cultural arena in the first half of the twentieth century languished with the advent and consolidation of Communist rule after 1949. The contradictory demands that the women of "New China" faced and the stubborn tenacity of patriarchal behaviors in the post-liberation era tended to be concealed beneath the emergent socialist iconography of muscular iron maidens (*tie guniang*) and happy peasant women. Dissident intellectual and creative voices offering (or who might well have offered) notions of womanhood, sexuality, or a gendered modernity that deviated from the prescribed socialist ideal were discouraged, if not altogether silenced, by the newly installed regime. Meanwhile, official state institutions (chief among them, the All-China Women's Federation, or *Fulian*) charged with the mandate of representing women's interests to some degree seem to have contributed to women's on-going oppression by undermining their gendered awareness and agency. Li Xiaojiang, a leading figure in contemporary Mainland Chinese women's studies circles (*funü yanjiu*) makes the case that party-state control of women's issues throughout the Maoist era stunted the growth of women's political self-consciousness and fostered a debilitating dependence on the part of women such that egalitarian policies could be (and indeed often were) easily rescinded whenever it suited the needs and interests of the state.[1] Mayfair Yang suggests that despite its professed commitment to the tenets of gender equalitarianism, the party-state's dominant discourse on liberated women in the post-49 period bred a dangerous disjunction between rhetoric and reality: so conspicuously did socialist public culture promote the ideals of female equality through slogans and media images that when women did encounter discrimination in the workplace or home, it was often difficult to explain or articulate their lived experience.[2] And Lydia Liu, among others, has noted that the CCP's formal ideology of gender was to a large degree premised on a false egalitarianism, insofar as women were expected to conform to a male standard (all the while continuing to fulfill normative domestic and familial roles).[3] Women's feminist consciousness appears to be making something of a comeback in the post-Mao reform era, fueled by the new rise of women's studies in Chinese academia and non-government organizations (NGOs), and as eased restrictions on political and aesthetic expression in general once again make it possible for literary intellectuals to resurrect explicitly gendered themes and restore womanhood as a dynamic site of ideological contestation and debate. But even so, as contemporary commentators note, the dominant Maoist discourse on women's liberation has left behind a complex legacy for Chinese feminism today.

Indeed, because of this legacy, rather than gloss over the Maoist years as a protracted hiatus in the history of Chinese feminism, it is imperative that we continue the work of historical and literary historical excavation and interrogation. The point is not to absolve the CCP from responsibility of having co-opted women's causes for ulterior political ends, or to downplay the contradictions women experienced under the Maoist gender order. Rather, it is to acknowledge that the revolutionary past is relevant to our understanding of the present and that there are a number of interesting and potentially significant questions that remain unanswered, especially when it comes to the literary realm. For example: what actually became of veteran feminist writers and cultural activists in the post-49 era? With the advent of "state feminism," and in particular the *Fulian*, to what extent did culture remain a viable site for the production and maintenance of new knowledges of gender? Is it possible to discern any continuities with feminist cultural practices of the pre-socialist era? For instance, how does the genre of personal narrative and memoir featured in the *Fulian*-sponsored magazines such as *Xin Zhongguo funü* (New Chinese women, later simply *Zhongguo funü*) compare with women's self-writings of the previous decades? And finally, can we detect a feminist strain in women's creative literary output from the post-revolutionary period and, if so, what kinds of rhetorical and aesthetic strategies characterize it? In the literary production during this period, did women ever represent themselves in ways that deviated from the orthodoxy?

I want to use these questions to suggest potential avenues of inquiry for future research that uses these as starting points. The underlying premise, however, is that the notion of a state-controlled gender discourse that became immediately fixed and all-pervasive in the post-49 period warrants further scrutiny. In this concluding chapter, three specific examples are accordingly examined as preliminary evidence that feminism did not simply disappear from the map of liberation after 1949. First, I look briefly at the official journal sponsored by the national Women's Federation, *Zhongguo funü*, drawing in part on new historical evidence that reveals that far from passively transmitting Party policy, the early *Fulian* actively sought to carve out (both in terms of the activities it conducted and in its mass media) a semi-autonomous space in which to debate and analyze women's issues. As far as this specific magazine is concerned, in the early fifties ideological disagreements were apparently tolerated, competing viewpoints welcomed, and the articulated agenda was *not* necessarily always in complete alignment with that of the CCP.[4] Next, I consider the "propaganda" narratives generated for the purpose of promulgating the 1950 Marriage Law in the Chinese countryside, the *Fulian*'s first major national initiative. And finally, looking beyond the official parameters of state feminism, I comment on three remarkable autobiographical novels by veteran feminist writers Chen Xuezhao (1906–1991), Wang Ying (1915–1974), and Yang Gang (1905–1957), each of which is marked by a desire on the part of the author to write her-story (back) into the history of the Chinese Revolution.

* * *

Founded in April of 1949, the initial aim of the All-China Democratic Women's Federation ("democratic" subsequently being dropped from its official name in 1957) was to recruit and unite the great many women intellectuals, social activists, and grassroots organizers who had been engaged in feminist-related work prior to Liberation.[5] A major organizational meeting had convened a month earlier in Beijing, when members of the CCP-led Preparatory Committee met with delegates from other leading (nonsocialist) women's associations. In attendance were delegations representing both the Young Women's Christian Association (*Zhonghua jidujiao nü qingnianhui*) and the Women's Christian Temperance Union of China (*Zhonghua funü jiezhihui*), two major philanthropic organizations long committed to advancing women's interests, having been established in 1890 and 1925, respectively. Both groups would become charter members of the *Fulian* at its inception.[6] Representatives from the relatively younger Women's Friendship Association (*Zhongguo funü lianyi hui*), founded in 1945 as a united front organization for progressive middle- and upper-class urban women, were also in attendance.

Interestingly, in terms of individual members, in addition to high-profile veteran cadres from the CCP leadership, a number of well-known seasoned intellectuals also became affiliated with the *Fulian* in the early years of its existence. Ding Ling, for instance, who had been an outspoken critic of the rampant male chauvinism at Yan'an, was evidently considered a key figure of the new state agency, perhaps lending credibility to the organization in the eyes of educated urban women who would have been familiar with her name. Official documents from the first Congress cite her biography alongside those of Deng Yingzhao (1904–1992), Cai Chang (1900–1990), and He Xiangning (1878–1972) and proudly applaud her contributions to the Chinese women's movement.[7] Other prominent veteran cultural activists with ties to the *Fulian* in the early post-liberation period include, for example:

- Shen Zijiu (1898–1989) who (as the reader may recall) had been a central figure in the running of the Shanghai-based Women's Bookstore in the 1930s as well as the founding editor of *Funü shenghuo* (1935–1941), an influential progressive women's publication at the time. Having returned from Singapore in 1948, in time to take part in the preparatory work for the *Fulian*, Shen was recruited to direct the Federation's Propaganda and Education section (with Luo Qiong as her deputy director).[8] In this capacity, she was to serve simultaneously as the editor-in-chief of the organization's central mouthpiece, *Xin Zhongguo funü* (f. 1949; later renamed *Zhongguo funü*) from 1949–1956.
- Liu-Wang Liming (1897–1970) was a prominent nonpartisan social activist who had been involved in feminist circles in Shanghai from the 1920s. Prior to 1949, her accomplishments included serving as the secretary-general of the Chinese Women's Christian Temperance Union, founding the progressive women's magazine *Nüsheng*, and authoring one of the first comprehensive histories of Chinese feminism (*Zhongguo funü yundong*, 1933). Liu was appointed to the standing committee of the *Fulian* in 1949, among other important positions.[9]
- Zhang Xiuyan (1901–1968), an early member of the Chinese Communist Party who organized women and female students in Tianjin in the 1930s. At that time, she worked for two feminist publications, *Funü yuandi* (Women's garden) and *Tianjin funü* (Tianjin women), and collaborated on the first translation of Bebel's *Women and Society*. On the eve of the founding of the People's Republic in 1949, she took part in the preparatory work for the *Fulian* and was later appointed as a member of the standing committee.
- Du Junhui (1904–1981), who had made a name for herself publishing articles and translations on *funü wenti* topics in the post-May Fourth era. In 1934, she worked alongside Shen Zijiu editing *Funü yuandi*, a supplement to *Shenbao* Daily, in which she also published a well-received series of articles on the Chinese women's movement. The following year, again with Shen, she helped launch the magazine *Funü shenghuo*. Du attended the first national congress of the *Fulian* in Beijing in 1949 as an alternate member of the Executive committee.
- Lu Jingqing (1907–1993), the May Fourth writer who coedited *Qiangwei zhoukan* (The wild rose literary supplement) with fellow writer Shi Pingmei before getting involved in the Nationalist Central Women's Department under He Xiangning. Lu reportedly remained deeply concerned about women's issues upon her return from Europe in 1948 and attended the *Fulian* Congresses (Fulian daibiao dahui) in the early fifties, even (reportedly) delivering a speech at one of them.[10]
- Yang Mo (1914–1995) an activist and writer who would go on to write the hugely popular but controversial novel *Qingqun zhi ge* (Song of youth,

1958). Yang was appointed to a high position in the Beijing Branch of the *Fulian* in the years immediately following liberation, before transferring to a job in the film industry.

• Feng Yuanjun (1900–1974), the May Fourth writer, was elected as the vice chair of the Shandong Province *Fulian*.

One of the central charges leveled against the Women's Federation in recent years is that it colluded in the creation of a dominant egalitarian rhetoric about gender that served the state but, in the long run, paradoxically, disempowered women. This rhetoric (to be crystallized in such Cultural Revolution slogans as "Women hold up half the sky" [Funü neng ding banbiantian] and "Whatever men can accomplish, women can too" [Nanren neng bandao de shi, nüren ye bande dao]) is said to have underpinned a false (or at the very least premature) sense of "emancipation" on the part of Chinese women that ultimately neutralized gender as a meaningful category of identity and political organization. There is truth in this assessment, to be sure. It might, however, be useful to point out that in the beginning the *Fulian*'s agenda was centrally informed by concern with ideological transformation. As in the pre-49 period, the Communist Party's discourse on women's liberation (*funü jiefang*) throughout the Maoist era was couched in orthodox Marxist terms predicating female equality on entry into the public sphere of production and labor; but increasing stock was now also placed on the notion that the enduring discrimination against women in Chinese society was attributable to deeply rooted cultural attitudes and values.[11] Only through concerted ideological struggle would these residual beliefs (or "*fengjian sixiang*" as they were often called) be thoroughly eradicated, and it was the *Fulian* that was to take the lead in this effort. In other words, the *Fulian* seems to have been conceived to a large degree as a *cultural* institution whose function was "*xuanchuan*," to promote new attitudes and inculcate modes of consciousness among the female subjects upon whom the Chinese State now formally bestowed equal social, political, and economic rights. Note, for example, what one commentator had to say in an early article appearing in *New Women of China*:

> The measures taken by the People's Government guarantee the social conditions for women's emancipation. But if women want to put these rights into practice and use this opportunity, they must rely on their own efforts and continuously struggle against traditional thought and the habits of the old society; they must continuously transform the weaknesses bred in them by the old society . . . and use their utmost effort to accomplish this.[12]

It might be recalled from chapter 1 that Qiu Jin once exhorted women to reimagine themselves in order to overcome present inequities; a half century later Chinese women were again being urged to transform their self-images and expectations, this time, however, in order to avail themselves of the equalities and opportunities society now (ostensibly) offered.

It was perhaps with the fundamental objective of ideological transformation in mind that as part of its first order of business the Preparatory Committee of the All-China Women's Federation launched the ten-volume book series *Fuyun congshu* (Women's movement series) on the eve of liberation in 1949, featuring such titles as *Zhongguo jiefangqu nongcun funü fanshen yundong sumiao* (Depictions of the rural women's fanshen movement in China's liberated areas); *Xin shehui de xin nügong* (New women workers of the new society); and *Zhongguo jiefangqu de Nandinggeermen* (Nightingales of China's liberated zones).[13] The stated purpose of these volumes was to introduce readers to the recent accomplishments of the women's movement in the so-called liberated areas, as well as in KMT-controlled areas. The titles alone, however, indicate the central emphasis placed on new positive archetypes. By far the most significant channel for disseminating socialist gender ideology to emerge in the early post-Liberation era, however, was *Xin Zhongguo funü* (Women of new China), launched in July of 1949 as the official national magazine of the *Fulian*.[14] Veteran feminist publisher and activist Shen Zijiu was appointed as the editor-in-chief, with Dong Bian and Xu Keli as vice editors. Because independent women's magazines had virtually disappeared by 1950, *Xin Zhongguo funü* occupied an enormously influential place in the public discourse on gender and sex-related matters during this time.[15] According to Dong Bian, under Shen's editorship the print-run of the magazine grew from approximately 10,000 in 1949 to an impressive 300,000 by 1955.[16] By 1957, that number had multiplied to more than three quarters of a million.[17] Much of the readership no doubt consisted of *Fulian* constituents, although copies could be purchased at bookstores and post offices throughout the country.[18] Yang Yun, who was on the magazine staff at the time attributes the growing popularity to the relevance of the topics covered.[19] In the early years of its existence, the magazine embarked on the task of consciousness-raising by introducing readers to new standards of socialist womanhood, which emphasized mobilization into the labor force and full-fledged participation in economic/political campaigns (including, first and foremost, Land Reform).[20] A variety of different textual formats were employed, including editorials; reports from the leadership; official party documents and directives; letters from readers; cartoons; regular columns (e.g., on women's health and hygiene; model Soviet women; the new-style housewife); and special series (such as one on the history of Chinese women's oppression). Narrative forms such as fictional stories, reportage, biographies, and profiles of remarkable women also worked to advance the still unconventional public feminine images of the model worker and model housewife. But it would be misleading to characterize the magazine as simply a mouthpiece for State propaganda: as Dong Bian also recalls, under Shen's tenure the magazine often contained content at odds with the official Party line. For instance, in opposition to the State's pro-natalist stance in the early fifties and the dominant discourse on sexuality that defined and legitimized sex primarily in terms of procreation, the magazine carried important and specific information on birth control devices and practices.

Dong Bian further remembers that the magazine defied the trend of uncritically eulogizing the new society by publicizing the troubling phenomenon of suicide among the ranks of female cadres.[21] One particular article that appeared in 1954, "Zhang Yun weishenme zisha" (Why Zhang Yun committed suicide), for instance, called attention to the complex case of a revolutionary cadre whose husband demanded a divorce when they were reunited after a decade-long separation during the war. The article sparked a flurry of responses from readers in the following months on such issues as marital fidelity and the priorities of women cadres. Furthermore, despite the preponderance of affirmative stories of female success in *Zhongguo funü* (and across the national media, for that matter), the magazine explicitly acknowledged gender contradictions within the existing social order. It was not uncommon, for instance, to find in editorials, articles, and even published reports by *Fulian* leaders themselves critical remarks condemning the persistence of conventional discriminatory views of women. In 1957, to take just one example, in response to Mao's famous speech "On the Correct Handling of the Contradictions among the People," the *Fulian* leadership used the magazine to issue an official report addressing the present inequalities between men and women, both within the family and in production. This was followed by a lively print debate in subsequent issues on the very question of whether or not Chinese women had been "liberated" by the advent of the Chinese Communist state with contributors weighing in on both sides of the argument. While there is evidence pointing to a certain hardening of the official line on women by late 1950s, even as late as 1963, for instance, the author of an article in *Zhongguo funü* commented that "[t]he ideological and habitual influence of the exploitation class in the old society will still play its role in a rather long period of time to come."[22] For instance, the author goes on to point out, such retrograde ideas as " 'the husband is responsible for supporting a family, while the wife is responsible for household chores' and 'man is superior to woman,' are reflected consciously or unconsciously in the thought of a large number of people, and are shown frequently in everyday life in the form of contradiction among the people." The explicit emphasis on positive imagery and rhetoric in the pages of *Zhongguo funü*, in other words, may mark a deliberate and strategic valorization of heroic models for the purpose of inspiring and guiding the reader toward a more liberated future rather than a purported reflection of present conditions.

The success of *Zhongguo funü* in keeping gender roles and sexuality alive as a legitimate arena of public debate in the early post-liberation era is underscored, paradoxically, by the vehemence with which it came under attack at the beginning of the Cultural Revolution in the early 1960s—an attack that would eventually lead to its demise. The initial volley came from the theorist Chen Boda, who published a blunt denunciation of *Zhongguo funü* in *Hongqi* (Red flag) magazine.[23] According to Chen, the magazine had overstated the gender-specific conflicts contemporary Chinese women faced (including, in his view, the alleged double burden of domestic and public labor) and was therefore guilty of leading readers astray by encouraging them to privilege women's well-being over class struggle. Chen also singled out for attack then current editor-in-chief Dong Bian (1916–), a veteran activist who had participated in the Preparatory Committee for the All-China Women's Federation on the eve of Liberation. She now stood accused of espousing a narrow feminism that placed undue attention on women's issues in the domestic realm, and for having failed to adequately address social solutions to the various domestic burdens women faced. Unable to withstand the accusations in the politically charged atmosphere, Dong Bian was forced to step down from the magazine in 1966. Some effort was subsequently made to revamp the magazine (including giving the cover a whole new look, complete with the title inscribed in Mao's distinctive calligraphy), but, having abandoned virtually all gender-specific content, it no longer functioned as a viable forum for feminist issues. By March of 1967, *Zhongguo funü* ceased publication altogether. The national *Fulian* itself had been disbanded a few months earlier, and would not be reinstated until 1978.

NARRATIVIZING THE MARRIAGE LAW

Another topic that would prove illuminating with regard to the relationship between feminism and cultural practice in the immediate post-liberation era is the massive propaganda campaign mounted by the *Fulian* during that period on behalf of the new Marriage Law (*hunyin fa*). Passed by the CCP in May 1950, the law aimed to legislate many of the freedoms and prohibitions Chinese social reformers had been pressing for since the turn of the century: freedom of choice in heterosexual marriage, gender equality within the family; easier access to divorce, and the abolition of arranged marriage, the child bride system, concubinage, polygamy, and prostitution.[24] The Marriage Law famously begins in article one by declaring that "The feudal marriage system based on arbitrary and compulsory arrangements and the supremacy of man over woman, and in disregard of the interests of the children, is abolished."[25] The CCP's underlying motive in enacting this law continues to be widely debated among contemporary scholars, who astutely observe that the legislation served the state's political and economic interests in addition to upholding the principle of gender equality (Croll, 1981; Evans, 1997; Diamont, 2000). Commentators also point out the inherent limitations of the law: Harriet Evans, for instance, argues persuasively that the model of free choice, heterosexual monogamy on which the law was predicated "reasserted hierarchical gender boundaries" by defining marriage and reproduction as women's natural duty (6). Nevertheless, the *way* in which the *Fulian* went about publicizing the law at the grassroots level in the countryside in the early 1950s again seems to point to the continuing priority the *Fulian* attached to cultural and psychological emancipation.[26] For what the media campaign implicitly recognized was, first of all, that national liberation and the official end of class oppression had *not* fully eradicated many of the discriminatory customs and attitudes specifically oppressive to women.[27] Nor had female participation in productive labor necessarily remedied women's suffering. And finally, the campaign presupposed that the legal provisions protecting women's rights in marriage were not, in and of themselves, sufficient; real and lasting change in actual social behaviors and values would only occur if women and men could overcome the ideological constraints hindering egalitarian relations between the sexes and absorb brand new cultural paradigms.[28] Thus at the start of one major push in March of 1953 (coinciding with the *Fulian's* second National Congress), a nationwide publicity campaign was announced with the following rationale:

> It is to remove that hindrance to our progress that a great publicity campaign will be undertaken for the full operation of the Marriage Law . . . this movement will be directed against the *remnants of feudal thinking* in regard to marriage and women and for the democratic reform of marriage. It differs in character from the land reform movement which aims at the elimination of the landlord as a class. *It is essentially a movement to remold backward outlooks, a movement for "ideological remolding" to eliminate the influence of reactionary social customs within the consciousness of the people.* Its purpose is to end the feudal state of marriage with its attendant evils handed down from the old society and to replace it by a system of free and happy marriages; to overcome the remnants of feudal ideology in relation to marriage and to institute the democratic idea of equality between men and women; bringing about the thorough emancipation of Chinese women, ensuring that every Chinese has a chance of a happy family life and can in consequence participate more actively in the large-scale planned economic construction as well as other fields of activity now going forward in the country.[29] (my emphases)

Throughout the early 1950s, local branches of the *Fulian* helped oversee and orchestrate the massive printing and distribution of a wide range of propaganda materials. In addition to the wide use of pictorial representations (posters, cartoons, billboards, and the like) visually illustrating the difference between the old and new marriage systems, such materials also often took the print form of small booklets featuring a selection of stories, plays, ballads or any number of regional performative genres (tanci, clapper talk tales, *kuaiban*, *sanbanggu*). Ono Kazuko estimates that some twenty-million Marriage Law pamphlets were distributed nationwide.[30] Short narrative forms and the use of highly colloquial (even rudimentary) language seem to predominate; a strong local flavor pervades many stories, which are typically set in specific actual locales, and there is overt concern for the ideologically correct over artistry. In terms of content, the stories often depict how women suffered under traditional arranged marriage and/or patriarchal feudal customs and the steps needed to acquire the freedoms to which they were now legally entitled as citizens of New China. In some cases, the narrative features a young maiden who wishes to choose her own marriage partner; in others, we find widows boldly asserting their right to remarry or unhappy wives who seek divorce. If the fundamental sentiments of these representations are reminiscent of early progressive fiction about peasant women, one obvious and crucial difference is that these actually reached a rural audience: the campaign was bolstered by traveling propaganda teams and drama troupes, which performed short skits and plays on these topics in small villages and towns, and by the wide incorporation of propaganda material in newspaper reading clubs, radio broadcasts, and in local literacy and study groups.[31] In the preface of one typical booklet, for instance, the authors state: "We have made every effort to popularize the language and to include illustrations so that those who only recognize one or two thousand characters can read it, and those who are illiterate can understand it. Teachers of literacy classes can also use it as supplementary reading material for their students."[32]

There is no denying the practical didactic intent of Marriage Law stories; the variation on the level of both form and content, however, would seem to work against a reading of them as mere "propaganda." At the very least, the consideration paid to adapting indigenous folk forms would require that we take into account the pleasure that they might have elicited from their audience. The practice of borrowing popular local genres to transmit new ideological content had already proven effective during the war period as a means of mobilizing the rural populace, a fact that no doubt informed the strategies of the Marriage Law campaign. Analysis of the plots, crude as they may be, also reveals a fascinating heterogeneity in the way women are positioned vis-à-vis the new regime. To be sure, in some cases the narrative logic is highly troubling in this respect: women characters are drawn as utterly helpless, powerless victims of feudal rural culture, and dependent on benevolent Party intervention on their behalf. The Marriage Law in many such stories is tantamount to a gift bestowed from above (*enci*) upon women. In these cases, it could easily be argued, the primary textual aim is to bolster the authority of the CCP (and Mao Zedong's leadership in particular) and to draw a clear distinction between the "new society" and the oppressive, feudal past. But not all stories neatly fit this description. Some represent the emancipation of the peasant heroine from the clutches of the patriarchal family as a process involving active individual resistance against dictatorial fathers, husbands, or mothers-in-law. Others carefully detail the content of the law as opposed to simply celebrating its authorship. Obviously without additional research one must be cautious about drawing overly broad conclusions about the cultural meanings of such examples, but at the very least they would seem to indicate a need to go beyond a homogenous account of the *Fulian* as simply subordinating women's interests to those of the Maoist state.

Consider, for example, a simple folk *tanci* entitled "Yonggan de Lin Yuxiu" (The courageous Lin Yuxiu, 1953) included in a collection published by the Committee for Implementing the Marriage Law of Hunan Province.[33] The story centers on a feisty peasant maiden from Linjiazhuang Village by the name of Yuxiu who learns something of the new Marriage Law in her literacy class. Her budding autonomy (evidenced by her attendance at nightly meetings and study sessions), however, arouses the concern of her feudal-minded father, who in turn hastily engages the services of the local marriage broker. In keeping with the usual portrait of the go-between as a greedy mercenary, Matchmaker Wang strikes a deal with a former itinerant merchant (*pao jianghu de*) named Master Chen, a widower significantly older than Yuxiu. Impressed by the man's wealth (and especially the bride price he has reportedly agreed to pay), Yuxiu's father settles on the match without so much as discussing the betrothal with his daughter. As he cavalierly exclaims to his wife, "even though we've been liberated, this doesn't mean parents no longer have the right to control our own daughters!" (10). When at last Yuxiu is informed of her father's plans for her, she is seized with indignation: "When Lin Yuxiu had heard her father out, she was so angry her eyes turned red. 'Father, you are treating my marriage like a business transaction!'" (11).

Seeing that the father is not to be swayed by her protests, Yuxiu takes matters into her own hands, slipping out of the house at the earliest opportunity. Before long, her absence is noticed and her parents panic, fearing she may have committed suicide (traditionally, of course, not an uncommon resort of unwilling brides). In fact, knowing that forced arranged marriages are now illegal, she has gone off to report the case to a cadre in the local *Fulian* branch who in turn shows up to mediate the dispute. Confident of his paternal prerogative, initially the father defends his decision. In response, the cadre delivers a stern lecture in which she spells out the cruel and coercive nature of feudal marriage customs, emphasizing that the wealthy treat women like trinkets and that matchmakers' sole motive in arranging marriages is not the mutual compatibility or affection between the two parties involved but money. By contrast, she concludes, under the laws of the new society (*xin shehui*) of new China (*xin Zhongguo*), marriage is to be a matter of choice and women are thus authorized to marry according to their own free will. The parents are at last persuaded to annul the match and allow their daughter to choose her own husband.

As unsurprising an outcome this may be, there are several aspects of the narrative worth noting. For one thing, even though the opening verse clearly establishes that the peasant family in question has undergone the process of emancipation (*fanshen*), and clearly doesn't belong to the category of class enemy, the reader soon learns that the father suffers from an untransformed patriarchal mentality. His newly awakened class consciousness, in other words, would appear to have done little to dislodge his chauvinistic outlook. More importantly, while the lament of brides is certainly nothing new to the Chinese cultural tradition, here we find a heroine empowered not only to speak out in protest—directly reproaching her father for selling her off like so much property, for instance—but, more crucially, to then seek help to settle her grievance.[34] Knowledge (acquired in her literacy class) combined with institutional support (the *Fulian* cadre) enable her to successfully circumvent paternal authority, reject the proposed marriage, and to positively alter the outcome of her personal situation. None of this would have been possible, it should further be noted, without the heroine's own tenacity and grit in bringing the matter to the attention of the local party cadres. In other words, she emerges as the linchpin in translating the abstract principle of equality into a concrete reality in her own life. Clearly a story such as this does not conform to the dominant Communist Party salvation narrative, noted by Lu Tonglin and others, whereby women are inscribed as passive objects of male patronage/rescue.

Although historians have shown that the new government sought to publicly downplay the sharp rise in divorce rates fueled by the Marriage Law, divorce was actually not an uncommon theme in the *Fulian* propaganda literature. "Qiugu gaijia" (Sister Qiu remarries), a narrative verse form identified as Hunanese *sanbang gu*, for instance, recounts the saga of a young woman whose otherwise kind parents are duped by a fast-talking match-maker into an ill-suited match for their daughter.[35] In a classic wedding-day scene, she is forced into the bridal sedan hired to transport her to the groom's home, sobbing uncontrollably. And as expected, the husband turns out to be an unsavory scoundrel who beats her every time she urges him to mend his ways. On a visit home, she pleads with her parents for permission to divorce, only to be rebuked on customary grounds that decent women "obey their fathers at home and their husbands after marriage" and live by the "three obediences and four virtues." Such an invocation of the older gender rhetoric within the story may reflect just how entrenched traditional views of feminine behavior remained in the Chinese countryside in the 1950s but of course also furnishes a foil to the contemporary political terminology the text introduces shortly thereafter.[36] Later on, a way out of the heroine's "living hell" (*huokang*) manifests itself when Communist cadres arrive in the village to propagandize the Marriage Law (the contents of which, including women's right to divorce, are detailed at this point in the narrative). The long-suffering Qiu musters up the courage and files for divorce. At the end of the story, the reader is told that she later falls in love with one Wang Chunsheng, the decent, hardworking chief of the village Peasant Association, and the two get married.

More so than the previous example, it appears that the plot structure of this narrative positions the CCP as a *deus ex machina* that arrives to rescue the victimized heroine from her plight. This is in keeping with the dominant affirmative representation of state intervention in matters of love and marriage and in protecting women from male power. Yet a closer reading shows that the story again makes a point of highlighting the woman's own agency in seeking redress to her unfortunate lot and in taking control over her own life. The encounter between the heroine and the team of visiting cadres is not represented; indeed the role of the Party cadres is conspicuously de-emphasized, mentioned in passing only once. Instead, what is emphasized is that it is the new knowledge of the law that brings about a new attitude in the heroine herself which, in turn, prompts her to take the critical step of petitioning for divorce.[37]

As a final example, consider "Zhang Qingmei nüban nanzhuang" (Zhang Qingmei impersonates a man) a tale worth mention if only because of its rather curious premise. Set in Liancheng County in Fujian Province, the tale involves a girl forced by circumstance to cross-dress as a man (a familiar trope, it will be recalled, in traditional Chinese literature).[38] The basic plot goes like this: Mei's parents were originally blessed with two sons and two daughters, but both of the sons died and the girls had long been sold off as child brides. As they desperately yearn for a male descendent to carry on the family name, they try again, but again have a girl. Worried that society will look down on them for being without male offspring, they pass the baby girl Mei off as a boy. When the time comes, according to local custom, they even go so far as to purchase a child bride for "him." When Mei reaches the age of sixteen, her father dies, and she assumes the role of man of the house, taking charge of farming the family land. Life is not easy. On one occasion, she is drafted into the army, and the mother must scrape together a huge sum of money to hire a replacement for "him." As Mei gets older, it becomes increasingly difficult to conceal her anatomical sex and her fellow villagers, for instance, constantly harass and tease "him" for looking so feminine. Needless to say, for her part Mei is not happy. In 1950, during Land Reform, Mei begins to observe the freedoms many women in the village have acquired and she becomes increasingly self-aware of the extent to which she too had been victimized by sexist ideology (*zhongnan qingnü*). Armed with this realization, she finally reveals to the world the truth of her identity. After that, not only is she much happier, but her work ethic shows signs of improvement as well. Before long she meets an eligible bachelor and they marry. Her "wife," having attained emancipation in the process, happily remarries as well.

Aside from its sheer entertainment value (which obviously exceeds the purely practical aims of political propaganda), what is interesting about this narrative is the way it explicitly foregrounds sexual difference as socially constructed. Note that Mei is depicted as being perfectly capable of performing conventional masculine roles (insofar as she encounters obstacles they have to do with the threat of discovery of her biological sex). Hence, rather than explain gender discrimination in terms of inherent difference, it is shown to stem from external social values. For instance, the priority attached to sons dictates that families without male offspring will be at a disadvantage and suffer the loss of social prestige. With the advent of the sexually egalitarian socialist order, however, such advantages are said to have disappeared, and with them Mei's need to pass as a man. But the tale also raises an intriguing question: that is, why would Mei be happier as a woman? Since she is (presumably) long accustomed to the privileges that accrue to male identity (privileges socialist women now also enjoy), what is the reader to infer from the heroine's newfound happiness? Could the story be subtly suggesting that new marriage was to be a source of emotional fulfilment, perhaps even improved sexual relations (as opposed to simply an economic unit of compatible workers)? Obviously such a small sample of examples can tell us little about the actual ideological effect the Marriage Law propaganda may have had on rural audiences in the post-liberation era; given the magnitude of the campaign, not to mention its unprecedented reach, it is a topic that clearly begs serious consideration if we are to understand this juncture of Chinese feminist cultural history.

Female Literary Intellectuals in the Post-Revolutionary Context

If the campaign to publicize the Marriage Law in the early 1950s attests to an ambitious endeavor on the part of *Fulian* cadres to harness the symbolic power of narrative to raise the consciousness of the rural masses, one wonders where this left female artists and writers in terms of their role in "representing" women and women's interests. Surely the fact that the post-revolutionary era bore witness to a new state apparatus that presented itself as the officially ordained advocate for women must be taken into account when assessing feminist discourse of the post-liberation period? But whether it was for this reason or owing to the artistic controversies and political uncertainties that marked the early 1950s, one is immediately struck by how few women writers explicitly addressed feminist themes in their work relative to earlier periods in modern Chinese literary history. Of the writers discussed in previous chapters, for instance, some more or less ceased writing in the post-revolutionary era. Bai Wei, for instance, reportedly volunteered for service in the Great Northern Wilderness (*Beidahuang*) shortly after the founding of the PRC, and later worked in the remote northwest province of Xinjiang. She would return to Beijing in the early 1960s, at which time her formal application for Party membership was rejected, despite her seemingly impeccable revolutionary credentials. Like many veteran intellectuals, she was severely beaten by Red Guards during the Cultural Revolution, and was left partially crippled. Guan Lu, who had been involved in underground party work in Shanghai throughout the war, using her editorship at a women's magazine as her cover, published just one novel before being imprisoned by the authorities of the new regime.[39] The short novel *Pingguo yuan* (The apple orchard, 1951) faithfully observes Mao's injunction for socialist literature to serve the masses in the way it recounts in elementary language the changing fortunes of a guileless poor lad during the war and after liberation. Guan Lu was not rehabilitated until the post-Mao era when her name was officially cleared in 1982. Wang Yiwei, the fiercely independent feminist intellectual who edited the popular nonpartisan magazine *Nüsheng* in Shanghai from 1932 to 1935, and again from 1945 to 1947, virtually withdrew from the public cultural arena after Liberation fearing persecution for having never formally joined the Communist Party. When Mainland Chinese historian Wang Zheng interviewed her just prior to her death in 1993, her remarks exposed the bitter resentment women like her harbored toward the CCP for having failed to publically recognize her contributions to the cause of women's liberation in the pre-revolutionary period.[40]

In other cases, women writers turned away from creative writing to take up scholarly research: May Fourth writer Feng Yuanjun, mentioned above, had long since stopped writing to conduct research on traditional Chinese literature, and devoted herself to teaching at Shandong University after 1949. Similarly, Lu Jingqing took a position in the Chinese department at Jinnan University (later part of the Shanghai Academy of Finance and

Economics) after having returned from a sojourn in Europe in 1948. Yang Jiang, who along with her husband Qian Zhongshu turned down several offers to teach abroad in order to remain in Mainland China, took refuge in translation work while at Qinghua University—among other projects, she immersed herself in learning Spanish in order to translate the picaresque novels *La Vida de Lazarillo de Tormes* and *Don Quixote*. She had completed work on the Cervantes novel in the 1950s, though it would not be until some twenty years later that the novel made its way into print. Despite Yang Jiang's self-censorship and her cautious efforts to steer clear of politically sensitive intellectual and literary projects, however, she was still not immune from political persecution. In 1958, she was forced to undergo a brief "re-education" program outside of Beijing and again found herself a target of persecution during the Cultural Revolution. Between 1969–1972, she was relocated to a so-called cadre school in the Henan countryside. Yang resumed her creative writing in the post-Mao period, producing, among other works a brilliant satirical novel about Chinese intellectuals in the 1950s (*Xizao* [Taking a bath]) as well as a poignant memoir of her experience during the Cultural Revolution (*Ganxiao liuji* [Six chapters from a cadre school]), but gender relations no longer figure among her primary concerns.

Others continued producing creative literature in the early post-liberation era but reigned in the feminist themes that had characterized their earlier work. Su Qing, for instance, got involved in the drama world, writing and publishing numerous scripts (including a great many rewritings of works of classical drama) in early 1950s. Although she reportedly joined two of the newly established CCP women's organizations in Shanghai (the *Funü shengchany cujin hui* and the *Jiating fulian*) after 1949, her writing does not sustain the feminist critique that had distinguished her wartime fiction.[41] Su Qing made the mistake of publishing several essays in the Shanghai Daily, a Hong Kong-based newspaper, that were openly critical of the new regime. This, and possibly lingering suspicions about her past, led to her arrest in 1955 by the Shanghai Public Security Bureau on counterrevolutionary charges. She was released from jail in June of 1957. Su Qing died in relative obscurity in Shanghai in 1982. Her name was officially cleared two years later.

And still others who had participated in feminist literary culture prior to 1949 left China along with the exodus to Taiwan in the late 1940s or emigrated overseas, though not necessarily for ideological reasons. Chen Ying, for instance, relocated to Taibei in 1949 after having finally divorced her husband, a man who had long disapproved of her literary vocation. Prior to leaving the country she reportedly told Zhao Qingge that her reason for leaving the country was to put as much distance between the two of them as possible.[42] The previous year Xie Bingying, who had mobilized a female nursing brigade at the beginning of the Sino-Japanese War before assuming the editorship of *Huanghe wenyi yuekan* (Yellow river literature and art monthly) and *Heping ribao* (Peace daily news), also departed for Taiwan shortly before the fall of the KMT. Over the next few years, she led a relatively quiet life teaching Chinese literature in Taiwan and Malaysia. She immigrated to the

United States with her husband in 1974. Xie continued writing after leaving Mainland China (with output that included fiction, children's literature, essays, and travel writings), although she would continue to be most closely identified with her 1936 autobiography. And of course Eileen Chang (Zhang Ailing) fled the People's Republic for Hong Kong in 1952, where she proceeded to publish two explicitly anticommunist English-language novels (*The Rice-Sprout Song* and *Naked Earth*) while under the employ of the U.S. Information Agency. A few years later she would emigrate to the United States though her work continued to appear in the Taiwanese and Hong Kong press.

And yet for all these examples, there are a few interesting instances of Mainland women writers who, despite increasingly challenging circumstances, managed to continue producing work in a feminist vein in the years leading up to and immediately following Liberation. Here I focus on just three, the prominent leftist literary intellectuals Chen Xuezhao (1906–1991), Wang Ying (1915–1974), and Yang Gang (1905–1957). Veteran writers who had been personally involved in organized revolutionary politics prior to 1949, each completed by the early 1950s an autobiographical novel that, like Yang Mo's more well-known *Qingchun zhi ge* (Song of youth, 1958), takes up the experience of the individual female intellectual in the context of revolutionary change. As such these works not only depart from the socialist literary mainstream (which specifically aimed to serve the workers, peasants, and soldiers—*wei gongnongbing fuwu*), but also emplot recent history and past personal experience in ways that complicate the official account of Women and the Revolution. Indeed, if, as David Wang argues, Mainland fiction of the 1950s can be understood in terms of a project to remake national history in support of the Chinese Communist Party, these examples critically engender that project by representing the formation of female revolutionary consciousness as an integral part of that history.[43] For instance, their narratives subversively foreground gender consciousness (consciousness that is often depicted as preexisting collaboration with the Communist Party) and the role of agency in revolutionary struggle. The heroines of these novels, in other words, are represented not simply as hapless victims waiting to be rescued by the Party but as active protagonists who help to propel the historical transformation of society. Implicitly, furthermore, these novels also assert that gender struggle is a significant aspect of recent historical narrative. The fight against social oppression thus includes personal resistance against oppressive gender norms, including conventional forms of marriage and motherhood. As such, these novels stand in sharp contrast to some of the most prominent works of fiction from the late 1940s and early 1950s that, according to Irene Eber, emphasized the reconsolidation of conventional family structure and hierarchies.[44] On the other hand, the publication histories of these three texts (two of which did not make it into print until the post-Mao era), however, also bespeak the perils of publicly voicing such stories at this particular moment in twentieth-century Chinese literary history. What rendered the production and reception of these autobiographical texts so difficult?

And what is the relevance of such novels to us today as we seek to better understand this critical juncture in Chinese feminism?

* * *

Compared to some of her contemporaries, Chen was fairly late in declaring a formal allegiance to the Communist Party.[45] Living in France up until the mid-1930s, she secured a reputation in progressive literary/intellectual circles back in China through her regular contributions to avant-garde journals and was considered by many to be something of a radical, even though she was personally removed from the political activities that Ding Ling, Bai Wei and so on were being drawn into at the time. It was not until her return to China in 1935, amid the deepening national crisis and under surveillance by KMT authorities, that her sympathies for the Left grew. In 1938, she accepted a journalism assignment from *Guoxun* (National dispatch) to travel to Yan'an to gather material and conduct interviews for a book of reportage—which would eventually be published under the title *Yanan fangwenji* (Interviews at Yan'an, 1940). In 1940 she returned to Yan'an, this time not as a correspondent but to stay, and worked alongside Ding Ling, Ai Siqi, and Bai Lang and others at the *Jiefang ribao* (Liberation daily). She was formally accepted into the Party in 1945 and in the years leading up to liberation she worked on several major literary projects, including a reportage collection based on first-hand observations of the so-called liberated areas in northern China entitled *Manzuo jiefangqu* (Wandering through the liberated zones) and a novel *Gongzuozhe shi meili de* (To be working is beautiful). Both were published on the eve of Communist victory in 1949. The novel, which I examine briefly here, was reissued in 1954 by Zuojia chubanshe.[46]

Structured as a third-person realist *Bildungsroman*, *Gongzuozhe shi meili de* traces the evolution of a petty-bourgeois student Li Shanshang from a quintessentially May Fourth-esque New Woman into a mature and loyal member of the Chinese Communist Party. The narrative can be divided into roughly three parts: part one depicts the youthful rebellion of the heroine as she leaves the comforts of home and goes in search of fulfillment (intellectual, romantic, and professional) in Europe; part two covers life in the KMT-controlled interior during the war and her growing disaffection as a young wife who subordinates her own interests to her husband's career; and part three examines the changes she undergoes at the Communist base camp at Yan'an. In its sequence of events as well as many of the narrative details, the novel bears an unmistakable resemblance to the author's own biography, in my view a fact that powerfully attests to the abiding influence of the pre-49 era women's literary tradition on Chen's literary output at the time.[47] The foregrounding of the life of a single protagonist and the use of realist psychological description to convey the heroine's complex and highly idiosyncratic personality, for instance, are typical of the narrative practices of earlier women writers. In particular, it echoes such works as Bai Wei's *Beiju shengya*, in which the author offers a personal account not so much as a celebration of the individual self or personal enlightenment as an attempt to unfold a representative portrait of the female intellectual's progress at a crucial moment in modern Chinese history. In the case of Chen's novel, that progress is represented as overcoming intellectual solipsism and bourgeois sensibilities to embrace a more collectivist ethos in line with socialist principles. Also characteristic of the critical strain of subjective fiction certain Chinese women writers favored in the 1930s is the objective narrative voice that, on balance sympathetic to the heroine's struggles and internal contradictions, also periodically intervenes to comment critically on the flawed and contradictory aspects of her personality, warning the reader against easy identification. Insofar as Chen Xuezhao had spent the better part of the previous decade at Yan'an and was undoubtedly well-versed in socialist literary and aesthetic doctrine (having personally attended Mao's famous "Talks on Literature and the Arts" in 1942), it may come as something of a surprise, in fact, just how little the novel conforms to the basic tenets of socialist realist literary creation. The novel does not, for instance, purport to reflect the interests and emotions of the people or to construct "positive" role models. Nor does the novel seem to cater to the kind of mass audience Mao enjoined writers to serve. Judging from the abundant references to European literature and classical music, not to mention the exotic Parisian backdrop (Notre Dame, the Luxembourg Gardens, the Latin Quarter, and so forth) in the early chapters of the novel, for instance, it would appear not to have been written with the "broad masses" in mind. Instead the work probes the delicate (and soon to be taboo) topic of the relationship between the intelligentsia and the revolutionary transformation of Chinese society.

In commenting on the origins of the novel, Chen herself commented that from as early as the late 1930s she had wanted to write about "a May Fourth era Chinese woman, a female protagonist who marched across several great eras up to the War of Resistance, and who *continued to make progress*. I felt that such a woman could reflect one angle of these historical eras" (my emphases, Preface, 1). The specific history Chen has in mind, obviously, is that of the Chinese Communist revolution, from the early struggles against repressive Nationalist rule to efforts to liberate the nation from the clutches of semi-feudal exploitation and Japan's military aggression to ultimate victory, a trajectory covered in a great many novels of the period. By mediating this national narrative through the gendered experiences of the female intellectual, however, the novel re-presents revolutionary history in a rare, and, on occasion, surprising way.

Of particularly interest, for instance, are the chapters describing life at Yan'an, where the heroine eventually makes her way, along with a small child and a self-absorbed, opportunistic husband (Lu Xiaoping), having returned from a lengthy sojourn in France. She ventures to Yan'an in part out of political conviction but above all in search of an alternative to her deepening sense of alienation and meaninglessness in her life as a young middle-class mother and wife. Richer in detail than Ding Ling's (in)famous critique of gender relations at the Communist base camp, Chen's account shows how the idealistic and romantically inclined heroine soon finds herself

overburdened with domestic responsibilities (made all the more taxing by
the rustic living conditions at Yan'an), cut off from the larger revolutionary
community (in part because she feels obliged to mediate between her husband,
a nonparty member and the Yan'an authorities), and feeling more and more
like a passive bystander than a useful participant. While many a modern Chinese
woman writer has protested the stifling effects of marriage/domesticity on
the educated woman, what is unexpected is how Chen lays bare the persistence of the customary gendered division of labor within the Yan'an context:
"Shanshang had thought that once they reached Yan'an, they would embark
on a new kind of life; that she would be able to break free from home and
go out and work independently, it didn't matter what kind of work she did,
for as long as it was work, she would be contributing to the war effort. But
now it wasn't this way at all, for she still had the burden of two lives on her
shoulders and her heart still felt as though it were tightly fettered" (170).
Merely taking up residence at the revolutionary stronghold, the author
insists, does not automatically bring the empowered sense of self for which
the heroine vaguely yearns; on the contrary, internalized notions of the priority of marriage and motherhood in a woman's life continue to impede her
entry into radical history-in-the-making, the revolutionary community all
the while indifferent to her struggle. Even after her husband Lu Xiaoping
unsuccessfully schemes to poison her and then brazenly carries on an extramarital affair with a young nurse at the hospital, she steadfastly resists divorce
(which she seems to believe would represent her failure as a woman); her
comrades, meanwhile, appear to view her situation not as symptomatic of the
masculinist gender order, but as merely a private domestic squabble that does
not warrant their attention.

The protagonist's consciousness does gradually evolve (or, rather,
undergo ideological remolding, *gaizao*), but not according to the standard
formulae of socialist realism. For instance, there is considerable emphasis
placed on how Li Shanshang's political growth precipitates a reevaluation of
a gendered sense of self. In the context of the Rectification Campaign
(launched by Mao in 1942 in order to reform the Yan'an intelligentsia),
Shanshang honestly examines what she really wants and what would make
her happy.[48] For the first time, it occurs to her that her constant anxiety and
despair—all for the sake of a man whom she has never even truly loved, may
not be worth it. Amid much angst and wavering, she eventually does divorce
her husband, but she does not go on to partner up with a more ideologically
enlightened Communist Party partner, a highly symbolic act of union so
often found in Chinese socialist literature.[49] When friends urge her to
remarry, it is clear that she no longer equates happiness with the nuclear
family but with a wider revolutionary collectivity. At the same time, however,
the reader is made privy to the fact that she is still in love with an old
boyfriend back in France (an apolitical albeit sensitive intellectual), even as
she realizes that this love is at profound odds with the new life she has
chosen.[50] This figure clearly marks an ambivalence in Shanshang's psyche
(as a compelling alternative to her current life), and through it the author

hints at a certain internal wavering on the part of her heroine: just as Li Shanshang suffers pangs of maternal guilt and regret when her work requires her to leave her small child in someone else's care, up until the end of the novel we find her torn between her feelings for the old boyfriend and her commitment to serving the people.[51] In a more typical socialist novel, such a rival for the heroine's heart and loyalties would almost certainly be vilified for luring the heroine away from her true revolutionary calling and would be dealt with accordingly within the narrative;[52] here, the author leaves the contradictory urges her heroine experiences unresolved.[53]

Ostensibly consistent with the Maoist directive for intellectuals to "go to the masses," the novel posits the heroine's first-hand experience (*tiyan*) of manual labor and contact with rural women as clearly transformative. Being submerged in the life of ordinary working people, however, does not bring about the anticipated identification with the female masses but, on the contrary, accentuates the enormous gulf that inevitably divides the heroine's own class subjectivity from theirs. During a production campaign in which she is assigned manual labor, Li Shanshang apprehends for the first time the nature of her own class privilege as she begins to compare the hardships of her own life to those of the working-class women with whom she labors. She finds herself contemplating how radically her own mindset must differ from her fellow comrades as, for instance, we see on one occasion as she escapes the monotony of work by daydreaming about bygone days in Paris: "on one sunny windless spring day, as the warm sun shone into cave and her hand was working the spinning wheel, but her thoughts had flown off toward the sky 'it must be around the time of Easter!' She thought about when she was young, in Paris, where everywhere it smelled of flowers, when she was a college student, when she was free and unmarried, had she been sitting in the classroom with weather like this her heart would have flown off to the boulevards, to the woods, to the riverbanks . . . when she looked around at the female comrades next to her wholly absorbed in their spinning, she reproached herself for this leisurely mind set, this mind set of the leisure class, the exploiting class. 'What is it that still prevents me from being a natural (*zizi ranran de*) member of the revolutionary ranks . . .?'" (270)[54] Further real-life perspective is gained when Shanshang travels with a military brigade through the liberated areas (*jiefangqu*) of Northern China in the wake of the Japanese surrender, exposing the heroine to the impoverished peasantry and rural realities that bear little relation to the cosmopolitan China of her privileged youth.

> their group crossed natural barrier made by the Yellow River, and they crossed the blockade line, and they trekked across rugged mountain paths of Huabei. They saw with their own eyes many villages destroyed by the enemy and people, *now liberated*, who had been trampled; they heard lots of wise, mythical anecdotes, and stories about how the heroes of the revolutionary army had killed the enemy. And for the first time, Shanshang, who had grown up in the south in the first city exposed to capitalist influence, saw the desolate and scattered villages and feudal society in its entirety. (282)[55]

What occupies the narrator's attention in particular are the conventional patriarchal attitudes and practices that apparently remain intact in rural villages. Peasant women, Li Shanshang observes in her journal, for example, "attach absolute priority to the family, a normal view produced under feudalism. A woman without a husband or a family is nothing. Women don't lead independent lives of their own, and they don't have their own, independent destiny" (283). What she does not say, although the attentive reader would be sure to notice, is that up until that point the narrator's own sense of self-worth has been firmly tied to the family as well. The experience does, however, afford her a more mature insight about her own "suffering": as she records in the notes she keeps of the tour: "The more contact I have with this great people who have been trampled upon and oppressed, the guiltier I feel about what I have done in the past and the life I have led. One could say that I was one hundred percent an upper-class woman. Now, the closer I get to the lower classes, the more I feel the need to completely overturn this unjust, irrational, uncivilized, brutal old order, old society . . ." (284). In the end, this knowledge contributes to a greater self-consciousness of her identity and duty as an intellectual/writer: Li Shanshang may never become one with the people but she may be better equipped to articulate a more self-reflexive empathy when she reports on the lives of the masses.

And indeed, as if to prove her commitment to the new literary orthodoxy, Chen Xuezhao did in fact go on to write two more conventional socialist realist novels, *Chuncha* (Spring camellias) and *Tudi* (The land), that represent the changes taking place in the life of the broad rural masses in the early post-liberation period. It is interesting, however, that neither work was nearly as successful a publication as *Gongzuozhe shi meilide*, which was reprinted in 1954 and yet again (in slightly revised form) in the post-Mao era.[56] And even after Chen was publically denounced as a rightist in 1957 and expelled from the Party, she set about writing a sequel to the novel (in secret), which was she able to publish in the post-Mao era.

* * *

Another significant post-49 novel that engages recent Communist history through the story of female self-realization is Wang Ying's *Baogu* (Precious girl).[57] Whereas Chen Xuezhao's narrative covers the era leading up to the eve of Liberation, this autobiographical novel chronicles the early decades of the twentieth century, in particular the heady years of the revolutionary upsurge of the mid-1920s.

A veteran party member, writer, and progressive stage, and film actress, Wang Ying (1915–1974) returned to China from the United States in 1954 with her husband Xie Hegeng. Earlier that year, in a high-profile incident that sparked a public outcry from a number of leading American intellectuals, the couple had been detained in New York for refusing American citizenship. Once back on Chinese soil, Wang Ying immediately set about revising the manuscript of her autobiographical novel *Baogu*, which she had begun writing while in the United States at the encouragement of Pearl Buck. A Ying and Tian Han, close friends of Wang Ying who were now high-ranking Communist officials, were among those who would read the manuscript and urge Wang Ying to finish the revisions and get the novel into print. This plan was derailed, however, when Xie Hegeng was branded a rightist in 1957 (for having proposed, among other "heretical" views, that the leadership compound at Zhongnanhai be converted into a public park) and was subsequently sent off to the northeast to undergo reform through labor. He was finally released in the fall of 1959, but the ordeal came as such a great shock to them both that they subsequently withdrew from public cultural life altogether, taking refuge in a modest residence located in the Fragrant Hills west of Beijing. As it turned out, their self-imposed exile proved productive for Wang Ying in creative terms. By 1964, she had not only completed the revisions to her first novel but had also finished a second, *Liang zhong Meiguoren* (Two kinds of Americans) (based on her experience living in the United States). The timing, however, could not have been worse: on the eve of the Great Proletarian Cultural Revolution, her close friends now advised her against publishing the work. Instead, she set about writing a sequel to *Baogu* (this manuscript was unfortunately confiscated during a raid on her home in May 1966, along with research materials she had compiled on Chinese immigrants in the United States and interviews conducted in New York's Harlem).[58] The following year both Wang Ying and Xie Hegeng were arrested on charges of espionage and sent to prison; Wang Ying died after being kept in solitary confinement in March 1974 (just five days short of her sixtieth birthday).[59] After his release the next year, her husband took it upon himself to edit her extant manuscripts, and eventually arranged to have them published:[60] *Baogu* was finally serialized in the prestigious Shanghai literary journal *Shouhuo* (Harvest) in 1981 and was issued as a single volume the following year; the English version of the novel, entitled *The Child Bride*, on which Wang Ying had worked in collaboration with Ida Pruitt while in the United States, was also subsequently published. In addition to numerous positive reviews hailing the literary merits of the novel, cultural luminary Mao Dun inscribed the title while Xia Yan provided a preface. A full-length biography of Wang Ying appeared in 1987.[61]

Baogu recounts the author's experiences from youth to early adulthood, giving particular weight to the ways gender shaped that experience and ultimately informed her political consciousness. Like *Gongzuozhe shi meilide*, it is structured as a novel of development and chronicles the I-narrator's progress as a process of overcoming the social/ideological constraints of the patriarchal family before embracing a more affirmative public identity as a member of the Communist Party in the late 1920s. The author opens by characterizing the narrative as an act of recollection, comprised of memories of past events that, it is implied, remain relevant in the present: "this story happened long ago and far away. But these events are as alive and fresh in my memory as if they happened yesterday, even though, like the years and the months, they have disappeared without sound or smell, without shadow or trace" (3). Needless to say, a statement about personal memory is intriguing at a moment when the recent past was increasingly conceived in terms of class struggle and collective resistance. Among the author's memories are those that reveal how influential the women in her life have been: the early part of the novel includes stories of her maternal grandmother, ostracized from the family for having had the audacity to remarry after being widowed at a young age, and of the author's mother, who suffered from depression and ill-health due to her husband's constant infidelities. Positive female role models, however, are also shown to have made a strong impression on the narrator as a young girl: for example, the I-narrator's aunt, a successful educator who defies conventional feminine roles by founding a modern school for girls and raising a daughter singlehandedly, provides an important counterexample to the dependent, tradition-bound women in her immediate family. Wang's portraits prove more nuanced than the usual dichotomized depiction of the modern versus traditional woman: for all her apparent liberation, the aunt clings to deeply conventional moral views and thus, along with the rest of the family severs relations with her mother (the I-narrator's grandmother) when the latter remarries. This same aunt also forces her own daughter into a loveless arranged marriage, a decision she eventually comes to regret. And the mother, for all her passive acquiescence to a conventional marital arrangement, is a staunch advocate of modern female education who dreams that her daughter will one day go to college. Unfortunately, the mother's early death leaves the I-narrator at the mercy of a jealous stepmother, who promptly packs her off to a strict convent boarding school before betrothing her (for a handsome sum) to an affluent Wuhu merchant family as a child bride (*yang xifu*). The narrator recalls her instinctive aversion to the idea of arranged marriage, but also points out that the tides of change had yet to reach the world she inhabited:

> I thought and thought and in my frustration I thought about flying out of this big iron cage to a new way of life, one different from the one Father and my step-mother had chosen for me. But where could I fly? Not a single road was open to me. Though grandmother and I were two generations apart and the even though the world had changed, the system and customs of the family and of society hadn't changed that much. From the time I was little, my surrounding environment and the school that I attended were like high walls, so tight and close that not even one breath of air could reach me. New currents had been stirring in the outside world, but I had never experienced them. (208)[62]

Attesting to the legacy of May Fourth feminist thought, much of Wang Ying's narrative dwells on the personal ordeal that follows the protagonist's move to the Shao family as a child bride. As was customary, she learns to dutifully wait on her mother-in-law as well the elderly Mrs. Shao. Before long, however, her true status in the family becomes evident: Mrs. Shao, for instance, expects her to look after the spoiled younger children and overworks her (not unlike the maids in the family) with sewing and knitting, and various other household chores. Even when she is allowed to resume her schooling, the endless tasks her mother-in-law piles on make it hard for her to concentrate on her studies. As the narrator observes, such tactics were precisely a means of maintaining control over her:

> Those knitting needles and balls of yarn weighed more heavily on me than any scale could ever tell. Mother-in-law, to this day I cannot but admire you—you were so clever, you knew so well how to gain the advantage. You thought of everything—not only was I so ground down that I could not lift my head while in your home, even when I went to school you did not loosen your grip. It did not matter whether you were there or not—neither my body nor my mind could escape your grasp. (209)

Within a year, the constant scolding and humiliation she suffers at the hands of Mrs. Shao reduce to the I-narrator to a pitiful state of despair, eventually giving rise to suicidal impulses.

Interestingly, while the new ideas and information she absorbs at school heighten her sense of personal grievance, in the narrative what triggers the protagonist's escape from the Shaos are not lofty political ideals but a mean-spirited letter from her husband-to-be Zhongyao. Up until that point she had maintained a cordial, even affectionate, relationship with him; now, however, with an adolescent broken heart and wounded pride she resolves to leave the family for good. What follows echoes the classic May Fourth plot of female rebellion: the I-narrator dramatically escapes to the provincial capital Changsha, aided *en route* by sympathetic female relatives on her mother's side, to embark on a new path of freedom and independence. As if to signal her reentry into the social world, she assumes a brand new name, Lu Biling (Lu, significantly, being her maternal aunt's surname).[63]

Having charted the heroine's individual plight, and her bid for personal freedom, it is only in the last fifth of the novel that the author joins this gripping, if familiar, story to the history of the Chinese revolution. On one level, the narrator points to a certain historical inevitability in the merging of the personal and national narrative at this point in the story: when the revolutionary tide reaches Changsha, where the heroine is now attending school, she cannot help but be swept up by the historical current: "peoples' destinies cannot be separated from the times in which they live. The times are like the ocean and the destiny of a person like a grain of sand—in periods of great confusion, when winds blows and the waves beat, the grains of sand are scattered in all directions. I and everyone else of my generation were all blown about by the story of revolution that was breaking" (345). What makes the heroine's political transformation convincing, however, is that it is presented as an outgrowth of her newfound sense of personal empowerment and self-confidence. It is the *embodied* experience of gender discrimination, in other words, that makes her so acutely attuned to social injustice, and that fosters a spirit of resistance and commitment to fighting for change. Together, these propel her to join forces with the growing anti-imperialist progressive movement calling for wide sociopolitical reform.

Significantly, one specific explanation the novel provides for why the young protagonist feels so emotionally drawn to the cause is the possibility for egalitarian male–female relationships. Not only do the revolutionaries she meets often champion new roles for women but in her interaction with them she is continually impressed by the empathy her fellow comrades show her. Her association with a former teacher-turned-activist, Mr. Wei, and her newly cropped hair, however, also put her at great risk during the White Terror of 1927 and she is forced to decide whether or not to commit to the (relatively dangerous) life of an activist. Eventually, Wei introduces her to an underground revolutionary cell in Shanghai and she takes up residence with two female labor activists in the French Concession. In the final chapters of the novel, we read of her growing self-confidence and sharpened political resolve, and finally (on International Workers' Day) her official acceptance into the CCP. Her feelings for Wei, who meanwhile has been off carrying out his own revolutionary assignments, remain steadfast, but she also comes to realize that her activism has, in the present context, greater significance than any romantic pursuit:

> . . . [E]ven though the matter of personal love was important, compared with my social ideals and duties, it was insignificant. In the future, perhaps I would have the opportunity to see Wei again on the path of Revolution; perhaps we would even fall in love; he was a revolutionary with more knowledge and experience than me, and I was sure he understood the problem of revolution and love even more clearly. Even if we were never to see each other again because of our revolutionary work, I hoped, and believed, that he would find someone else to love who cherished the same ideals as he; and that I too would find a young man on the same path as me. (440)

The narrator leaves open the possibility that, circumstances permitting, she and Wei might some day develop a romantic partnership, but in the meantime her desires for mutually beneficial relationships seem to be satisfied by her "revolutionary family" (*geming de jiating*, 438)—Elder Sister and Second Sister. The novel closes with a verse by the Hungarian poet Petőfi, which the I-narrator invokes to express her passionate devotion to revolution: "Life is precious/Love is all the more precious/But for the cause of revolution/I can lose either or both." The ending of the English version of the novel, interestingly, differs quite significantly: in that version, Wei is arrested and the I-narrator finds work at an elementary school while she anxiously awaits his release. Later she receives word that Wei has been executed, news that is said to spur her to vow to carry on "his unfinished cause." To the extent that such a resolution seems to rely on a troubling elision of sexual and revolutionary desire and, in turn, defines revolutionary desire as male (she is reduced to a mere surrogate carrying on his cause) it is significant that Wang Ying altered this part when she revised the novel. By leaving the heroine to make her choice in the revised Chinese edition the author reasserts the importance of women's feminist self-identity and independence.

Like Chen Xuezhao, Wang Ying's narrative carries on the textual tradition of writing female self-identity as it had developed in China in the first half of the twentieth century, albeit with some crucial differences. Perhaps most important, whereas we have seen in many earlier texts that the quest for identity typically culminates in the painful self-awareness of the abiding socio-historical conditions that impede alternative gender roles and subjectivities, in the final pages of this novel the I-narrator exudes a palpable sense of purpose and political camaraderie. The more interesting point that might be made, however, involves the way Wang Ying's account as a whole implicitly interrogates the myth of the CCP's "emancipation" of women by fore-grounding the origins and evolution of a young, bourgeois woman's politi-cal activism amid the social, cultural, and political transformations of the early twentieth century. Here, the I-narrator is not presented in any simple sense as the product of the Party's instruction or rescue, but rather as the protagonist of a complex and arduous personal journey forged by her own choices and personal history, which ultimately leads her to the revolutionary cause. The value of personal experience is underscored toward the end of the novel, when the narrator voices not a lament of past suffering but appreciation for the lessons this has taught her:

> I no longer resented the people in my past who had mistreated and tormented me, not even Zhongyao's mother, the one who had been the most cruel of all. All the hardships and suffering I had endured had made me go far, and had opened my mind; I understood that if weren't for our family and social systems, systems in which one person tramples the next, where the powerful insulted the weak, and the rich oppressed the poor, how could I have been sent off to the Shaos like an object . . . I had no desire for personal vengeance, but I had grown to hate the unjust system. (239–240)

And, as if to amplify the point that women need to be inscribed as partici-pants in the formation of the CCP, the author leaves us with the powerful image of the three "sisters" toward the end of the novel. At an exuberant get-together they host on International Workers' Day to celebrate the narrator's formal acceptance into the Party, for instance, Elder Sister toasts, "We three sisters, from the three provinces of Hubei, Hunan, and Anhui, are not the same age but we share the same aspirations. We have become a rev-olutionary family, and we are completely happy and content" (438). This sense of belonging to a common cause is reiterated by the I-narrator in the final passage of the novel.

*   *   *

As a final example, let us briefly consider the finely crafted autobiographical novel *Daughter* by Yang Gang (1905–1957). A student activist at Yanjing University, Yang Gang joined the CCP in 1928 and soon became actively involved in left-wing cultural politics in Beijing in the 1930s. After her brief detainment in 1931 for demonstrating on International Workers' Day, she helped to launch the Beijing Branch of the League of Left-Wing Writers. With the outbreak of the War of Resistance, she rose to prominence as a progressive journalist, succeeding Xiao Qian as literary editor of the influential *Dagongbao* (L'Impartial) in 1939. From 1944 to 1948, she worked in the United States as a special foreign correspondent for that newspaper, during which time she also attended classes at Radcliff College and at Harvard. She also used the opportunity to observe and analyze contemporary American society, publishing a collection (1951) of incisive reportage pieces on topics ranging from American racism in the deep south to McCarthyism. Upon her return to China, Yang Gang worked as a deputy editor for the paper in Tianjin and later for the *Renmin ribao* (People's daily). She also held posts in the Ministry of Foreign Affairs and the Ministry of Propaganda. *Daughter* is the autobiographical novel she had begun composing (in English) during her stay in the United States; from the information available, it is unclear whether or not she worked on a Chinese version after her return to the People's Republic. Since Yang Gang committed suicide in 1957, nor will we ever know whether she would have finished the project at some future date.[64] The first edition of the novel was eventually published in 1988 when an extant typed copy of the English language manuscript surfaced. It was issued both in its original English form by the Beijing Foreign Languages Press, and in Chinese translation under the title *Tiaozhan* by Renmin chubanshe.

Like *Gongzuozhe shi meilide, Daughter* is an autobiographical novel structured as a third-person female *Bildungsroman*. Whereas in the former novel the heroine's subjective viewpoint tends to dominate the narrative, Yang Gang employs an omniscient narrator to achieve a comparatively more detached and ironic point of view from which to unfold her story of the self. Looking back to the mid-1920s, amid the revolutionary upsurge in the author's native Hubei province, the narrative opens just as the naive, pampered, and politically inexperienced central protagonist Pingsheng takes leave of her wealthy upper-class home to attend Lindgren, a modern boarding school for girls run by European missionaries. An early scene depicting her dismay at the sparsely furnished dormitory room where she is to live and her utter helplessness without servants there to wait on her vividly captures the aristocratic lens through which the protagonist, as we first encounter her, views and experiences the world. By the end of the novel, the female protagonist has finally, though not without tremendous pain, come to accept the bitter truth about her elite gentry family, incipient knowledge that prompts her to leave home for good to enlist in the revolution.

How does the privileged daughter of a wealthy landowner turn into a political revolutionary? That is the story the novel takes up as it traces the protagonist's Confucian upbringing to her youthful fascination with Christianity, and finally as she slowly moves from a somewhat naive progressive humanitarianism (based on a perception of the peasants' desire for dignity) to a more radical political stance based on an incipient awareness of class oppression. The trajectory is nothing new, nor is the romantic subtext that fuels the protagonist's political desire (she falls in love with a radical political organizer of peasant origins).[65] What is particularly salient, however, is the author's candid examination of the possibilities for revolutionary consciousness. One of serious questions the novel as a whole raises is whether intellectual theories and ideals can be a sufficient foundation for revolutionary consciousness or whether embodied experience of the oppressed alone generates such consciousness. True consciousness of social oppression cannot be derived merely from ideas, the author seems to suggest, but must be rooted in lived experience.

Much of the novel's strength lies in its presentation of the psychological turmoil of the female protagonist as she confronts the realities of social oppression. Unlike the New Woman fiction popular in the pre-49 era, however, here the narrative focus no longer centers sympathetically on the anguish of the middle-class woman striving for economic and sexual autonomy. Instead, a great deal of the narrative is taken up with Ping's struggle to come to terms with her class privilege and the ways in which her own affluent upbringing separates her from her school mates, the majority of whom are poor work study students who are required to labor (mainly doing painstaking embroidery work) in exchange for tuition. On the one hand, the protagonist naively assumes that the education her less advantaged classmates have been afforded will bring them equal opportunities and she resents the fact that her friends dismiss her "problems" as trivial as compared to theirs. Yet, when she reluctantly admits that she can never truly know what their grim lot might be like, she is left feeling alienated and lonely in their midst. She experiences "a strange distance" from her classmates, even her closest friends: "it was as though she were really separated from them, a different kind of person" (177). An awareness of class difference is arguably one of the most important lessons she learns, and in this respect Yang Gang's representation of modern school life departs dramatically from the May Fourth feminist trope of the school as a liberating space of female community and solidarity. At the same time, the reader is shown the enormous difficulty the protagonist has in fully accepting the grim truth about her family's wealth, in particular the values for which her father stands. Indeed, even when he is taken into custody by the newly formed Peasant Association (a key organizer of which is Zhongyuan, the young man she loves) at the height of the revolutionary insurgency, she rushes to his defense and seeks to secure his release. And later, when Zhongyuan urges her to flee Hankou with him, she again resists out of sentimental attachment and loyalty to her father. It is not until the final pages of the novel when the bondmaid, Laixiang, whom Ping has gradually learned to treat with respect and human compassion, is almost raped by her father that she wakes up to the tyranny and moral depravity he embodies. Only at this point does Ping begin to break away from her vague and abstract intellectual appreciation of revolution (and her position as a spectator watching from the sidelines) into the realm of active progressive struggle: now, for example, she defies her father by helping the maid escape and ultimately, armed with a new outlook on the world, decides to sever ties with the family herself and strike out on her own.

Unlike many eulogistic socialist realist novels of the 1950s designed to glorify the heroic revolutionary past, at no point does the author romanticize the revolutionary movement: instead, more akin to the spirit of 1930s critical realism, the author exposes the rampant opportunism, the superficiality and limits of youth understanding, and the way "revolution" simply represented the latest fashion for many of its practitioners during this era. Even the heroine herself is not spared the author's critique, which time and again draws attention to the character's ambivalence and irresolution as she struggles to identify with the aims of a cause which spells the demise of her own family's way of life. Indeed, throughout most of the story, though the heroine likes to think of herself as having compassion for those less fortunate, she watches the political upheaval that engulfs the community from the sidelines all the while stubbornly clinging to the naive belief that her father is a good and decent man. Only in the end is she forced to confront her own passivity:

> And what has she done throughout all this? Inactivity . . . there had been no real effort at abandoning the comforts and the services of home. No attempt to bring her father out of the brutal way of life which based its luxury and security on other people's toil and suffering . . . Change had, like an icy blade, cut open her eyes but not deeply enough to sever her heart from its birthplace. She had seen, she had timidly felt out, she had lingered, she had not moved one step. The past had lived in her like the grave of four thousand years of history, quietly seeking to extend itself and to embrace the future. (461–462)

The author provocatively questions but ultimately provides no easy answers to the fraught relationship between the radical female intellectual and processes of historical change.

*   *   *

The above analysis only begins to fathom the various developments that would reconfigure the relationship between literary women and feminist ideology in China in the early Maoist era in the 1950s. What I have attempted to suggest in this final chapter, however, through a series of concrete examples, is that the history of women's literary feminism does not simply come to a halt with the establishment of the People's Republic of China. As momentous a turning point this date was in many respects, we need to resist the temptation to read 1949 as an absolute cut-off date that neatly divided one historical era from the other. For one thing, as we gain critical distance from the history of the Maoist era, it seems increasingly clear that a new gender order was not simply decreed from above but that the period was characterized, at least in the early years, by a greater interplay between women intellectuals and the State. Using the tools and resources made available to them by the State, *Fulian* activists and female writers contested the CCP's self-aggrandizing myth of *jiefang funü* in narratives that reinscribed women's agency in the history of the Chinese Revolution; they developed new textual practices and rhetorical strategies to encourage nonelite women at the grassroots level to actively pursue and take advantage of their new rights; and they protested the limits of official State rhetoric by drawing attention to the incomplete nature of gender struggle and the contemporary obstacles to an egalitarian society. In retrospect, and especially in light of socialism's much decried failure to live up to its grand promises to women, we would do well to keep such symbolic acts of resistance in perspective; yet they also powerfully attest to the struggles and capacity for self-invention and a vision of gendered social change in women's texts. Indeed, this is the important alternative narrative that I have sought to privilege throughout this book.

NOTES

INTRODUCTION: WOMEN AND FEMINISM IN THE LITERARY HISTORY OF EARLY-TWENTIETH-CENTURY CHINA

1. These various renderings of "feminism" can be found in texts from the period covered in this study. While often used interchangeably, they carry slightly different connotations.
2. In addition to calling for a radical transformation of Confucian social mores and values prejudicial to women, early feminists also demanded concrete recognition of women's social and political rights. Prominent among these were the eradication of foot binding, equal rights in inheritance, access to education and the professions, marital freedoms, including the right to choose one's own partner and to divorce, the right to vote and be elected to public office, and the abolition of the practice of child-brides, concubinage, and prostitution.
3. Charlotte Beahan, "The Women's Movement and Nationalism in Late Ch'ing China" (Ph.D. diss., Columbia University, 1976); Elisabeth Croll, *Feminism and Socialism in China* (New York: Schocken Books, 1978); Phyllis Andors, *The Unfinished Liberation of Chinese Women: 1949–1980* (Bloomington: Indiana University Press, 1983); Judith Stacey, *Patriarchy and Socialist Revolution in China* (Berkeley: University of California Press, 1983); Margery Wolf, *Revolution Postponed: Women in Contemporary China* (Stanford: Stanford University Press, 1985); Christina Gilmartin, *Engendering the Chinese Revolution: Radical Women, Communist Politics, and Mass Movements in the 1920s* (Berkeley: University of California Press, 1995).
4. See, for example, David Der-wei Wang, "Feminist Consciousness in Modern Chinese Male Fiction," in Michael Duke, ed., *Modern Chinese Women Writers* (Armonk, NY: M.E. Sharpe, 1989), 236–256; Stephen Chan, "The Language of Despair: Ideological Representation of the 'New Woman' by May Fourth Writers," *Modern Chinese Literature* 4 (Spring and Fall 1988): 19–38; Rey Chow, *Woman and Chinese Modernity* (Minneapolis: University of Minnesota Press, 1991); Yue Ming-Bao, "Gendering the Origins of Modern Chinese Fiction," in Lu Tonglin, ed., *Gender and Sexuality in Twentieth-Century Chinese Literature and Society* (Albany: SUNY Press, 1993); Sally Lieberman, *The Mother and Narrative Politics in Modern China* (Charlottesville: University Press of Virginia, 1998); Kam Louie, *Theorizing Chinese Masculinity: Society and Gender in China* (Cambridge: Cambridge University Press, 2002).
5. Lu Tonglin, *Gender and Sexuality in Twentieth-Century Chinese Literature and Society* (Albany: SUNY Press, 1993), introduction; Meng Yue, "Female

Images and National Myth," in Tani Barlow, ed., *Gender Politics in Modern China: Writing and Feminism* (Durham: Duke University Press, 1993).

6. Critics who have explored these issues include: Ma Ning, "The Textual and Critical Difference of Being Radical: Reconstructing Chinese Leftist Films of the 1930s," *Wide Angle* 2, no. 2 (1989); Lydia Liu, "The Female Body and Nationalist Discourse: Manchuria in Xiao Hong's *The Field of Life and Death*," in Angela Zito and Tani Barlow, eds., *Body, Subject, and Power* (Chicago: University of Chicago Press, 1994); Liu Kang, "The Language of Desire, Class, and Subjectivity in Lu Ling's Fiction," in Lu (1993); Zhang Yingjin, ed., "Prostitution and Urban Imagination," *Cinema and Urban Culture in Shanghai, 1922–1943* (Stanford: Stanford University Press, 1999).

7. Feminist scholarship is also transforming the study of literature and culture prior to the twentieth century, as scholars challenge the stereotypes of "traditional Chinese women." Recent studies include Ellen Widmer and Kang-i Sun Chang, eds., *Writing Women in Late Imperial China* (Stanford: Stanford University Press, 1997); Dorothy Ko, *Teachers of the Inner Chambers: Women and Culture in Seventeenth Century China* (Stanford: Stanford University Press, 1994); Susan Mann, *Precious Records: Women in China's Long Eighteenth Century* (Stanford: Stanford University Press, 1997); Susan Mann and Yu-Yin Cheng, eds., *Under Confucian Eyes: Writings on Gender in Chinese History* (Berkeley: University of California Press, 2001).

8. *Documents of the Women's Movement of China* (All China Democratic Women's Federation, 1952), 41–42. Quoted in Irene Eber, "Images of Women in Recent Chinese Fiction," *Signs* 2, no. 1 (1976): 27.

9. This rhetoric of equality seems to have contributed to the overly idealistic assessments by nonspecialist Western feminists of the achievements of the women's emancipation movement in China in the 1970s. See, e.g., Sheila Rowbatham, *Women, Resistance, Revolution* (New York: Vintage Books, 1974); and Claudie Broyelle, *Women's Liberation in China* (Atlantic Highlands, NJ: Humanities Press, 1977).

10. For an overview of the recent developments in the women's movement in Mainland China and the legacy of state-sponsored feminism, see Naihua Zhang, "Discovering the Positive within the Negative: The Women's Movement in a Changing China," in Amrita Basu, ed., *The Challenge of Local Feminisms* (Boulder: Westview Press, 1995), 25–57.

11. Since the late 1990s, a number of doctoral dissertations (several of which have now been published) have been completed, which focus on modern Chinese women writers from feminist perspectives and in so doing contribute to the paradigm shift that the present work calls for. Noteworthy recent publications include Liu Jianmei, *Revolution Plus Love: Literary History, Women's Bodies, and Thematic Repetition in Twentieth-Century Chinese Fiction* (Honolulu: University of Hawaii Press, 2003); and Tze-lan D. Sang, *The Emerging Lesbian: Female Same-Sex Desire in Modern Chinese Literature and Culture* (Chicago: University of Chicago Press, 2002). See also Nicole Huang, "Written in the Ruins: War and Domesticity in Shanghai Literature of the 1940s" (Ph.D. diss., Los Angeles, UCLA, 1998); Megan Ferry, "Chinese Women Writers of the 1930s and Their Critical Reception" (Ph.D. diss., St. Louis, Washington University, 1998); Wang Lingzhen, "Modern and Contemporary Chinese Women's Autobiographical Writing" (Ph.D. diss., Cornell University, 1998); and Wang Jing, "Strategies of Modern Chinese Women Writers' Autobiography" (Ph.D. diss., Ohio State University, 2000).

12. Patricia Yaeger, *Honey-Mad Women: Emancipatory Strategies in Women's Writing* (New York: Columbia University Press, 1988). This engaging book argues that while the trope of the silenced, muted, or lost female voice has been central to feminism's critique of women's relation to language and writing in patriarchal culture, it has also become something of a liability to feminist scholarship.

13. Lu, *Gender and Sexuality in Twentieth-Century Chinese Literature and Society* (1993), 18. Lu elaborates on this position in her book *Misogyny, Cultural Nihilism, and Oppositional Politics: Contemporary Chinese Fiction* (Stanford: Stanford University Press, 1995). For instance, she argues that "in traditional China, a woman could speak only through the voice of her husband, who assigned her the honorable social function as mother of his male descendants. Ironically, in socialist China, the emancipated second sex also remains largely silenced. This time, women must speak though the voice of the new patriarchal order, the Communist Party" (5). The danger of making such a general claim, in my view, is that it obscures the complexities of feminist discourse in twentieth-century China and erases the efforts by women (and men) to redress the gender injustices of their culture.

14. For instance, in two important critical anthologies on gender issues in modern Chinese culture, *Gender and Sexuality in Twentieth-Century Chinese Literature and Society* (1993) and *Gender Politics in Modern China* (1993), only one essay (Rey Chow's "Virtuous Transactions") deals specifically with a woman writer active before the contemporary period. Michael Duke begins his edited volume *Modern Chinese Women Writers* (1989) by remarking that few early-twentieth-century women writers "have been considered the equal of male writers," and accordingly includes just two essays (on Ding Ling and Zhang Ailing) on pre-contemporary writers.

15. Scholarship in Chinese tends to engage a much wider range of writers. See, e.g., Bai Shurong, *Shiwei nüzuojia* (Ten women writers) (Tianjin: Chunzhong chubanshe, 1986); Meng Yue and Dai Jinhua, *Fuchu lishi dibiao* (Emerging from the horizon of history) (Zhengzhou: Henan renmin chubanshe, 1989); Qiao Yigang, *Zhongguo nüxing de wenxue shijie* (The literary world of Chinese women) (Wuhan: Hubei jiaoyu chubanshe, 1993); and Wang Jialun, *Zhongguo xiandai nüzuojia lungao* (A discussion of modern Chinese women writers) (Beijing: Zhongguo funü chubanshe, 1992). The current flurry of re publications of pre-49 literature, especially from the 1920s to 1940s, has also dramatically facilitated access to a much broader range of early women writers. Recently issued collections include the multivolume *Minguo nüzuojia xiaoshuo jingdian* (Fiction classics by Republican era women writers), Ke Ling, ed. (Shanghai: Guji chubanshe, 1999) and *Zhongguo xiandai cainü jingdian wencong* (Collection of literary classics by modern Chinese literary women), Fu Guangming, ed. (Beijing: Yanshan chubanshe, 1998).

16. My analysis here takes its cue from the insights of historian Judith Newton, who has shown how feminist critiques of patriarchal history have inadvertently given rise to a "tragic essentialism in regard to male domination." See her essay "Making—and Remaking—History: Another Look at Patriarchy," in Shari Benstock, ed., *Feminist Issues in Literary Scholarship* (Bloomington: Indiana University Press, 1987).

17. Laurie Finke develops the notion of "complexity" as a way of countering the tendency in women's literary history to construct totalizing narratives. See her *Feminist Theory: Women's Writing* (Ithaca: Cornell University Press, 1992).

18. While I have benefitted enormously from Wang Zheng's research, the one criticism I have is that she underestimates the scope of women's literary feminism during the period under question. Even the rationale she provides for her particular methodology—to "use women's own words to reconstruct the subject position of the May Fourth new women, rather that merely search texts produced by men to find women's subjectivity" (7)—seems to derive from an assumption that May Fourth era women left no significant textual legacy of their struggles. This assumption is, of course, widespread, and is precisely the point of intervention of my own study.

19. Like many, I am suspicious of critical efforts to delineate a specifically "female" literary tradition, since such attempts usually rest on essentialized notions of the relationship between gender and writing. This is not to say, however, that there is not an urgent need for a thorough, empirical literary history of women's writing in twentieth-century China in English (akin to Meng Yue and Dai Jinhua's book), especially since the theoretical concerns and problems many feminist scholars in Chinese studies are now raising often seem to outstrip the basic historical knowledge of this writing.

20. Maria Lauret, *Liberating Literature: Feminist Fiction in America* (London: Routledge, 1994).

21. Sandra M. Gilbert and Susan Gubar, *The Madwoman in the Attic: The Woman Writer and the Nineteenth-Century Literary Imagination* (New Haven: Yale University Press, 1979).

22. Rachel Blau DuPlessis, *Writing Beyond the Ending: Narrative Strategies of Twentieth Century Women Writers* (New York: Oxford University Press, 1985).

23. As Lydia Liu points out in her essay "Invention and Intervention: The Making of a Female Tradition in Modern Chinese Literature," in Ellen Widmer and David Wang, eds., *From May Fourth to June Fourth* (Cambridge: Harvard University Press, 1993), this phenomenon clearly needs to be historicized within the particular context of contemporary PRC feminism and its efforts to reestablish gender as a site of difference.

24. Meng Yue and Dai Jinhua, *Fuchu lishidibiao* (Emerging on the horizon of history) (Zhengzhou: Henan renmin chubanshe, 1989). Also part of Li Xiaojiang's women's studies series, Yue Shuo's *Chidao de chaoliu* (The belated tide) (Zhengzhuo: Henan renmin chubanshe, 1989), contends that it is only in the contemporary post-Mao era that women writers have achieved creative independence from the dominant male culture.

25. Lauret, *Liberating Literature*, 3.

26. Elaine Showalter, *A Literature of Their Own: British Women Novelists from Brontë to Lessing* (Princeton: Princeton University Press, 1977).

27. Rosalind Coward, "Are Women's Novels Feminist Novels?," in Elaine Showalter, ed., *The New Feminist Criticism* (London: Virago, 1985); Rita Felski, *Beyond Feminist Aesthetics: Feminist Literature and Social Change* (Cambridge: Harvard University Press, 1989); Anne Cranny Francis, *Feminist Fiction: Feminist Uses of Generic Fiction* (New York: St. Martin's Press, 1990); Ann Ardis, *New Women, New Novels* (New Brunswick: Rutgers University Press, 1990); Gayle Greene, *Changing the Story: Feminist Fiction and the Tradition* (Chicago: University of Chicago Press, 1991); Maria Lauret, *Liberating Literature: Feminist Fiction in America* (London: Routledge, 1994); Eve Taylor, *The Domestic Revolution: Enlightenment*

Feminisms and the Novel (Baltimore: Johns Hopkins University Press, 2000); Anna Wilson, *Persuasive Fictions: Feminist Narrative and Critical Myth* (Lewisburg: Bucknell University Press, 2001).

28. Greene, *Changing the Story*, 2.

29. Gynocriticism is a term coined by Elaine Showalter to refer to the critical project of studying "woman as writer—with woman as the producer of textual meaning, with history, themes, genres and structures of literature by women." See her "Towards a Feminist Poetics," in Mary Jacobus, ed., *Women Writing and Writing about Women* (London: Croom Helm, 1979), 25. "L'écriture féminine" refers to the theory of feminine textuality developed by French feminists.

30. Felski, *Beyond Feminist Aesthetics*, 19.

31. There are striking parallels between the early formation of Chinese feminism and feminist movements in other Asian countries that also developed alongside anti-imperialist nationalist movements. Kumari Jayawardena's groundbreaking study of Third World feminist movements shows that male nationalists often took the lead in advocating reform for women. See her *Feminism and Nationalism in the Third World* (London: Zed Press, 1986). For another useful cross-cultural perspective on non-Western feminisms, see also Amrita Basu, ed., *The Challenge of Local Feminisms: Women's Movements in Global Perspective* (Boulder: Westview Press, 1995).

32. "Zhongguo de funü yundong wenti" (The problem of China's women's movement) (1924), in *Lu Yin xuanji* (Fuzhou: Fujian renmin chubanshe, 1985), 16–28. Lu Yin elaborated on the importance of women's self-liberation in her later essay "Jinhou funü de chulu" (The future of women) (1936).

33. Lauret, *Liberating Literature*, 83.

34. "Funü wenti yanjiuhui xuanyan" (Manifesto of the Woman Problem Research Association), *Funü pinglun* (August 2, 1922).

35. Michel Foucault, *The History of Sexuality Volume I: An Introduction*, trans. Robert Hurley (New York: Vintage Press, 1980), 101.

36. For more on this and other early Japanese feminist activities, see Sharon Sievers, *Flowers in Salt: The Beginnings of Feminist Consciousness in Modern Japan* (Stanford: Stanford University Press, 1983).

37. The founders of the Women's Bookstore were Huang Xinmian and her husband Yao Mingda, a professor at Fudan University. Other prominent female members included Zhao Qingge, Fengzi, Wu Shutian, and Chen Baiping. See Zhao Qingge, *Changxiang ji* (Forever recalling each other) (Shanghai: Xuelin chubanye, 1999), 191–194. For additional information see Zhu Lianbao, ed., *Jinxiandai Shanghai chubanye yinxiangji* (Impressions of the modern Shanghai publishing industry) (Shanghai: Xuelin chubanye, 1993), 61.

38. The mini-storybooks distributed by the Women's Federation (*Fulian*) to promulgate the Marriage Law in the early 1950s represent another example of a consciously propagandistic textual practice. See chapter 5.

39. Cranny-Francis, *Feminist Fiction*, 2.

40. Lauret, *Liberating Literature*, 4.

41. The attention to narrative discourse in contemporary feminist theory, it should be pointed out, has specific roots in the strong associations between women and the novel in the Western literary tradition. Nancy Armstrong,

among others, has argued that the novel constituted one of the primary sites of the ideological production of bourgeois gender codes. The conventional romance narrative, e.g., of which middle-class women were not only the primary consumers but also (somewhat ironically) producers, helped consolidate the domestic ideals of womanhood by figuring love and marriage as solely legitimate female concerns. To expose these plots, as it were, has been among the chief projects of feminist critics and writers. When we turn to the Chinese context, the relationship between the novel (or fiction in general) and women looks quite different. For a fascinating discussion on this very issue, see the exchange between Ellen Widmer and Nancy Armstrong in Widmer and Kang-i Sun Chang, eds., *Writing Women in Late Imperial China* (1997).

42. The term is Judith Fetterly's, who was one of the first to theorize the relationship between the female reader and male-authored (and masculinist) texts in her book *The Resisting Reader: A Feminist Approach to American Fiction* (Bloomington: Indiana University Press, 1978).

43. Teresa de Lauretis, *Technologies of Gender: Essays on Theory, Film, and Fiction* (Bloomington: Indiana University Press, 1987), 109.

44. Felski, *Beyond Feminist Aesthetics*, 6.

45. In his article "The Seeds of Change: Reflections on the Condition of Women in the Early and Mid Ch'ing," *Signs* 2 (1976), Paul Ropp examines this and several other examples, which he suggests are proof that the origins of feminism in China are not simply Western in nature. For other attempts to uncover a feminist consciousness in late imperial literature, see the collections Anna Gerstlacher et al., eds., *Women and Literature in China* (Bochum: Studienverlag Brockmeyer, 1985); Ellen Widmer and Kang-i Sun Chang, ed., *Writing Women in Late Imperial China*; and Marina Sung, *Narrative Art of Tsai-sheng-yuan: A Feminist Vision in Traditional Confucian Society* (Taiwan: Chinese Materials Center, 1994).

46. While the intricacies of this history are still in the process of being documented, there are already a number of outstanding studies, both general and on particular facets of Chinese feminist politics. Pioneering works include those by Ono Kazuko (1975), Bobby Siu (1975), Elisabeth Croll (1974, 1978), and Judith Stacey (1983), which trace the evolution of gender debates and political alliances of the women's movement from their origins in the late Qing nationalist movement up to and into the Communist era. Charlotte Beahan's unpublished doctoral dissertation, "The Chinese Women's Movement and Nationalism in Late Ch'ing China" (1976) and Hu Ying's *Tales of Translation: Composing the New Woman in China, 1899–1918* (2000) are among the most important English-language studies that look specifically at the late Qing period, although several well-researched histories, including Liu Jucai's *Zhongguo jindai funü yundongshi* (1989) and Lu Meiyi and Zheng Yongfu's *Zhongguo funü yundong: 1840–1921* (1990), both published in Mainland China, also contain rich detail for that historical period. Roxane Witke's doctoral dissertation "Transformation of Attitudes toward Women During the May Fourth Era of Modern China" (1970) remains an influential source for the study of May Fourth feminism, despite the regrettable fact that it was never published in book form; Wang Zheng's more recent *Women in the Chinese Enlightenment* (1999), also on May Fourth culture, marks a valuable contribution to our knowledge of that period. In her eloquent book,

Christina Gilmartin (1995) explores in detail the relationship between feminism and the Chinese Communist Party in the context of the 1920s. Research that addresses feminism in the post-1949 and contemporary periods is also becoming available. For an excellent analysis of the Chinese Women's Federation see Zhang Naihua's doctoral dissertation "The All-China Women's Federation: Chinese Women and The Women's Movement: 1949–1993" (1996) and Ellen Judd's *The Chinese Women's Movement: Between State and Market* (2002). See also Harriet Evans, *Women and Sexuality in China: Female Sexuality and Gender since 1949* (1997).

47. Late Qing discussions on women were not confined to topics of education and foot binding. The topics listed here are taken from a survey of magazines published in the late 1890s to 1900s. By the late 1920s, major publishing houses such as the Shanghai Commercial Press also published many works devoted to the Women Question. The following is a list of titles that appeared in an advertisement from 1927: *Funü wenti* (The woman question); *Funü yu jiating* (Women and the family); *Funü yundong* (The women's movement); *Nüzi jiaoyu zhi wenti ji xianzhuang* (The female education problem and its present condition); *Nüzi yingyou de zhishi* (What women should know); *Oumei nüzi jiaoyushi* (The history of women's education in Europe and America); *Funü zhiye yu muxinglun* (Discussions on women's professions and motherhood); *Jiating wenti* (The family problem); *Xiyang jiazu zhidu yanjiu* (Research on the family system in the West).

48. "*Xin qingnian* zazhi xuanyan" (Manifesto of the *New Youth* magazine), Winter (1919). Quoted in Chow Tse-tsung, *The May Fourth Movement: Intellectual Revolution in Modern China* (Cambridge: Harvard University Press, 1960), 175.

49. In his article "Jianshe de wenxue geming lun" (Toward a constructive theory of literary revolution), which first appeared in *Xin qingnian* IV, no. 4 (April, 1918).

50. Foreign feminists whose writings were translated include Ellen Key, Yosano Akiko, Yamakawa Kikue (the Japanese feminist-socialist who translated Bebel's *Women Under Socialism*), Margaret Sanger, and Charlotte Perkins Gilman.

51. For a bibliography of women's magazines, including those of a feminist persuasion, see Jacqueline Nivard, "La Presse féminine Chinoise de 1898 a 1949," *Etudes Chinoises* 5 (1986). For a more descriptive introduction to May Fourth women's organizations and their publications, see Liu-Wang Liming, *Zhongguo funü yundong* (The Chinese women's movement) (Shanghai: Shanghai Commercial Press, 1934), 181–191.

52. One of the earliest and most radical of such May Fourth feminist periodicals, *Funü pinglun* (launched in 1921), had among its contributors several soon-to-be prominent May Fourth writers, including Ye Shengtao and Mao Dun.

53. "Du '*Shaonian Zhongguo*' funü hao" (Reading the issue on women in *Young China*), reprinted in *Mao Dun quanji* (Beijing: Renmin wenxue chubanshe, 1985), vol. 14, 89.

54. Mao Dun was put in charge of the magazine in 1919, although he left the position in 1920 to take over *Xiaoshuo yuebao* (Short story monthly). For an informative article that traces the changing nature of this magazine, see Jacqueline Nivard, "Women and the Women's Press: The Case of the *Ladies' Journal*," *Republican China* X, no. 16 (1984): 37–55.

55. An advertisement for the press lists, e.g., such titles as *Zhongguo jinshi funü canzheng yundong shi* (The history of the modern Chinese women's suffrage movement) by Zhong Guiyang; *Funü wenti mingzhu jieshao* (Introduction to famous works on the Women Question) by Jin Zhonghua; *Zhongguo funü shi* (The history of Chinese women) by Huang Xinmian and Yao Mingda; *Zhongguo funü laodong wenti* (The problem of Chinese women's labor) by Zhong Guiyang; *Shijie funü yundong shi* (A history of the global women's movement) by Lu Yunzhang nüshi.

56. *Nüzi shijie* (1904), *Zhongguo xinnüjie* (1907), *Zhongguo nübao* (1907), and *Shenzhou nübao* (1907), for instance, all featured "xiaoshuo," columns.

57. I would again refer the reader to Jayawardena's *Feminism and Nationalism* (1986) and Basu's *The Challenge of Local Feminisms* (1995), which trace the formation of feminist movements within specific Third World contexts.

58. Wang Weiqi, *Shijie nüquan fada shi* (The world history of the development of women's rights) (Shanghai: Shanghai wenming shuju, 1905).

59. Vera Schwartz, *The Chinese Enlightenment: Intellectuals and the Legacy of the May Fourth Movement of 1919* (Berkeley: University of California Press, 1986), 116.

60. I am reminded here of an anecdote about the progressive playwright Ouyang Yuqian who, after recasting the traditionally despised femme fatale Pan Jinlian in a more sympathetic light, so identified with the heroine that he decided to perform the role himself. Not an entirely unusual occurrence in a culture in which female parts were traditionally played by male actors, the anecdote provides a useful analogy for the potential peripheralization of women in a male-dominated feminism. On one level, the anecdote bespeaks a commendable effort by the modern male intellectual to challenge traditional ideas about women—in this case, he appropriates a famous narrative about the dangers of uncontrolled female sexuality to critique the constraints on women in feudal marriage. On another, however, the author's unyielding control over his representation—he not only created the new image but seeks to control its proper interpretation by occupying the role himself—consigns women to their (traditional) space of silence all over again.

61. Chris Gilmartin makes a similar point in her invaluable work on radical women in the early Communist movement. Citing the example of *Funü zhi sheng* (Women's voice), a left-wing magazine edited and written by women for women readers in 1921, she also finds evidence of an awareness of the need for female agency in feminist causes: "they instinctively realized the importance of making their first order of business the creation of their own organs of mass propaganda. They did not merely parrot men's voices but through their writings often asserted a female perspective on a number of issues" (204). Gilmartin does not romanticize these efforts, however, but stresses that in conjunction with this remarkable agency was a more problematic pattern of compliance and thus complicity with patriarchal hierarchy within the party.

62. *Zhongguo funü yundong*, 181.

63. "Jiefang de funü yu funü de jiefang" (Emancipated women and women's emancipation), *Mao Dun quanji*, 14 (1984–1993), 64; original article in *Funü zazhi* (1919).

64. Alice Jardine, *Gynesis: Configurations of Woman and Modernity* (Ithaca: Cornell University Press, 1985), 25.

65. Eide, *China's Ibsen: From Ibsen to Ibsenism* (London: Curzon Press, 1987).
66. Chang-Tai Hong, "Female Symbols of Resistance in Chinese Wartime Spoken Drama," *Modern China*, 15 (April 1989), 149–177.
67. Nor, I would add, is it uniquely Chinese. Both Jardine and Felski, e.g., have published studies on the "imaginative centrality" of the feminine in Western modernity.
68. Liu, "The Female Body and Nationalist Discourse," 175.
69. Yaeger, *Honey-Mad Women*, 41.
70. The appearance of liberal feminist groups who, like their early Western counterparts, were chiefly devoted to achieving legal equality with men, was the exception.
71. Liu-Wang, *Zhongguo funü yundong*, 156.
72. The need to address historiographic conventions as a part of feminist literary scholarship has been raised by numerous critics. For an excellent discussion of these issues, see Margaret Ezell's *Writing Women's Literary History* (Baltimore: Johns Hopkins University Press, 1993).
73. Examples of this include both the more theoretically inclined scholarship in the essays in collections such as *Gender and Sexuality in Modern Chinese Literature and Society* (1993) and *Gender Politics in Modern China* (1993), as well as more standard literary histories of women's writing like Meng Yue and Dai Jinhua's *Fuchu lishi dibiao* (1989) and Qiao Yigang's *Zhongguo nüxing de wenxue shijie* (1993).
74. Wendy Larson, *Women and Writing in Modern China* (Stanford: Stanford University Press, 1998), 166–197.
75. I have in mind here such stories as Xie Bingying's "Paoqi" (Abandoned, 1932) and Yang Gang's "Riji shiyi" (Fragment from a lost diary, 1936), both of which foreground the experience of pregnant activists.
76. Edward Gunn, *Unwelcome Muse: Chinese Literature in Shanghai and Peking, 1937–1945* (New York: Columbia University Press, 1980).

CHAPTER 1   NATIONAL IMAGINARIES: FEMINIST FANTASIES AT THE TURN OF THE CENTURY

1. Many women's organizations were dedicated to this dual agenda. The *Gongaihui* (Mutual love association) for instance, an early all-women's political association, which was formed in Tokyo in the wake of the Russian occupation of Manchuria in 1903, linked the questions of woman and nation by locating the importance of women's emancipation in the resulting creation of patriotic female citizens (*nüguomin*). As their charter stated, their objective was "to enhance the status of the two-hundred million women of China and to regain their natural rights so that every woman, imbued with a concern for the nation, will be able to fulfill her duty as a citizen." Quoted in Liumei Ching, "The Forerunners of Chinese Feminism in Japan" (Ph.D. diss., Leiden University, 1988), 288. The charter of this organization was first published in *Zhejiang chao* (Tides of Zhejiang) (1903), 3.
2. Lian Shi (Luo Yanbin), "Fakanci," *Zhongguo xinnüjie* (China's new women), no. 1 (1907): 2.

3. This journal was edited by Tang Qunying (1871–1938), who would later spearhead the Women's Suffrage Alliance (*Nüzi canzheng tongmenghui*) and launch *Nüquan ribao* (Women's rights daily) in 1913 in Hunan. Despite its mission statement, the contents of this journal reveal a fairly broad array of concerns, including marriage reform, education, labor, and ethics.

4. "Liuri nüxuehui zazhi fakanci" (Publication announcement of the magazine of the overseas women students in Japan organization) as cited in full in Tan Sheying, *Zhongguo funü yundong tongshi* (A comprehensive history of the Chinese women's movement) (Shanghai: Funü gongming she, 1936), 18–23. This book is an invaluable resource, containing many political manifestos and prefaces of feminist journals of the period.

5. Another article that explores the minor strand of anarcho-feminism, by historian Peter Zarrow, reiterates this conclusion: "The content of this feminism was perhaps radical for its day: feminist demands included the end to foot binding and the right to modern education. But the form of this feminism was confined to China-as-nation: changes were needed ultimately not for the sake of Chinese women but for the sake of Chinese wealth and power." Peter Zarrow, "He Zhen and Anarcho-feminism in China," *Journal of Asian Studies* 47, no. 4 (November 1988): 796–813.

6. Charlotte Beahan, "Feminism and Nationalism in the Chinese Women's Press, 1902–1922," *Modern China* 1, no. 4 (1975): 414. For a much earlier account of feminist publications in China by a woman activist involved in the early Republican suffrage campaign, see Tan Sheying, *Zhongguo funü yundong tongshi*. More recent Chinese scholarship that touches on the subject includes Liu Jucai's well-researched *Zhongguo jindai funü yundongshi* (History of the modern Chinese women's movement) (Liaoning: Zhongguo funü chubanshe, 1989) and Lu Meiyi and Zheng Yongfu, *Zhongguo funü yundong: 1840–1921* (The Chinese women's movement) (Zhengzhou: Henan renmin chubanshe, 1990). The latter includes useful profiles of many women activists of the late Qing.

7. Tani Barlow, "Theorizing Women: Funü, Guojia, Jiating (Chinese Women, State, and Family)," *Genders* 10 (Spring 1991): 132–160. Using as her primary example a typical late Qing pro-reformist publication, the *Xin nüzi duben* (New woman reader), Barlow illustrates how women's loyalties are symbolically realigned from the domestic to the public sphere in stories celebrating traditional Chinese and Western heroines who dedicate themselves, in varying capacities, to the cause of national salvation (*jiuguo*). She argues that while such narratives might at first appear to represent a radical reemplotment of feminine roles—transgression of the narrow domestic categories of daughter, wife, and mother in which women's lives were traditionally organized—upon closer inspection it becomes obvious that they are, in fact, merely an extension of conventional gender paradigms into a more public, political sphere of activity. In these stories, as Barlow rightly discerns, women's participation in national affairs does not replace or even render problematic their traditional duties as wives or mother but rather is depicted as an expression of those fundamental roles. Barlow's example sharply illustrates the conservative ideological underpinnings of the idealized *nü guomin* of the early nationalist movement; however, what Barlow fails to address in her otherwise insightful discussion is how feminists wrote very different kinds of narratives of the nation.

8. An article on modern women's writing by the mainland feminist critic Li Ziyun, for instance, makes the following claim: "Ding Ling, the leading female

figure in modern Chinese literature, might be said to be the first woman to express an awareness of the sexual inequality underlying patriarchal oppression" (300). See "Women's Consciousness and Women's Writing," in Christina Gilmartin et al., eds., *Engendering China: Women, Culture, and the State* (Cambridge: Harvard University Press, 1994), 299–317. Statements like these abound in current scholarship.

9. Meng Yue and Dai Jinhua, *Fuchu lishi dibiao* (Emerging on the horizon of history) (Zhengzhou: Henan renmin chubanshe, 1989), 29–35.

10. See, for, instance, Recheng Aiguoren, *Nüzi jiuguo meitan* (A beautiful tale of a girl who saves the nation) (Shanghai: Xinminshe, 1902). This short novel retells the story of Joan of Arc, or Jende, and concludes by lamenting the lack of such patriotic spirit in China.

11. *Nüyuhua* (Flowers in the female prison), a short 12 linked-chapter (*hui*) novel, was published in 1904 in Shanghai and is, to my knowledge, the earliest known feminist novel by a woman author, Wang Miaoru (1877–1903, a.k.a. Xihu nüshi). Aside from the few facts provided in the brief biography appended at the end of her novel, which was published posthumously, little is known about this writer from Zhejiang. Prior to her novel, she is said to have written, and presumably published, a chuanqi entitled *Xiao taoyuan chuanqi* (*The tale of little Taoyuan*) as well as a collection of poetry; she died not long after completing *Nüyuhua* at the tender age of 26. Although Wang Miaoru's novel is, as a work of creative fiction, flawed in several respects, as the first explicitly feminist treatment of the conditions of women by a woman writer, it represents a significant cultural event that deserves greater attention in literary histories of modern China than it has hitherto received. Citations here are from a photo reprint in *Zhongguo jindai xiaoshuo daxi* (Compendium of modern Chinese fiction) (Nanchang: Baihuazhou wenyi chubanshe, 1991).

Jingweishi (1905–1907) (Stones of the Jingwei bird) is an ambitious *tanci* that the renowned feminist pioneer and nationalist martyr Qiu Jin began writing during her radical student days in Tokyo in 1904–1905 and continued composing off and on until the time of her execution for plotting to overthrow the Qing government in 1907. Qiu Jin only completed the first part of her utopian narrative: the drafts of chapter 5 and part of chapter 6 were discovered among her belongings when she was arrested by local officials in Datong and were later submitted as material evidence of her revolutionary intentions during the trial that led to her conviction and subsequent beheading. Citations here are from *Qiu Jin ji* (Shanghai: Shanghai guju chubanshe, 1960).

Published in 1907 by the Zuoxinshe, *Nüziquan* (Women's rights) is by Siqi Zhai (Zhan Kai) a little known male author with feminist sympathies. He is also the author of another vernacular feminist novel, *Zhongguo xinnühao* (The new heroine of China, 1907). Citations here are from a reprint in *Zhongguo jindai xiaoshuo daxi* (Nanchang: Baihuazhou wenyi chubanshe, 1991). For a recently published article analyzing Siqi Zhai's work see Ellen Widmer, "Inflecting Gender: Zhan Kai/Siqi Zhai's 'New Novels' and 'Courtesan Sketches,'" *Nan Nü: Men, Women, and Gender in China* 6, no. 1 (2004).

12. Rosemary Jackson, *Fantasy: The Literature of Subversion* (London and New York: Methuen, 1981), 3–4. Jackson acknowledges the fact that fantasy can provide an outlet for (and thus a sublimation of) subversive social desire, but also stresses its productive potential in generating desire for social change.

13. I do not include *Nü Wa shi* in my analysis below because it represents, to my mind, a satire of the feminist agenda rather than an earnest feminist text *per se*.

For a brief synopsis of this text, see Liu Jucai, *Zhongguo jindai funü yundongshi*, 171–175.

14. Siqi Zhai's *Nüziquan* (1907) is a futuristic novel set in the 1940s, by which time China has undergone dramatic social restructuring such that the major economic and political woes of the late Qing, among them foreign monopoly of railroads and mines, the unstable tax system, and the technological weakness of the Chinese military, have been remedied. China's national revolution, however, is incomplete, for the female population remains as subjugated as it has been in the past. The main narrative chronicles the quest of a prototypical New Woman named Zhenniang to promote the rights of women, a task she (predictably) accomplishes, thus finally realizing China's historical bid to join the family of modern nation states.

15. For nationalists like Liang Qichao and Yan Fu, *qun*, or association, referred to the unification of political participants based on common loyalties and commitment to the nation; it was seen as a fundamental prerequisite for effective social change and the basis of democracy. The lack of *qun*, in the minds of late Qing nationalists, was a major contributing factor in China's failure to attain the status of strong, modern nationhood and, in turn, in China's subjection to foreign imperialism. From the turn of the century, however, this key term of nationalist discourse also crops up in new feminist magazines such as *Nüxuebao* and *Zhongguo nübao*. On one level, *hequn*—the act of association—is advocated as an important foundation for the transformation of the *nüjie*: the solidarity of women based in part on a unity of emotion. Yet on another level, the concept of *qun* as the basis for nationhood is reenvisioned in terms of certain "unique" female attributes. For example, Chen Xiefen, a close associate of Qiu Jin in Japan and the founding editor of *Nüxuebao*, wrote a provocative article entitled "Qun" (Association) (*Nüxuebao* no. 1, 1903) in which she argues that women possess unique qualities of benevolence, resoluteness, and vengefulness, and thus are *better* equipped to unite in opposition to the various forces of domination: not just men, but also the Manchu regime and foreign powers. In other articles, women radicals used the argument that the lack of unity among women (often described with the familiar metaphor of loose sand) is in part to blame for the dismal state of China's national affairs in order to demand greater rights and freedoms for women—including their right to associate in public with men.

16. I would note that the importance of women's physical fitness also emerged as a popular topic in late Qing reform debates, and several fictional works, including *Nüziquan* and *Ershi shiji nüjie wenmingdeng* (The torch of civilization of the twentieth-century women's world, 1911) feature women who participate in athletic competitions.

17. For recent feminist analyses of national formations, see, for instance, Mohanty et al., eds., *Third World Women and the Politics of Feminism* (Bloomington: Indiana University Press, 1991); McClintock et al., eds., *Dangerous Liaisons: Gender, Nation, and Postcolonial Perspectives* (Minneapolis: Minnesota University Press, 1997); and Parker et al., eds., *Feminisms and Sexualities* (London: Routledge, 1992).

18. McClintock et al., *Dangerous Liasons*, 109.

19. Timothy Brennan, "The National Longing for Form," in Homi Bhabha, ed., *Nation and Narration* (London: Routledge Press, 1990), 44–70.

20. The first waves of Chinese foreign students in Japan coincided with the "Bunmei Kaika" period, a period of fervent translation of Western philosophical

and political texts, including those of Spencer and Mill. One of the primary forums for debate on these new ideas was the *Meirokuzasshi*, the journal founded in 1877 by the Meirokuzasha, whose members included Mori Arinori (1847–1889) who wrote on the need for marriage reform and the outspoken proponent of women's educational reform, Fukuzawa Yukichi (1833–1901).

21. Zeng Jihui, "Buchanzuhui boyi" (Dispute of the anti-footbinding society) in *Xiangbao*, no. 151. Quoted in Lu Meiyi, *Zhongguo funü yundong*, 75.

22. Liang Qichao, "Chang she nüxuetang qi" (Proposal calling for the establishment of women's schools) as quoted in Liu Jucai, *Zhongguo jindai funü yundongshi*, 91.

23. The historical data here is drawn from research on the feminist press by Charlotte Beahan (1975), Liu Jucai (1989), Li Youning (1981), and Jacqueline Nivard (1984), as well as my own research at the Guomindang Party History Archives and the Modern History Institute of Academia Sinica in Taibei and Beijing University Library.

24. Founding members included Kang Tongwei, the daughter of Kang Youwei; Li Huixian, the wife of Liang Qichao; Qiu Yufang, the female editor of an early vernacular language reform newspaper, the *Wuxi baihuabao* (Wuxi vernacular journal); and Li Run, wife of Tan Sitong. The previous year this group had founded the *Zhongguo nüxuehui* as well as a school for women.

25. By 1911, there were 450, according to R.S. Britton's estimate. See *The Chinese Periodical Press, 1880–1912* (Taibei: Chengwen, 1966).

26. The prevalent use of pseudonyms makes it difficult at times to determine the gender of the contributors to the feminist press, although I have verified that many of the editors and/or frequent contributors were women.

27. "Funü shixing geming ying yi ansha wei shouduan" (Women in the revolutionary movement ought to use assassination as a method), *Zhongguo xinnüjie*, no. 6 (1907).

28. In 1907, *Shenzhou nübao* was launched in Shanghai by several of her close friends, both in commemoration of her life and to carry on the mission of her journal.

29. From the editorial pages, it would appear that many feminist journals intended to generate funds through advertisements, though the extant copies I have examined tend to carry few (if any) ads. One issue of *Nüzi shijie* that I examined advertised textbooks for women students and other women's magazines (in this case, *Zhongguo nübao* and *Zhongguo xinnüjie*). Ads for products relating to women's education, according to the guidelines, were half price.

30. Liu Jucai, *Zhongguo jindai funü yundongshi*, 184.

31. The slightly later *Shenzhou nübao* (1912–1913) lists distributors as far flung as London, Paris, and the University of Illinois (!). No doubt the "distributors" were individuals studying abroad.

32. The connection between modern linguistic reform and gender politics has been little studied. The fact that many of the earliest calls for vernacular writing were made in reference to women readers, however, seems to suggest an important link between gender and the rise of modern vernacular Chinese as a literary language.

33. Liang Qichao, "Lun baoguan youyiyu guoshi" (On the value of the periodical press in national affairs) (1896). Translated in Britton, 88.

34. Qiu Jin, "Fakanci" (Foreword), *Zhongguo nübao*, no. 1 (1907).

35. Luo Yanbin, "Benbao wuda zhuyi yanshuo" (A speech on the five major principles of this paper), 2 (1907). Translation from Leslie Collins, "The New Woman: A Psychohistorical Study of the Chinese Feminist Movement from 1900 to the Present" (Ph.D. diss., Yale University, 1976), 270.

36. These include the American educator Mary Lyon (1797–1849), who paved the way for higher education for women; Lucretia Mott (1793–1880), an abolitionist and feminist who helped organize the Women's Rights Convention at Seneca Falls with Elizabeth Cady Stanton; Margaret Fuller (1810–1850), the first female foreign correspondent for a major American newspaper; and Florence Nightingale (1820–1910), British pioneer of the nursing profession.

37. See, in particular, Dolezelova-Velingerova, ed., *The Chinese Novel at the Turn of the Century* (Toronto: University of Toronto Press, 1980); Chen Pingyuan, *Zhongguo xiaoshuo xushi moshi de zhuanbian* (The narrative transformation of Chinese fiction) (Beijing: Jiuda wenhua chuban, 1990); and David Wang, *Fin-de-Siècle Splendors: Repressed Modernities of Late Qing Fiction, 1849–1911* (Stanford: Stanford University Press, 1997).

38. Liang Qichao, "Lun xiaoshuo yu qunzhi zhi guanxi" (On the value of the periodical press in national affairs) (1896). Translated in C.T. Hsia, "Yen Fu and Liang Ch'i-ch'ao as Advocates of New Fiction," in Adele Rickett, ed., *Chinese Approaches to Literature: From Confucius to Liang Chi-chao* (Princeton: Princeton University Press, 1978), 222–223.

39. According to Chen Xianggong, Qiu Jin planned to serialize *Jingweishi* in her own magazine *Zhongguo funü*. See *Qiu Jin nianpuji chuanji ziliao* (Biographical materials on Qiu Jin) (Beijing: Zhongguo shuju, 1983), 32.

40. Qiu Jin, "Yanshuo de haochu" (The merits of speeches), *Baihuabao*, no. 1 (1904).

41. Magazines like *Nüxuebao* and *Nüzi shijie* frequently reported on public speeches by women, and featured articles promoting the practice of public speaking.

42. Given the conspicuous absence of women in the development of other fictional narrative forms (the vernacular and *wenyan* short story and the novel, for instance) prior to the twentieth century, the relationship between women and the *tanci* has, not surprisingly, generated considerable interest among scholars of Chinese women's literary history. Although this is not the place to review the literature on this topic, I would note two theoretical tendencies which, as they relate to the important issue of the gender/genre nexus, have a direct bearing on both the general subject of this study and the specific question at hand, Qiu Jin's political deployment of the *tanci* form. The first and clearly least convincing explanation posits an inherent link between literary form and "feminine nature": this view (which has obvious parallels with the early Western feminist literary theory discussed in the introduction) claims that women's emotional and expressive "nature" results in their affinity for poetic form. The *tanci*, as a basically poetic narrative genre (unlike other more strictly prose narrative forms) is thus naturally suited to women. Another, slightly different view reaches essentially the same conclusion (i.e., that women have excelled in the *tanci* because of their poetic capacities) but via a different explanation: namely, it links women's historically oppressed status to their literary productions by asserting that the restricted realm of feminine experience limited women to private poetic expression, and disabled them from writing in the more public, social narrative genres. Aside

from the problematic dichotomy of poetry/private and narrative/social and the naive assumption that experience alone provides the basis of art, this view verges on a form of historical essentialism. Specifically, rather than explain how women's literary practices have shifted in relation to specific moments in patriarchal history, this view attempts to define female creativity using a totalized vision of "patriarchy."

43. *Ershi shiji nüjie wenmingdeng* (The torch of civilization of the twentieth-century women's world) (Shanghai: Mingming she, 1911), in A Ying, *Wanqing wenxue congchao: shuochang wenxue yuan* (A compendium of late Qing literature: volume of "shuochang" literature) (Beijing: Zhonghua shuju, 1960), 173–201.

44. Once again, we find a similar trope in *Nüziquan*, in which the daily paper *Women Citizen's News* launched by the central protagonist captures instant national attention, reaching an astonishing circulation of half a million readers within the first week, and provides a much-needed platform for her (inter)national campaign to promote women's rights.

45. Published by the Shaonian Zhongguo xuehui chubanshe, the latter is one of the earliest published tracts on women's equality in China. Using natural rights theory and social Darwinism, this treatise argues that: (1) women are naturally equal to men; (2) their apparent incompetence stems from their lack of access to education; and (3) China's national development is connected to women's social status.

46. The following statement, for instance, is typical: "Let us not forget that it cannot be expected that women will become aware of their subservience, of what it really means to be called a 'worthy wife,' if their situation is not explained to them, if they are not shown that their idea of this situation as a state of happiness is illusory." Yi Qin, *Jiangsu*, no. 4.

47. Adrienne Rich, "When We Dead Awaken: Writing as Revision," in *On Lies, Secrets, and Silence: Selected Prose, 1966–1978* (New York: Norton, 1979), 35.

48. I use the term "subjectivity" in the sense described by Chris Weedon's concise definition, as "the conscious and unconscious thoughts and emotions of the individual, her sense of herself and her ways of understanding her relation to the world." Weedon, *Feminist Practice and Poststructuralist Theory* (Oxford: Basil Blackwell, 1987), 32.

49. Several other feminist fantasies of this period feature enlightened deities. For instance, *Huiguanguo* (Return of the sweet fruit) features an enlightened Nü Wa who turns a stone into "the daughter of freedom" whom she sends to China, along with three mentors Hua Mulan, Qin Liangyu, and Liang Hongyu. *Ershi shiji nüjie wenmingdeng*, another *tanci*, is framed by a story involving a fascinating encounter between the now immortal Harriet Beecher Stowe and Confucius's mother, who discuss the plight of Chinese women.

50. Whereas *Jingweishi* and *Nüyuhua* both use the convention of geographical displacement to construct an alternative perspective on contemporary "reality," other fantasy novels from the period rely on the common device of temporal displacement. *Nüziquan*, described above, for instance imagines a prosperous, post-reform China in the not-too-distant future (1940s), when the unhealthy symptoms of China's *fin-de-siècle* malaise have been successfully remedied: a constitutional monarchy governs the nation; the tax system stabilized; the unequal treaties with foreign nations rescinded; domestic control over the mining industry and railways restored; and a modern military

installed to protect national security. One major difference is said to separate China from the modern civilized world—its entrenched patriarchy. Though the worst customs such as foot binding have been eradicated, women remain second-class citizens of a male-dominated regime.

51. The heroine of Chen Duansheng's (1751–1796) tanci, *Zaisheng yuan* (A story of rebirth).

52. The famous satirical episode of the "Kingdom of Women" in Li Ruzhen's *Jinghuayuan* (Flowers in the mirror), in which the hero is taken captive in a state in which conventional gender roles have been reversed, may seem the exception to the rule, but the progressive implications of this scene are arguably canceled out by the emphatic association between female domination and sociopolitical upheaval framing the novel as a whole.

53. A number of scholars have commented on the influence of Sophia Perofskaya as a new female model (not unlike Nora in the May Fourth Era). See, e.g., Fudan daxue zhongwenxi jindai wenxue yanjiushi ed. *Zhongguo jindai wenxue yanjiu* (Baihuazhuo wenyi chubanshe, 1991), 262–281, which discusses Luo Pu's *Dong'ou nühaojie* (Heroine of eastern Europe) in this connection. For an even more thorough account of foreign models and the construction of the Chinese New Woman around the turn of the century, see Hu Ying, *Tales of Translation: Composing the New Woman in China: 1899–1918* (Stanford: Stanford University Press, 2000).

54. While Qiu Jin was certainly not alone in mistaking certain conventions of etiquette in Western European culture for an indication women's equal social status, some of her contemporary were far less impressed by Western practices. As an interesting counterexample, Wang Miaoru's *Nüyuhua* contains a conversation between Pingquan and her fiancé in which the two acknowledge the fact that while Western women enjoyed a higher social standing than their Chinese counterparts, they too were far from having achieved social parity with men.

55. In *Nüyuhua*, the advent of the new social order also enables the fulfilment of a more personal form of desire: Xu Pingquan, having vowed to postpone her marriage until her mission to educate the *nüjie* had been accomplished, is finally able to complete her romantic union. A similar resolution can be found in *Nüziquan*: Zhenniang, now protected by the constitution, is able to legitimately marry the man of her own, rather her parents', choosing. The issue of romantic freedom would soon emerge as a central concern of intellectuals and writers in the May Fourth era.

56. Angelika Bammer, *Partial Visions: Feminism and Utopianism in the 1970s* (New York: Routledge, 1991).

57. Quoted in Bammer, *Partial Visions*, 51.

58. For instance, although Kang Youwei's utopian philosophical treatise *Datongshu* projects a vision of the future in which gender inequalities have been eradicated, there is little indication that women have played a significant role in this achievement. The author's paternalistic desire to "save" women is unmistakable: "I now have a great wish: to save the eight hundred million women of my own time from drowning in [the sea] of suffering, I now have a great desire: to bring the incalculable inconceivable numbers of women of the future the happiness of equality, complete unity, and independence." Laurence G. Thompson, *Ta T'ung-shu: The One World Philosophy of K'ang Yu-wei* (London: Allen and Unwin, 1958), 150.

59. In *Nüziquan*, Zhenniang's suitor mobilizes his military comrades to demonstrate in support of women's rights; in *Nüyuhua*, Pingquan's fiancee takes to writing feminist novels, and in the fragmented portion of *Jingweishi*, Huang Jurui's progressive tutor Master Yu provides clandestine assistance in the heroines' escape to Japan.

CHAPTER 2   THE NEW WOMAN'S WOMEN

1. Wendy Larson, *Women and Writing in Modern China* (Stanford: Stanford University Press, 1998).
2. See Marston Anderson, *The Limits of Realism: Chinese Fiction in the Revolutionary Period* (Berkeley: University of California Press, 1990); and David Wang, *Fictional Realism in 20th-Century China: Mao Dun, Lao She, and Shen Congwen* (New York: Columbia University Press, 1992).
3. "Wenxue yu rensheng" (Literature and life), in Zhao Jiabi, ed., *Zhongguo xin wenxue daxi* (Compendium of modern Chinese literature). 10 vols. (Taibei: Yeqiang chubanshe, 1990). English translation appears in Kirk Denton, ed., *Modern Chinese Literary Thought: Writings on Literature, 1893–1945* (Stanford: Stanford University Press, 1996), 190–195.
4. Anderson, *The Limits of Realism*, 25.
5. "Zhongguo de funü yundong wenti" (Problems of China's women's movement), *Lu Yin xuanji* (Selected works of Lu Yin) (Fuzhou: Fujian renmin chubanshe, 1985), 16–28. Originally published in *Minze* 5, no. 1 (1924).
6. Translations appeared regularly in publications such as *Funü pinglun, Funü zhoubao, Funü zazhi*, and *Xin nüxing*.
7. The woman translator Zhang Xian (dates unknown) would later publish an important collection of essays by Yosano Akiko. See Zhang Ruogu, "Zhongguo xiandai de nüzuojia" (Contemporary Chinese women writers), *Zhenmeishan* (1928): 49–50, for additional information on her and other May Fourth women translators.
8. Zhang launched this journal in 1926 after a dispute with the Commercial Press over his controversial issue on sexual morality, and his suspected involvement in a strike at the Press led to his dismissal as editor-in-chief. The same year, he opened the Kaiming Bookstore, which published several influential translations of foreign feminist books, including Bebel's *Women and Socialism* (translated by Shen Duanxian in 1929).
9. Key's writings remained popular throughout the early 1930s. A full translation of *The Women's Movement* was translated by Lin Yuanwen and published by the Shanghai Commercial Press in 1936.
10. Li Junyi, "Cong Ai Lunkai dao Ke Luntai" (From Ellen Key to Kollontai) *Funü zazhi*, no. 6 (June 1931): 131–136.
11. Stephen Chan, "The Language of Despair: Ideological Representation of the 'New Women' by May Fourth Writers," *Modern Chinese Literature*, 4 (1988).
12. Chan, "The Language of Despair," 27.
13. Rey Chow, *Woman and Chinese Modernity: The Politics of Reading between West and East* (Minneapolis: University of Minnesota Press, 1991), 103–107.
14. Sally Lieberman, *The Mother and Narrative Politics in Modern China* (Charlottesville: University Press of Virginia, 1998).

15. See his "Bing Xin lun" and "Lu Yin lun" both originally published in *Wenxue* (Literature) (1934). Mao Dun published a similar essay on Ding Ling ("Nüzuojia Ding Ling") the previous year in *Zhongguo luntan*.

16. Yue, 62. Meng Yue and Dai Jinhua make a similar argument in their book *Fuchu lishidiao* (Emerging from the horizon of history) (Taibei: Shibao chubanshe, 1993). See the introduction and chapter 1 in particular.

17. Although overstating the case in the opposite direction is also problematic, as is the case of Meng Yue and Dai Jinhua in their otherwise useful book (1993). Contrasting the "traditional" woman's repressed position under the Confucian order to "modern" women, they make the following, rather simplistic, claim: "That short, six word sentence 'I am my own person' is woman's challenge to the entire symbolic order, for in that single instant when the name 'I' and the female are connected into one symbol, in that one instant when the Zijuns (the female protagonist of Lu Xun's 'Shangshi') become subjects, the long two-thousand-year history of women's objectification and commodification ends and the era of women as subjects commences . . . the emergence (*chuxian*) of women in the symbolic order transforms the relationship between women and society as a whole, for she is no longer in a subject/object relationship with men, but one of subject/subject" (36).

18. Rita Felski, *Beyond Feminist Aesthetics: Feminist Literature and Social Change* (Cambridge: Harvard University Press, 1989), 42.

19. Chan, "The Language of Despair," 48.

20. Felski, *Beyond Feminist Aesthetics*, 156–157.

21. Felski, *Beyond Feminist Aesthetics*; and Maria Lauret, *Liberating Literature: Feminist Fiction in America* (London: Routledge, 1994). See also Penny Boumelha's essay, "Realism and the Ends of Feminism," in Susan Sheridan, ed., *Grafts: Feminist Cultural Criticism* (London: Verso, 1988), 77–91.

22. Felski, *Beyond Feminist Aesthetics*, 159.

23. David Wang makes a compelling argument for this point in his *Fictional Realism* (1992).

24. According to the editors of the short-lived *Nüzuojia zazhi* (Woman writer magazine), this edition of *Zhenmeishan* sold over 10,000 copies within two months, which marked a record-breaking number. One particularly useful article in the issue is Zhang Ruogu's lengthy "Zhongguo xiandai de nüzuojia" (Contemporary Chinese women writers), 1–73, which provides a comprehensive introduction to women's literary production of the period (including writers of children's literature, translation, poetry, and literary history).

25. Jin Zhonghua, "Jinshi funü jiefang yundong zai wenxueshang de fanying," *Funü zazhi*, no. 6 (June 1931): 2–12.

26. Larson, *Women and Writing in Modern China*.

27. Zhou Zuoren, "Nüzi yu wenxue," *Funü zazhi*, no. 8 (August). Citations here are from the translation in Kirk Denton, ed., *Modern Chinese Literary Thought: Writings on Literature 1893–1945*, 228–234.

28. Tan Zhengbi, *Zhongguo nüxing de wenxue shenghuo* (The literary life of Chinese women) (Shanghai: Guangming shuju, 1931).

29. Tao Qiuying, *Zhongguo funü yu wenxue* (Chinese women and literature) (Shanghai: Beixin shuju, 1933).

30. Tao, *Zhongguo funü yu wenxue*, 305–306.

31. To illustrate the extent to which traditional patriarchal values were internalized by women themselves he quotes a line by the famous song poetess

Zhu Shuzhen on the incompatibility between women and writing: "When a woman dabbles in literature, that is truly evil/How can she 'intone the moon' or 'chant into the wind'?/Wearing out the inkstone is not our business/Let us rather be skilled at needlework and embroidery." What Yi Zhen, and others who echoed his view, of course fail to acknowledge is the sharp irony that underlies Zhu's poem, which flouts the very message it ostensibly delivers. See his article "Ji wei dangdai Zhongguo nü xiaoshuojia" (Several contemporary women novelists), *Funü zazhi* (1930). The essay was anthologized several times over the next few years, including in Chen Si, ed., *Zhongxue wenxue duben* (Chinese literature reader) (Shanghai: Tingtaoshe, 1931) and in Huang Renying's *Dangdai Zhongguo nüzuojia lun* (On contemporary Chinese women writers) (Shanghai: Guanghua shuju, 1933).

32. For a compelling feminist critique of the May Fourth reception of Ling Shuhua, including her characterization as a *guixiu* writer, see Rey Chow's "Virtuous Transactions: A Reading of Three Stories by Ling Shuhua," *Modern Chinese Literature* 4 (1988): 71–86.

33. The 1935 film *Xin nüxing* (New women), starring Ruan Lingyu, makes a fascinating reference to the contemporary commodification of the modern woman writer. One scene, e.g., reveals that the heroine Weiming's publisher cares more about the glamorous photo of Weiming that will appear on the jacket of the novel than the novel itself.

34. Editorial preface, Shi Xisheng, ed., *Nüzuojia xiaocongshu* (Shanghai: Guangyi shuju, 1930).

35. What is also ironic about the above attitudes, of course, is the fact that at the time many of the most prolific—and certainly most vociferous—voices in the media torrent about the modern woman were male. As an editor of *Xin qingnian* wistfully points out, alluding to the journal's short-lived *funü wenti* column, "We seek women contributors who can boldly study and solve the woman problem, analyze woman's true nature, understand woman's true positions, and discuss the close relationships between woman and state and society. But such women are as rare as phoenix feathers and unicorn horns." Cited in Wang Zheng, *Women in the Chinese Enlightenment: Oral and Textual Histories* (Berkeley: University of California Press, 1999), 49. While this last point no doubt rang truer in 1917 than a decade or two later, an uncomfortable awareness surfaces from time to time throughout the period that women's feminist voices had somehow been usurped. Women literary intellectuals, in particular, were sensitive to this contradiction and, as I will suggest below, developed specific narrative strategies in their fiction in response.

36. Originally published in her collection *Meigui de ci* (The thorns of the rose) (Shanghai: Zhonghua shuju, 1933). Reprinted in *Lu Yin xiaoshuo* (Shanghai: Guji chubanshe, 1999), 139–155.

37. Reprint in *Lu Yin daibiaozuo* (Representative works by Lu Yin) (Beijing: Huaxia chubanshe, 1998), 200–352. The novel is based on the life of the May Fourth writer Shi Pingmei. Lu Yin and Shi Pingmei were classmates at Beijing Women's Normal College but became especially close friends beginning in 1925, when they worked together as teachers at the affiliated highschool. See Xiao Feng, *Lu Yin zhuan* (Biography of Lu Yin) (Beijing: Beijing shifan daxue chubanshe, 1982), 61.

38. Chen Xuezhao, *Xingfu* (Shanghai: Shenghuo shudian, 1933).

39. Originally published in her collection *Manli* (1928). Reprinted in *Lu Yin xuanji* (Selected works by Lu Yin) (Fuzhou: Fujian chubanshe, 1985), 332–337.

40. In *Shi Pingmei wenji* (Collected works of Shi Pingmei) (Hailar: Neimenggu chubanshe, 2000), 490.

41. Even Chen Dongyuan, a liberal thinker when it came to gender politics, considered the phenomenon of the single woman to be an alarming symptom of the "diseased" condition (bingxiang, 404) of the Chinese family and contemporary society itself, and listed "bachelor teachers" alongside prostitutes as two major problems within contemporary female existence. See the postface of the original edition of his *Zhongguo funü shenghuo shi* (The history of Chinese women's lives) (Shanghai: Shangwu chubanshe, 1937).

42. Originally published in *Xiaoshuo yuebao* (1927). Reprinted in *Lu Yin daibiaozuo*, 128–134.

43. *Nanfeng de meng* (Dreams of southern winds) (Shanghai: Zhenmeishan shudian, 1929).

44. This novel was partially serialized in Lu Xun's journal *Benliu* (Torrents) between 1928–1929 and was subsequently issued as a single volume by Beixin shuju in 1929.

45. In this they also bear a strong resemblance to European New Women writers whose work was being introduced to Chinese readers at the time. For instance, Olive Schreiner's short stories were masterfully translated into Chinese by the woman writer CF (a.k.a. Zhang Jinfen), while the names of Edith Wharton, Virginia Woolf, Stella Cather, and Rebecca West were also familiar to readers at the time, either through the translation of their works or discussions in critical literature.

46. Yi-tsi Feuerwerker, "Women as Writers in the 1920's and 1930's," in Margery Wolf and Roxane Witke, eds., *Women in Chinese Society* (Stanford: Stanford University Press, 1975), 167.

47. See Xiao Feng, *Lu Yin zhuan*.

48. Chen Xuezhao, *Surviving the Storm: A Memoir*. Trans. Hua Ti and Caroline Green (Armonk: M.E. Sharpe, Inc., 1990).

49. Cao Ye, *Xiandai Zhongguo nüzuojia* (Modern Chinese women writers) (Tianjin: Renwen shudian, 1932).

50. See, e.g., Zhang Ruogu's description of her work, 25.

51. Jian Shen, "Du Bingying nüshi *Congjun Riji*" (Reading Miss Bingying's *War Diary*), in Huang Renying, ed., *Dangdai nüzuojia lun* (Shanghai: Guanghua Shuju, 1933), 108.

52. Domna Stanton, *The Female Autograph* (Chicago: University of Chicago Press, 1987), 4. Other feminist critics have pointed out that this critical tendency is grounded in several stereotypes of women, chief among them, feminine narcissism and the relative lack of creative (as opposed to procreative) abilities.

53. Larson, "The End of 'Funü Wenxue': Women's Literature from 1925–1935," *Modern Chinese Literature* 4 (1988).

54. Lu Yin, for instance, often gave her characters names that encouraged readers to identify them with herself. For example, in Lu Yin's 1927 story "Lantian de chanhuilu," which I analyze below, the I-narrator's name is Yin. Lu Sha is a character who appears in several of Lu Yin's fictional works, but is also the name by which Shi Pingmei addressed her in the lyrical letters the two jointly published in the early 1920s.

55. Lauret, 107.
56. All of these stories first appeared in *Chuangzao zhoukan* (Creation weekly) and were subsequently included in Feng's first short story collection *Juanshi* (Juanshi grass) (Beixin shuju chubanshe, 1926). The collection was so popular it was reprinted again in 1928, with two new stories. Reprinted in *Feng Yuanjun chuangzuo yiwenji* (Collected writings and translations of Feng Yuanjun) (Jinan: Shandong renmin chubanshe, 1983). For an insightful discussion of these same works in terms of their shifting treatment of the maternal figure, see Sally Lieberman, *The Mother and Narrative Politics in Modern China*.
57. Feng's literary debut occurred in the early 1920s shortly after graduating from the prestigious Beijing Women's Normal College, a hotbed of feminist ideas, thanks in part to faculty members like the progressive male scholar Li Dazhen. Feng would go on to become a prominent scholar of Chinese literature.
58. Qiao Yigang, *Zhongguo nüxing de wenxue shijie* (The literary world of Chinese women) (Wuhan: Hubei jiaoyu chubanshe, 1993), 195.
59. Lu Yin was particularly popular with female readers at the time. According to Su Xuelin, one of her classmates at Nü Shida, there were few educated women of their generation who did not read her fiction. See "'Haibin guren' de zuozhe Lu Yin nüshi," *Su Xuelin wenji* 2 (1994), 353–357.
60. Lu Yin attended the inaugural meeting of the association in Beijing in 1921, and much of her early writing was subsequently published in the journal connected with that group, the *Xiaoshuo yuebao* (Short story monthly).
61. "Chuangzao de wo jian" (My opinions on creativity) in *Xiaoshuo yuebao* (1921). Reprinted in *Lu Yin xuanji* (Fujian renmin chubanshe, 1985), 60–61. This translation is from Kirk Denton, ed., *Modern Chinese Literary Theory: Writings on Literature*, 235–237.
62. Denton, *Modern Chinese Literary Theory*, 237.
63. Marston Anderson examines the importance of the concept of "tongqing" in May Fourth theories of realism, especially that of the critic/writer Ye Shaojun. See in particular, chapters 2 and 3 of his book *The Limits of Realism* (1990).
64. Mao Dun, who would later criticize Lu Yin for what he viewed as the excessive emotionalism of her writing, held a strikingly similar view with regard to the moral responsibility of the realist writer: "To use intelligible language in this way to awaken the masses is not bad, but merely to criticize without interpreting can cause melancholy and deep sorrow, and these can to lead to despondency." Quoted in Anderson, *The Limits of Realism*, 42.
65. Sandra Lee Bartky, *Femininity and Domination: Studies in the Phenomenology of Oppression* (New York: Routledge, 1990), 14.
66. See Anderson, *The Limits of Realism*, chapter 3. Anderson argues that such endings are in fact self-conscious and ironic, designed to expose and undermine the "realist project."
67. As I discuss in the Introduction, in making their arguments, several contemporary critics paint precisely such a gloomy picture. Stephen Chan, for instance, suggests that May Fourth intellectuals "failed" to posit a textual (in addition to sociohistorical) place for the New Women, 23; Tonglin Lu writes of the May Fourth debates about social transformation, "women . . . were excluded from this great battlefield. Or, their presence served mainly as a means of representation," 6.

68. First published in *Xiaoshuo yuebao* 18, no. 2 (1927). Reprinted in *Lu Yin xuanji* (Fujian renmin chubanshe, 1985), 282–294. Translations here are from Dooling and Torgeson, eds., *Writing Women in Modern China* (New York: Columbia University Press, 1998). For details on this period of Lu Yin's life, see Xiao Feng, *Lu Yin zhuan*, 19–36.

69. Lu Yin, "Jinhou funü de chulu" (The future of women), in *Lu Yin daibiaozuo* (Beijing: Huaxia chubanshe, 1998). Originally published in her collection *Dongjing xiaopin* (Beixin shuju, 1936).

70. Lu Yin, "Huaping shidai" (The flower vase generation), in *Lu Yin daibiaozuo*. Originally published in *Qingguang* (a supplement to *Shishi xinbao*), August 11, 1933.

71. Like many other May Fourth women writers, Lu Yin explicitly addressed contemporary gender issues in many critical articles that she wrote in addition to her creative writing. Besides those already mentioned, other notable articles include "Zhongguo de funü yundong wenti" (The problem of the Chinese women's movement) (1924).

72. This collection, edited by Tao Qiuying (Shijie shuju, 1930) was obviously a hit, as it was already in its fifth reprinting by 1933. The volume is divided into different "genres" of letters that the emancipated women were to master, including letters to family, relatives, spouses, teachers, classmates, and society.

73. In a reading of "Haibin guren" (Seaside friends) (1923), Wendy Larson also notes the importance of "an all-female society" in Lu Yin's fiction, 157. The trope of the compassionate female community in fact appears throughout women's fiction of this period. Other notable examples include Ding Ling's "Shujiazhong" (Summer break) (1928) and her unfinished novel *Muqin* (Mother) (1933); and Ling Shuhua's "Shuo you zhemme yihui shi" (Once upon a time) (1928).

74. Katherine Carlitz, "The Social Uses of Female Virtue," *Late Imperial China* 12, no. 2 (December 1991).

75. It was discussed in publications such as *Xin nüxing zazhi* (New woman magazine). For a feminist defense of "dushen zhuyi" from this period, see Chen Xuezhao's essays "Gei nanxing" (To men), *Xin nüxing* (December 1926) and "Xiandai nüxing de kumen wenti" (Woes of the modern woman), *Xin nüxing* (January 1927).

76. First published in *Xiaoshuo yuebao* 17, no. 1 (1927). Reprinted in *Lu Yin xuanji*, 295–306.

77. For more on the trope of illness in New Women narratives, see chapter 3.

78. Lu Yin of course could have made Lantian's fate much worse. In a fascinating scene involving a heated discussion over Kollontai's notion of "trial marriage" (*shiyan hunyin*) in her novella *Xingfu*, Chen Xuezhao's new woman heroine Yu Fen contemplates the potential hazards New Women face in "free" sexual unions without legal protections, 23–25. Two risks in particular concern her: unwanted pregnancy and sexual disease.

79. This story was published posthumously in Ding Ling's *Hong he hei banyuekan* (Red and black) in 1928, shortly after Shi Pingmei's unexpected death from encephalitis. It has been reprinted in Yang Yang, ed., *Shi Pingmei zuopinji* (A collection of Shi Pingmei's work) (Beijing: Shumu wenxian chubanshe, 1984), 239–250.

80. The story rewrites Shi Pingmei's earlier story "Qifu" (Abandoned woman) (1925), in which a New Woman I-narrator expresses sympathy for her cousin's

wife, an unintended victim of the May Fourth revolt against the traditional family.

81. An excellent comparison to this story is Ye Shaojun's famous short story "Chunguang bushi tade le" (No longer hers, the spring) (1924), which also revolves around a young woman abandoned by her "modern" husband. In the story, the husband encourages his ex-wife to return to school, where she is initially ostracized by other students who look down on her for being a divorcee. Eventually, however, as she begins to grasp the idea of independence (in part through contact with other women at school), she decides to cut economic ties with her ex-husband. Although she graduates and lands a job, she suffers from depression and loneliness.

82. Lu Yin also attacks the modern male intellectual (whom Chen Xuezhao once dubbed mockingly as the "new man" or *xin nanxing*) in her 1928 story "Yimu" (One scene), in which a self-styled progressive male intellectual who champions women's equality hypocritically mistreats his wife and invites a prettier younger concubine into their home.

83. Examples abound. In Yu Dafu's "Niaoluo xing" (The cypress vine trip) (1923), for instance, the I-narrator laments *his* own fate as a victim of the cruel traditional family system; several of the young heroes of Ba Jin's *Jia* are also so preoccupied with their own personal rebellions they seem oblivious to the far more precarious position of women within the traditional family structure.

84. Felski, *Beyond Feminist Aesthetics*, 100.

85. Lu Yin and Shi Pingmei discussed whether or not women were better off living in blissful ignorance of their oppression in public letters they exchanged in 1925. Lu Yin, in response to Shi Pingmei's suggestion that she become more politically involved, expressed reservations: "They [i.e., downtrodden Chinese women] are living their lives contentedly, so how can I bear to tear open the thin veil shielding them [from such knowledge], only to make them recognize their own misfortune? People find the blind pitiful because they are unable to see, but in fact those who see are as pitiful as the mute who eats bitter medicine yet is unable to complain." See "Haibin xiaoxi—ji Bowei" (News from the seashore—a letter to Shi Pingmei), *Jingbao fukan, funü zhoukan*, 1925.3.

86. Yi-tsi Mei Feuerwerker, *Ding Ling's Fiction: Ideology and Narrative in Modern Chinese Literature* (Cambridge: Harvard University Press, 1982), 19.

87. "Gei S-mei de yifeng xin," *Xie Bingying zuopinxuan*, 553–569.

88. By appearing to conceal the true identity of S-, the author further lends a sense of authenticity to the text.

89. What constitutes a "lesbian" representation is currently a matter of great critical dispute and need not, according to some theorists, include an explicitly erotic dimension (viz. Adrienne Rich's concept of the lesbian continuum). Here, the relationship is described primarily in terms of emotional affection rather than erotic attraction, although there are some references to physical contact such as embracing. The theme of schoolgirl lesbianism was explored in stories by several other May Fourth women writers, including Ling Shuhua ("Shuo you zhemme yihui shi" [Once upon a time]) and Lu Yin ("Li Shi de riji" [Li Shi's diary]). For an unsightful analysis on this topic, see Tze-lan D. Sang's *The Emerging Lesbian: Female Same-Sex Desire in Modern Chinese Literature and Culture* (Chicago: University of Chicago Press, 2002).

90. In certain ways, the narrative conforms to the "romance and revolution" (*aiqing jia geming*) genre that gained popularity in the late May Fourth,

although the twist here is that the private relationship that competes with political responsibility is not a heterosexual romance between a woman and a man, but two close female friends. In the next chapter, I discuss further how Xie Bingying rewrites this genre in terms of the mother–daughter relationship.

91. "Yecao" (1929). Originally published in *Honghei* 6 (June 1929). Translations here are from Tani Barlow, ed., *I Myself am a Woman: Selected Writings of Ding Ling*, 105–111.

92. Barlow, 104.

93. Feuerwerker, *Ding Ling's Fiction*, 38.

94. A prolific New Woman writer whose work remains sadly neglected by contemporary scholars in China and abroad, Chen Xuezhao began her literary career as an essayist in the early twenties—her debut publication was a short essay entitled "Wo suo xiwang de xin funü" (The new woman of my dreams). By the time she published her first novel, she had already established herself as a staunch feminist who, among other things, openly questioned "modern" marriage: in contentious articles such as "Gei nanxing" (To men) (1926), published in the cutting edge journal *Xin nüxing* (New women), for instance, she attributed the failure of so many new-style marriages to the dearth of emancipated "new men"(*xin nanxing*) asserting that "Chinese men have yet to free themselves from the servile nature inculcated by Confucianism, which remains deeply entrenched in our culture." From 1927–1935, Chen went abroad to study literature in France, a venture she financed with income from her writing, including what she earned as a foreign correspondent for the newspaper *Dagongbao*. Overall, it was an extremely productive period in her literary career: in addition to a steady stream of essays (many of which were collected in book form), she also completed *Nanfeng de meng* (published by *Zhenmeishan*). The novel, briefly described above, has strong autobiographical overtones.

CHAPTER 3   LOVE AND/OR REVOLUTION?: FICTIONS OF THE FEMININE SELF IN THE 1930S CULTURAL LEFT

1. The collection in which this essay appeared is a classic example of the growing critical disdain of the "personal" orientation of women's writing (especially writers like Bing Xin and Lu Yin) and the new affirmation of writers like Ding Ling and Xie Bingying, whose work was seen as a promising alternative to the "feminine" limitations of *funü wenxue*. Fang Ying, "Bai Wei lun" (On Bai Wei), in Huang Renying, ed., *Dangdai Zhongguo nüzuojialun* (Shanghai: Guanghua shuju, 1933), 59–78.

2. See Bai Shurong and He You, *Bai Wei pingzhuan* (A critical biography of Bai Wei) (Changsha: Hunan renmin chubanshe, 1982), 103.

3. *Beiju shengya* was published by Shenghuo shudian, perhaps the most progressive publishing house in Shanghai in the 1930s. *Nübing zizhuan* was published by the prominent Liangyou tushu chuban gongsi, which represented such writers as Lu Xun, Mao Dun, and Ba Jin.

4. Although Bui Shurong and He You's critical biography of Bai Wei appeared in 1982, her work has only recently begun to capture the attention of scholars abroad.

5. Lydia Liu's phrase. See her "Narratives of Modern Selfhood: First-Person Fiction in May Fourth Literature," in Ellen Widmer and David Wang, eds.,

From May Fourth to June Fourth: Fiction and Film in Twentieth-Century China (Cambridge: Harvard University Press, 1993), 102.

6. Other examples of diary-form fiction include Shi Pingmei's "Lin Nan de riji" (Lin Nan's diary) (1928); Lu Yin's "Lishi de riji" (Lishi's diary) (1923); and "Manli" (Manli) (1927). Epistolary fiction includes Su Xuelin's "Ge'er de tongxin" (Pigeon letters) (1928); Chen Xuezhao's "Zuihou de xin" (The last letter) (1928); and Xie Bingying's "Gei S de yifeng xin" (A letter to S-) (1929).

7. There are important examples of women's autobiographical writing in the 1940s and 1950s as well. In addition to works by Chen Xuezhao, Wang Ying (1915–1974), and Yang Gang (1905–1957), which I examine in chapter 5, Guan Lu's autobiographical novel *Xin jiu shidai* (Era of the old and new), originally serialized in *Shanghai funü* magazine in 1939, was published in book form in 1940, while Ling Shuhua, whose well-crafted short stories won considerable critical acclaim in the 1920s, published her memoir *Ancient Melodies* (also originally in English) in 1953.

8. Wang Lingzhen's forthcoming *Personal Matters: Women's Autobiographical Practice in Twentieth-Century China* will fill in an important chapter in modern Chinese literary history.

9. Feuerwerker, "Women as Writers in the 1920's and 1930's," in Margery Wolf and Roxane Witke, eds., *Women in Chinese Society* (Stanford: Stanford University Press, 1975), 143–168. Feuerwerker's main points have been widely cited by other scholars in the field.

10. Feuerwerker, "Women as Writers," 158.

11. Feuerwerker, "Women as Writers," 168.

12. Rey Chow, "Virtuous Transactions: A Reading of Three Stories by Ling Shuhua," *Modern Chinese Literature* 4 (1988).

13. Compare this, e.g., to essays on May Fourth male writers such as Lydia Liu's "Narratives of Modern Selfhood: First-Person Fiction in May Fourth Literature," in Widmer and Wang, eds., *From May Fourth to June Fourth*, and Michael Egan, "Yu Dafu and the Transition to Modern Chinese Literature," *Modern Chinese Literature in the May Fourth Era* (Cambridge: Harvard University Press, 1977).

14. Feuerwerker, "Women as Writers," 155.

15. Feuerwerker applies a more nuanced model of self writing in her more recent research; unfortunately, she does not examine any female writers. See "Text, Intertext, and the Representation of the Writing Self in Lu Xun, Yu Dafu, and Wang Meng," in Widmer and Wang, eds., *From May Fourth to June Fourth*, 167–193.

16. Croll, *Changing Identities of Chinese Women* (London: Zed Press, 1995).

17. The examples she examines in the section on the pre-1949 period are predominantly by nonliterary women, whose works were published in English (or English translation) apparently for a Western audience. These include: Wong Su-ling's *Daughter of Confucius* (London: Farrar, Straus and Young, 1952); Chao Buwei Yang's *Autobiography of a Chinese Woman* (New York: The John Day Company, 1947); and Chow Ching-li's *Journey into Tears: Memory of a Girlhood in China* (New York: McGaw Hill, 1978). Although she does not address this point, it would be interesting to consider how the specific (foreign) context of publication also shaped the ways in which these authors represented their lives as Chinese women.

18. Croll's approach, for all its limitations, remains common, particularly among American feminist critics.

19. This remark appears in Croll's preface to the reprinted translation of one of the key autobiographical examples she uses in her book, Xie Bingying's *Autobiography of a Chinese Girl* (London and New York: Pandora, 1986).

20. Maria Lauret, *Liberating Literature: Feminist Fiction in America* (London: Routledge, 1994), 106. For other recent feminist accounts of women's autobiography see also Sidonie Smith, *Subjectivity, Identity and the Body: Women's Autobiographical Practices in the Twentieth-Century* (Bloomington: Indiana University Press, 1993); Rita Felski, *Beyond Feminist Aesthetics: Feminist Literature and Social Change* (Cambridge: Harvard University Press, 1989); and Domna Stanton, *The Female Autograph: Theory and Practice of Autobiography from the Tenth to the Twentieth Century* (Chicago: University of Chicago Press, 1987).

21. See also Carolyn Heilbrun, *Writing a Woman's Life* (New York: Ballantine Books, 1988), in which she argues that women's autobiographies are typically informed by particular dominant cultural scripts such as heterosexual romance and marriage.

22. Liu, "Narratives of Modern Selfhood," 120.

23. An account of her experience as a woman propagandist on the Northern Expedition, this text was serialized in the *Wuhan zhongyang ribao* (Wuhan central daily) in 1927 (with translations, by Lin Yutang, appearing simultaneously in the English edition of the paper) and was published in book form the following year. It went into multiple reprintings and was soon available abroad in various foreign language editions.

24. Ai Yi, editorial postscript, *Xie Bingying wenji*, vol. 3, p. 460.

25. See, for instance, discussions of Bai Wei in Huang Renying, ed., *Dangdai Zhongguo nüzuojia lun* (1933).

26. Yang Hansheng remembers her, in the preface he wrote for *Bai Wei pingzhuan*, as the most prominent woman in leftist cultural circles along with Ding Ling. Zhao Qingge, in her recent collection of memoirs, refers to Bai Wei as one of the revolutionary writers she most admired. See *Changxiang yi* (Forever recalling each other) (Shanghai: Xuelin chubanshe, 1999.) See also Bai Shurong and He You, *Bai Wei pingzhuan* (A critical biography of Bai Wei) (Changsha: Hunan renmin chubanshe, 1982).

27. Qu Qiubai, for instance, argued in 1931 that most writers remained "captives of the bourgeois 'May Fourth Movement'." Quoted in Paul Pickowitz, "Qu Qiubai's critique of the May Fourth Generation: Early Chinese Marxist Literary Criticism," in Merle Goldman, ed., *Modern Chinese Literature in the May Fourth Era* (Cambridge: Harvard University Press, 1977), 373.

28. Quoted in *Bai Wei pingzhuan*, 148–149.

29. As early as 1919, Li Dazhao had linked the analysis of class to women's oppression. However, as his essay "Zhanhou zhi furen wenti" (The woman question after the war) reveals, certain issues remained murky. For instance, while he recognized that women of the bourgeoisie and the working classes were allies in terms of their struggle against patriarchy, he also asserted that the proletariat had to overthrow the middle class. For a brilliant analysis of the role of feminism in the formation of early Chinese Marxism, see Christina Gilmartin, *Engendering the Chinese Revolution: Radical Women, Communist Politics, and Mass Movements in the 1920s* (Berkeley: University of California Press, 1995).

30. Gilmartin, *Engendering the Chinese Revolution*, 215.

31. See, e.g., Kirk Denton, *The Problematic of Self in Modern Chinese Literature: Hu Feng and Lu Ling* (Stanford: Stanford University Press, 1998).

32. Chen traces this through the work of Mao Dun, although her remarks are relevant to many leftist writers at this time. See her essay "False Harmony: Mao Dun on Women and the Family," *Modern Chinese Literature* 7, no. 1 (Spring 1993): 131–152.

33. See her article "The End of 'Funü Wenxue': Women's Literature from 1925–1935," *Modern Chinese Literature* 4, (1988): 50.

34. Lu Yin's ambivalence toward revolutionary politics, I would note, may have something to do with her negative perception of the experience of educated women like her close friend Lu Jingqing (1907–1993) who worked for the Wuhan Central Women's Department during the revolutionary upsurge of 1926–1927. In her 1928 story "Manli," the title character pours her heart into her work only to be disenchanted by the greed, corruption, and opportunism she observes among her "comrades." In the end, she winds up hospitalized after suffering a mental breakdown.

35. She published several volumes of fiction in the late 1920s and 1930s, including *Xiyan zhihou* (After the banquet) (Shanghai: Beixin shuju, 1929); *Nüxing* (Women) (Shanghai: Shenghuo shudian, 1934); and *Yige nüzuojia* (A woman writer) (Shanghai: Beixin shuju, 1935).

36. An advertisement for the press lists, e.g., such titles as *Zhongguo jinshi funü canzheng yundong shi* (The history of the modern Chinese women's suffrage movement) by Zhong Guiyang; *Funü wenti mingzhu jieshao* (Introduction to famous works on the women question) by Jin Zhonghua; and *Zhongguo funü shi* (The history of Chinese women) by Huang Xinmian and Yao Mingda; and *Zhongguo funü laodong wenti* (The problem of Chinese women's labor) by Zhong Guiyang; *Shijie funü yundong shi* (The history of the global women's movement) by Lu Yunzhang nüshi.

37. According to Wang Yiwei, the magazine had a monthly print run of 2,000. It folded due to censorship and financial difficulties in 1935, but resumed publication for two years after the end of War of Resistance. For an interview with Wang, see Wang Zheng, *Women in the Chinese Enlightenment*, 221–257.

38. See, Tan Sheying, *Zhongguo funü yundong tongshi* (Shanghai: Funü gongming shc, 1936).

39. As Tani Barlow and Yi-tsi Feuerwerker have both shown, Ding Ling's embrace of Marxism ca. 1930 was accompanied by a gradual peripheralization of feminist issues in her creative writing.

40. See, chapter 5 for a more detailed analysis of this work.

41. See, e.g., Feng Keng's "Yi tuan rou" (A piece of flesh) (1930), and Guan Lu's "Yi taitai de riji" (Diary of a concubine) (1935). Feng Keng joined the Communist Party in 1929 and was an active member of the League of Left-Wing Writers in Shanghai serving, among other things, on the Preparatory Committee for the First Conference of the Soviet Representatives. On January 17, 1931, she was arrested by the KMT police after attending a secret executive committee meeting of the League (along with Rou Shi, Hu Yepin, Li Weisen, and Yin Fu) and was executed several weeks later. Best known for her poetry, Guan Lu was a versatile writer who published essays, fiction, translations, and literary criticism. She even wrote the lyrics for the popular theme song of the 1937 progressive film *Shizi jietou* (Crossroads). During the Japanese occupation of Shanghai, having been assigned by the CCP to carry out underground

cultural work, she became the editor of the Japanese-supported magazine *Nüsheng* (no relation to Wang Yiwei's journal by the name same). Her publications during this period include her autobiographical novel *Xinjiu shidai* (first serialized in *Shanghai funü* magazine), which recounts her experience growing up in a bourgeois family and the struggles following the death of her father. After 1949, Guan Lu was imprisoned after falling victim to internal party struggles, and was not officially "rehabilitated" until after Mao's death.

42. See e.g., Luo Shu's stories "Shengren qi" (A stranger's wife) (1929) and "Liu Sao" (Auntie Liu) (1936), and Xiao Hong's *Shengsi chang* (Field of life and death) (1935).

43. *Funü shenghuo* (Women's life) was edited by Shen Zijiu (b. 1898), an activist in the women's movement. After the outbreak of the war, the magazine relocated to Chongqing. For more on Shen's activities in the post-1949 period, see chapter 5.

44. Quoted in Shanghai shehui kexueyuan wenxue yanjiusuo, ed., *Sanshi niandai zai Shanghai de zuolian zuojia* (Leftist writers in Shanghai in the 1930s) (Shanghai: Shanghai shehui kexueyuan chubanshe, 1988), 396. Originally from Bai Wei's essay "Wo xie ta de dongji" (My motives for writing it) published in *Funü shenghuo* 2, no. 1 (1935).

45. Leo Lee briefly discusses leftist writers and their "love plus revolution" stories (including Jiang Guangci, Mao Dun, and Ding Ling) in *The Romantic Generation of Modern Chinese Writers* (Cambridge: Harvard University Press, 1973).

46. The other is her novel *Wei Hu*, in which the hero, a sophisticated Communist, eventually decides to end his romance with his liberated new woman girlfriend because of its negative effect on his political work. Yi-tsi Feuerwerker discusses both works in *Ding Ling's Fiction* (Cambridge: Harvard University Press, 1982), 52–60.

47. *Ding Ling wenji* (Changsha: Hunan renmin chubanshe, 1983), 211.

48. In Mao Dun's novel *Ziye* (Midnight), e.g., Wu Sunfu's wife carries around a copy of the novel wherever she goes, a habit that identifies her as being out of touch with the times. According to Leo Lee, this text, first translated by Guo Moruo in 1921, was one of the main inspirations behind the flood of highly subjective, romantic writings in 1920s. For more, see Lee, 283–286.

49. Throughout the autobiography, in fact, Xie pays close attention to texts and the ideological systems they uphold.

50. As for literary influences on her own writing, Xie cites Agnes Smedley's autobiographical novel *Daughter of Earth* (1928; translated into Chinese in the early 1930s) as among her favorite literary works, praising in particular its realism and its "courageous, naked (*chiluoluo*) description."

51. Significantly, in the opening scene of the text, as the "naughty" young Xie recovers from one of her mother's beatings, her grandmother tells her that this discipline reflects her mother's love for her.

52. Huang Dinghui, another important feminist activist of this period, provides a virtually identical explanation for her motivation in joining the National Revolution in Wuchang in 1926. See Wang Zheng's interview with her in *Women in the Chinese Enlightenment*, 296.

53. In the spring of 1927, conservative factions within the Guomindang cracked down on Communist organizations. Considered "radical" elements, women activists became an immediate target of persecution and it is estimated that thousands lost their lives at this time. Several prominent leaders in the

women's movement at the time, including Xiang Jingyu (1895–1928), were executed. Later in *Nübing zizhuan*, Xie Bingying reports on how she herself was thrown in jail as a suspected Communist and was only released because of a lucky family connection to one of the local authorities. For more on the White Terror, see Gilmartin, 194–199.

54. See, e.g., Feng Yuanjun's "Gejue" (Separation). Xie Bingying also wrote a short story in 1932, "Xinhun zhi ye" (Wedding night), in which the unwilling bride commits suicide after being forced to marry a physically repulsive older man.

55. This translation, a more literal rendering of the original, is from *Girl Rebel: The Autobiography of Hsieh Pingying* (1940) (New York: De Capo Press, 1975), 125–126.

56. The translation was arranged by Lin Yutang, who also had a hand in the publication of *Congjun riji*. The actual translation of the text was done by his two daughters and was published in a volume that also included *Xin congjun riji* (The new war diary), which tells of Xie Bingying's involvement mobilizing women in the war against Japan. See *Girl Rebel* (1975), an unabridged republication of the translation. A new translation, by Xie's daughter and son-in-law, has recently been published under the title *A Woman Soldier's Own Story* (New York: Columbia University Press, 2001).

57. Xie Bingying explores this theme in her haunting novella "Paoqi" (Abandoned) (1932), in which two impoverished young radicals face the problem of the woman's pregnancy and the subsequent birth of a baby daughter.

58. Bai Wei interrogates both romance and revolution as viable options for the modern woman in her first full-length novel *Zhadan yu zhengniao* (The bomb and the expeditionary bird) (1928), which contrasts the experiences of two sisters who join the 1926 revolution. Although not explicitly autobiographical, the novel may draw upon Bai Wei's personal observations during the period she spent in Wuhan in 1927 working in the Revolutionary government. Unfortunately, the complete novel is no longer extant since significant portions of it were lost when *Benliu* was shut down by the KMT censors. For a more extensive discussion of this work, see Jianmei Liu, *Revolution Plus Love: Literary History, Women's Bodies, and Thematic Repetition in Twentieth-Century Chinese Fiction* (Honolulu: University of Hawaii Press, 2003).

59. *Beiju shengya*, 2.

60. In doing so, Bai Wei departs from the dominant trend that Wendy Larson terms the "circumstantial autobiography," i.e., the emphasis in modern Chinese autobiographical practice on locating the autobiographical subject within specific temporal and spacial origins.

61. "Wo toudao wenxue quanli de chuzhong" (My original intentions for joining the literary world), in Zhen Zhengduo, ed., *Wo yu wenxue* (Shanghai: Shenghuo shudian, 1934).

62. This is the same school Xie Bingying would attend in 1920.

63. In the late 1920s, Yang Sao (1900–1957) began publishing progressive works and was, by the 1930s, actively involved in leftist cultural circles. According to some biographers, Bai Wei was instrumental in his political "conversion." He is today remembered primarily as a poet, but he also authored numerous plays, works of criticism, and translations. For a brief biography of his life and literary career, see *Sanshiniandai zai shanghai de*

zuolian zuojia (Leftist writers in 1930s Shanghai) (Shanghai: Shanghai shehui kexueyuan chubanshe, 1988).

64. Liu, "Narratives of Modern Selfhood," 103.

65. For more on this issue see Rey Chow's *Woman and Chinese Modernity* (Minneapolis: University of Minnesota Press, 1991), chapter 3; Jaroslav Průšek, *The Lyrical and the Epic: Studies of Modern Chinese Literature* (Bloomington: Indiana University Press, 1980); Marston Anderson, *The Limits of Realism* (Berkeley: University of California Press, 1990); Leo Lee, *The Romantic Generation* (1973).

66. Yu Dafu perhaps enunciated this view most explicitly in his oft-quoted comment "All literary works are autobiographies of their authors."

67. A typical example occurs in section 2, where Bai Wei inserts a series of diary excerpts from 1927. Although the narrative has already clearly established that Zhan is not to be trusted, the diaries reveal how Bai Wei continues to delude herself about the nature of her lover and their relationship.

68. *Zuoye* (Last night) (Shanghai: Nanqiang shuju, 1933). For quite different historical reasons, there has been a recent revival of interest in these public-private writings of the May Fourth generation. Many of the love letter collections from the 1920s–1930s have been reprinted in Mainland China in recent years, including *Zuoye*, which was reissued in 1994 by the Hebei jiaoyu chubanshe.

69. For more on this genre see David Raoul Findeisen, "From Literature to Love: Glory and Decline of the Love Letter genre," in Michael Hockx, ed., *The Literary Field of Twentieth Century China* (Honolulu: University of Hawaii Press, 1999).

70. *Aimei xiaozha* was republished in 1994 by the Dongfang chubanshe.

71. In fact, there is little doubt that Bai Wei's motives in writing *Beiju shengya* were at least in part financial, and that she wrote it to help offset the cost of the medical treatment she was undergoing at the time.

72. In the preface to a later edition of her autobiography, Xie Bingying refers to the immense satisfaction she derived from knowing that her readers sympathized (*tongqing*) with her plight. See "Guanyu *Nübing zizhuan*" (About *Autobiography of a woman soldier*), in *Nübing zizhuan* (Sichuan wenyi chubanshe, 1985), 1–10.

73. Bai Wei's scathing depiction of Zhan's insidious sexual politics places him squarely in the company of a number of prominent modern intellectuals whose patriarchal dispositions were made public by the women they mistreated. Yu Dafu, e.g., who cultivated a romantic self-image in his writing, was represented as an abusive husband in the memoir his wife Wang Yingxia later wrote (*Wo yu Yu Dafu* [Yu Dafu and I], 1988). The text includes the open letters Wang published in *Dafeng* magazine in the late 1930s in which she divulged Yu's infidelity and abusive behavior during the course of their marriage. In the late 1940s, the Shanghai-based feminist magazine *Nüsheng* (which had resumed publication after the defeat of Japan) also featured exposés of degenerate "new" men.

74. Wei recalls one particularly violent scene, in which rape is implied albeit never named as such: "It was in their little room, in the morning. Zhan's image, as if drunk or crazy. His tender and innocent entreaties, his passionate, explosive desire, his domination, his recklessness. Wei struggled against him, quarreled with him; finally his strong pair of hands, gripping her like a wooden puppet,

throwing her on the bed; her head on the bed, her feet hanging over the side, and her back pressed against the edge; he laughed, and laughed, and madly laughed revealing his horse-like teeth . . . Wei would never forget this heartbreaking (*cixin*) scene," 297.

75. Leo Lee discusses cinema, advertising, and the popular print media that comprised the "modern" urban culture of Shanghai during this period in his book *Shanghai Modern: The Flowering of a New Urban Culture in China 1930–1945* (Cambridge: Harvard University Press, 1999).

76. Margaret Sanger's lectures at Beijing University in the early 1920s sparked a flurry of debate and activism around issues of birth control in Beijing and Shanghai while translations of studies by European sexologist Edward Carpenter and Havelock Ellis also contributed to Republican era sexual discourse. Among new Chinese intellectuals vocal in such debates was Zhang Jingsheng, a philosophy professor from Beida, who played an instrumental role in promoting modern sex education with his magazine *Xin wenhua* (New culture) and his best-selling book *Mei de renshengguan*. *Xin nüxing* (New woman), another magazine in circulation at the time, also tapped into the growing public interest in sexuality, sexual anatomy, and physical hygiene. In the 1930s, articles on these topics also appeared in feminist magazines such as *Nüzi yuekan* and *Gongming yuebao* (Women's sympathetic understanding). For a discussion of these and related topics, see Gail Hershatter, *Dangerous Pleasures: Prostitution and Modernity in Twentieth-Century Shanghai* (Berkeley: University of California Press, 1997) and Peng Xiaoyan, *Chaoyue xieshi* (Beyond realism) (Taibei: Lianjing, 1993).

77. For a discussion of Lu Xun's use of syphilitic imagery, see Lung-kee Sun, "The Fin-de-Siècle Lu Xun," *Republican China* 18, no. 2 (April 1993) 64–98. Two of the most interesting, albeit highly problematic, texts that link sexual disease and figure of the female revolutionary are Mao Dun's *Shi* (Eclipse) (1930) and Jiang Guangci's *Chongchu yunwei de yueliang* (Moon emerging from the clouds, 1930). The latter, Jiang's most popular novel, features a female activist who drifts into a life of prostitution and later takes to sleeping with the enemy in order to infect them with venereal disease (the novel's cruel twist being that she eventually discovers she doesn't have the disease after all).

78. Bai Wei offers a similar vision in a short piece of reportage, almost certainly drawn from her own experience, entitled "Sandeng bingfang" (The third-class hospital ward) (1936). In it, the author describes a ward of patients suffering from venereal disease and other physical ailments—women of all social classes, ages, and physical type—to suggest that no woman is immune to the social ills of patriarchy. For another, somewhat later, feminist literary treatment of venereal disease, see Mei Niang's short story "Dong shoushu zhi qian" (Before the operation) (1943).

79. Feminist literary critics Gilbert and Gubar, among others, have commented on the prevalence of metaphors of disease and paralysis in the Western female literary tradition, which they read as symptomatic of women's condition in patriarchal culture. See *Madwoman in the Attic* (1979).

80. It is interesting to note that despite critical attacks on May Fourth women's writing in the 1930s, there was obviously still a strong market for this literature. In 1935, for instance, the Women's Bookstore (*Nüzi shudian*) reissued Lu Yin's fiction from the early 1920s.

81. Chen Bo'er (1910–1951), a socialist involved in Shanghai theater and film circles; Wang Ying (1915–1974), a progressive writer and actress who starred in several successful Left-wing films in the 1930s, including *Ziyou shen* (The goddess of liberty) and *Nüxing de nahan* (Woman's scream); Guan Lu, see above; Du Junhui (1904–1981), a feminist activist and essayist who had helped Shen Zijiu launch *Funü shenghuo* in 1935. Du joined in the CCP in 1928. Li Lan (dates unknown) was a well-known translator whose publications included a translation of Alexandra Kollontai's "Three Generations" (1923). Also included on the list are Ji Hong (1913–), a member of the CCP involved with *Funü shenghuo* and who assumed its editorship when the magazine moved inland (to Wuhan then Chongqing) during the war; Dong Zhujun (1901–), a wealthy divorcee with leftist sympathies who helped finance several progressive women's magazines and underground CCP activities; and Lan Ping (a.k.a Jiang Qing, 1914–1991), then pursuing her acting career in Shanghai. This impressive list of women, many of whom were Bai Wei's personal friends, reads like a who's who on the progressive female left.

82. Tragically, Bai Wei had no sooner arrived in Beijing than the Japanese army occupied the city. Despite the urging of friends, including Wang Huiwu and her husband Li Da, at whose house she recuperated, she decided not to flee south but instead remained there until March of 1938 to continue her treatment. During this time, she wrote a patriotic five-act play which, according to her biographers Bai Shurong and He You, was destroyed.

CHAPTER 4   OUTWITTING PATRIARCHY: COMIC NARRATIVE STRATEGIES IN THE WORKS OF YANG JIANG, SU QING, AND ZHANG AILING

1. First published in *Xiju erzhong* (Shanghai: Shijie shuju, 1944). Reprinted in *Xiju erzhong* (Fuzhou: Fujian renmin chubanshe, 1982). Yang Jiang wrote a third comedy *Youxi renjian* (Sporting with the world), which was staged in the summer of 1944 under the direction of Yao Ke, but which has regrettably never appeared in print. When I contacted Yang Jiang's daughter in Beijing in the summer of 1995 to inquire about the possibility of examining the manuscript of the unpublished play, I was informed that Yang Jiang had never been satisfied with the script and had not even kept a copy for herself.

2. *Jiehun shinian* (Shanghai: Tiandi chubanshe, 1944). Citations here are from a 1948 edition issued by Sihai chubanshe.

3. "Qingcheng zhi lian" (Love in a fallen city) (1943), *Zhang Ailing wenji*, vol. 2 (Hefei: Anhui wenyi chubanshe, 1992), 48–84. Translations cited here are from Karen Kingsbury, *Renditions: Special Issue, Eileen Chang*, 62–92.

4. Critical biographies of both Yang Jiang and Su Qing have recently been published, a promising sign that their work will receive the thorough critical evaluation they deserve. See Kong Qingmao, *Yang Jiang pingzhuan* (A critical biography of Yang Jiang) (Beijing: Xiahua chubanshe, 1998) and Wang Yixin, *Su Qing zhuan* (Biography of Su Qing) (Shanghai: Xuelin chubanshe, 1999). For more on Yang Jiang, see also Edward Gunn, *Unwelcome Muse: Chinese Literature in Shanghai and Peking, 1937–1945* (New York: Columbia University Press, 1980), 231–243; and Zhuang Haoran, "Lun Yang Jiang xiju de wailai yingxiang he minsu fengge" (On the foreign influences and national

characteristics of Yang Jiang's dramas), in *Huaju wenxue yanjiu* (Beijing: Zhongguo xiju chubanshe, 1987) 111–128. On Su Qing, see Gunn, 69–77; Meng Yue and Dai Jinhua, *Fuchu lishi dibiao* (Emerging from the horizon of history) (Taipei: Shibao wenhua chubanshe, 1993), 301–319; Yingjin Zhang, *The City in Modern Chinese Literature and Film: Configurations of Space, Time, and Gender* (Stanford: Stanford University Press, 1996), 249–255; Chen Qingsheng, *Kangzhan shiqi de Shanghai wenxue* (Shanghai literature during the War of Resistance) (Shanghai: Shanghai renmin chubanshe, 1995), 243–245. Zhang Ailing has received substantial critical attention. In addition to C.T. Hsia, who devotes an entire chapter to her in his *A History of Modern Chinese Fiction, 1917–1957* (New Haven: Yale University Press, 1961), see also Karen Kingsbury, "Reading Eileen Chang's Early Fiction: Art and a Female Sense of Self" (Ph.D. diss., Columbia University, 1995); Wang Xiaoming, "The 'Good Fortune' of Eileen Chang," *Renditions* (Spring 1996); Rey Chow, *Woman and Chinese Modernity*, 112–120; and Gunn, *Unwelcome Muse*, 200–231.

5. The theater groups that produced Yang's plays, the Shanghai United Arts Troupe (*Shanghai lianyi jutuan*), the Tong Mao Theatrical Company (*Tongmao yanjutuan*), and the Struggle Company (*Kugan jutuan*) all operated within this commercialized cultural arena.

6. Those involved in the resistance were not the only ones at risk. Writers Liu Na'ou (1900–1939) and Mu Shiying (1912–1940), for instance, both of whom served in cultural apparatuses controlled by the Wang Jingwei regime, were assassinated in 1939 and 1940.

7. His study remains the definitive English-language study of occupation-period literary culture (in both Shanghai and Beijing) to date. Poshek Fu's *Passivity, Resistance, and Collaboration: Intellectual Choices in Occupied Shanghai, 1937–45* (Stanford: Stanford University Press, 1993), also examines male writers and intellectuals of this era, but from the perspective of intellectual history. For more on publishing in Shanghai during the occupation, see also Chen Qingsheng, *Kangzhan shiqi de Shanghai wenxue* (1995).

8. See Poshek Fu, *Passivity, Resistance, and Collaboration* (1993), for an account of the ways in which male writers responded to the Japanese occupation. Although he mentions the writers examined here in passing, he does not engage the issue of what the occupation meant from the standpoint of women intellectuals.

9. In 1944, the *Shijie shuju* issued a volume under the title *Xiju erzhong* with both plays. They were also selected for inclusion in Kong's *Juben congkan* (Script series) (Shanghai: Shijie shuju, 1943–1945). Because some of the plays in this important collection included patriotic themes, Kong was arrested by the Japanese authorities and held until the end of the war. See *Shanghai gudao wenxue huiyilu* (Memoirs of Shanghai gudao literature) (Shanghai: Shanghai shehui kexueyuan chubanshe, 1985), 101–102.

10. The novel was first serialized in 1943 in the influential monthly literary journal *Fengyu tan* (Talks amid hardship), a periodical that like many of its day had backing from the Nanjing regime. For more on the contemporary reception of Su Qing's writing, see Wang Yixin, *Su Qing zhuan*.

11. See Ke Ling, "Yaoji Zhang Ailing" (Sent to Zhang Ailing), in *Zhang Ailing wenji*, vol. 4, 421–429. The novella was also made into a film in Hong Kong in 1984.

12. Of the three, Su Qing was the most openly engaged with feminist issues. In addition to her fiction, she published numerous essays on such topics as women's education, divorce, and sexual discrimination. For a fascinating discussion between Su Qing and Zhang Ailing on a number of contemporary gender issues, including the much-debated problem of women's employment, see their joint interview in 1944 "Su Qing, Zhang Ailing duitanlu: guanyu funü, jiating, hunyin wenti" (A dialogue between Su Qing and Zhang Ailing: on women, family, and marriage), in *Zhang Ailing wenji* (1992), 392–404.

13. Meng and Dai, 292. For more on the three distinct strands of women's writing in the 1940s (i.e., literature in KMT areas, in CCP territory, and in occupied Shanghai), see chapter 12 in Meng Yue and Dai Jinhua's study.

14. Prior to the war, Guan Lu had known ties to the cultural left, so her decision to stay in Shanghai and to accept a position as an editor at *Nüsheng*, a women's magazine backed by Japan and overseen by Toshiko Sato, came as a surprise to some. In 1982, the CCP finally disclosed that this had been a cover for the underground work she was carrying out for the party.

15. Although several May Fourth feminist writers, including Ding Ling and Chen Xuezhao, turned their attention to resistance during the war, the relationship between feminism and literary production is more complex than most literary histories have suggested. Beyond Shanghai, Yang Gang (1909–1957) and Wang Ying (1915–1974), both affiliated with the Left, went abroad to the United States in the early 1940s, and worked on major literary projects. In occupied Beijing, Mei Niang (1920–) came to prominence with the publication of two volumes of fiction, *Yu* (Fish) (1943) and *Xie* (Crabs) (1945). Both volumes reveal the distinct influence of May Fourth feminist thought. And in Chongqing, where many of the most vocal women's organizations were based during the war, the young author Yu Ru (1921–) rose to success. Her first novel *Yaoyuan de ai* (Remote love) (1944), a fascinating rewriting of Mao Dun's earlier new woman novel *Hong* (Rainbow), was a tremendous hit and went into multiple reprintings in the following years. In addition to Tan Zhengbi's 1944 collection *Dangdai nüzuojia xiaoshuo xuan*, which introduced many young new writers from this period, including Zhang Ailing, Su Qing, Yang Xiuzhen, Zeng Wenqiang, and Shi Jimei, see also Zhao Qingge's immediate postwar anthology *Wutiji* (Untitled) (1947) for new work by veteran writers such as Lu Jingqing, Wang Ying, and Xie Bingying. For translations of women's writing from the war period, see Dooling, ed., *Writing Women in Modern China: The Revolutionary Years, 1936–76* (New York: Columbia University Press, 2005).

16. Rey Chow, "Against the Lures of Diaspora: Minority Discourse, Chinese Women, and Intellectual Hegemony," in Lu Tonglin, ed., *Gender and Sexuality in Twentieth-Century Chinese Literature and Society* (Albany: SUNY Press, 1993), 26.

17. Chow, "Against the Lures of Diaspora," 28.

18. The phrase is from Teresa de Lauretis, "The Violence of Rhetoric: Considerations on Representation and Gender," in Nancy Armstrong and Leonard Tennenhouse, eds., *The Violence of Representation: Literature and the History of Violence* (London: Routledge, 1989), 239–258.

19. Chow, "Against the Lures of Diaspora," 35.

20. Yue Ming-bao, "Gendering the Origins of Modern Chinese Fiction," in Lu Tonglin (1993), p. 54.
21. Yue, "Gendering the Origins of Modern Chinese Fiction," 53.
22. Xianglin Sao is one of the most frequently invoked modern female literary characters in feminist scholarship, a fact that attests to the power of her image. In addition to Feuerwerker, see also Ono Kazuko, *Chinese Women in a Century of Revolution: 1850–1950* (Stanford: Stanford University Press, 1989), 97–100, and Rey Chow, *Woman and Chinese Modernity: The Politics of Reading Between West and East* (Minneapolis: University of Minnesota Press, 1991), 107–112.
23. Chow, "Against the Lures of Diaspora," 110.
24. For more on Li Jianwu during the war, see Fu, *Passivity, Resistance, and Collaboration,* chapter 2.
25. Given the enormous success of her plays (some of which, reportedly, were performed outside of Shanghai), it is curious that Yang Jiang was not more prolific in these years, producing a total of just four plays. One explanation, suggested by her biographer Kong Qingmao, is that after the success of his wife's second play in 1944, Qian Zhongshu decided to write a novel (his soon-to-be acclaimed satire *Weicheng* [Fortress besieged]) and that Yang spent much of her time assisting him with his manuscript and managing their household affairs. Reportedly, in order to allow Qian to scale back on his teaching load, she let go of the domestic help to economize and took over the work herself. See Kong, *Yang Jiang pingzhuan,* 83–84.
26. The lead role of Li Junyu was played by the famous actress Lin Binshi.
27. Quoted in Meng Du's review "Guanyu Yang Jiang de hua" (On Yang Jiang), *Zazhi* (May 1945): 111.
28. Newell Sawyer, *The Comedy of Manners from Sheridan to Maugham* (Philadelphia: Philadelphia University Press, 1931), 172. This early full-length study of the genre is a thorough, if somewhat dated, treatment of the manners genre.
29. See, e.g., Zhuang Haoran, "Lun Yang Jiang xiju de wailai yingxiang he minsu fengge" (1987).
30. Joseph S.M. Lau dates the birth of Chinese *huaju* in 1907, with the founding of the small Western-style drama group, the Spring Willow Society. See Introduction in Lau, *Ts'ao Yu* (Hong Kong: Hong Kong University Press, 1970).
31. Luce Irigaray, *This Sex Which Is Not One.* Trans. Catharine Porter (Ithaca: Cornell University Press, 1985), 76.
32. Hélène Cixous puts this notion into practice by refiguring the horrific image of the snake-haired Medusa into a beautiful *and laughing* woman, as a way of appropriating this misogynistic stereotype for feminist ends. Her influential essay, "The Laugh of the Medusa," is reprinted in Elaine Marks and Isabelle de Courtivon, eds., *New French Feminisms* (New York: Schocken Books, 1981).
33. The contrast is suggestive: a typical May Fourth rebel, Junyu's mother defied her family to marry a poor artist and subsequently died in poverty. Junyu chooses an altogether different strategy.
34. Another interesting comparison could perhaps be drawn between Yang Jiang and another contemporary woman playwright like Yuan Changying

(1894–1973). Yuan's 1935 tragedy *Kongque dongnan fei* (Southeast flies the peacock, 1930), a feminist revision of the classical narrative poem by the same name, e.g., explores the ways in which traditional marriage and family relations produce female suicide, madness, and self-sacrifice.

35. Regina Barecca, *Untamed and Unabashed: Essays on Women and Humor in British Literature* (Detroit: Wayne State University Press, 1994), 145.

36. Yang Jiang's female trickster differs fundamentally from the traditional "fox fairy" (*hulijing*) figure of traditional fiction in that the depiction of her actions is not intended to accentuate the virtues of the hero.

37. Hu Shi, "Zhongshen dashi" (Life's greatest event), *Zhongguo xiandai dumu huaju xuan 1919–1949* (A selection of modern Chinese one act plays 1919–1949) vol. 1 (Beijing: Renmin wenxue chubanshe, 1984).

38. While many of the popular plays produced in Shanghai during the late 1930s and 1940s also feature assertive and convention-defying women, the narrative focus is not necessarily women's sexual liberation but rather national liberation. For a discussion of these patriotic characters, see Chang-Tai Hong, "Female Symbols of Resistance in Chinese Wartime Spoken Drama," *Modern China* 15 (April 1989): 149–177.

39. This question was the title of a lecture that Lu Xun delivered in December 1923 at the Beijing Women's Normal College. While the debate over women's emancipation often focused on the "liberated" women themselves, Lu Xun's question suggests provocatively that the issue relates not just to "Nora" but to those she leaves behind and the society she aims to join. See Lu Xun, "Nala zouhou zenyang?" *Funü zazhi* (August 1924).

40. A similar scene appears in Qian Zhongshu's novel *Weicheng*, which he began writing in 1944. See chapter 9, in which Fang Hongjian and Miss Sun are forced into a traditional marriage ceremony.

41. Some critics have argued that an ambivalent comic ending, and particularly the absence of a joyous resolution, is characteristic of feminist comedy, whose primary aim is to dismantle rather than preserve or celebrate the status quo.

42. For a feminist critique of fictional romance, see Anne Cranny-Francis, *Feminist Fiction* (New York: St. Martin's Press, 1990), chapter 6.

43. "Nüzuojia jutanhui" (Colloquium of women writers), *Zazhi* (April 1944): 54. Su Qing goes on to remark that the tendency to conflate the content of women's writing with the actual lives of female authors inhibits many women writers. As for herself, she comments "I've never really paid attention to this [in my writing], so people have always had lots to say about me." Su Qing reiterated this point in the postscript she added to the book version of the novel.

44. See Su Qing's comments in the roundtable discussion with other women writers, "Nüzuojia jutanhui," *Zazhi* (April 1944).

45. See Elisabeth Croll, *Changing Identities of Chinese Women* (Hong Kong University Press, 1995) for specific examples. Edward Gunn makes an insightful comparison between Xie Bingying's autobiography (1936) and Su Qing's novel, although an interesting parallel might also be drawn with Xie Bingying's later first-person novella *Lihun* (Divorce), first published in Zhao Qingge's postwar collection of women's writing *Wutiji* (1947). Set during the war, the story also charts the awakening of a naive and adoring wife after discovering that her husband Guoqiang (Nation-strengthener) is not the heroic man she imagined him to be. Like Su Qing's novel, the story ends with the heroine's "triumphant" divorce.

46. For a review from the 1940s, see Meng Du, "Guanyu Yang Jiang de hua," *Zazhi* (May 1945): 110–112. Zhuang Haoran notes in his article that prior to the early 1980s, Yang Jiang's name was rarely mentioned in Chinese literary histories. As part the revival of interest in her work, Yang Jiang's collected works were published in 1993.

47. In a round table symposium of women writers in 1944, Zhang Ailing cited Su Qing as her favorite modern woman writer ("Nüzuojia jutanhui," *Zazhi* (April 1944): 49–56). For a more personal reflection on Su Qing, see also Zhang Ailing, "Wo jian Su Qing" (My views on Su Qing), in *Zhang Ailing wenji* (Hefei: Anhui wenyi chubanshe, 1992), 226–239. This essay originally appeared in *Tiandi* Magazine in April 1945.

48. *Xu jiehun shinian* (Sequel to ten years of marriage) (Shanghai: Sihai chubanshe, 1947), 4.

49. Gunn, *Unwelcome Muse*, 76. Su Qing's main crime was an alleged affair with Chen Gongbo, the mayor of Shanghai under the Wang Jingwei regime. Chen was a backer of *Tiandi*, the literary magazine Su Qing edited beginning in 1944, but whether or not her relationship with him extended beyond this remains unclear.

50. Su Qing wryly notes in the preface to the sequel, however, that sales of the novel picked up dramatically after rumors started circulating that it was "pornographic" (*seqing de*), 4.

51. Gunn, *Unwelcome Muse*, 75.

52. Barecca, *Untamed and Unabashed*, 14.

53. In the tabloids, Su Qing was accused of being an actual prostitute, as well as being physically unattractive, stingy, and pro-Japanese.

54. M.M. Bakhtin, *The Dialogic Imagination* (Austin: University of Texas Press, 1981), 23.

55. Bergson's "Laughter," in Wylie Sypher, ed., *Comedy* (New York: Doubleday Anchor: 1956), 97.

56. Hardly erotic, Su Qing's candid representations of the female body and physical experiences of pregnancy, childbirth, and breast-feeding nevertheless contributed to the novel's reputation as a titillating and sleazy book about sex.

57. The theme of unwanted pregnancy was treated by a number of women writers in the 1920s and 1930s, including Chen Ying ("Qi" [Woman, 1929]), Xie Bingying ("Paoqi" [Abandoned, 1932]), and Xiao Hong ("Qi'er" [Abandoned child, 1933]).

58. Judith Butler develops her highly influential "performative theory of gender" in her book *Gender Trouble: Feminism and the Subversion of Identity* (New York: Routledge, 1990).

59. And the narrative tradition it established. An excellent contrast to Su Qing's defiant laughter in this novel is the short story by Zhu Ziqing entitled "Xiao de lishi" (The history of laughter), which traces the transformation of a happy-go-lucky girl into an unsmiling, despondent wife/mother.

60. Both Gunn and Zhang Yingjin comment on this.

61. Born into an elite Shanghai family, Zhang Ailing enjoyed a privileged, if not entirely carefree, upbringing: her parents divorced when she was just ten years old and she was left, after her mother went abroad to study in France, in the care of her opium-addicted father and his concubine. Zhang eventually had a bitter falling out with her father herself over the question of her schooling,

but she later admitted a certain nostalgia for the decadent atmosphere—"the opium smoke, hazy sunlight, the disorderly piles of tabloid newspapers"—of her father's house. Zhang made her literary debut in the early 1940s, after her college studies in Hong Kong were cut short by the Japanese invasion and she reluctantly returned to Shanghai. Appearing in major journals *Zazhi*, *Ziluolan*, and *Tiandi* (Su Qing's literary journal), her essays and fiction quickly captured a devoted following and propelled the young Zhang Ailing to a prominent position in the literary world within a few short years.

62. This novella was first published in two serial installments for *Zazhi* Magazine in 1943.

63. Lim Chin-Chow, "Reading 'The Golden Cangue': Iron Bourdoirs and Symbols of Oppressed Confucian Women," *Renditions: Special Issue on Zhang Ailing* 45 (Spring 1996): 143.

64. The locus classicus of this phrase is the *Hanshu* (History of the former Han dynasty), in reference to the Emperor Xiaowu's consort: "In the north there is a beauty without peer. One glance from her could topple a city wall, another glance could topple a state." Quoted in Anne E. McLaren, *The Chinese Femme Fatale: Stories from the Ming Period* (Sydney: Wild Peony Press, 1994), 1.

65. Let me note here that the traditional *femme-fatale* trope did not necessarily attribute power or personal agency to the woman in question. In many of the earliest stories, the devastation the state-toppler wreaks on the state is less the product of deliberate feminine wiles than the unwitting consequence of the erotic charm she wields over the man (or men) around her.

66. Chow, "Virtuous Transactions," 113.

67. Zhang, *The City in Modern Chinese Literature and Film* (1996), 247.

68. Zhang explains her preference for writing about "ordinary" people, as opposed to heroic figures, in her essay "Ziji de wenzhang" (My essays) (1944), in *Zhang Ailing wenji*, vol. 4, 173–178.

69. See Ke Ling, "Yaoji Zhang Ailing," 428.

CHAPTER 5   A WORLD STILL TO WIN

1. Li Xiaojiang, *Nüren de chulu* (The future of women) (Shenyang: Liaoning renmin chubanshe, 1989).

2. Mayfair Yang, ed., "From Gender Erasure to Gender Difference: State Feminism, Consumer Sexuality and Women's Public Sphere in China," *Spaces of Their Own: Women's Public Sphere in Transnational China* (Minneapolis: University of Minnesota, 1999).

3. In Liu's view, "In the emancipatory discourse of the state, which always subsumes woman under the nationalist agenda, women's liberation means little more than equal opportunity to participate in public labor. The image of the liberated daughter and the figure of the strong female Party leader celebrated in the literature of socialist realism are invented for the purpose of abolishing the patriarchal discriminatory construction of gender, but they end up denying difference to women." Liu, "Invention and Intervention: The Making of a Female Tradition in Modern Chinese Literature," in Widmer and Wang, eds., *From May Fourth to June Fourth: Fiction and Film in Twentieth-Century China* (Cambridge: Harvard University Press, 1993), 196.

4. For an informative discussion of the formation and evolution of the *Fulian*, see Zhang Naihua, "The All-China Women's Federation: Chinese Women and the Women's Movement: 1949–1993" (Ph.D. diss., Michigan State University, 1996).
5. There is evidence that activists formally affiliated with the Guomindang in the pre-1949 era were not included. For example, Zhu Su'e (1901–), interviewed by historian Wang Zheng in the early 1990s, a lifelong activist and member of the Women's Movement Committee was arrested and imprisoned after liberation on (counter-revolutionary) charges. She would play no role whatsoever in the development of Chinese feminism after 1949. See *Women in the Chinese Enlightenment*, chapter 5.
6. Davin, *Woman-Work*, chapter 2.
7. Documents from the first Congress also list among its most important leaders Zhang Qinqiu, Li Dequan, and Kang Keqing, all of whom were veteran women activists.
8. Luo Qiong (1911–) was a contributor to *Funü shenghuo* in the 1930s, and had collaborated with Shen on a translation of Alexandra Kollontai's *Novayia zhenshchina*. After going to Yan'an in 1940, she became the editor of the "Chinese woman" supplement to *Jiefang ribao*.
9. For a brief biography, see Wang Zheng, *Women in the Chinese Enlightenment* (1999), 135–143.
10. Zhao Qingge, *Changxiang yi* (Shanghai: Xuelin chubanshe, 1999), 93.
11. For further discussion of the shifting meanings inscribed in the Communist discourse on "funü jiefang" see Harriet Evans, "The Language of Liberation: Gender and *Jiefang* in early Chinese Communist Party Discourse," *Intersections* (September 1998). URL: http:// wwwshe. murdoch.edu.au/ intersections/back_issues/harriet.html.
12. "Zenme yang zuo yige xin shehui de xin funü" (How to become a new woman of the new society), *Xin Zhongguo funü*, 7, no. 20 (1949).
13. For a list of the titles see the preface of *Zhongguo jiefangqu nongcun funü fanshen yundong sumiao* (Sketches of the turning over movement among peasant women in the liberated areas) (Shanghai: Xinhua shudian, 1949).
14. In 1956, the name was changed to *Zhongguo funü*.
15. Fulian also published two magazines for internal circulation among its cadres in the early post-revolutionary period: *Funü gongzuo tongxun* (later renamed *Funü gongzuo*) and *Fuyun jianguang* (Briefing of the women's movement). In 1956, it also launched the magazine *Women of China* for overseas readers that, despite the similarity in title, differed from *Zhongguo funü*. Another important new journal that regularly covered sex-related topics was *Zhongguo qingnian*.
16. Dong Bian, "Keqin kejin de Shen Dajie" (Beloved and respected sister Shen), in *Nüjie wenhua zhanshi Shen Zijiu* (Women's cultural warrior, Shen Zijiu) (Beijing: Zhongguo funü chubanshe, 1991), 163.
17. Evans, "The Language of Liberation," 17.
18. Evans, "The Language of Liberation," 17.
19. Yang Yun, "Shen dajie jiao wo ban kanwu," in *Nüjie wenhua zhanshi Shen Zijiu* (1991), 169–170.
20. When the Women's Federation was disbanded at the beginning of the Cultural Revolution in 1966, *Zhongguo funü* also halted publication. In the months leading up to this, a fierce (and highly public) struggle against the Editor-in-Chief Dong Bian took place, with adversaries denouncing her as a

"black gang element" and for having advanced a bourgeois approach to women's issues. The magazine resumed publication in 1978.

21. Dong, "Keqin Kejin de Shen dajie," 161–162.

22. According to Zhang Naihua, the "high tide" of the *Fulian* came to an end around the time of the Third National Women's Congress in 1957. Under the tense milieu of the unfolding anti-rightist campaign, it appeared increasingly difficult to openly criticize the gender order under the Party or Socialism, and instead hyperbolic official statements were issued such as "A brand new social system has been set up, the roots of women's oppression have been forever eliminated, women in our country have been liberated, equality between men and women has been achieved." As quoted by Zhang, 249.

23. Zhang Naihua, 353.

24. See Neil Diamant, *Revolutionizing the Family: Politics, Love and Divorce in Urban and Rural China, 1949–1968* (Berkeley: University of California Press, 2000). Most of Diamant's research is based on court archives from that period, though the author says little about the propaganda literature issued at the time.

25. Croll, *The Women's Movement in China: A Selection of Readings* (London: Anglo-Chinese Educational Institute, 1974), 110. The full text of the 1950 Marriage Law and other important documents and articles from the time are collected in this volume.

26. A common view contends that the law served as a means through which the CCP as a whole and Mao in particular strove to consolidate their reputation and authority. For additional interpretations of the Marriage Law, see Evans (1997).

27. This sticky issue was addressed in the contemporary press. An article published in 1951 in the *Renmin ribao*, for instance, asked: "In the new China, where the revolution has already been victorious and the people have stood up (*fanshen le*), and where women's rights have gained the protection of the law, why is it that we continue to have serious incidents of women being maltreated?" Interestingly, though the author cites as the first reason the familiar lingering influences of feudal culture, insufficient support and understanding on the part of grassroots party cadres is also offered as a contributing factor. "Jianjue guanche hunyinfa, baozhang funü quanli" (Resolutely implement the Marriage Law, ensure women's rights) (September 30, 1951), reprinted in *Hunyin fa cankao ziliao* (Reference material for the Marriage Law): 3 (Propaganda Department of the Women's Federation of Nanjing, 1953), 10.

28. It is perhaps in this respect that the CCP's Marriage Law differed most dramatically from the New Civil Code passed by the KMT in 1930, which also outlawed arranged marriage, child-brides, polygamy, and so forth.

29. Originally published in *People's China* (March 1953); reprinted in Croll, ed., *The Women's Movement in China*, 31–34.

30. Ono Kazuko, *Chinese Women in a Century of Revolution: 1850–1950* (Stanford: Stanford University Press, 1989), 183. The following analysis is based on materials held at the Beijing Library.

31. See Davin, *Woman-Work*, 86–67.

32. *Liu Yingjiao zhengqu hunyin ziyou* (Liu Yingjiao demands marital freedom) (Fuzhou: Fujian renmin chubanshe, 1953), preface.

33. *Xuanchuan guanche hunyin fa yanchang cailiao* (Singing materials for publicizing and implementing the Marriage Law) (Changsha: Hunan tongsu duwu

chubanshe, 1953). This collection begins with a typical propaganda song that explains the contents of the Marriage Law.

34. For an informative examination of the revolutionary practice of "speaking bitterness" (*shuku*) in terms of the tradition of female grievance genres, see Anne E. McLaren, "The Grievance Rhetoric of Chinese Women: From Lamentation to Revolution," in *Intersections: Gender, History and Culture in the Asian Context*, no. 4 (Sept 2000) URL: http://www.murdoch.edu.au/intersections/ issue4/mclaren.html.

35. Also included in *Xuanchuan guanche hunyin fa yanchang cailiao*.

36. While Diamont's study emphasizes the uneven implementation and effects of the Marriage Law, his examination of court archives also presents ample evidence of how the Marriage Law afforded rural women an empowering new political vocabulary.

37. Anthropologist Ellen Judd notes that in oral accounts of women who faced marital disputes during that era, the new law and state policy were often downplayed while women's own actions in changing their lives were emphasized. See *The Chinese Women's Movement Between State and Market* (Stanford: Stanford University Press, 2002), 6–7.

38. This story appears in the collection *Liu Yingjiao Zhengqu hunyin ziyou* (1953). Most of the texts are reprinted from *Fulian* materials. A better known example of female-crossing dressing in Chinese revolutionary narrative is the Cultural Revolution model opera *Zhiqu weihushan* (Taking tiger mountain by strategy) in which the heroine Chang Bao is forced to disguise herself as a man until the arrival of the Communist Party.

39. Not to be confused with the earlier journal edited by Wang Yiwei, this magazine was entitled *Nüsheng* and had the official backing of Japanese authorities. See chapter 4 for more information.

40. Wang, *Women in the Chinese Enlightenment*, 221–242.

41. According to her biographer, this was primarily an expedient measure to ensure a salary. See *Su Qing zhuan*, 250.

42. Zhao, *Changxiang yi*, 106.

43. "Reinventing National History: Communist and Anti-Communist Fiction of the Mid-Twentieth Century," in Pang-yuan Chi and David Wang, eds., *Chinese Literature in the Second Half of a Modern Century, A Critical Survey* (Bloomington: Indiana University Press, 2000), 39–64.

44. In the set of novels she examines, including Zhou Libo's *Baofeng zhouyu* (Hurricane) (1948), Liu Qing's *Tongqiang tiebi* (Impregnable fortress) (1951), and Zhao Shuli's *Sanliwan* (1955), Eber finds that a reassuring vision of social harmony is projected through traditional (i.e., unequal) familial relationships in which women occupy the subordinate position. See "Social Harmony, Family and Women in Chinese Novels, 1948–1958," *China Quarterly* 117 (March 1989).

45. For an informative overview in English of Chen Xuezhao's career, see Jeffrey Kinkley's introduction to *Surviving the Storm*, the English translation of her post-Mao memoir (Armonk: M.E. Sharpe, 1990).

46. Despite the proletarian-sounding title, Chen notes it was inspired by the French expression "Qu'l est beau quand on travaille." For a complete bibliography of her work from this period, see Ding, *Chen Xuezhao yanjiu zhuanji* (1983).

47. The early chapters overlap considerably with her earlier novel *Nanfeng de meng* (1929), which also involves a rebellious young woman who goes abroad in search of economic, romantic, and intellectual freedom and fulfillment during heady May Fourth era. See chapter 2.

48. For more on the Rectification Movement (1942–1944), see Ellen Judd, "Prelude to the Yan'an Talks: Problems in Transforming a Literary Intelligentsia," *Modern China* 11 (July 1985).

49. See Meng Yue, "Female Images and National Myth," in Tani Barlow, ed., *Gender Politics in Modern China: Writing and Feminism* (Durham: Duke University Press, 1993).

50. The fictional character, Zhang Dewei, appears to be based on the real life Cai Boling, one of Chen's close male companions in Paris.

51. One might note that the national public debate carried out in *Zhongguo funü* in 1963–1964 attests to the continuing relevance of the question of what constitutes women's happiness in a revolutionary context. Readers who wrote in to the magazine to express their opinions on the matter were not in accord as to whether personal well-being derived from the family (as opposed to revolution or production). See Croll, *The Women's Movement in China*, 82–83.

52. As we find, for instance, in case of the character Yu Yongze in Yang Mo's *Qingchun zhi ge*. For an informative analysis of the novel, see Meng, "Female Images and National Myth".

53. The revised edition published upon Chen's "rehabilitation" in the post-Mao era, however, contains a somewhat contrived scene in which the heroine learns that her old boyfriend Dewei is the son of an impoverished academic and not, as she had long assumed, a rich KMT official. By endowing the character with a more "politically correct" class status, it's almost as though the author wants to minimize the tension between the heroine's sexuality and political aspirations in the original novel.

54. In the revised post-Mao version, Chen inserted an entirely new chapter at this point in the narrative (chapter 43), which elaborates the heroine's grooming by Party superiors and her subsequent induction into the CCP. It is interesting that the author did not feel the need to foreground the aspect of the heroine's political development when the novel was originally composed.

55. I would note here that the term "liberation" is being used in the narrow sense of being freed from foreign aggression.

56. By her own account in her later memoir *Fuchen zayi* (Surviving the storm), Chen was eager to take part in the rural Land Reform campaigns in her native Zhejiang province in the immediate post-liberation era and therefore requested an assignment in the countryside with thoughts of literary projects always on her mind. Her request was initially denied, however, on grounds that her intellectual training better suited her to an academic post, and she was accordingly sent to teach and oversee "political" classes at Zhejiang University. Chen's persistence eventually paid off, however, and within a year she was permitted to move to Xieqiao, in Haining county, to begin research for a new novel. Around that time she was also accorded the status of professional writer by the Central Research Institute of Literature and thus ensured a steady income. In 1953, in accordance with Party directives she published a slim novel entitled *Tudi*. The novel involves the collaboration of a land reform brigade and the members of the Village Peasant Association to overturn the lingering influence of the reactionary local landowners.

Although the novel provides a straightforward account of the process—complete with scenes of "speaking bitterness" sessions, public trials of land-lords and unrepentant rich peasants, and the redistribution of land—neither the characters nor the plot are sufficiently developed, and the novel generated little critical attention. More disappointing in terms of the issue at hand, the novel alludes to a number of topical gender issues (the fate of women characters such as A'E, a young woman of peasant origins who marries into a rich landlord family and the special challenges faced by female peasants—such as Zhou Xuefeng, the local Women's Association Representative, for instance—who are politically mobilized by Land Reform, and how the movement positively impacted social/political roles of peasant women) only to leave them undeveloped as themes.

57. *Baogu* (Beijing: Zhongguo qingnian chubanshe, 1982).

58. Xie Hegeng, postface to the novel, 444.

59. It is widely believed that the harsh treatment she endured came at the behest of Jiang Qing herself. Back in the early 1930s, the two women had both pursued acting careers (in left-wing theater and film) and Jiang Qing (then known as Lan Ping) is said to have bitterly resented the fact that Wang Ying often landed the better roles. She was particularly jealous when the lead part in Xia Yan's play *Sai Jinhua* went to Wang when it was staged in Shanghai in 1936.

60. According to her biographer Li Ruixin, he relied on the manuscript Ida Pruitt had kept of the English translation to supplement the incomplete Chinese manuscript that survived the Cultural Revolution. See *Wang Ying* (Beijing: Zhongguo qingnian chubanshe, 1987), 437.

61. Li, *Wang Ying*.

62. Translation is from the English edition, with slight modifications based on the Chinese text.

63. Wang Ying (born Yu Zhihua) signaled a severing of tics with her father's side of the family by assuming her mother's surname.

64. According to John Fairbank, who knew her personally, Yang Gang committed suicide in 1957 after being seriously injured in a car accident and not, as one might assume from the date, because of the difficulties she encountered during the anti-Rightist campaign. See *Chinabound: A Fifty-year Memoir* (New York: Harper and Row, 1983), 418. Xiao Qian appears to hold a different view, reminding us that the rescission of her status as a deputy to the National People's Congress, along with that of Feng Xuefeng, made headline news in October 1957, right around the time she died.

65. Before their budding cross-class romance has a chance to blossom into anything serious, however, he disappears (in all likelihood having been executed) following the brutal suppression of a local uprising, and she vows to follow in his footsteps. In this final turn of events, of course, the reader will detect a certain resemblance to Yang Mo's *Qingchun zhige* in which the heroine Lin Daojing similarly reaffirms her commitment to the struggle after her revolutionary lover dies in prison.

BIBLIOGRAPHY

A Ying. *Xiaoshuo xiantan sizhong* 小说闲谈四种 (Four chats on fiction). Shanghai: Shanghai guji chubanshe, 1985.

———. *Wanqing xiaoshuo shi* 晚清小说史 (History of late Qing fiction). Shanghai: Shangwu yinshuguan, 1937. Reprint. Beijing: Dongfang chubanshe, 1996.

———. *Wanqing wenxue congchao: xiaoshuo xiju yanjiujuan* 晚清文学丛钞：小说戏剧研究卷 (A compendium of late Qing literature: volume of fiction and drama). Beijing: Zhonghua shuju, 1960.

———. *Wanqing wenxue congchao: shuochang wenxue juan* 晚清文学丛钞：说唱文学卷 (A compendium of late Qing literature: volume of shuochang literature). Beijing: Zhonghua shuju, 1960.

Anderson, Marston. *The Limits of Realism: Chinese Fiction in the Revolutionary Period*. Berkeley: University of California Press, 1990.

Andors, Phyllis. *The Unfinished Liberation of Chinese Women: 1949–1980*. Bloomington: Indiana University Press, 1983.

Ardis, Ann. *New Women, New Novels: Feminism and Early Modernism*. New Brunswick: Rutgers University Press, 1990.

Bai Shurong. *Shiwei nüzuojia* 十位女作家 (Ten women writers). Tianjin: Chunzhong chubanshe, 1986.

Bai Shurong and He You. *Bai Wei pingzhuan* 白薇评传 (A critical biography of Bai Wei). Changsha: Hunan renmin chubanshe, 1982.

Bai Wei. *Bai Wei zuopinxuan* 白薇作品选 (Selected works of Bai Wei). Changsha: Hunan renmin chubanshe, 1985.

———. *Beiju shengya* 悲剧生涯 (Tragic life). Shanghai: Wenxue chubanshe, 1936.

———. *Linli* 琳丽 (Linli). Shanghai: Shanghai shangwu shuju, 1926.

———. "Wo toudao wenxue quanli de chuzhong" 我投到文学圈里的初衷 (My original intentions for joining the literary world). Zhen Zhengduo ed. *Wo yu wenxue*. Shanghai: Shenghuo shudian, 1934.

———. "Wo xie ta de dongji" 我写它的动机 (My motives for writing it). *Funü shenghuo* no. 1 (1935).

———. *Zhadan yu zhengniao* 炸弹与征鸟 (A bomb and an expeditionary bird). Shanghai: Beixin shuju, 1929.

———. *Zuoye* 昨夜 (Last night). Shanghai: Nanqiang shuju, 1933. Reprint. Shijiazhuang: Hebei jiaoyu chubanshe, 1994.

Bakhtin, M.M. *The Dialogic Imagination: Four Essays*. Ed. Michael Holquist. Austin: University of Texas Press, 1981.

Bammer, Angelika. *Partial Visions: Feminism and Utopianism in the 1970s*. New York: Routledge, 1991.

Barecca, Regina. *Untamed and Unabashed: Essays on Women and Humor in British Literature*. Detroit: Wayne State University Press, 1994.

Barlow, Tani, E. "Gender and Identity in Ding Ling's *Mother*." In *Modern Chinese Women Writers: Critical Appraisals*, ed. Michael S. Duke 1–24. Armonk: M.E. Sharpe, 1989.

———. ed. *Gender Politics in Modern China: Writing & Feminism*. Durham: Duke University Press, 1993.

———. "Theorizing Women: Funü, Guojia, Jiating [Chinese Women, State and Family]." *Genders* 10 (Spring 1991), 132–160.

Bartkowski, Frances. *Feminist Utopias*. Lincoln: University of Nebraska Press, 1989.

Bartky, Sandra Lee. *Femininity and Domination: Studies in the Phenomenology of Oppression*. New York: Routledge, 1990.

Basu, Amrita, ed. *The Challenge of Local Feminisms: Women's Movements in Global Perspective*. Boulder: Westview Press, 1995.

Bhabha, Homi, ed. *Nation and Narration*. London: Routledge Press, 1990.

Beahan, Charlotte. "Feminism and Nationalism in the Chinese Women's Press 1902–1922." *Modern China* 1, no. 4 (October 1975), 379–416.

———. "The Chinese Women's Movement and Nationalism in Late Ch'ing China." Ph.D. Dissertation. Columbia University, 1976.

Beijing nübao 北京女报 (Beijing women's paper). Beijing, 1905–1906.

Beijingshi funü lianhehui, ed. *Beijing funü baokan kao, 1905–1949* 北京妇女报刊考 (An investigation of the Beijing women's press). Beijing: Guangming ribao chubanshe, 1990.

Bing Xin. *Bing Xin quanji* 冰心全集 (Complete works of Bing Xin). 8 vols. Haixia wenyi chubanshe, 1994.

Boumelha, Penny. "Realism and the Ends of Feminism." In *Grafts: Feminist Cultural Criticism*, ed. Susan Sheridan, 77–91. London: Verso, 1988.

Britton, R.S. *The Chinese Periodical Press, 1800–1912*. Taibei: Chengwen, 1966.

Brown, Carolyn. "Woman as Trope: Gender and Power in Lun Xun's Soap." *Modern Chinese Literature* 4 (Spring 1988), 55–70.

Brownell, Susan and Jeffrey N. Wassestrom. *Chinese Femininities, Chinese Masculinities: A Reader*. Berkeley: University of California Press, 2002.

Broyelle, Claudie. *Women's Liberation in China*. Atlantic Highlands, N.J.: Humanities Press, 1977.

Butler, Judith. *Gender Trouble: Feminism and the Subversion of Identity*. New York: Routledge, 1990.

Cao Ye. *Xiandai Zhongguo nüzuojia* 现代中国女作家 (Modern Chinese women writers). Tianjin: Renwen shudian, 1932.

Carlitz, Katherine. "The Social Uses of Female Virtue." *Late Imperial China* 12, no. 2 (December, 1991), 117–152.

Chan, Stephen. "The Language of Despair: Ideological Representation of the New Woman by May Fourth Writers." *Modern Chinese Literature* 4 (Spring 1988), 19–38.

Chang, Yvonne. "Yuan Qionggiong and the Rage for Zhang Ailing." *Modern Chinese Literature* 4 (Spring 1988), 201–223.

Chen Dongyuan. *Zhongguo funü shenghuo shi*. 中国妇女生活史 (The history of Chinese women's lives). Shanghai: Shanghai Commercial Press, 1937. Reprint. Taipei: Taiwan Commercial Press, 1994.

Chen Jingshi. *Xiandai wenxue zaoqi de nüzuojia* 现代文学早期的女作家 (Early modern women writers). Taipei: Chengwen chubanshe, 1980.

Chen Mingshu, ed. *Ershi shiji Zhongguo wenxue dadian: 1930–1965* 二十世纪中国文学大典 (Compendium of twentieth-century Chinese literature, 1930–1965). Shanghai: Shanghai jiaoyu chubanshe, 1996.

Chen Pingyuan. *Zhongguo xiaoshuo xushi moshi de zhuanbian* 中国小说叙事模式的转变 (The narrative transformation of Chinese fiction). Beijing: Jiuda wenhua chuban, 1990.

Chen Qingsheng. *Kangzhan shiqi de Shanghai wenxue* 抗战时期的上海文学 (Shanghai literature during the war of resistance). Shanghai: Shanghai renmin chubanshe, 1995.

Chen Xianggong. *Qiu Jin nianpu ji chuanji ziliao* 秋瑾年谱及传记资料 (Biographical materials on Qiu Jin's life). Beijing: Zhongguo shuju, 1983.

Chen Xiefen. "Qun" 群 (Associations). *Nüxuebao* 2, no. 1 (1903).

Chen Xuezhao. *Surviving the Storm: A Memoir*. Translated by Hua Ti and Caroline Green, ed. and intro. by Jeffrey C. Kinkley. Armonk, NY: M.E. Sharpe, 1990.

———. *Chuncha* 春茶 (Spring camellias). Beijing: Zuojia chubanshe, 1957.

———. "Funü yundong de yimian guan" 妇女运动的一面观 (The one-sided view of the women's movement). In *Xiandai funü pinglun ji*, ed. Fan Xiangshan. Shanghai: Shijie shuju, 1930.

———. "Gei nanxing" 给男性 (To men). *Xin nüxing* (December 1926).

———. *Gongzuozhe shi meili de* 工作者是美丽的 (Working is beautiful, 1949). Hangzhou: Zhejiang renmin chubanshe, 1979.

———. *Nanfeng de meng* 南风的梦 (Dream of southern winds). Shanghai: Zhenmeishan shudian, 1929.

———. *Tudi* 土地 (The land). Beijing: Renmin wenxue chubanshe, 1953.

———. "Wo suo xiwang de xin funü" 我所希望的新妇女 (The new woman of my dreams, 1923). In *Yanxia banlu*, 1–3.

———. "Xiandai nüxing de kumen wenti" 现代女性的苦闷问题 (Woes of the modern woman). *Xin nüxing* (January 1927). Translation in Amy D. Dooling and Kristina M. Torgeson eds. *Writing Women in Modern China*, 1998, 169–173.

———. *Xingfu* 幸福 (Happiness). Shanghai: Shenghuo shudian, 1933.

———. *Yi Bali* 忆巴黎 (Remembering Paris). Shanghai: Beixin shuju, 1929.

———. *Yan'an fangwenji* 延安访问记 (Interviews at Yan'an). Hong Kong: Beiji, 1940.

———. *Yanxia banlu* 烟霞伴侣 (Travel companion in the twilight mist). Beijing: Beijing guangbo xueyuan chubanshe, 1993.

———. "Zuihou de xin" 最后的信 (The last letter). *Zhenmeishan: Nüzuojia hao* (1928).

Chen Ying. "Qi" 妻 (Wife, 1929). Translated as "Woman" in Amy D. Dooling and Kristina M. Torgeson eds. *Writing Women in Modern China*. New York: Columbia University Press, 1998, 279–298.

Chen, Yu-shih. *Realism and Allegory in the Early Fiction of Mao Dun*. Bloomington: Indiana University Press, 1986.

———. "False Harmony: Mao Dun on Women and the Family." *Modern Chinese Literature* 7 (1993), 131–152.

Ching Liumei. "The Forerunners of Chinese Feminism in Japan." Ph.D. Dissertation, Leiden University, 1988.

Chow, Lim Chin. "Reading 'The Golden Cangue': Iron Bourdoirs and Symbols of Oppressed Confucian Women." *Renditions* 45 (Spring 1996), 153–176.

Chow, Rey. "Virtuous Transactions: A Reading of Three Stories by Ling Shuhua." *Modern Chinese Literature* 4, no. 1–2 (Spring–Fall 1988), 71–86.

———. *Woman and Chinese Modernity: The Politics of Reading Between West and East*. Minneapolis: University of Minnesota Press, 1991.

———. "Against the Lures of Diaspora: Minority Discourse, Chinese Women, and Intellectual Hegemony." In *Gender and Sexuality*, ed. Lu Tonglin, 23–45. Albany: SUNY Press, 1993.

Chow Tse-tung. *The May Fourth Movement: Intellectual Revolution in Modern China*. Cambridge: Harvard University Press, 1960.

Collins, Leslie. "*The New Women: A Psychological Study of the Feminist Movement from 1990 to the Present*." Ph.D. Dissertation. Yale University, 1976.

Coward, Rosalind. "Are Women's Novels Feminist Novels?" In *The New Feminist Criticism: Essays on Women, Literature, and Theory*, ed. Elaine Showalter, 225–239. London: Virago, 1985.

Cranny-Francis, Anne. *Feminist Fiction: Feminist Uses of Generic Fiction*. New York: St. Martin's Press, 1990.

Croll, Elisabeth. *Feminism and Socialism in China*. New York: Schocken, 1978.

———. *Changing Identities of Chinese Women: Rhetoric, Experience, and Self-Perception in Twentieth Century China*. London: Zed Press, 1995.

———. *The Women's Movement in China: A Selection of Readings*. London: Anglo-Chinese Educational Institute, 1974.

Cuadrado, Clara Yu. "Portraits by a Lady: The Fictional World of Ling Shuhua." In *Women Writers of 20th-Century China*, ed. Angela Jung Palandri, 41–62. Eugene: University of Oregon, 1982.

Davin, Delia. *Woman-Work: Women and the Party in Revolutionary China*. Oxford: Oxford University Press, 1976.

De Lauretis, Teresa. *Technologies of Gender: Essays on Theory, Film, and Fiction*. Bloomington: Indiana University Press, 1987.

———. "The Violence of Rhetoric: Considerations on Representation and Gender." In *The Violence of Representation: Literature and the History of Violence*, ed. Nancy Armstrong and Leonard Tennenhouse, 239–258. London: Routledge, 1989.

Denton, Kirk A. *Modern Chinese Literary Theory: Writings on Literature*. Stanford: Stanford University Press, 1996.

———. *The Problematic of Self in Modern Chinese Literature: Hu Feng and Lu Ling*. Stanford: Stanford University Press, 1998.

Diamant, Neil J. *Revolutionizing the Family: Politics, Love, and Divorce in Urban and Rural China, 1949–1968*. Berkeley: University of California Press, 2000.

Dikotter, Frank. *Sex, Culture and Modernity in China*. Honolulu: University of Hawaii Press, 1995.

Ding Ling. *Ding Ling wenji* 丁玲文集 (The collected works of Ding Ling). 10 vols. Changsha: Hunan renmin chubanshe, 1983.

———. *I Myself Am a Woman: Selected Writings of Ding Ling*. Ed. Tani E. Barlow and Gary J. Bjorge. Boston: Beacon Press, 1989.

———. "Yecao" (1929). In *I Myself am a Woman: Selected Writings of Ding Ling*, ed. Tani E. Barlow and Gary J. Bjorge, 105–111. Boston: Beacon Press, 1989.

———. "Yijiusanling nian chun Shanghai" 一九三零年春上海 (Shanghai, Spring 1930, 1930). In *Ding Ling wenji*. Changsha: Hunan renmin chubanshe, 1983.

Ding Maoyuan, ed. *Chen Xuezhao yanjiu zhuanji* 陈学昭研究专集 (A collection of research on Chen Xuezhao). Hangzhou: Zhejiang wenyi chubanshe, 1983.

Dolezelova-Velingerova, Milena. *The Chinese Novel at the Turn of the Century*. Toronto: University of Toronto Press, 1980.

Dong Bian, ed. *Nüjie wenhua zhanshi Shen Zijiu* 女界文化战士沈兹久 (Women's cultural warrior, Shen Zijiu). Beijing: Zhongguo funü chubanshe, 1991.

Dooling, Amy and Kristina Torgeson, eds. *Writing Women in Modern China: An Anthology of Women's Literature From the Early Twentieth Century*. New York: Columbia University Press, 1998.

Dooling, Amy. "Reconsidering the Origins of Modern Chinese Women's Writing." In *The Columbia Companion to Modern East Asian Literatures,* ed. Joshua Mostow and Kirk A. Denton, 371–377. New York: Columbia University Press, 2003.

———. "Desire and Disease: Bai Wei and the Thirties Literary Left." In *Contested Modernities in Chinese Literature,* ed. Charles Laughlin. New York: Palgrave Macmillan Press, 2005.

———. "In Search of Laughter: Yang Jiang's Feminist Comedy." *Modern Chinese Literature* 8, no. 1/2 (1994), 41–68.

———. *Writing Women in Modern China: The Revolutionary Years, 1936–76.* New York: Columbia University Press, 2005.

Duke, Michael, ed. *Modern Chinese Women Writers: Critical Appraisals.* Armonk, NY: M.E. Sharpe, 1989.

Dunker, Patricia. *Sisters and Strangers: An Introduction to Contemporary Feminist Fiction.* Oxford: Blackwell, 1992.

DuPlessis, Rachel Blau. *Writing Beyond the Ending: Narrative Strategies of Twentieth Century Women Writers.* New York: Oxford University Press, 1985.

Eber, Irene. "Social Harmony, Family and Women in Chinese Novels, 1948–1958." *China Quarterly,* no. 117 (March 1989), 71–96.

———. "Images of Women in Recent Chinese Fiction: Do Women Hold up Half the Sky?" *Signs* 2, no. 1 (1976), 24–34.

Eide, Elisabeth. *China's Ibsen: From Ibsen to Ibsenism.* London: Curzon Press, 1987.

Evans, Harriet. *Women and Sexuality in China: Female Sexuality and Gender Since 1949.* New York: Continuum, 1997.

———. "The Language of Liberation: Gender and *Jiefang* in early Chinese Communist Party Discourse." *Intersections* (September 1998). URL: http:// wwwshe. murdoch.edu.au/intersections/back _issues/harriet.html.

Ezell, Margaret J.M. *Writing Women's Literary History.* Baltimore: Johns Hopkins University Press, 1993.

Fairbank, John King. *Chinabound: A Fifty-Year Memoir.* New York: Harper and Row, 1982.

Fang Hanqi. *Zhongguo jindai baokanshi* 中国近代报刊史 (A history of the modern Chinese press). Taiyuan: Shanxi jiaoyu chubanshe, 1981.

Felski, Rita. *Beyond Feminist Aesthetics: Feminist Literature and Social Change.* Cambridge: Harvard University Press, 1989.

Feng Keng, "Yituan rou" 团肉 (A piece of flesh, 1930). In *Chenguang: Rou Shi Feng Keng yigao,* 313–316. Beijing: Shumu wenxian chubanshe, 1986.

Feng Yuanjun. *Feng Yuanjun chuangzuo yiwenji* 冯沅君创作译文集 (The collected writings and translations of Feng Yuanjun). Jinan: Shandong renmin chubanshe, 1983.

———. "Cimu" 慈母 (Benevolent mother, 1924). In *Juanshi.* Beixin shuju chubanshe, 1926.

———. "Gejue" 隔绝 (Separation, 1923), in *Writing Women in Modern China,* ed. Amy D. Dooling and Kristina M. Torgeson, New York: Columbia University Press, 1998, 105–113.

———. "Gejue yihou" 隔绝以后 (After the separation, 1923) in *Juanshi.* Beixin shuju chubanshe, 1926.

Ferry, Megan. "Chinese Women Writers of the 1930s and Their Critical Reception." Ph.D. dissertation. St. Louis, Washington University, 1998.

Fetterly, Judith. *The Resisting Reader: A Feminist Approach to American Fiction.* Bloomington: Indiana University Press, 1978.

Feuerwerker, Yi-tsi Mei. "Women as Writers in the 1920s and 1930s." In *Women in Chinese Society,* ed. Margery Wolf and Roxane Witke, 143–168. Stanford: Stanford University Press, 1975.

Feuerwerker, Yi-tsi Mei. *Ding Ling's Fiction: Ideology and Narrative in Modern Chinese Literature.* Cambridge: Harvard East Asian Series, 1982.

———. "Text, Intertext, and the Representation of the Writing Self in Lu Xun, Yu Dafu, and Wang Meng." In *From May Fourth to June Fourth*, ed. Ellen Widmer and David Wang, 167–193. Cambridge: Harvard University Press, 1993.

Findeisen, Raoul David. "From Literature to Love: Glory and Decline of the Love Letter Genre." In *The Literary Field of Twentieth Century China*, ed. Michel Hockx, 79–112. Honolulu: University of Hawaii Press, 1999.

Finke, Laurie. *Feminist Theory: Women's Writing.* Ithaca: Cornell University Press, 1992.

Foley, Barbara. *Radical Representations: Politics and Form in U.S. Proletarian Fiction, 1929–1941.* Durham: Duke University Press, 1993.

Forsas-Scott, Helen, ed. *Textual Liberation: European Feminist Writing in the Twentieth Century.* London: Routledge, 1991.

Foucault, Michel. *The History of Sexuality Volume I: An Introduction.* Translated by Robert Hurley. New York: Vintage Press, 1980.

Funü pinglun 妇女 评论 (Women's review). Supplement of Shanghai *Minguo ribao*, 1921–1923.

Funü shenghuo 妇女生活 (Women's life). Shanghai, 1935–1937.

"Funü wenti yanjiuhui xuanyan" 妇女 问题 研究会.宣言 (Manifesto of the Woman Problem Research Association) *Funü pinglun*, August 2, 1922.

Funü zazhi 妇女 杂 志 (Ladies' journal). Shanghai, 1915–1931.

Funü zazhi: funü wenxue zhuanhao 妇女 杂 志：妇女 文学 专号 (Ladies' journal: special issue on women's writing) 7 no. 17 (1931).

Fu, Poshek. *Passivity, Resistance, and Collaboration: Intellectual Choices in Occupied Shanghai: 1937–1945.* Stanford: Stanford University Press, 1993.

Galik, Marian. "On the Literature Written by Chinese Women Prior to 1917." *Asian and African Studies* XV (1979).

Gechang hunyinfa. 歌唱婚姻法 (Songs about the marriage law). Sichuan Province Democratic Women's Federation Preparatory Committee, Propaganda and Education Department: 1953.

Gerstlacher, Anna, ed. *Women and Literature in China.* Bochum, West Germany: Studienverlag Brockmeyer, 1985.

Gilbert, Sandra M. and Susan Gubar. *The Madwoman in the Attic: The Woman Writer and the Nineteenth-Century Literary Imagination.* New Haven: Yale University Press, 1979.

Gilmartin, Christina Kelley. *Engendering the Chinese Revolution: Radical Women, Communist Politics, and Mass Movements in the 1920s.* Berkeley: University of California Press, 1995.

Gilmartin, Christina K., Gail Hershatter, Lisa Rofel, and Tyrene White, eds. *Engendering China: Women, Culture, and the State.* Cambridge: Harvard University Press, 1994.

Gipoulon, Catherine. "The Emergence of Women in Politics in China, 1898–1927." *Chinese Studies in History* 23 (1989/90), 47–67.

Goldblatt, Howard. *Hsiao Hung.* Boston: Twayne Publishers, 1976.

Goldman, Merle. *Literary Dissent in Communist China.* Cambridge: Harvard University Press, 1967.

————. *Modern Chinese Literature in the May Fourth Era*. Cambridge: Harvard University Press, 1977.

Gu Yanling. *Nüxing zhuyizhe Qiu Jin* 女性主义者秋瑾 (The feminist Qiu Jin). *Funü yu liangxing xuekan* 1 (1990), 27–45.

Guan Lu. *Guan Lu xiaoshuo: Zhongxia ye zhimeng* 关露小说：仲夏夜之梦 (Guan Lu's fiction: midsummer's night dream). Shanghai: Guji chubanshe, 1999.

————. *Pingguo yuan* 苹果园(The apple orchard). Beijing: Gongren chubanshe, 1951.

————. "Yi taitai de riji" 姨太太的日记(Diary of a concubine, 1935). In *Zhongxia ye zhi meng*. 10–27, Shanghai: Guji chubanshe, 1999.

Gunn, Edward. *Unwelcome Muse: Chinese Literature in Shanghai and Peking, 1937–1945*. New York: Columbia University Press, 1980.

Guo Yanli. *Qiu Jin wenxue lungao* 秋瑾文学论槁 (A manuscript on Qiu Jin's literature). Xi'an: Shanxi renmin chubanshe, 1987.

Guo Zhenyi. *Zhongguo funü wenti* 中国妇女问题 (The Chinese woman question). Shanghai: Shangwu yinshuguan, 1937.

Greene, Gayle. *Changing the Story: Feminist Fiction and the Tradition*. Chicago: University of Chicago Press, 1991.

He Yubo. *Zhongguo xiandai nüzuojia* 中国现代女作家 (Modern Chinese women writers). Shanghai: Fuxing shuju, 1936.

Heilbrun, Carolyn. *Writing a Woman's Life*. New York: Ballantine Books, 1988.

Hershatter, Gail. *Dangerous Pleasures: Prostitution and Modernity in Twentieth-Century Shanghai*. Berkeley: University of California Press, 1997.

Hite, Molly. *The Other Side of the Story: Structures and Strategies of Contemporary Feminist Narrative*. Ithaca: Cornell University Press, 1989.

Hockx, Michael, ed. *The Literary Field of Twentieth Century China*. Honolulu: University of Hawaii Press, 1999.

Hong, Chang-Tai. "Female Symbols of Resistance in Chinese Wartime Spoken Drama." *Modern China* 15 (April 1989), 149–177.

Hu Lanqi. *Hu Lanqi huiyilu 1901–1936* 胡兰畦回忆录 (Memoirs of Hu Lanqi). Chengdu: Sichuan renmin chubanshe, 1985.

Huang, Nicole. "Written in the Ruins: War and Domesticity in Shanghai Literature of the 1940s." Ph.D. dissertation. Los Angeles: UCLA, 1998.

Hunan sheng guanche huyinfa bangongshi. *Xuanchuan guanche hunyin fa yanchang cailiao* 宣 传贯彻婚姻法演唱材料 (Singing materials to publicize and implement the marriage law). Changsha: Hunan tongsu duwu chubanshe, 1953.

Hunyin fa cankao ziliao: 3. 婚姻法参考资料 (Reference material for the marriage law). Propaganda Department of the Women's Federation of Nanjing: 1953.

Hu Shi. "Jianshe de wenxue geming lun" 建设的文学革命论 (Toward a constructive theory of literary revolution). *Xin qingnian* 4, no. 4 (April 1918).

————. "Zhongshen dashi" 终身大事 (Life's greatest event, 1919). *Zhongguo xiandai dumu xuan, 1919–1949*. Beijing: Renmin wenxue chubanshe, 1984.

Huang Renying, ed. *Dangdai Zhongguo nüzuojia lun* 当代中国女作家论 (On contemporary Chinese women writers). Shanghai: Guanghua shuju, 1933.

Huang Yixin. *Ding Ling xiezuo shengya* 丁玲写作生涯 (Ding Ling's literary career). Tianjin: Baihua wenyi chubanshe, 1984.

Hu Ying. *Tales of Translation: Composing the New Woman in China, 1899–1918*. Stanford: Stanford University Press, 2000.

Hsia, C.T. *A History of Modern Chinese Fiction*. 2nd ed. New Haven: Yale University Press, 1971.

Hsia, C.T. "Residual Femininity: Women in Chinese Communist Fiction." In *Chinese Communist Literature*, ed. Cyril Birch. New York: Praeger, 1963.

———. "Yen Fu and Liang Chi-chao as Advocates of New Fiction." In *Chinese Approaches to Literature: From Confucius to Liang Chi-chao,* ed. Adele Rickett, 221–257. Princeton: Princeton University Press, 1978.

Irigaray, Luce. *This Sex Which is Not One.* Translated by Catharine Porter. Ithaca: Cornell University Press, 1985.

Jackson, Rosemary. *Fantasy: The Literature of Subversion.* London and New York, Methuen, 1981.

Jardine, Alice. *Gynesis: Configurations of Woman and Modernity.* Ithaca: Cornell University Press, 1985.

Jayawardena, Kumari. *Feminism and Nationalism in the Third World.* London: Zed Press, 1986.

Jian Shen. "Du Bingying nüshi *Congjun riji*" 读冰莹女士从军日记 (Reading Miss Bingying's *War Diary*). In *Dangdai nüzuojia lun*, ed. Huang Renying, 108–118. Shanghai: Guanghua Shuju, 1933.

Jin Zhonghua. "Jinshi funü jiefang yundong zai wenxueshang de fanying" 近世妇女解放运动 在文学上的反映 (The reflection of the modern women's emancipation movement in literature). *Funü zazhi* no. 6 (June 1931), 2–12.

Judd, Ellen. *The Chinese Women's Movement: Between State and Market.* Stanford: Stanford University Press, 2002.

———. "Prelude to the Yan'an Talks: Problems in Transforming a Literary Intelligentsia." *Modern China* 11 (July 1985), 377–408.

Ke Ling. "Yaoji Zhang Ailing" 遥寄张爱玲 (Sent to Zhang Ailing). In *Zhang Ailing wenji,* Vol. 4. Hefei: Anhui wenyi chubanshe, 1992, 421–429.

Kingsbury, Karen. "Reading Eileen Chang's Early Fiction: Art and a Female Sense of Self." Ph.D. Dissertation. Columbia University, 1995.

Ko, Dorothy. *Teachers of the Inner Chambers: Women and Culture in Seventeenth-Century China.* Stanford: Stanford University Press, 1994.

Kong Qingmao. *Yang Jiang pingzhuan* 杨绛评传 (A critical biography of Yang Jiang). Beijing: Huaxia chubanshe, 1998.

Kubin, Wolfgang. "Sexuality and Literature in the People's Republic of China: Problems of Chinese Women prior to and since 1949 as seen in Ding Ling's *Diary of Sophia* (1928) and Xi Rong's Story *An Unexceptional Post* (1962)." In *Essays in Modern Chinese Literature and Literary Criticism,* ed. Wolfgang Kubin and Rudolf Wagner, 168–191. Bochum: Brockmeyer, 1982.

Lan R. Hua and Vanessa L. Fong, eds. *Women in Republican China: A Sourcebook.* Armonk, NY: M.E. Sharpe, 1999.

Lanser, Susan. "Toward a Feminist Narratology." In *Feminisms: An Anthology of Literary Theory and Criticism,* ed. Robin Warhol and Diane Herndl. New Brunswick: Rutgers University Press, 1991.

Larson, Wendy. "The End of 'Funü Wenxue': Women's Literature from 1925–1935." *Modern Chinese Literature* 4, no. 1–2 (Spring–Fall 1988), 39–54.

———. "Female Subjectivity and Gender Relations: The Early Stories of Lu Yin and Bing Xin." In *Politics, Ideology, and Literary Discourse in Modern China,* ed. Liu Kang and Tang Xiaobing, 124–143. Durham: Duke University Press, 1993.

———. *Literary Authority and the Modern Chinese Writer: Autobiography and Ambivalence.* Durham: Duke University Press, 1991.

———. *Women and Writing in Modern China.* Stanford: Stanford University Press, 1998.

Lau, Joseph. *Ts'ao Yu*. Hong Kong: Hong Kong University Press, 1970.

Lauret, Maria. *Liberating Literature: Feminist Fiction in America*. London: Routledge, 1994.

Lee, Leo Ou-fan. *The Romantic Generation of Modern Chinese Writers*. Cambridge: Harvard University Press, 1973.

———. *Shanghai Modern: The Flowering of a New Urban Culture in China: 1930–1945*. Cambridge: Harvard University Press, 1999.

Lee, Lily Xiao Hong ed. *Biographical Dictionary of Chinese Women: The Twentieth Century 1912–2000*. Armonk, NY: M.E. Sharpe, 2003.

Li Dazhao. "Zhanhou de funü wenti" 战后的妇女问题 (The postwar woman question, 1919). In *Women in Republican China: A Sourcebook*, eds. Hua R. Lan and Vanessa Fong. Armonk, NY: M.E. Sharpe, 1999, 187–193.

Li Ju-Chen. *Flowers in the Mirror*. Translated by Lin Tai-yi. Berkeley: University of California Press, 1965.

Li Junyi. "Cong Ai Lunkai dao Ke Luntai" 从爱伦凯到科伦泰 (From Ellen Key to Kollontai). *Funü zazhi* no. 6 (June 1931), 131–136.

Li Ruixin. *Wang Ying* 王莹. Beijing: Zhongguo qingnian chubanshe, 1987.

Li Xiaojiang. *Zouxiang nüren* 走向女人 (Moving toward women). Hong Kong: Qingwen shushi, 1993.

———. *Nüren de chulu* 女人的出路 (The future of women). Shenyang: Liaoning renmin chubanshe, 1989.

Li Youning. *Zhongguo xinnüjie zazhi de chuangkan ji neihan* 中国新女界杂志的创刊内涵 (The founding and content of *China's New Women* magazine). In *Zhongguo funüshi lunwenji* (Collected essays on Chinese women's history), ed. Li Youning and Zhang Yufa, 179–241. Taipei: Taiwan Shangwu yinshuguan, 1981.

Li, Youning and Zhang Yufa, eds. *Jindai Zhongguo nüquan yundong shiliao, 1842–1911* 近代中国女权运动史料 (Documents on the feminist movement in modern China, 1842–1911). 2 vols. Taipei: Zhuanji wenxueshi, 1975.

Li Youning and Zhang Yufa, eds. *Zhongguo funushi lunwenji* 中国妇女史论文集 (Collected essays on Chinese women's history). Taipei: Taiwan Shangwu yinshuguan, 1981.

Li Ziyun. "Nüzuojia zai dangdai wenxueshi suoqi de xianfeng zuoyong" 女作家在当代文学史所起的先锋作用 (The vanguard role of women writers in contemporary literary history). *Dangdai zuojia pinglun* 6 (1987), 4–10.

Liang Qichao. "Lun baoguan youyiyu guoshi" 论报官有益于国事 (On the value of the periodical press in national affairs, 1896). In *Liang Qichao xuanji*. Shanghai: Shanghai renmin chubanshe, 1983.

———. "Lun xiaoshuo yu qunzhi zhi guanxi" 论小说与群众之关系 (The relationship between fiction and popular sovereignty, 1902). In *Liang Qichao xuanji*. Shanghai: Shanghai renmin chubanshe, 1983, 349–353.

Liang Yizhen. *Qingdai funü wenxue shi* 清代妇女文学史 (A history of women's literature in the Qing dynasty). Shanghai, 1927. Reprint. Taipei: Zhonghua shuju, 1979.

Lieberman, Sally. *The Mother and Narrative Politics in Modern China*. Charlottesville: University Press of Virginia, 1998.

Liu Jianmei. *Revolution Plus Love: Literary History, Women's Bodies, and Thematic Repetition in Twentieth-Century Chinese Fiction*. Honolulu: University of Hawaii Press, 2003.

———. "Feminizing Politics: Reading Bai Wei and Lu Yin." *Journal of Modern Literature in Chinese* 5, no. 2 (2002), 55–80.

Liu Jucai. *Zhongguo jindai funü yundongshi* 中国近代妇女运动史 (The history of the modern Chinese women's movement). Liaoning: Zhongguo funü chubanshe, 1989.

Liu, Lydia H. "Invention and Intervention: The Making of a Female Tradition in Modern Chinese Literature." In *From May Fourth to June Fourth: Fiction and Film in Twentieth-Century China*, eds. Ellen Widmer and David Der-wei Wang, 194–220. Cambridge: Harvard University Press, 1993.

———. *Translingual Practice: Literature, National Culture, and Translated Modernity–China, 1900–1937*. Stanford: Stanford University Press, 1995.

———. "The Female Body and Nationalist Discourse: Manchuria in Xiao Hong's *Field of Life and Death*." In *Body, Subject, and Power in China*, eds. Angela Zito and Tani Barlow, 157–177. Chicago: University of Chicago, 1994.

———. "Narratives of Modern Selfhood: First-Person Fiction in May Fourth Literature." In *Politics, Ideology and Literary Discourse in Modern China*, ed. Kang Liu and Tang Xiaobing, 102–123. Durham: Duke University Press, 1993.

Liu-Wang Liming. *Zhongguo funü yundong* 中国妇女运动 (The Chinese women's movement). Shanghai: Shanghai Commercial Press, 1934.

Liu Yingjiao zhengqu hunyin ziyou 刘英娇争取婚姻自由 (Liu Yingjiao demands marital freedom). Fuzhou: Fujian renmin chubanshe, 1953.

Louie, Kam. *Theorizing Chinese Masculinity: Society and Gender in China*. Cambridge: Cambridge University Press, 2002.

Lu Fangshang. "Kangzhan shiqu de nüquan lunbian" 抗战时期的女权论辩 (A discussion of women's rights during the war of resistance). *Jindai zhongguo funü shi yanjiu* 2 (1994).

Lu Jingqing. *Liulangji* 流浪集 (Wandering). Shanghai: Chunyu shudian, 1932.

Lu Meiyi and Zheng Yongfu. *Zhongguo funü yundong: 1840–1921* 中国妇女运动: 1840–1921 (The Chinese women's movement: 1840–1921). Zhengzhou: Henan renmin chubanshe, 1990.

Lu, Tonglin, "The Language of Desire, class, and Subjectivity in Lu Ling's Fiction," ed. *Gender and Sexuality in Twentieth-Century Chinese Literature and Society*, 67–83. Albany: SUNY Press, 1993.

———. *Misogyny, Cultural Nihilism, and Oppositional Politics: Contemporary Chinese Fiction*. Stanford: Stanford University Press, 1995.

Lu Yin. "Chuangzao de wojian" 创造的我见 (My views on creativity) (Original in *Xiaoshuo yuebao*, 1921). *Lu Yin xuanji*, 60–61.

———. *Lu Yin zizhuan* 卢隐自传 (The autobiography of Lu Yin). Shanghai: Shanghai diyi chubanshe, 1934.

———. *Lu Yin daibiaozuo* 卢隐代表作 (Representative works by Lu Yin). Beijing: Huaxia chubanshe, 1998.

———. *Lu Yin xuanji* 卢隐选集 (The selected works of Lu Yin). 2 vols. Ed. Hong Qian. Fuzhou: Fujian renmin chubanshe, 1985.

———. "Haibin xiaoxi—ji Bo Wei" 海滨消息--寄波微 (Seaside news—a letter to Bo Wei, 1925). In *Lu Yin xuanji*, 397–399.

———. "Huaping shidai" 花瓶时代 (The flower case generation, 1933). In *Lu Yin daibiaozuo*, 373–374.

———. "Hechu shi guicheng" 何处是归程 (Which way back, 1927). In *Lu Yin daibiaozuo*, 128–134.

———. "Jinhou funü de chulu" 今后妇女的出路 (The future of women, 1936). In *Lu Yin daibiaozuo*, 367–369.

———. "Lantian de chanhuilu" 兰田的忏悔录 (Lantian's confession, 1927). In *Lu Yin xuanji*, 295–306.

———. "Lishi de riji" 丽石的日记 (Lishi's diary, 1923). In *Lu Yin daibiaozuo*. Beijing: Huaxia chubanshe, 1998, 69–79.

———. "Manli" 曼丽 (Manli, 1928). In *Lu Yin daibiaozuo*. Beijing: Huaxia chubanshe, 1998, 146–156.

———. "Neige qieruo de nüren" 那个怯弱的女人 (That weak woman, 1931). In *Lu Yin: Lin Shi de riji*. Beijing: Yanshan chubanshe, 1998, 302–312.

———. "Qilu" 歧路 (Forked road, 1933). In *Lu Yin xiaoshuo*. Shanghai: Guji chubanshe, 1999, 139–155.

———. "Shidai de xishengzhe" 时代的牺牲者 (Sacrificed to the era, 1928). In *Lu Yin daibiaozuo*. Beijing: Huaxia chubanshe, 1998, 135–145.

———. "Shengli yihou" 胜利以后 (After victory, 1925). Translation in *Writing Women in Modern China*, ed. Dooling and Torgeson, 1998, 143–156.

———. *Xiangya jiezhi* 象牙戒指 (Ivory rings, 1934). In *Lu Yin daibiaozuo*. Beijing: Huaxia chubanshe, 1998, 200–352.

———. "Yimu" — 幕 (A scene, 1928). In *Lu Yin xuanji*. Fuzhou: Fujian Vermin chubanshe, 1985, 332–337.

———. "Zhongguo de funü yundong wenti" 中国的妇女运动问题 (China's women's movement problem, 1924). In *Lu Yin xuanji*. Fuzhou: Fujian renmin chubanshe, 1985, 16–28.

Lu Yunzhang. *Shijie funü yundong shi* 世界妇女运动史 (A history of the global women's movement). Shanghai: Nuzi shudian, 1935.

Lu Xiaoman. *Aimei xiaozha* 爱眉小札 (Love letters to Mei, 1936). Reprint. Beijing: Dongfang chubanshe, 1994.

Lu Xun. *Lu Xun quanji* 鲁迅全集 (The complete works of Lu Xun). Beijing: Renmin wenxue chubanshe, 1982.

Luo Shu. *Luo Shu xuanji* 罗淑选集 (The selected works of Luo Shu). Chengdu: Sichuan renmin chubanshe, 1980.

———. "Shengren qi" 生人妻 (A stranger's wife, 1929). In Shengren qi, 1–20. Beijing: Renmin wenxue chubanshe, 1964.

Luo Yanbin. "Benbao wuda zhuyi yanshuo" 本报五大主义演说 (The five cardinal principles of this paper). *Zhongguo xinnüjie* 2 (1907).

Ma Ning. "The Textual and Critical Difference of Being Radical: Reconstructing Chinese Leftist Films of the 1930s." *Wide Angle* 2, no. 2 (1989), 22–31.

Mann, Susan. *Precious Records: Women in China's Long Eighteenth Century*. Stanford: Stanford University Press, 1997.

Mann, Susan and Yu-Yin Cheng, eds. *Under Confucian Eyes: Writings on Gender in Chinese History*. Berkeley: University of California Press, 2001.

Mao Dun. "Bing Xin lun" 冰心论 (On Bing Xin). In *Mao Dun lun Zhongguo xiandai zuojia zuopin*, 114–132.

———. *Mao Dun lun Zhongguo xiandai zuojia zuopin* 茅盾论中国现代作家作品 (Mao Dun on modern Chinese authors and their works). Ed. Yue Daiyun. Beijing: Beijing daxve chubanshe, 1980.

———. *Mao Dun quanji* 茅盾全集 (Complete works of Mao Dun), 14 vols. Beijing: Renmin chubanshe, 1984–1993.

———. "Du *Shaonian Zhonguo* funü hao" 读少年中国妇女号 (Reading the issue on women in *Young China*). *Funü zazhi* 6, no. 1 (1920), 1–4. Reprint. *Mao Dun quanji* (The collected works of Mao Dun). Beijing: Renmin wenxue chubanshe, 1987. Vol. 14, 89–93.

———. "Jiefang de funü yu funü de jiefang" 解放的妇女与妇女的解放 (Emancipated women and women's emancipation). *Mao Dun quanji*, 14, 63–69.

Mao Dun. "Lu Yin lun" 庐隐论 (On Lu Yin). In *Mao Dun lun Zhongguo xiandai zuojia de zuopin*, 106–113.

———. "Nüzuojia Ding Ling" 女作家丁玲 (Woman writer Ding Ling). In *Mao Dun lun Zhongguo xiandai zuojia de zuopin*, 101–105.

Marks, Elaine, and Isabelle de Courtivon, eds. *New French Feminisms*. New York: Schoken Books, 1981.

McClintock, Anne et al. eds. *Dangerous Liaisons: Gender, Nation, and Postcolonial Perspectives*. Minneapolis: University of Minnesota Press, 1997.

McLaren, Anne E. *The Chinese Femme Fatale: Stories from the Ming Period*. Sydney: Wild Peony Press, 1994.

———. "The Grievance Rhetoric of Chinese Women: From Lamentation to Revolution." *Intersections: Gender, History and Culture in the Asian Context* no. 4 (September 2000). URL: http://www. murdoch.edu.au/intersections/ issue4 /mclaren.html.

Mei Niang. "Dong shoushu zhi qian" 动手术之前 (Before the operation, 1943). In *Mei Niang daibiaozuo*. Beijing: Huaxia press, 1998.

Meng Du. 孟度 "Guanyu Yang Jiang de hua" 关于杨绛的话 (On Yang Jiang). *Zazhi* (May 1945), 110–112.

Meng Yue and Dai Jinhua. *Fuchu lishidibiao.* 浮出历史地表 (Emerging from the horizon of history, 1989). Taibei: Shibao wenhua chubanshe, 1993.

Meng Yue. "Female Images and National Myth." In *Gender Politics in Modern China: Writing and Feminism*, ed. Tani Barlow, 118–136. Durham: Duke University Press, 1993.

Mezei, Kathy, ed. *Ambiguous Discourse: Feminist Narratology and British Women Writers*. Chapel Hill: University of North Carolina Press, 1996.

Miller, Nancy. *Subject to Change: Reading Feminist Writing*. New York: Columbia University Press, 1988.

Minguo nüzojia xiaoshuo jingdian 民国女作家小说经典 (Fiction classics by Republican era women writers). 20 vols. Shanghai: Guji chubanshe, 1999.

Mohanty, Chandra et al. *Third World Women and the Politics of Feminism*. Bloomington: Indiana University Press, 1991.

Moi, Toril. *Sexual/Textual Politics: Feminist Literary Theory*. London: Methuen, 1985.

Newton, Judith. "Making—and Remaking—History: Another Look at Patriarchy." In *Feminist Issues in Literary Scholarship*, ed. Shari Benstock. Bloomington: Indiana University Press, 1987.

Nivard, Jacqueline. "Women and the Women's Press: The Case of the *Ladies' Journal* (Funü Zazhi) 1915–1931 [1]." *Republican China* X, no. 16 (November 1984), 37–55.

———. "La Presse féminine Chinoise de 1898–1949." *Etudes Chinoises* 5 (1986) 156–235.

Nübao 女报 (The women's paper). Shanghai, Tokyo. 1899–1905. Changes its name to *Nüxuebao* 女学报 (Women's Studies paper) in 1903.

Nüsheng 女声 (Women's voice). Shanghai, 1932–1935, 1945–1947.

Nüzi shijie 女子世界 (Women's world). Shanghai, 1903–1907.

"Nüzuojia jutuanhui" 女作家聚团会 (Colloquium of women writers). *Zazhi* (April 1944).

Ono, Kazuko. *Chinese Women in a Century of Revolution, 1850–1950*. (1978) Edited and translated by Joshua A. Fogel. Stanford: Stanford University Press, 1989.

Peng Xiaoyan.*Chaoyue xieshi* 超越写实 (Beyond realism). Taibei: Lianjing, 1993.

Pickowitz, Paul. "Qu Qiubai's critique of the May Fourth Generation: Early Chinese Marxist Literary Criticism." In *Modern Chinese Literature in the May Fourth Era*, ed. Merle Goldman. Cambridge: Harvard University Press, 1977.

Průšek, Jaroslav. *The Lyrical and the Epic: Studies of Modern Chinese Literature*, Ed. Leo Ou-fan Lee. Bloomington: Indiana University Press, 1980.

Qiao Yigang. *Zhongguo nüxing de wenxue shijie* 中国女性的文学世界 (The literary world of Chinese women). Wuhan: Hubei jiaoyu chubanshe, 1993.

Qing He. *Yang Sao zhuan* 杨骚传 (Biography of Yang Sao). Shanghai: Haixia wenyi chubanshe, 1998.

Qiu Jin. "Fakanci" 发刊词 (Foreward). *Zhongguo nübao* 1 (1907).

———. *Qiu Jin ji* 秋瑾集 (The collected works of Qiu Jin). Shanghai: Shanghai guji chubanshe, 1960.

———. "Yanshuo de haochu" 演说的好处 (The merits of speeches). *Baihuabao* 1 (1904).

Quanguo minzhu funü lianhehui choubei weiyuanhui, ed. *Zhongguo jiefangqu nongcun funü yundong sumiao* 中国解放区农村妇女翻身运动素描 (Sketches of the 'turning over' movement among peasant women in the liberated areas). Shanghai: Xinhua shudian, 1949.

Rankin, Mary Backus. "The Emergence of Women at the End of the Ch'ing: The Case of Ch'iu Chin." In *Women in Chinese Society*, ed. Margery Wolf and Roxane Witke, 39–66. Stanford: Stanford University Press, 1975.

Recheng Aiguoren. *Nüzi jiuguo meitan* 女子救国美谈 (A beautiful tale of a girl who saves the nation). Shanghai: Xinminshe, 1902.

Renditions: Special Issue, Eileen Chang 45 (Spring 1996).

Rich, Adrienne. "When We Dead Awaken: Writing as Revision." In *On Lies, Secrets, and Silence: Selected Prose, 1966–1978*. New York: Norton, 1979, 33–49.

Ropp, Paul S. "The Seeds of Change: Reflections on the Condition of Women in the Early and Mid Ch'ing." *Signs* 2 (1976), 5–23.

Rowbatham, Sheila. *Women, Resistance, Revolution*. New York: Vintage Books, 1974.

Sang, Tze-lan D. *The Emerging Lesbian: Female Same-Sex Desire in Modern Chinese Literature and Culture*. Chicago: University of Chicago Press, 2002.

Sawyer, Newell. *The Comedy of Manners from Sheridan to Maugham*. Philadelphia: Philadelphia University Press, 1931.

Schwarcz, Vera. *The Chinese Enlightenment: Intellectuals and the Legacy of the May Fourth Movement of 1919*. Berkeley: University of California Press, 1986.

Schyns, Joseph. *1500 Modern Chinese Novels and Plays*. Hong Kong: Lung Men Bookstore, 1966.

Shanghai gudao wenxue huiyilu. 上海孤岛文学回忆录 (Memoirs of the Shanghai gudao literature). Shanghai: Shanghai shehui kexue chubanshe, 1985.

Shanghai shehuikexue yuan wenxue yanjiusuo, ed. *Sanshiniandai zai Shanghai de zuolian zuojia* 三十年代在上海的左联作家 (Leftist writers in 1930s Shanghai). Shanghai: Shanghai shehui kexueyuan chubanshe, 1988.

Sheng Ying. *Zhongguo nüxing wenxue xintan* 中国女性文学新探 (A new exploration of Chinese women's literature). Beijing: Zhongguo wenlian chubanshe, 1999.

Shenzhou nübao 神州女报 (Shenzhou women's paper), Shanghai, 1912.

Sheridan, Susan, ed. *Grafts: Feminist Cultural Criticism*. London: Verso, 1988.

Shi Pingmei. *Shi Pingmei zuopin ji* 石评梅作品集 (The collected works of Shi Pingmei). 3 vols. Ed. Yang Yang. Beijing: Shumu wenxian chubanshe, 1984–1985.

———. "Linnan de riji" 林楠的日记 (Linnan's diary, 1928). In *Shi Pingmei zuopinji*. Beijing: Shumu wenxian chubanshe, 1984, 239–250.

Shi Pingmei. "Ouran lailin de guifuren" 偶然来临的贵妇人 (Unexpected visit of a distinguished lady). In *Shi Pingmei wenji*. Hailar: Neimenggu chubanshe, 2000, 490–492.

———. "Qifu" 弃妇 (Abandoned woman, 1925). In *Shi Pingmei wenji*. Hala'er: Neimenggu chubanshe, 2000, 378–383.

———. *Shi Pingmei wenji* 石评梅文集.. Hala'er: Neimenggu chubanshe, 2000.

Shih Shu-mei. *The Lure of the Modern: Writing Modernism in Semicolonial China, 1917–1937*. Berkeley: University of California Press, 2001.

Shi Xisheng, ed. *Nüzuojia xiaocongshu* 女作家小丛书 (Women writers mini-book series). Shanghai: Guangyi shuju, 1930.

Showalter, Elaine. *A Literature of Their Own: British Women Writers from Brontë to Lessing*. Princeton: Princeton University Press, 1977.

———. "Towards a Feminist Poetics." In *Women Writing and Writing about Women*, ed. Mary Jacobus, 22–41. London: Croom Helm, 1979.

Siqi Zhai. *Nüziquan* 女子权 (Women's rights). Shanghai: Zuoxinshe, 1907. Reprint. *Zhongguo jindai xiaoshuo daxi*. Nanchang: Baihuazhou wenyi chubanshe, 1991.

Sievers, Sharon L. *Flowers in Salt: The Beginnings of Feminist Consciousness in Modern Japan*. Stanford: Stanford University Press, 1983.

Siu, Bobby. *Women of China: Imperialism and Women's Resistance*, 1900–1949. London: Zed Press, 1981.

Smith, Sidonie. *Subjectivity, Identity and the Body: Women's Autobiographical Practices in the Twentieth-Century*. Bloomington: Indiana University Press, 1993.

Spence, Jonathan. *The Search for Modern China*. New York: W.W. Norton and Co., 1990.

Stacey, Judith. *Patriarchy and Socialist Revolution in China*. Berkeley: University of California Press, 1983.

Stanton, Domna. *The Female Autograph*. Chicago: University of Chicago Press, 1987.

Su Qing. *Jiehun shinian* 结婚十年 (10 years of marriage). Shanghai: Sihai chubanshe, 1944.

———. *Su Qing sanwen* 苏青散文 (Su Qing's essays). Ed. Yu Liqing. Taibei: Wusi shudian, 1989.

———. *Xu jiehun shinian* 续结婚十年 (Sequel to 10 years of marriage). Shanghai: Sihai chubanshe, 1947.

Su Qing xiaoshuo ji 苏青小说集 (A collection of Su Qing's fiction). Hefei: Anhui wenyi chubanshe, 1996.

Su Xuelin. *Ersanshi niandai de zuojia yu zuopin* 二三十年代的作家与作品 (Writers of the twenties and thirties and their works). Taibei: Guangdong chubanshe, 1979.

———. "'Haibin guren' de zuozhe Lu Yin nüshi" 海滨古人的作者庐隐 (Lu Yin, author of "Seaside Friends"). In *Su Xuelin wenji*. Hefei: Anhui wenyi chubanshe, 1994. Vol. 2, 353–357.

———. "Ge'er de tongxin" 鸽儿的通信 (Pigeon letters, 1928). In *Su Xuelin wenji*. Hefei: Anhui wenyi chubanshe, 1994. Vol. 1, 227–245.

———. *Su Xuelin wenji* 苏雪林文集 (Collected works of Su Xuelin). Hefei: Anhui wenyi chubanshe, 1994.

Sun Zhaoxian. *Nüxingzhuyi wenxue* 女性主义文学 (Feminist literature). Shenyang: Liaoning daxue chubanshe, 1987.

Sun, Jiang Guanci. *Chongcha yunerie de yueliang* (Moon emerging from the clouds, 1930).

Sung, Marina H. *The Narrative Art of Tsai-sheng-yuan: A Feminist Vision in Traditional Confucian Society.* Taiwan: Chinese Materials Center, 1994.

Sypher, Wylie. *Comedy.* New York: Doubleday Anchor, 1956.

Tan Sheying. *Zhongguo funü yundong tongshi* 中国 妇女 运动 通 史 (A comprehensive history of the Chinese women's movement). Shanghai: Funü gongmingshe, 1936.

Tan Zhengbi. *Dangdai nüzuojia xiaoshuo xuan* 当代女作家小说选 (Selected fiction by contemporary women writers). Shanghai: Taiping shuju, 1944.

———. *Zhongguo nüxing de wenxue shenghuo* 中国 女性 的 文学 生活 (The literary life of Chinese women). Shanghai Guangming Shuju, 1931. Reprint. Taipei: Zhuangyan chubanshe, 1982.

———. *Zhongguo nüxing wenxue shihua* 中国 女性 文学 史 话 (A history of Chinese women's literature). Tianjin: Baihua wenyi chubanshe, 1984.

Tao Qiuying. *Zhongguo funü yu wenxue* 中国 妇女 与 文学 (Chinese women and literature). Shanghai: Beixin shuju, 1933.

Taylor, Eve. *The Domestic Revolution: Enlightenment Feminisms and the Novel.* Baltimore: Johns Hopkins University Press, 2000.

Thakur, Ravni. *Rewriting Gender: Reading Contemporary Chinese Women.* London: Zed Books, 1997.

Thompson, Laurence G. *Ta Tung-shu: The One World Philosophy of Kang Yu-wei.* London: Allen and Unwin, 1958.

Tianyi bao 天 义 报 (Journal of natural justice). Tokyo, 1907.

Timothy Brennan, "The National Longing for Form," in Homi Bhabha, ed., *Nation and Narration* (London: Routledge Press, 1990), 44–70.

Wang Der-wei David. *Fictional Realism in Twentieth-century China.* New York: Columbia University Press, 1992.

———. *Fin-de-Siècle Splendors: Repressed Modernities of Late Qing Fiction, 1849–1911.* Stanford: Stanford University Press, 1997.

———. "Feminist Consciousness in Modern Chinese Male Fiction." In *Modern Chinese Women, Writers*, ed. Michael Duke, 236–256. Armonk, NY: M.E. Sharpe, 1989.

———. "Reinventing National History: Communist and Anti-Communist Fiction of the Mid-Twentieth Century." In *Chinese Literature in the Second Half of a Modern Century, A Critical Survey*, ed. Pang-yuan Chi and David Wang, 139–164. Bloomington: Indiana University Press, 2000.

———. *Xiaoshuo Zhongguo: Wanqing dao dangdai de Zhongwen xiaoshuo* 小说中国：晚清 到当代的中文小说 (Narrating China: Chinese novels from the late Qing to the present). Taibei: Maitian chubanshe, 1993.

Wang Jialun. *Zhongguo xiandai nüzuojia lungao* 中国 现代 女 作家 论 稿 (A discussion of modern Chinese women writers). Beijing: Zhongguo funü chubanshe, 1992.

Wang Miaoru. *Nüyuhua* 女 狱 花 (Flowers in the female prison). n.p. 1904. Reprinted in *Zhongguo jindai xiaoshuo daxi.* Nanchang: Baihuazhou wenyi chubanshe, 1991.

Wang Xiaoming. "The 'Good Fortune' of Eileen Chang." *Renditions* (Spring 1996), 136–140.

Wang Weiqi, trans. *Shijie nüquan fada shi* 世界女权发达史 (The world history of the development of women's rights). Shanghai: Wenming shuju, 1905.

Wang Yixin. *Su Qing zhuan* 苏青传 (Biography of Su Qing). Shanghai: Xuelin chubanshe, 1999.

Wang Ying. *Baogu* 宝姑 (Precious girl). Beijing: Zhongguo qingnian chubanshe, 1982.

———. *The Child Bride.* Beijing: Foreign Language Press, 1989.

Wang Yingxia. *Wo yu Yu Dafu* 我与郁达夫 (Yu Dafu and I). Xi'an: Huayue wenyi chubanshe, 1988.

Wang Zheng. *Women in the Chinese Enlightenment: Oral and Textual Histories.* Berkeley: University of California Press, 1999.

———. "Maoism, Feminism, and the UN Conference on Women." *Journal of Women's Studies,* 8 (Winter 1997), 126–152.

Weedon, Chris. *Feminist Practice and Poststructuralist Theory.* Oxford: Basil Blackwell, 1987.

Widmer, Ellen. "Inflecting Gender: Zhan Kai/Siqi Zhai's 'New Novels' and 'Courtesan Sketches.'" *Nan Nü: Men, Women, and Gender in China* 6, no. 1 (2004).

Widmer, Ellen and David Wang. *From May Fourth to June Fourth: Fiction and Film in Twentieth-Century China.* Cambridge: Harvard University Press, 1993.

Widmer, Ellen and Kang-i Sun Chang, eds. *Writing Women in Late Imperial China.* Stanford: Stanford University Press, 1997.

Wilson, Anna. *Persuasive Fictions: Feminist Narrative and Critical Myth.* Lewisburg: Bucknell University Press, 2001.

Witke, Roxane. "Transformation of Attitudes toward Women During the May Fourth Era of Modern China." Ph.D. Dissertation. University of California at Berkeley, 1970.

Wolf, Margery. *Revolution Postponed: Women in Contemporary China.* Stanford: Stanford University Press, 1985.

Wolf, Margery and Roxane Witke, eds. *Women in Chinese Society.* Stanford: Stanford University Press, 1975.

Woolf, Virginia. "Professions for Women." (1931) Ed. Michele Barrett. *Women and Writing.* New York: Harcourt Brace Jovanovich, 1979, 57–63.

Xiao Feng. *Lu Yin zhuan* 庐隐传 (Biography of Lu Yin). Beijing: Beijing shifan daxue chubanshe, 1982.

Xiao Hong. *The Field of Life and Death and Tales of Hulan River.* Translated by Howard Goldblatt and Ellen Yeung. Bloomington: Indiana University Press, 1979.

Xiao Hong. *Market Street: A Chinese Woman in Harbin.* Translated by Howard Goldblatt. Seattle: University of Washington Press, 1986.

———. "Qi'er" 弃儿 (Abandoned child, 1933). Translated in Amy D. Dooling and Kristina M. Torgeson eds. *Writing Women in Modern China.* New York: Columbia University Press, 1998, 347–361.

———. *Selected Stories of Xiao Hong.* Panda Books. Beijing: Chinese Literature Press, 1982.

———. *Xiao Hong quanji* 萧红全集 (The complete works of Xiao Hong). 2 vols. Harbin: Ha'erbin chubanshe, 1991.

Xie Bingying. *Autobiography of a Chinese Girl.* With an introduction by Elisabeth Croll, 1943. London and New York: Pandora, 1986.

———. *Congjun riji* 从军日记 (War diary, 1928). In *Xie Bingying wenji.* Vol. 1. Hefei: Anhui wenyi chubanshe, 1998.

———. "Gei S-mei de yifeng xin" 给 S 妹的一封信 (A letter to S-, 1929). *Xie Bingying zuopinxuan.* Changsha: Hunan renmin chubanshe, 1985, 553–569.

———. *Girl Rebel: The Autobiography of a Chinese of Hsieh Pingying, with Extracts from Her New War Diaries.* New York: De Capo Press, 1975.

———. "Guanyu *Nübing zizhuan*" 关于女兵自传 (About the *Autobiography of a woman soldier*). In *Nübing zizhuan,* 1–10. Chengdu: Sichuan wenyi chubanshe, 1985.

———. "*Lihun*" 离婚 (Divorce). In *Wutiji* 无题集 (Untitled), Ed. Zhao Qingge. Shanghai: n.p. 1947.

———. *Nübing zizhuan* 女兵自传 (Autobiography of a woman soldier, 1936). In *Xie Bingying weniji*. Vol. 1. Hefei: Anhui wenyi chubanshe, 1998, 3–283.

———. "*Paoqi*" 抛弃 (Abandoned, 1936). In *Xie Bingying daibiaozuo.* Beijing: Huaxia chubanshe, 1999, 323–363.

———. *Xie Bingying sanwen xuanji* 谢冰莹散文集 (The selected essays of Xie Bingying). Ed. Demin Fu. Tianjin: Baihua wenyi chubanshe, 1992.

———. *Xie Bingying weniji* 谢冰莹文集 (Collected works of Xie Bingying). 3 vols. Hefei: Anhui wenyi chubanshe, 1998.

———. *Xie Bingying zuopin xuan* 谢冰莹作品选 (Selected works of Xie Bingying). Changsha: Hunan renmin chubanshe, 1985.

Xie Yu'e, ed. *Nüxing wenxue yanjiu: jiaoxue cankao ziliao* 女性文学研究：教学参考资料 Kaifeng: Henan daxue chubanshe, 1990.

Xinxing de jiating funü 新型的家庭妇女 (New style housewives). Beijing: Zhongguo funü zashi she, 1956.

Xin nüxing 新女性 (New woman). Beijing: 1926–1929.

Xin Qing. *Ershi shiji nüjie wenmingdeng tanci* 二十世纪女界文明灯弹词 (The torch of civilization in the twentieth century women's world). Shanghai: Mingming she, 1911.

Xin Zhongguo funü 新中国妇女 (Chinese women). Beijing, 1949–1956 (Changed name to 中国妇女 in 1956).

Xuanchuan guanche hunyin fa yanchang cailiao 宣传贯彻婚姻法演唱材料 (Singing materials for publicizing and implementing the marriage law). Changsha: Hunan tongsu duwu chubanshe, 1953.

Yaeger, Patricia. *Honey-Mad Women: Emancipatory Strategies in Women's Writing.* New York: Columbia University Press, 1988.

Yang Gang. *Daughter.* Beijing: Foreign Languages Press, 1988.

———. "Fragment from a Lost Diary." In Living China: Modern Chinese Short Stories, ed. Edgar Snow, 302–318. New York: Reynal and Hitchcock, 1936.

———. *Meiguo zhaji* 美国札记 (Notes from America). Beijing: Shijie zhishi she, 1951.

———. *Tiaozhan* 挑战 Beijing: Renmin wenxue chubanshe, 1988.

———. *Yang Gang xiaoshuo: Huan Xiu waizhuan* 杨刚小说：桓秀外传 (Yang Gang's fiction: an unofficial biography of Huan Xiu). Shanghai: Guji chubanshe, 1999.

———. *Yang Gang wenji* 杨刚文集 (Collected works of Yang Gang). Beijing: Renmin wenxue chubanshe, 1984.

Yang Hsienyi and Gladys Yang. *Selected Stories of Lu Xun.* Beijing: Foreign Language Press, 1978.

Yang Jiang. *Chenxin ruyi* 称心如意 (As you desire). Beijing: Shijie shuju, 1943. Reprint. *Xiju erzhong.* Fuzhou: Fujian renmin chubanshe, 1982.

———. *Ganxiao liuji* 干校六集 (Six chapters from a cadre school). Hong Kong: Guangjiao chubanshe and Sanlian shuju, 1981.

———. *Nongzhen chengjia* 弄真成假 (Forging the truth). Shanghai: Shijie shuju, 1944. Reprint. *Xiju erhong.* Fuzhou: Fujian renmin chubanshe, 1982.

———. *Yang Jiang zuopinji* 杨绛作品集 (Collected works of Yang Jiang). 3 vols. Beijing: Zhongguo shehui kexue chubanshe, 1993.

———. *Xiju erzhong* 戏剧二种 (Two plays). Fuzhou: Fujian renmin chubanshe, 1982.

———. *Xizao* 洗澡 (Taking a bath). Beijing: Sanlian shudian, 1988.

———. *Women sa* 我们仨 (We three). Beijing: Sanlian shudian, 2003.

Yang, Mayfair. "From Gender Erasure to Gender Difference: State Feminism, Consumer Sexuality and Women's Public Sphere in China." In *Spaces of Their Own: Women's Public Sphere in Transnational China*, ed. Yang, 35–67. Minneapolis: University of Minnesota, 1999.

Yang Mo. *Qingchun zhige* 青春之歌 (Song of youth). Beijing: Shiyue wenyi chubanshe, 1992.

Yang Yun. "Shen dajie jiao wo ban kanwu" 沈大姐教我办刊物 (Sister Shen taught me how to run a journal). In *Nüjie wenhua zhanshi Shen Zijiyu*, 1991.

Ye Shaojun. "Chunguang bushi tade le" 春光不是她的了 (No longer hers, the spring). In Ye Shengtao wenji, 130–152. Beijing: Renmin wenxue chubanshe, 1958.

Yi Zhen. "Ji wei dangdai zhongguo nü xiaoshuojia" 几位当代中国女小说家 (Several contemporary women novelists). In *Dangdai Zhongguo nüzuojia lun*, ed. Huang Renying, 1–36. Beijing: Guanghua shuju, 1933.

Young, Marilyn B., ed. *Women in China: Studies in Social Change and Feminism*. Ann Arbor: Center for Chinese Studies, University of Michigan, 1973.

Yu Ru. *Yaoyuan de ai* 遥远的爱 (Remote love). Chongqing: Ziqiang chubanshe, 1946.

Yuan Changying. *Kongque dongnan fei ji qita dumuju* 孔雀东南飞及其他独幕剧 (Southeast flies the peacock and other one act plays). Ed. Su Xuelin. Taipei: Shangwu yinshuguan, 1983.

———. *Yuan Changying xuanji* 袁昌英选集 (Selected works of Yuan Changying). Ed. Su Xuelin. Taipei: Hongfan shudian, 1986.

Yue Ming-bao. "Gendering the Origins of Modern Chinese Fiction." In *Gender and Sexuality in Twentieth-Century Chinese Literature and Society*, ed. Lu Tonglin, 47–65. Albany: SUNY Press, 1993.

Yue Shuo. *Chidao de chaoliu* 迟到的潮流 (The belated tide). Zhengzhou: Henan renmin chubanshe, 1989.

Zarrow, Peter. "He Zhen and Anarcho-feminism in China." *Journal of Asian Studies* 47, no. 4 (November 1988), 796–813.

Zhang Ailing. *Zhang Ailing wenji* 张爱玲文集 (The works of Zhang Ailing). 4 vols. Hefei: Anhui wenyi chubanshe, 1992.

———. *Naked Earth*. Hong Kong: Union Press, 1956.

———. "Qingcheng zhi lian" 倾城之恋 (Love in a fallen city). *Zazhi* (September–October 1943). Translated by Karen Kingsbury. Renditions 95 (Spring 1996).

———. *The Rice-Sprout Song* (1955). Berkeley: University of California Press, 1998.

———. "Wo jian Su Qing" 我看苏青 (My views on Su Qing). In *Zhang Ailing wenji*. Hefei: Anhui wenyi chubanshe, 1992, 226–239.

———. "Ziji de wenzhang" 自己的文章 (My writing). *Liuyan*. Shanghai: Wuzhou shubao she, 1944.

Zhang Ailing and Su Qing. "Su Qing, Zhang Ailing duitanlu: guanyu funü jiating, hunyin went" 苏青张爱玲对谈录：关于妇女，家庭，婚姻问题 (A dialogue between Su Qing and Zhang Ailing: on women, family and marriage) in *Zhang Ailing wenji* (1992), 392–404.

Zhang, Naihua. "The All-China Women's Federation: Chinese Women and The Women's Movement: 1949–1993." Ph.D. Dissertation. Michigan State University, 1996.

Zhang, Naihua with Wu Xu. "Discovering the Positive Within the Negative: The Women's Movement in a Changing China." In *The Challenge of Local Feminisms: Women's Movements in Global Perspective*, ed. Amrita, Basu, 25–57. Boulder: Westview Press, 1995.

Zhang Ruogu. "Zhongguo xiandai de nüzuojia" 中国现代的女作家 (Contemporary Chinese women writers) *Zhenmeishan* Magazine, (1928), 1–73.

Zhang Yingjin. *The City in Modern Chinese Literature and Film: Configurations of Space, Time and Gender.* Stanford: Stanford University Press, 1996.

———, ed. *Cinema and Urban Culture in Shanghai, 1922–1943.* Stanford: Stanford University Press, 1999.

Zhao Jiabi, ed. *Zhongguo xin wenxue daxi* 中国新文学大系 (Compendium of modern Chinese literature). 10 vols. Taibei: Yeqiang chubanshe, 1990.

Zhao Qingge. *Wutiji* 无题集 (Untitled). Shanghai. n.p, 1947.

———. *Changxiang yi* 长相忆 (Forever recalling each other). Shanghai: Xuelin chubanshe, 1999.

Zhenmeishan: Nüzuojia hao 真美善女作家号 (Zhenmeishan: special issue on women writers). Shanghai, 1928.

Zhong Xueping. *Masculinity Besieged? Issues of Masculinity and Male Subjectivity in Chinese Literature of the Late Twentieth Century.* Durham: Duke University Press, 2000.

Zhongguo funü yundong lishi ziliao 中国妇女运动历史资料 (Historical materials on the Chinese women's movement). Vol. 1: 1840–1918; Vol. 2: 1918–1937, Vol. 3: 1937–1945. Beijing: Zhongguo funü chubanshe, 1991.

Zhongguo jindai wenxue yanjiu 中国近代文学研究 (Research on modern Chinese literature). Ed. Fudan daxue zhongwenxi jindai wenxue yanjiushi. Baihuazhou wenyi chubanshe, 1991.

Zhongguo nübao 中国女报 (Chinese women's journal). Shanghai, 1906–1907.

Zhongguo funü zazhi she bianji. *Xinxing de jiating funü* 新型的家庭妇女. (The new style housewife). Beijing: Funü zazhi she, 1956.

Zhongguo xiandai cainü jingdian wencong 中国才女经典文丛 (Collection of literary classics by modern Chinese literary women). 8 vols. Beijing: Yanshan chubanshe, 1998.

Zhongguo xinnüjie 中国新女界 (New Chinese women). Tokyo, 1907.

Zhou Zuoren. "Nüzi yu wenxue" 女子与文学 (Women and literature). *Funü pinglun.* June 1922.

Zhu Lianbao. *Jinxiandai Shanghai chubanye yinxiangji* 近现代上海出版业印象记 (Impressions of the modern Shanghai publishing industry). Shanghai: Xuelin chubanshe, 1993.

Zhuang Haoran. "Lun Yang Jiang xiju de wailai yingxiang he minzu fengge" 论杨绛戏剧的外来影响和民族风格 (On the foreign influences and national characteristics of Yang Jiang's dramas). In *Huaju wenxue yanjiu.* Beijing: Zhongguo xiju chubanshe, 1987.

Zito, Angela and Tani Barlow, eds. *Body, Subject, and Power in China.* Chicago: University of Chicago Press, 1994.

INDEX